International Perspectives on Migration

South-South Migration

This book series serves the growing academic interests in South-South migration, offering a scholarly publication platform to scholars and practitioners globally. It advances a Southern perspective to migration studies. It encompasses distinct fields such as international migration, internal migration, remittances, migrant entrepreneurship, diaspora philanthropy, social cost of migration, political and environmental refugees, gender and migration, labor migration, migration policy, the political economy of migration, migrants' rights, and other migration-related issues in the global South. The series aims to address migration questions, employ critical analyses, and advance evidence-based migration scholarship. This book series takes an interdisciplinary approach to the causes, patterns, and implications of migration for countries and regions in the global South. This series invites original monographs and edited books. The series explicitly gives scholars from the global South more voice and visibility in academic publications.

Kawser Ahmed · Md. Rafiqul Islam
Editors

Understanding the Rohingya Displacement

Security, Media, and Humanitarian Perspectives

Springer

Editors
Kawser Ahmed
University of Winnipeg
Winnipeg, MB, Canada

Md. Rafiqul Islam
Department of Peace and Conflict Studies
University of Dhaka
Dhaka, Bangladesh

ISSN 2214-9805 ISSN 2214-9813 (electronic)
International Perspectives on Migration
ISSN 2731-5045 ISSN 2731-5053 (electronic)
South-South Migration
ISBN 978-981-97-1423-0 ISBN 978-981-97-1424-7 (eBook)
https://doi.org/10.1007/978-981-97-1424-7

This Springer imprint is published by the registered company Springer Nature Singapore Pte Ltd.
The registered company address is: 152 Beach Road, #21-01/04 Gateway East, Singapore 189721, Singapore

Contents

Editors and Contributors

About the Editors

Kawser Ahmed is an adjunct professor at University of Winnipeg (Political Science) and University of Manitoba (NRI). He received his Ph.D. in Peace and Conflict Studies from University of Manitoba in 2017 and completed his Social Science and Humanities Research Council (SSHRC) of Canada's post-doctoral fellowship at University of Winnipeg. He was an exchange officer with the Turkish Armed Forces (TSK), an observer-Peacekeeper to the United Nations Missions in Western Sahara (MINURSO), and an alumnus at the Near East South Asia Center for Strategic Studies (NESA) in Washington DC. He is associated with the Center for Defence and Security Studies (CDSS) as a research fellow and a member of the Writers Union of Canada. He leads a Winnipeg based not-for-profit organization named Conflict and Resilience Research Institute, Canada (CRRIC). His research interests are social conflict and peace building, radicalism and violent extremism prevention, and UN peacekeeping operations.

Md. Rafiqul Islam is a professor at the Department of Peace and Conflict Studies, University of Dhaka, Bangladesh. He has a Ph.D. from Flinders University, Australia, and his thesis was awarded the John Lewis Silver Medal in South Australia. He had previously completed his bachelor's degree in political science and has a master's and an M.Phil. in peace and conflict studies from the University of Dhaka, Bangladesh. He has also completed an M.A. degree in environmental security and peace from the University for Peace, Costa Rica. His primary research interests include climate change, migration, refugees, peace, conflict, and development. Dr. Islam also has a keen interest in global politics, security, and peace issues and has published 40 articles and chapters across several publications based globally. Dr. Islam is currently involved in research in the field of Rohingya issues and statelessness in the Bengali borderland. Dr. Islam's first book on *Climate Change, Migration and Conflict in Bangladesh* was published in 2023 by Routledge.

Contributors

Etu Ahmed, after completing her BSS and MSS in early 2023 at the Department of Peace and Conflict Studies, University of Dhaka, is currently working as a Lecturer, Department of Peace, Conflict and Human Rights, Bangladesh University of Professionals (BUP), Bangladesh.

Md. Nazmul Arefin is a doctoral student in the field of sociology-criminology at the University of Alberta, Canada. The Canadian Sociological Association (CSA) has honoured him with a Congress Graduate Merit Award for 2023. In 2019, he also received a fellowship from the University of Kassel in Germany as a visiting researcher. His research interests include terrorism and radicalization studies, global south criminology, identity politics, right-wing populism, social justice, Islamophobia, and visual criminology.

Muhammad Mazedul Haque is a researcher specializing in conflict resolution and management. He holds a Bachelor's and Master's degree from the Department of Peace and Conflict Studies at the University of Dhaka, Bangladesh. Currently serving as a Research Officer at the Bangladesh Institute of International and Strategic Studies (BIISS), Haque has made significant contributions to the field of peace and conflict studies.

Rukiya Hassan holds a Bachelor's degree in Social Science from Bangladesh University of Professionals. She specializes in mass communication and media studies. She made a substantial contribution to initiatives examining the circumstances of women and children in Bangladesh while working as a research assistant at the renowned nongovernmental Manusher Jonno Foundation. She is currently enrolled into a Master's program at the same university.

Maria Hussain is an Assistant Professor in the Department of Peace and Conflict Studies, University of Dhaka, Bangladesh. She completed her BSS and MSS in Peace and Conflict Studies at the University of Dhaka, Bangladesh. As a Commonwealth Scholar, she also completed her MA in Peace Studies at the University of Bradford, United Kingdom.

Amena Khatun is currently studying as a Ph.D. student in the Department of Peace and Conflict Studies at the University of Dhaka, Bangladesh. She is also teaching as an Associate Professor in the Department of Mass Communication and Journalism at the University of Rajshahi, Bangladesh. She is currently working on the *Stateless Rohingyas in the Bengali Borderlands* project, funded by the Norwegian Refugee Council (NRC).

Lamia Islam is an Assistant Professor in the Department of Political Science at Jagannath University. She holds an M.Sc. from the University of Antwerp in Belgium, and an MSS from the University of Dhaka. e-mail: lamiaislam@pol.jnu.ac.bd

Rehnuma Mahjabin graduated with a Bachelor of Science from the Department of Geography and Environment, University of Dhaka, Bangladesh in 2017. She completed her Master of Science at the Department of Geography and Environment, University of Dhaka, Bangladesh in 2020. With an interest in working in human, environmental, and social research, she started pursuing another M.Sc. at the Natural Resources Institute, University of Manitoba, Canada in 2021. Currently, she is working on a thesis focused on the Forcibly Displaced Myanmar Population (FDMN) influx and resettlement in Bangladesh.

Mahabuba Islam Meem completed her Bachelor's and Master's at the Department of Peace and Conflict Studies, University of Dhaka. She is currently enrolled in the Ph.D. program in Sociology at North Carolina State University, USA. Her research interests include gender, crime, and inequality. e-mail: meem.mahabuba@gmail.com

Khandaker Farzana Rahman is an Associate Professor of the Department of Criminology, University of Dhaka. She has completed LLB and LLM from the same university, and her MA from Erasmus University in Rotterdam. Her research centers on Displacement and Crime, Criminal Justice and Gender, Youth Justice, Correction and Prison, Criminal Procedure and Law, and Organized Crime and Drugs.

Lieutenant General (Retired) Mohammad Mahfuzur Rahman, Ph.D. retired as Principal Staff Officer to the Bangladeshi Prime Minister on 29 November 2020. He was commissioned from Bangladesh Military Academy in the year 1981 in the corps of Infantry. He has served in various capacities in Bangladesh Army's Command, Staff, and Instructional appointments. He is a graduate of Staff College and Armed Forces War Course. He has also graduated from National Defence College, New Delhi and Royal College of Defence Studies, London. As the head of Armed Forces Division, he was directly involved with the UN Peacekeeping Affairs (Preparation, Pledges, Gender Perspective, Deployment etc.) of Bangladesh Armed Forces. Besides writing articles in magazines and dailies on contemporary security issues, he has edited a book on *Indo-Bangladesh Trade Relations*, and his second book, *A Study on Drug Proliferation in Bangladesh* was published in 2016.

Md. Zillur Rahman is currently pursuing his Ph.D. at Bangladesh University of Professionals (BUP). Having successfully completed the 18th Bangladesh Civil Service (BCS) examination, Rahman serves as a Superintendent of Police (SP) within the Cox's Bazar Region. Rahman's research interests primarily revolve around security studies, where he focuses on understanding and analyzing the multifaceted challenges faced by law enforcement agencies. His doctoral research delves into exploring innovative strategies for enhancing security and addressing emerging threats within the context of the Cox's Bazar Region.

Rafa Nailah Sattar is a Fulbright Scholar to India. She graduated from Macaulay Honors at CUNY Hunter College in 2020 as salutatorian with a BA in Political Science. She is currently pursuing her Master's in Nonprofit Management at Columbia University. At Columbia, Rafa was one of two winners of the Excellence in Academic Leadership Award. She is founder and president of the FERA Foundation, an international nonprofit committed to educational equity and a partner of the Conflict and Resilience Research Institute Canada. Today, she serves on the steering committee of Project HOPE, CRRIC's pilot initiative to deliver a remote education to Rohingya refugee girls. She also serves on the board of trustees of the EmpowerEd Program, a UK charity seeking to deliver training modules to domestic violence shelters. Rafa aims to dedicate her career to securing the rights of marginalized children and women to an education and social mobility.

Umme Wara is an Associate Professor in the Department of Criminology, University of Dhaka. She is a Ph.D. candidate at the University of Warwick, UK, as of November 2022. After completing her LLB and LLM at the University of Dhaka with First Class honors, she received AusAID's scholarship to pursue her second Master's on Transnational Crime Prevention at the University of Wollongong, Australia. Later she completed another Master's at the University of Torino, Italy, on International Crime and Justice, with a scholarship.

Abu Salah Md. Yousuf is the Research Director at Bangladesh Institute of International and Strategic Studies (BIISS), Old Elephant Road, Ramna, Dhaka-1000. Bangladesh.

Chapter 1
Setting the Stage and Addressing Conceptual Issues

Kawser Ahmed and Md. Rafiqul Islam

Refugees represent the very best of the human spirit... And we need much stronger political will to make peace, so refugees can return safely to their homes. This year's theme is "Hope Away from Home." I call on the world to harness the hope that refugees carry in their hearts. Let's match their courage with the opportunities they need, every step of the way.
António Guterres
UN Secretary General
20 June 2023

Abstract The chapter introduces the book, delving into the complex and multi-faceted Rohingya crisis. It emphasizes the importance of understanding the issue from various perspectives including security, media, and humanitarian efforts. The aim is to build on existing research by exploring the historical roots of the crisis, responses to it, and potential resolutions. This work addresses how security concerns, media representation, and humanitarian aspects intersect rather than solely focusing on human rights issues. In particular, it focuses on Bangladesh's experience as the primary host country for Rohingya refugees and its impact on foreign policy. Additionally, this text discusses challenges within refugee camps in Bangladesh such as organized crime, humanitarian effort, respect towards women and groups with hostile intentions. The objective is to present a detailed understanding of the Rohingya crisis that contributes valuably to academic discussions while pursuing sustainable solutions. Starting with a historical context of displacement, this chapter outlines media coverage, humanitarian response, and security concerns, international law, and human rights. It also contains the methodology of the research upon which this book has been written.

K. Ahmed (✉)
University of Winnipeg, Winnipeg, Canada
e-mail: k.ahmed@uwinnipeg.ca

Md. R. Islam
University of Dhaka, Dhaka, Bangladesh
e-mail: rislampacs@du.ac.bd

K. Ahmed and Md. R. Islam (eds.), *Understanding the Rohingya Displacement*, International Perspectives on Migration, https://doi.org/10.1007/978-981-97-1424-7_1

1 Introduction

The Rohingya crisis (in this book, both "crisis" and "conflict" have been used interchangeably) has captured the attention of the international community due to its multifaceted and complicated nature. Over the past ten years, there has been a surge in scholarship on this group of forcibly displaced persons from Myanmar. This increase coincides with the massive influx of more than one million Rohingyas into Bangladesh in 2017. The literature about this issue covers various aspects such as identity politics, ethnic conflicts, statelessness, and the demographic decline experienced by Rohingya people within Myanmar's borders. Naturally, the question was asked: why is another book on this crisis required? We approach answering this question in two ways: firstly, we seek to draw on the existing body of research and develop an even more comprehensive understanding of this crisis; secondly, we aim to explore the issue from the perspective of three crucial aspects: security, media, and humanitarianism. In addition, we aim to delve into the historical origin of the crisis, the local and international responses so far, and potential solutions that might ensure a better future for the Rohingya people.

Most importantly, this book addresses a gap in the literature by examining how security, media, and humanitarian perspectives intersect in the Rohingya crisis. While existing studies have examined the crisis primarily from a human rights standpoint, few comprehensive studies have explored the problem from the perspective of foreign policy stances taken by host countries, media portrayals of the crisis, and the impact these factors have on humanitarian aid efforts. Bangladesh is the largest host country of Rohingya refugees in the world; our research also focuses on the impact of the displacement on Bangladesh, and how its foreign policy is affected by this crisis. With time, while it is already evident that the Rohingya crisis is undeniably a humanitarian calamity that has led to the displacement of millions, it is also increasingly becoming a potential threat to regional and international security. Even Rohingyas are not safe within their communities in Bangladesh camps, given the sub-standard quality of life and low level of human security (Cousins, 2018; Tripura, 2022; Ullah, 2011). Rohingyas are also victims of organized crime and gender-based violence within the camps. Moreover, various hostile groups—including the Arakan Rohingya Salvation Army (ARSA)—are also active in the camps, which often complicates the living environment (Islam & Wara, 2022). These emerging issues in the post-settlement period demand scholarly work to analyze the many factors and look for sustainable solutions to the Rohingya problem. As such, this book aims to contribute significantly to the scholarly discourse on the Rohingya crisis by offering a more nuanced and comprehensive understanding of this issue.

2 Historical Context of Rohingya Displacement

The Rohingya crisis, which has garnered international attention in the recent years, has its historical roots deeply embedded in Myanmar's sociopolitical landscape (Ullah, 2011). This crisis emerged as a result of decades-long discrimination and persecution faced by the Rohingya people, who are predominantly Muslim (Alam, 2019; Prasse-Freeman, 2017). The Myanmar government's denial of citizenship rights to the Rohingya, labeling them as "Bengalis" and claiming they are illegal immigrants from Bangladesh, has led to their statelessness and exclusion from society (Ullah, 2016). Such discrimination has had severe consequences for the Rohingya people, including restrictions on their access to education, employment, and health care (Ullah & Chattoraj, 2018). The exclusion of the Rohingyas from Myanmar and persecution by the state system has led to a large-scale displacement and migration of the Rohingyas to neighboring countries and beyond. These displaced and migrants lead miserable lives in the refugee receiving societies. Readers will find additional historical contexts in each chapter.

3 Media Coverage of the Conflict

The media has played a pivotal role in shaping global perceptions of the Rohingya crisis. While the media initially provided limited coverage of the crisis, it has gained broader attention in the recent years (Lee, 2021). The Rohingya crisis received extensive coverage between August 2017 (when the exodus occurred) and 2020 (before covid-19). Among some of the positive consequences of widespread coverage were that the crisis gained global recognition, and the international community was compelled to rally resources to support the Rohingya refugees. For example, the Canadian government, for the first time, appointed a special envoy—Mr. Bob Rae—for attending to the crisis, and allotted $3 million in aid. International support gained momentum as well in pushing the case for the recognition of genocide in various international forums and in Western countries such as the US and Canada. Although crisis observers opine that such recognition is merely a token gesture of support for the Rohingya cause, due to media coverage of the phenomenon of genocide, it has gained much attention and awareness among the general public. In an unprecedented way, the International Court of Justice (ICJ) proactively took up the case against Myanmar for committing genocide against Rohingya Muslims, which was a direct result of the extensive media coverage. In addition, a case in the International Criminal Court (ICC) against the chief of staff of the Myanmar military is also underway to hold those responsible accountable for their actions (Pedersen, 2019). On social media, hundreds of solidarity groups proliferated to support Rohingyas, and for the first time, the Rohingya diaspora groups gained global attention for their cause.

Despite the positive impacts, media coverage of the Rohingya crisis has also had some negative consequences (Mohanty, 2020). One such consequence is the potential for sensationalism in media reporting, which can distort and oversimplify complex issues. Media coverage is largely absent, though, in highlighting host country Bangladesh's predicaments for long-term hosting of the now nearly 1.3 million Rohingyas. Crucially, the issue of repatriation is also largely absent from the media in the West, while it remains the foremost concern in Bangladesh. It is crucial to acknowledge the complex diplomatic situation that Bangladesh finds itself in regarding the Rohingya crisis. Not only has Bangladesh been hosting over a million Rohingya refugees since 2017, but it also faces major challenges in maintaining a delicate balance between multiple key players on this issue. China's role as a mediator looms large, and there are concerns about escalating tensions with Myanmar. Interestingly, our research shows that the crisis has received the least attention in South and Southeast Asian countries in comparison to those in the West. Particularly, the Association of Southeast Asian Nations (ASEAN) pact and its member countries only made very limited efforts to address the Rohingya crisis, despite their geographic proximity and potential influence. Yet lately, ASEAN leaders have barred the Myanmar military chief from attending the yearly summit due to their concern over Myanmar's treatment of the Rohingya people. Still, none of the major media outlets in this region has endorsed "genocide" as the appropriate term to describe the atrocities committed against Rohingya Muslims in Myanmar. So far, all the media coverage has failed to garner support from the international community for repatriation.

Furthermore, media bias and framing can also influence public opinion on the issue. Some of the media outlets in the Global South covered news of the dubious ARSA, which might be tied to some terror activities. Media outlets both in the East and West also failed to cover the plights of other ethnic minority groups fighting the same opponents (i.e., against the Myanmar military). Unfortunately, media coverage of this matter tends to be inadequate and often fails to recognize these complexities. While much attention has been paid to the human rights violations against the Rohingya people themselves, which remain an urgent concern, less emphasis has been placed on how host countries like Bangladesh navigate foreign policy quagmires around international crises such as this one. In light of these factors, there is a growing recognition that addressing the Rohingya crisis must involve broader perspectives beyond just humanitarian aid or condemnation of atrocities committed by security forces in Myanmar. Instead, we need more nuanced analyses from different angles, including political diplomacy playing out among nations involved here, for prompt resolution and the betterment of lives affected by ongoing turmoil in the Rakhine State region.

4 Humanitarian Response to the Displacement

The Rohingya refugee crisis, which has seen over a million refugees displaced since its start in 2017, is an unparalleled humanitarian catastrophe that necessitates a worldwide effort for resolution. It is disconcerting to witness the absence of support from ASEAN and other neighboring countries, which could have more impact due to proximity and influence; their lack of action exacerbates the prevailing situation. To address this complex problem sustainably requires taking effective measures not just locally but on international levels to find viable solutions toward a resolution. Additionally, we must acknowledge the need for long-term solutions beyond simply providing immediate aid. There must be a push toward increased funding and support for development programs, education, healthcare initiatives, and economic opportunities to ensure the Rohingya community is integrated into society and has a viable future that extends beyond mere survival. As alluded to above, the issue of resolving the crisis is multidimensional, necessitating a comprehensive approach that considers not just humanitarian aid but also political diplomacy and economic sustainability. Although the conflict in Ukraine continues to dominate the news cycle, it is crucial not to overlook other pressing issues, such as the ongoing Rohingya settlement and repatriation crisis. Unfortunately, this topic has received little attention in policy discussions both locally and globally, despite its significant impact on affected populations and surrounding nations (Islam & Wara, 2022). Many researchers, however, have made note of this impact; Imtiaz Ahmed, Thomas K. Ragland, and David Scott Mathieson all write about "the Rohingya problems of violation of their human rights, their statelessness, critical deportation issues, and other related crises in border areas" (Rahman & Sakib, 2021).

One aspect that has been largely overlooked in discussions surrounding the Rohingya displacement crisis is the role of political diplomacy. This crisis is not just a humanitarian issue, but also one that requires political engagement, conflict resolution, and diplomatic negotiation. The lack of action from neighboring countries and regional organizations is a result of their failure to recognize the political dimensions of this crisis. As such, policymakers and political leaders must recognize the importance of engaging in meaningful dialog to address the Rohingya displacement crisis and take it beyond the humanitarian crisis. To effectively address the ongoing Rohingya displacement crisis, policymakers must prioritize far-reaching solutions beyond providing immediate humanitarian aid. Last, but most importantly, the core concern that acts as a stumbling block in all the efforts to resolve the Rohingya crisis is the lack of recognition of Rohingyas as citizens of Myanmar—or, in other words, the issue of statelessness. This issue not only affects their basic human rights, but also hampers their prospects of integration into society and economic sustainability. Therefore, addressing the issue of statelessness should be an integral part of any comprehensive solution to the Rohingya crisis. Take, e.g., the latest China-mediated repatriation initiative, where a select group of Rohingyas from Bangladesh traveled to Rakhine State to test the feasibility of repatriation and said unequivocally that they wouldn't go back unless their demand for citizenship was met.

5 Security Concerns in the Rohingya Crisis

The Rohingya crisis is not just a humanitarian issue; it also has significant security implications (Rahman, 2010). The large-scale displacement of Rohingya refugees has created social and economic challenges for host countries, especially Bangladesh. It poses a significant security threat to Bangladesh, as the refugees generate conflict, tensions, and insecurity in three ways. First, locally, within the Cox's Bazar area, several armed hostile groups are operating and vying for control of the refugee camps. Already, such groups were responsible for the killing of prominent Rohingya leader Mohibullah in 2021 and threatened to derail the repatriation process. Second, regionally, the area around Cox's Bazar has become known as a route for trafficking drugs and part of the "Golden Triangle" of the Southeast Asian drug trade. In July 2022, Bangladesh held an international seminar on drug trafficking in this area, and it portrayed a grim picture of the future if the existing trade goes unchecked. Third, the Rohingya crisis could potentially destabilize the entire region due to its proximity to major powers like India and China. The lack of legal refugee status for the Rohingya people increases their vulnerability and risks exposing them to harsher security measures. Additionally, it should be noted that the crisis also has implications for global security, as it allows extremist groups like the ISIS-inspired ARSA to exploit the situation and expand their presence in the region. Also, the military coup d'état in 2021 resulted in the creation of the National Unity Government (NUG) and its armed wing, the People's Defense Force (PDF), which vowed to dislodge the military from Myanmar. It must not be forgotten that 23 ethnic armed organizations have been embroiled in conflict with the Myanmar military since 1948. This adds additional layers to the already volatile situation in and around Myanmar and the southeastern part of Bangladesh. Therefore, the international community must address the security implications of this crisis along with its humanitarian aspects. It is important to note that the security concerns surrounding the Rohingya crisis are not solely limited to armed conflict. The director of the Bangladesh Institute of International and Strategic Studies (BIISS), Major General Md. Emdad-Ul-Bari, has highlighted that Rohingya refugees have shown a tendency to flare up conflicts and threaten national security in both transit and destination countries. The potential for civil unrest and a rift between the host community and the Rohingya community in the area can arise if the host community feels that government efforts to increase security in the region are insufficient.

6 International Law and Human Rights Violations

Although humanitarian and human rights perspectives have received extensive coverage regarding the Rohingyas, a comprehensive foreign policy perspective with respect to host countries has received much less attention. The Rohingya displacement crisis is also fundamentally a human rights issue, with countless reports of violence, persecution, and discrimination against this minority group. In addition to the multidimensional approach discussed earlier, it is important to consider the role of international law and human rights in addressing this crisis. The displacement of the Rohingya population is a clear violation of numerous international human rights standards, including the right to life, liberty, and security of person, freedom, and most importantly, freedom from genocide.

7 Role of Regional Actors vis-à-vis Bangladesh, the Largest Host Country in the Crisis

As discussed, the Rohingya displacement crisis has implications for regional stability and security. The crisis poses a significant threat to the stability of Bangladesh, which is currently hosting over a million refugees and facing challenges in managing the concomitant economic and security implications. Therefore, it is necessary to consider the role of regional actors in addressing this crisis, particularly neighboring countries like China and India, which have significant political and economic influence in the region. China's role in the crisis has not changed much since August 25, 2017. China has consistently maintained its position in the United Nations (UN) and elsewhere that it considers the crisis an internal matter of Myanmar, and has largely refrained from taking any concrete action toward resolving the crisis. India has maintained a similar stance to China, and has not made any significant efforts to resolve the crisis. Although both China and India have made some humanitarian aid contributions to Bangladesh, they have yet to take the necessary steps toward resolving the crisis at its root cause. Japan's role is also worth considering, as it is a significant donor to the region and has shown an interest in contributing to resolving the crisis. So far it has maintained its status of "investor" for Myanmar, and has only expressed interest in providing funds for humanitarian causes. It is worthwhile to remember that Bangladesh is a close diplomatic friend of both China and Japan, who are archrivals in the region's geopolitics, while it is surrounded by India in the east, west, and north. Both India and Japan are members of the newly formed coalition called the Quad (the Quadrilateral Security Dialog, or QSD), led by the USA, which has greatly upset China. Also, the brewing tension between the US and China has impacted the host country, Bangladesh, and has the potential to further complicate efforts to resolve the Rohingya crisis. On the eve of the sixth anniversary of the crisis, it is quite evident that China, India, and Japan, who are not only the key players in the region but also have significant global influence, have no interest in making significant efforts toward resolving the Rohingya crisis. Gradually, these countries come to view the Rohingya crisis as inevitable, and host countries like Bangladesh are left to bear the brunt of the crisis with its far-reaching consequences for security, the economy, and regional politics.

8 Methodology

This book is a collection of chapters from various authors. Each chapter has been written based on a robust methodology. However, most of the data for the book were collected from primary research conducted between 2020 and 2022 by a team of researchers and scholars from the Peace and Conflict Studies (PACS) Department, University of Dhaka, Bangladesh. Considering the complexities and diverse actors involved, their study applied a mixed-methods inquiry with multiple tools that were employed throughout its various stages. The mixed method is a process of collecting, analyzing, and presenting data by using both qualitative and quantitative methodologies (Morse, 2016). In a conflict situation, information from the micro (experiences and processes) and macro (trends and patterns) level is required to substantiate and validate any findings (Thaler, 2011). In the context of micro- and macro-level information, adopting both qualitative and quantitative methods provides greater scope to explore robust findings.

A combined research approach has been followed to explore a comprehensive set of information. This not only includes a review of wider secondary literature including books, journals, and publicly available policy documents, but also uses newspaper articles published on the Rohingya crisis and its impact on the lives of all communities in Cox's Bazar. Besides the secondary sources of data, the study has used four different approaches for collecting primary data both from the Rohingya camps and their surrounding areas, as well as from other relevant locations with regards to expert interviews. These four approaches include: (i) Surveys of Bengali people living near Rohingya camp settlements; (ii) Focus Group Discussions (FGDs) with Rohingya people in the camps of Cox's Bazar; (iii) Key Informant Interviews (KIIs) with involved and educated people in affected communities; and (iv) Expert Interviews (EIs).

This study employed FGDs among the Rohingyas because conducting surveys among the Rohingyas is a singularly difficult task due to language, access to the camps, security, and non-response tendency. Thus, FGDs were conducted with Rohingya respondents such as Majhis, Imams, community leaders, and teachers. This process enabled researchers to collect data from the Rohingya community required for this study. Key Informant Interviews and Expert Interviews were used to achieve an in-depth understanding about the Rohingyas, the current conflict situation, and potential for future conflict in Bangladesh.

In sum, it can be said that authors have used diverse methodologies–qualitative, quantitative, and mixed methods–for writing each chapter. However, this book as a whole is based on mixed methods by combining of narrative and descriptive statistics information for analyzing data and presenting information.

9 Geographic Area of the Study

The geographic area of the study includes the refugee camps located in Cox's Bazar (Map. 1) and the surrounding areas in the Noakhali district of Bangladesh.

Since the displacement of the Rohingyas, they have been living in Cox's Bazar district in Bangladesh. After 2017, more than millions of Rohingyas are living in this area. As of 2020, there are 34 camps located in Kutupalong and Nayapara of Cox's Bazar (tables in subsequent chapters offer information on the camp populations of the two locations); among them, five camps from Kutupalong/Ukhiya and five camps from Nayapara/Teknaf were been selected for this inquiry based on a random selection (Fig. 1). The random selection was performed with the help of a random number generator in order to ensure that the selection process constituted a fully random selection.

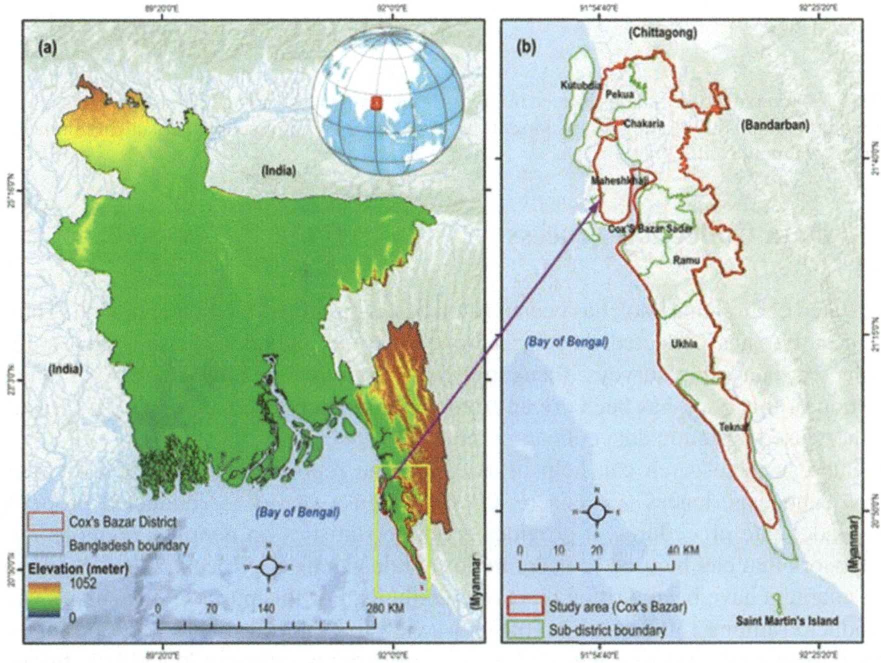

Map 1 **a** Location of the Cox's Bazar in Bangladesh and **b** the sub-districts of Cox's Bazar district. Digital elevation model (DEM). *Source* Adnan et al. (2020)

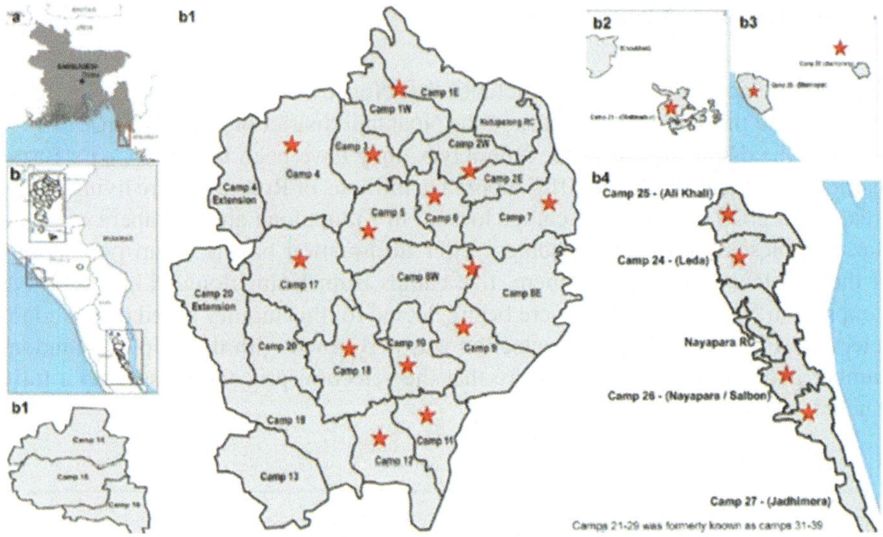

Fig. 1 Rohingya refugee camps located in Cox's Bazar, Bangladesh; as of 2023, Kutupalong is host to more than 800,000 Rohingyas, making it the most dense camp in people per square kilometer. *Source* Mahmud et al. (2019)

10 Data Collection Process

As stated earlier, this book has been written based on mixed-method approach. Thus, each author has collected data by adopting various methods. In sum, this study collected data using surveys, focus group discussions, and interviews. As a major portion of this book has been driven from the field study conducted in Cox's Bazar, authors used systemic data collection method.

Surveys in research can help in assessing the representativeness of individual views and experiences (Greenacre, 2016). When a survey is conducted properly with adequate procedures, it provides concrete statistics on people's opinions and behaviors that can be used to make important decisions (DeRoeck, 2004). Some of the chapters have been written on mixed methods. For this purpose, the survey was conducted among 150 Bengali people with a view to exploring their perceptions of the Rohingya people. Surveys among Bengali respondents were conducted in February 2022. Questions involved factors such as the way respondents view the Rohingya refugees' presence in their territory, what impacts the Rohingya people are having on the social, economic, and political affairs of the region, and how the presence of a large number of Rohingyas has influenced the livelihoods of the local people. Figure 1 illustrates the study locations involving the camps and their surrounding areas in Teknaf and Kutupalong. The participants, like the camp areas themselves, were randomly selected. However, the study conducted surveys only among people over 18 years of age.

For information to substantiate the data, 10 FGDs were conducted in 10 study locations in Cox's Bazar where the Rohingyas are living in close proximity to the local Bengalese. The FGDs involved Rohingya people living in the camps in Cox's Bazar. In each of the 10 camps, at least one FGD was held that included six to eight residents of the camp (see Appendix 1). Moreover, four FGDs were held with female residents of the camps to achieve sufficient feedback from both genders. The FGDs were undertaken at different times between April and May of 2022. The participants were willing to voluntarily participate in the FGDs. As this is long-term policy research, these FGDs are considered adequate in providing a comprehensive idea of the current conditions within the camps. The FGDs involved assessing the conflict potential between the host and refugee populations, from the side of the refugee population, in sociopolitical, economic and environmental, and security dimensions.

This study also conducted 15 KIIs in the Rohingya camps and among local residents during the time between February and May of 2022 (see Appendix 2). In each camp, at least two people were targeted for KIIs. For this study, stakeholders were interviewed who have knowledge of the conditions of the camps and perspectives of the resident Rohingyas. This list of KIIs includes participants from the community such as camp leaders (Majhi), educated Rohingya, female Rohingya leaders, people working in the camp areas to meet the needs of the Rohingya population, and law enforcement authorities, including police. In the context of local individuals, this study also targeted the people who are living close to the Rohingya camps such as school teachers, local representatives, journalists, shopkeepers, and student leaders. The key informants were highly cooperative during the interviews, conducted with the help of our skilled assistants in the field.

This study also conducted 10 EIs with experts possessing high levels of competence and working experience in this particular topic (see Appendix 3). Expert Interviews aid the research process in gaining and exploring contextual, implicit expert knowledge of a social issue (Döringer, 2020). In the study, the researchers interviewed experts who have significant knowledge and understanding from the academic, human rights, environmental, governance, and administrative perspectives of the crisis. Therefore, the list of EIs includes human rights activists, academicians, environmentalists, government officials, and nongovernmental organization (NGO) personnel. The researchers queried them for their opinions on the conflict potential of the Rohingya crisis in Cox's Bazar between the host and refugee populations. Questionnaires were specifically tailored to their respective fields of expertise, and the research team obtained their full cooperation in lengthy in-depth EIs. In Cox's Bazar, interviews were conducted with experts including officials working at the Rohingya camps, officials managing the construction work within the camps, NGO workers, and officials managing camp security. The EIs involved retrieving additional data that could reliably complement, guide, and elaborate upon the assessment of the conflict potential between the host and refugee population in sociopolitical, economic and environmental, and security dimensions, obtained via the surveys and the FGDs.

11 Limitations in Data Collection

Collecting data from any population on sensitive issues such as security and political problems poses a serious challenge to social research. For this reason, selecting the most suitable method of extracting the most reliable data from participants is a challenging task. Though pilot projects and expert consultations can provide insight into the method most suitable for the task of gathering the most consistent and reliable data for any social research, questions may arise regarding the reason behind the selection process between different populations. The FGD method has been deemed most suited to retrieving data from the Rohingya population, yielding qualitative data for the researchers to work with. On the other hand, surveys have been used to gather data from the Bengali participants, yielding quantitative data for the researchers to work with. These different methods were selected to extract data from within settings in which participants feel most comfortable with regards to discussing sensitive issues. Accuracy of the data has been prioritized over streamlining the process of comparing the same forms of data. However, issues with different data have been minimized as the key dimensions of the conflict potential—sociopolitical, economic and environmental, and security dimensions—have been kept consistent when comparing the two types of data.

12 Data Presentation

After completing the field study, FGDs, KIIs, and EIs, the survey data was entered into the computer-assisted software program Statistical Package for the Social Sciences (SPSS). This helped to explore any inconsistencies or faults of the data. The SPSS program also provided a summary of the indices of the data. First, survey data was presented using descriptive statistics, which is a powerful tool for presenting the data. This survey data illustrated the perceptions of the Bengali host population. The FGD data was transcribed to determine common themes, arguments, and information provided by the Rohingya people about the sociopolitical, economic, and environmental issues of Cox's Bazar. After presenting the survey information, the FGD information was similarly presented to see how the Rohingya and Bengali host people view the issues of conflict potentials, either differently or similarly. The KII data was interpreted manually and presented to corroborate, support, or contrast the information provided by the survey and FGDs. Finally, the EIs were transcribed and interpreted as well as corroborated with the survey, FGD, and KII information.

13 Ethical Considerations

Ethical concerns regarding the sensitive nature of the data collected for this study have been minimized, as the utmost care has been ensured in obtaining the full consent of the parties and participants involved in the data collection process. The sensitive nature of the data requires that all information with regards to traceable identities of participants remain anonymous, and the confidentiality aspect of the data collection process has been handled with care and consideration. Minimizing the ethical concerns greatly assisted researchers in obtaining reliable data from the participants with regards to assessing the conflict potential between host and refugee communities in Cox's Bazar, Bangladesh.

14 Contents

In this book, we seek to explore the complex dynamics surrounding the Rohingya crisis, analyzing the crisis from security, media, and humanitarian perspectives.

Part I discusses historical context and Rohingyas ethnic identity formation in Myanmar and abroad. In Chap. 2, the authors explain that Rohingyas, a historically oppressed group faced mistreatment and discrimination for generations. The 1982 Citizenship Act stripped them of citizenship, despite being recognized as an ethnic group. Chapter 2 explores the Rohingyas' origins, identity, and citizenship status, using secondary sources and historical records to provide a comprehensive understanding of their way of life and citizenship. Chapter 3 elaborates on the Rohingya settlement in Bangladesh, its history, and the current situation post-2017, focusing on measures taken by the government and international agencies to accommodate the growing Rohingya population.

Part II analyzes conflict dynamics and security implications. Chapter 4 offers a succinct overview of the potential for conflict between the Rohingya refugee population and the existing Bangladeshi host community. It pays particular attention to the changes engendered by the crisis in the social composition of Cox's Bazar, the region hosting the majority of the Rohingya refugees. Chapter 5 discusses how the Rohingya conflict in Bangladesh has significantly impacted the country's economy and environment due to increased demographic pressure. The conflict's potential areas include unmet demand for commodities, livelihood competition, price hikes, and environmental degradation. Chapter 6 illustrates how the Rohingya conflict in Bangladesh has escalated due to complex bilateral and multilateral relations. The conflict's potential includes mutual distrust, threat perception, insurgent activities, hampering cooperation, Bangladesh's vulnerability, illicit businesses, and human trafficking. The chapter focuses on key areas of conflict potential. Chapter 7 examines the sociopolitical conflict potential of the Rohingya crisis in Bangladesh, focusing on seven areas: population, resource scarcity, health care, education, public goods, gender issues, and political issues. We find that the conflict's impact on the host community is often negative. Chapter 8 covers the geopolitical context and security ramifications of the conflict with particular reference to inter-state relationship. Chapter 9 recalls how Myanmar experienced some normalcy in 2011, but the military staged a coup against the National League for Democracy (NLD) government in 2021, leading to chaos and violence. The dream of inclusive democracy was thus shattered, and the ethnic reconciliation process faces a bleak future. Factors contributing to this failed process include Burmanization, radical Buddhism, military hegemonic attitudes, constitutional alienation of minorities, and violence and discrimination against different ethnic groups. Chapter 10 explores the complex relationship between Rohingya camps, their environment, and their propensity for fostering criminal activities. It focuses on the crime and securitization challenges; the presence of criminal gangs, illegal weapons, and abduction; gender-based violence, extremism, and insecurity; refugee populations' impact on crime; and the overall impacts of the Rohingya camps on crime in Bangladesh. The chapter also examines the impact of refugee populations on crime rates, socioeconomic factors, resource constraints, and competition for limited resources. The overall impacts of the Rohingya camps on crime in Bangladesh are evaluated, emphasizing the need for holistic approaches that address socioeconomic, cultural, and security challenges to mitigate criminal activities and promote the well-being of the Rohingya population.

Part III covers the role of media in the conflict. Here, Chap. 11 explores the historical "othering" of Rohingyas, the conceptual ideas of propaganda, the propaganda model, and the major propaganda used against them. It provides a comprehensive analysis of the role of the media and propaganda in shaping negative narratives and perpetuating discrimination against the Rohingya community. The chapter explores the sociopolitical factors contributing to their exclusion and the construction of an "other" identity. The propaganda model is introduced to explain how media institutions serve as powerful actors and perpetuate biased narratives. The chapter also examines the tactics and narratives employed by state-controlled media, hate speech, social media platforms, books, and religious leaders to stigmatize and dehumanize the Rohingya community. Chapter 12 looks into media framing (Western and Oriental media coverage), critical discourse analysis, and the role of social media in conflict. It also covers hate speech and propaganda (the Ma Ba Tha movement) that fueled the anti-Rohingya conflict.

Chapter 13 examines the security issues faced by the Bangladesh Police as a law-enforcing agency in Cox's Bazar due to the Rohingya presence. Over 1.3 million Rohingyas live in the area, causing security threats to refugees and local communities alike. The study described in this chapter uses a mixed-method approach, including content analysis, a questionnaire survey, KII, and FGD, to assess the capabilities of the Armed Police Battalion (APBn) in handling the Rohingya camp's security concerns. The findings provide recommendations for policy directives to better equip the APBn to handle the evolving dynamics of the Rohingya presence in Cox's Bazar, Bangladesh.

Part IV details right to return, peace-building, and camp management. Chapter 14 discusses social cohesion and integration probability (although a hotly contested topic in Bangladesh) of Rohingyas within the host community. Chapter 15 critically examines the repatriation of Rohingya refugees from Bangladesh to Myanmar, focusing on the complexities and challenges surrounding the process. It analyzes the government of Bangladesh's humanitarian approach, the challenges faced in hosting a large refugee population, and the government's efforts to engage with Myanmar and the international community. It also includes expert opinions on the feasibility and challenges of repatriation, the perspectives of Rohingya refugees, Myanmar's position on the issue, and the government's efforts to address the crisis. It identifies key factors influencing the success or failure of repatriation efforts, such as a comprehensive citizenship framework, sustainable development in Rakhine State, and a trust-building mechanism. It also evaluates the role of regional and international stakeholders in supporting repatriation and discusses the potential impact of ongoing legal proceedings at the International Court of Justice. Chapter 16 elaborates on the fact that Myanmar signed an agreement with Bangladesh in November 2017 to repatriate the Rohingyas, but this initiative failed due to mistrust and fear. Two more initiatives under Myanmar's Suu Kyi regime failed due to opaque policies. The recent Myanmar military junta's initiative to repatriate the Rohingya group halted earlier repatriation talks. Chapter 17 discusses the relocation of Rohingyas to Bhasan Char island, and whether this is a practical step toward a sustainable resolution of the conflict internally for Bangladesh. Chapter 18 investigates the role of education in peace-building and fostering social cohesion in Rohingya refugee camps in Bangladesh. It examines how teachers can influence belonging and civic engagement for children, using critical design theory to determine the feasibility of civic education delivery given the unique legal status of Rohingya refugees.

15 Challenges for Sustainable Conflict Resolution

Although the book does not intend to suggest policy options, it aims to provide a comprehensive understanding of the crisis and its various dimensions, which will enable policymakers, academics, and activists to gain greater insights into potential solutions. It is imperative that the international community work toward preventing another situation like Palestine and put an end to the ongoing crisis that has been raging for six long years. The repercussions of allowing such crises to persist are far-reaching and inevitably lead to dire consequences in terms of human suffering, social unrest, economic instability, and political turmoil on a global scale. There are several challenges for the international community in coming up with a solution to the Rohingya crisis. First, finding a sustainable and safe way to repatriate Rohingya refugees back to Myanmar while ensuring they are not subjected to further persecution by the military junta. In this regard, finding a way to open a dialog with the current regime is important. It is not meant to legitimize the military junta, but rather to find a way to engage with them in constructive discussions that could lead to some form of resolution. Although some observers might opine that engagement should not be made with a regime that has committed atrocities against its people, it is important to remember the ultimate goal of achieving peace and justice for the Rohingya people. Also, given the existing situation where Suu Kyi and her NLD are largely underground and the NUG has persistent legitimacy issues both locally and globally, there is no viable pathway outside of talking to the military junta about a durable solution to the problem. Second, supporting host countries to negotiate a deal with Myanmar is important since they still maintain a reasonably balanced diplomatic relationship with Myanmar. Third, providing humanitarian assistance to Rohingya refugees in the host countries, such as Bangladesh and Malaysia, is critical given their limited resources and capacity to manage the influx of refugees. Fourth, often we hear the well-intentioned but meaningless phrase "we need to create more pressure on Myanmar to take back the Rohingyas" in various international forums; however, creating meaningful pressure requires coordinated efforts among international actors, such as using economic sanctions or diplomatic isolation. And here the role of the "Big Three" countries (China, Japan, and India) comes into play. Unless these countries change their positions beyond "realpolitik," there is hardly any hope for a lasting solution to the Rohingya crisis.

This book aims to provide a comprehensive analysis of the Rohingya displacement crisis from multiple perspectives. If the international community and the "Big Three" are not willing to take meaningful actions, this crisis will continue to threaten the stability of the region and exacerbate the already-dire humanitarian situation faced by the Rohingyas. We are, it must be said, also talking about the possibility of the extinction of an ethno-cultural group. The children born in Bangladesh and other countries hosting Rohingyas will remain stateless and without basic rights such as education and health care. Children who are born into crises, such as the Rohingya crisis, have no control over their circumstances. Therefore, the international community must take on its responsibility to safeguard and uphold their rights. By doing so, we can ensure a better future for these children despite the challenges they face due to forces beyond their control.

In conclusion, the Rohingya crisis is no longer just a humanitarian issue. It has regional security and stability implications that need to be addressed urgently. The international community must take concerted and meaningful actions to address this crisis in a comprehensive manner that considers all aspects of the issue. Focusing only on short-term solutions will not resolve the problem, but rather exacerbate it. We cannot allow ourselves to watch an ethno-cultural group disappear from the face of the Earth, especially when we are only talking about providing basic human rights such as education and health care for children born into crises like the Rohingya one. Therefore, all stakeholders must work together toward finding a lasting solution to the Rohingya crisis for the sake of both regional stability and the basic human rights of those affected. This book hopes to contribute to this goal by providing a detailed analysis of the Rohingya crisis from multiple angles, including security, media, and humanitarian perspectives.

Appendix 1 Focus Group Discussion (FGD) statistics

FGD number	Male	Female
FGD-1	5	0
FGD-2	6	0
FGD-3	5	0
FGD-4	0	6
FGD-5	0	7
FGD-6	3	4
FGD-7	0	5
FGD-8	5	4
FGD-9	6	0
FGD-10	0	5
Total	30	31

Appendix 2 Key Informant Interview (KII) statistics

No.	Identity	Age	Location
1	President of the local journalists' association	57	Tekhnaf
2	Member (a local representative)	40	Ukhia
3	Local businessman	44	Kutupalong camp, Ukhiya
4	School teacher	40	Shamlapur, Teknaf
5	A Majhi	45	Unchiparong, Teknaf
6	NGO worker	35	Ykhiya Sadar
7	A local journalist	40	Tekhnaf
8	Madrasa teacher	50	Ukhiya
9	Student	25	Tekhnaf
10	Housewife	32	Ukhiya
11	Women leader	30	Ukhiya
12	Member of a Union Parishad	40	Tekhnaf
13	Head Majhi	50	UKhiya
14	NGO worker	35	Ukhiya
15	A community leader	35	Tekhnaf

Appendix

See Appendices 1, 2 and 3.

Appendix 3 Expert Interview (EI) statistics

No.	Identity of the expert	Age	Gender	Location
1	Anthropologist and academician	45	M	Chittagong
2	Professor of International Relations, University of Dhaka	55	M	Dhaka
3	Director of an International Organization based in Bangladesh	50	M	Dhaka
4	Employee of the International Organization of Migration (IOM)	30	F	Cox's Bazar
5	Former diplomat and security expert	67	M	Dhaka
6	A journalist and activist	60	M	Cox's Bazar
7	An education policy analyst and researcher	37	F	Dhaka
8	Director of a Research Organization and academician	62	F	Dhaka
9	A Jailor	45	M	Cox's Bazar
10	A police officer stationed in Cox's Bazar	50	M	Cox's Bazar

References

Adnan, M. S. G., Rahman, M. S., Ahmed, N., Ahmed, B., Rabbi, M. F., & Rahman, R. M. (2020). Improving spatial agreement in machine learning-based landslide susceptibility mapping. *Remote Sensing, 12*(20), 3347.

Alam, J. (2019). The current Rohingya crisis in Myanmar in historical perspective. *Journal of Muslim Minority Affairs, 39*(1), 1–25.

Cousins, S. (2018). "People will die" as monsoon approaches Rohingya refugee camps in Bangladesh. *BMJ: British Medical Journal, 361*. https://doi.org/10.1136/bmj.k2040

DeRoeck, D. (2004). The importance of engaging policy-makers at the outset to guide research on and introduction of vaccines: The use of policy-maker surveys. *Journal of Health, Population and Nutrition, 22*(3), 322–330. https://www.jstor.org/stable/23499147

Döringer, S. (2020). 'The problem-centred expert interview': Combining qualitative interviewing approaches for investigating implicit expert knowledge. *International Journal of Social Research Methodology, 24*(3), 265–278. https://doi.org/10.1080/13645579.2020.1766777

Greenacre, Z. A. (2016). The importance of selection bias in internet surveys. *Open Journal of Statistics, 6*(3), 397–404. https://doi.org/10.4236/ojs.2016.63035

Islam, M. R., & Wara, U. (2022). Conflict potential of the Rohingya people in Bangladesh and beyond. *Journal of ASEAN Studies, 10*(1), 107–127. https://doi.org/10.21512/jas.v10i1.8215

Lee, M. J. (2021). Media influence on humanitarian interventions: Analysis of the Rohingya refugee crisis and international media coverage. *Journal of International Humanitarian Action, 6*(1), 20.

Mahmud, Z. H., Islam, M. S., Imran, K. M., Hakim, S. A. I., Worth, M., Ahmed, A., Hossan, S., Haider, M., Islam, M. R., Hossain, F., Johnston, D., & Ahmed, N. (2019). Occurrence of Escherichia coli and faecal coliforms in drinking water at source and household point-of-use in Rohingya camps, Bangladesh. *Gut Pathogens, 11*(1), 1–11.

Mohanty, B. (2020). Understanding media portrayal of Rohingya refugees. In N. Chowdhory & B. Mohanty (Eds.), *Citizenship, nationalism and refugeehood of Rohingyas in Southern Asia* (pp. 97–111). Springer.

Morse, J. M. (2016). *Mixed method design: Principles and procedures*. Routledge.

Pedersen, M. B. (2019). The ICC, the Rohingya and the limitations of retributive justice. *Australian Journal of International Affairs, 73*(1), 9–15.

Prasse-Freeman, E. (2017). The Rohingya crisis. *Anthropology Today, 33*(6), 1–2.
Rahman, U. (2010). The Rohingya refugee: A security dilemma for Bangladesh. *Journal of Immigrant & Refugee Studies, 8*(2), 233–239.
Rahman, M. S., & Sakib, N. H. (2021). Statelessness, forced migration and the security dilemma along borders: An investigation of the foreign policy stance of Bangladesh on the Rohingya influx. *SN Social Sciences, 1*(7). https://doi.org/10.1007/s43545-021-00173-y
Thaler, K. (2011). Mixed methods research in the study of violence and conflict. In *6th General Conference of the European Consortium on Political Research (ECPR), University of Iceland, Reykjavik.*
Tripura, E. (2022). Confined, controlled, and violated: The Rohingya women in Bangladesh refugee camps. *Feminist Encounters: A Journal of Critical Studies in Culture and Politics, 6*(2), 25. https://doi.org/10.20897/femenc/12348
Ullah, A. K. M. A. (2011). Rohingya refugee to Bangladesh: Historical exclusions and contemporary marginalization. *Journal of Immigrant and Refugee studies, 9*(2), 139–168.
Ullah, A. K. M. A. (2016). Rohingya crisis in Myanmar: Seeking justice for the 'stateless'. *Journal of Contemporary Criminal Justice, 32*(3), 285–301.
Ullah, A. A., & Chattoraj, D. (2018). Roots of discrimination against Rohingya minorities: Society, ethnicity and international relations. *Intellectual Discourse, 26*(2), 541–565.

Part I
Historical Context and Ethnic Identity

Chapter 2
A History of Rohingya Displacement, Rohingya Ethnicity, and Contested Identity in Myanmar and Bangladesh

Md. Rafiqul Islam and Amena Khatun

Abstract The Rohingya is one of the most oppressed and mistreated populations in the world. Despite living in Myanmar for centuries, today they have no state. The Myanmar government does not acknowledge them as citizens; they believe that the Rohingya people moved from Bengal to Arakan during the British colonial period. Accordingly, the country's 1982 Citizenship Act stripped the Rohingya of their citizenship, failing to even include them as one of the 135 government-recognized ethnic groups. There are many disagreements regarding the Rohingya's ancestry and ethnicity, as some factions believe they are illegal immigrants from Bangladesh, especially the then-East Pakistan, while other factions claim that they are the indigenous or native people of Arakan in Myanmar. However, historical evidence indicates that Rohingyas are the descendants of several mixed races and have long been living in the Arakan region. This chapter addresses the origin, identity, and citizenship status of the Rohingya population in Myanmar. It also details who the Rohingya are, what the term "Rohingya" means, where they come from, and why and how the Myanmar government refused them citizenship. The information contained here comes from secondary sources or historical records. A variety of scholarly journals, books, newspaper articles, and online materials are employed to illustrate the significance of the Rohingya and their origins, way of life, and questions of citizenship.

1 Introduction

The Rohingyas are a mostly Muslim population that descended from a variety of ancestors over many years, with historical ties to Bengali, Persian, and Arabian high cultures (Islam, 2018; Ullah, 2011). They are often classified as a South Asian

Md. R. Islam (✉)
University of Dhaka, Dhaka, Bangladesh
e-mail: rislampacs@du.ac.bd

A. Khatun
University of Rajshahi, Rajshahi, Bangladesh

K. Ahmed and Md. R. Islam (eds.), *Understanding the Rohingya Displacement*, International Perspectives on Migration, https://doi.org/10.1007/978-981-97-1424-7_2

ethno-linguistic and religious minority group who currently have no state, though they have lived in Myanmar for the past 200 years (Alam, 2018; Uddin, 2015). The United Nations (UN) has referred to the Rohingyas as the "most persecuted minority group" in the world due to the decades of forced migration, relocation, restrictions on their freedom of movement, brutality, and oppression by the Myanmar government (Sudheer & Banarjee, 2021). From 1978 to 2017, Rohingyas were sporadically forced to flee to different neighboring countries to avoid such persecution. At present, around 1.3 million Rohingyas are living in the different refugee camps in Cox's Bazar, a southern part of Bangladesh, as forcibly displaced people (Forcibly Displaced Myanmar Nationals), the majority of them having arrived after the mass exodus in 2017 to protect themselves from crackdowns by the Myanmar military (Alam, 2021). However, the history of Rohingyas in Myanmar has always been divisive and turbulent, and there are some controversies about the identity of this group of people in the country. For example, Dr. Eye Chan (2005) notes that in the 1950s, Bengali Muslim intellectuals who migrated from the Chittagong district of then-East Pakistan started to use the term "Rohingya" to describe themselves (Chan, 2005). Some academics, on the other hand, have written that the Rohingyas are the mixed descendants of Persians, Arabs, Turks, Moors, Mughals, and Bengalis who arrived via both maritime and land routes as pilgrims, traders, and soldiers (Uddin, 2020; Ullah & Chattoraj, 2018). While the Myanmar government refers to them as "Muslims in Rakhine State" rather than "Rohingya," some anti-Islamic radicals of the country refer to Rohingyas as "Bengalis"; nevertheless, the Muslims of Rakhine prefer to be referred to as "Rohingya" (Ebbighausen, 2017).

The official stance is unsurprising, as Myanmar not only officially does not recognize the Rohingya as an ethnic group, but also asserts that the Rohingyas were never residents of Burma; rather, that they migrated to Arakan during the British colonial era beginning in 1824 (Chan, 2005). This state narrative was instrumental in creating the 1982 Citizenship Act, which denied citizenship and fundamental rights to the majority of Rohingyas (The Guardian, 2014; Uddin, 2020). In addition, with the exception of the Rohingya, Myanmar's government recognizes 135 ethnic groups. This ethnic system was made possible by political compromise, negative influences, and the peculiarities of military leadership (Uddin Md Zahed & Jenkins, 2022). Indeed, the conflict surrounding the Rohingya people of Myanmar involves a multitude of factors involving identity, politics, and power struggles. However, by first focusing on the formulation of Rohingya identity and how it became contested later on, the nuances of the conflict up to its present stage can be better understood and its future trajectories better predicted.

The present chapter's goal is to analyze the name "Rohingya," as well as the history of the ethnic minority in Myanmar, its way of life, and its citizenship status there. As a research question, this chapter tends to answer what is the history of Rohingyas and how they have been excluded from the Rakhine state of Myanmar. In order to inform this aim, diverse sources have been drawn upon to properly illustrate the meaning of "Rohingya" and their roots, lives, and citizenship issues. Different secondary literature has been assessed and tried to answer the questions stated above. The structure of this chapter starts with a definition of the term "Rohingya," going on to describe their identity and life in Rakhine State. Then, this paper illustrates the citizenship status of the Rohingya people in Myanmar. Finally, a conclusion has been offered, summing up all the relevant issues.

2 What Does the Term "Rohingya" Mean?

Historically the term "Rohingya" refers to the Muslim Arakanese who have been living in the region for a several hundred years (Charney, 2005; Uddin, 2020). The term's origin has its roots in the word "Rohai," or "Rohangee," which denotes the Muslim people inhabiting historic Arakan (Uddin, 2020; Yunus, 1994). According to Aman Ullah (n.d.) Arakanese Muslims refer to their country as "Rohang" or "Roang" in their local language and identify themselves as "Rohangya," or "Roangya," which is short for "native of Rohang or Roang" (Ullah, n.d). However, Dr. Aye Chan (2005), a historian of ancient Burma and Arakan and professor at Kanda University of International Studies in Japan, states that the term "Rohingya" describes the ethnic and religious identity of the Muslims in the Rakhine State of Myanmar, and the name originated in the 1950s—and has been part of public debate ever since (Chan, 2005). Alternatively, some historians believe the term "Rohingya" was historically pronounced "Rwangya," and the name may be derived from "Rakhanga" or "Roshanga." These had been in use since before the British occupation of Arakan, and historian Francis Buchanan Hamilton wrote in 1799 that the name was common in Royal Burma (Hussain, 2018). Habibullah (2017) argues that the words "Rowai," "Rohingya," and "Rosang" have been modified so as to appear as "Rosang" to Bengali poets but as "Rowang" to the local people. Meanwhile, experts have different opinions about the origin of the word "Rowang" or "Rolang." Dr. Satyendranath Ghoshal, Dr. Ahmad Sharif, and others believe that the words "Roang/Rohang/Rosang" have been derived from the word "Mrohang," the former capital of Arakan (Habibullah, 2017).

In ancient times, Arakan was known as "Rakhaing," and later on this became the "Rakhang" or "Arkahang" of Muslim writers, finally becoming Arakan. The name of the last capital of Arakan was pronounced as "Mrohaung," which in the mouths of the local people of both Arakan and Chittagong become "Rohang" (Mohajan, 2018). In this way the people came finally to be known as "Rohangi" or Rohingya (Karim, 2016). Uddin (2020) also gave similar information about the origin of the word Rohingya. He identified that Mrohong was the original Arakanese root of Rohang, and Rohingyas were the inhabitants of Mrohong (Uddin, 2020). In the dialect of Chittagong, the word "Rakhine" came to be pronounced as "Rohong" or "Rohang," and the inhabitants of the region were therefore called Rohingya (Razzaq & Haque, 1995). In addition, there is a myth about the origin of the term Rohingya that claims that when an Arab ship capsized close to the Arakan coast, the passengers begged for assistance by saying "Raham, Raham," which in Arabic means "compassion, compassion"; locals then pronounced this word as "Rohang" and ever since, the inhabitants of the coast have been referred to as the Rohingya (Yin, 2005). According to the same myth, also mentioned by Froster and Chowdhury and cited by Zahed and Jenkins (2022), the locals saved the survivors of the sinking ship and brought them to then-king Maha Taing Chandra (788–810 CE) and the king allowed them to live in his kingdom while over time "Raham" changed to "Rohang" and finally became associated with the Rohingya.

The meaning of Rohingya is a contested one as the Myanmar authority does not acknowledge these people as Rohingya, but historical data and evidences prove that these people are recognized a "Rohingya". The displaced people who are living in the refugee camps and the diasporas also recognized them as Rohingya. Thus, the debate on labeling these people as "Rohingya" and "Bengali" is merely a political issue of the Myanmar authority to exclude them from the Myanmar. In terms of identity and racial attachment, these people are Rohingya who have distinctive identity and cultural attributes.

3 History of Rohingya Identity and Life in Rakhine State

Rohingyas are known as Arakanese Muslims in the Burmese constitution, and they are taken to represent a language-based nation who live in Arakan and speak a unified language (Ullah, 2017; Uddin, 2022). Indeed, a large portion of the population of Arakan are followers of Islam—Zerbadee, Kamein, Rohingya—but Rohingyas are the largest Muslim ethnic group among them (Akhanda, 2018; Alam, 2019). Even though the majority of the Rohingyas follow Sunni Islam or Sufism, a small number of them practice Hinduism and Christianity (International Christian Concern, 2021). Since not all Rohingyas are Muslims—as mentioned, some are Hindus and Christians—and they do not, in fact, speak the same language or have the same physical appearance, the creation of a homogenous image of this community obscures the astonishing diversity it contains (Nursyazwani & Freeman, 2020). The community arrived in Arakan in several phases and different times (Ullah, 2011). Some came as traders from as distant places as Arabia and Persia, while others came as conquerors and in the train of the invading army; still others came as victims of pirates and some even arrived in peaceful pursuits (Karim, 2016). The colonization of this area also invited people from the adjacent areas to come and work in the agricultural fields. Particularly, the British colonial power invited many people to work for them in the Rakhine state (Ullah, 2011). Therefore, the Rohingyas are not homogenous because they originated from various ethnic groups rather than simply one race or ethnicity (Habibullah, 1995).

The origin and ethnicity of the Rohingyas are, however, a matter of considerable debate (Kipgen, 2014). Some believe that Rohingyas are not Myanmar's citizens, but rather they are illegal immigrants from a neighboring country; others claim that they are indigenous to the country, but due to the lack of primary studies or supporting documentation, there is sufficient uncertainty to make the issue quite problematic (Washaly, 2019). Leider (2018) noted that "Rohingya" refers to an ethno-religious identity of Muslims in North Rakhine State in Myanmar, and they are different from the Burmese population in terms of religion and outward appearance (Leider, 2018). Due to their mixed ancestry, Rohingyas frequently have a nose that is not flat, eyes that are not as narrow as Rakhine Maghs and Burmans, a less prominent cheekbone, a darker complexion, and a little higher forehead that Rakhine Maghs (Alam, 1999). Additionally, it is claimed that Rohingyas are illegal immigrants from Bengal because they have a dialect similar to that of the Chittagong people; however, Yusuf (2018) argued regarding this issue that the Rohingyas language has Bengali influences because of the historical lack of borders in the northwest of modern-day Myanmar, which also had historically stronger political ties with Bengal (Yusuf, 2017). Minahan (2016), a reputable scholar from Spain who has written several volumes on statehood and identity, noted that the Rohingyas trace their descent from Arabs who settled the port cities in what is now Myanmar in 600 CE, and they are of mixed Arab, Bengali, and Burmese ancestry (Minahan, 2016). On the other hand, the Myanmar government defines only those who inhabited the region before the capture of Arakan in the first Anglo-Burma War in 1824 as their citizens—not the later population, as the Myanmar government and military leaders argue that the Rohingya were brought to the Rakhine region by the British Raj for farming and other jobs in the area, and the Rohingya people are their descendants (Hussain, 2018).

However, history reveals that the Rohingyas are not merely British-era immigrants, as Islam arrived in Arakan before 788 CE, and since then it appears that Rohingyas have been living there. As well, the Rohingya and the Buddhist Arakanese both speak the same language, which was the original lingua franca in Arakan (Jilani, cited in Sohel, 2017). In addition, Ludden, quoted by Ahmed and Biswas (2022), also notes that historical records indicate that the Rohingya peoples have been in the Arakan region since the eighth century. Moreover, a number of Arabic and Persian words that are present in the Burmese lexicon also attest to the presence of Muslims because they were supposedly used by Muslim traders who came to Burma between the ninth and the sixteenth centuries (Yegar, 1972). There is a myth about the identity of the Rohingyas that claims following the Karbala War in 680 CE, and Hazrat Ali's son Mohammad Bin Hanafi traveled to Arabshah para, which is very close to Maungdaw in Northern Arakan. At that time Kayapuri was ruler of the Cannibals, who, according to legend, controlled a neighboring forest and attacked as well as pillaged the Arkan population. Hanafi eventually converted Kayapuri to Islam and married her, and it is said that the followers of Hanafi and Kayapuri intermarried and coexisted amicably, and the ancestors of these mixed people are known as the Rohingya today (Alam, 1999). Hamilton (1820) identified that Arakan was known to the Moguls as Rakhang and the residents of this Rakhang were called "Rooinga," or the natives of "Aracan" (Hamilton, 1820). Late-eighteenth-century traveler Francis Buchanan also referred to the Rohingya as natives of Arakan (Buchanan, 1799).

Further, the much-contested origins of the identity of Rohingyas or Rohingya Muslims have its basis in this period, especially between the fifteenth and eighteenth centuries under Narmeikhla's rule (Bhonsale, 2015). When the Burmese king Myinsaing invaded Arakan in 1406, Narmeikhla escaped and sought safety in Gauda, the then Bengali capital, which was governed by the Ilyas Shahi dynasty. For around

24 years Narmeikhla remained in Gauda and became interested in Islamic history, politics, and civilization and changed his name to become known as Mohammad Solaiman Shah. After that, in 1430 Narmeikhla, with the help of Gauda Sultan Nasiruddin Shah, rescued his kingdom Arakan by sending twenty thousand soldiers under the command of Wali Khan. He later founded a dynasty called Mrauk-U in Arakan under the name of Mohammad Solaiman Shah, and thus, Arakan leaned toward the Muslim state, which later became Rosang and identified as an independent civilization (Ullah, 2017). Opposing the state narratives of Myanmar about Rohingyas, Uddin (2015, 2020) notes that the Arakanese first came into contact with Muslims when Arab traders stopped at an Arakan port while traveling to China in the ninth century, and the Rohingyas are said to be descended from this group of Muslims (Uddin, 2015, 2020). Mentioning anthropologist Fredrik Barth's "social organization of cultural differences," Uddin (2020) also underscored that Rohingyas should never be regarded as Bengalis based on their social, cultural, material, and non-material markers, because their behavior, attitudes, and interactions with others are completely different from those of Bengalis, who Barth's organizational framework emphasizes to be an ethnic group (Uddin, 2020, 2022).

The discussion above delineates two opposite accounts of the Rohingya's identity: one from the perspective of the Rohingya and the other from the Rakhine and Bamar people. The Rohingya version of the region's history emphasizes five key points, including the fact that ethnic Rohingya has lived in Rakhine for centuries, even before Islam arrived at the end of the eighth century, and the Rohingya language and culture predominated in Rakhine during the Mrauk-U Dynasty's rule of the region from the fifteenth to the eighteenth centuries. After the Mrauk-U Dynasty fell in 1785, the Burmese Empire conquered Rakhine, ending Muslim rule in the area. In 1826, Rakhine became a British colony, making the Rohingya British subjects. During World War II, many Rohingya enlisted in the British Army and engaged in guerrilla warfare against the Japanese with the hope of subsequently being given Rakhine as their own country; however, the British government broke its promise to establish the area as an independent country for the Rohingyas after war, so the Muslim region Rakhine remained a part of Myanmar (Tanenbaum Center for Interreligious Understanding, n.d.). On the other hand, the narratives of the Rakhine and Bamar peoples insist that the Rohingya are Bengali migrants, or "Chittagonians," who arrived in 1826 after the British conquest of Rakhine, while the few Muslims who lived in Rakhine prior to British colonialization were not the ancestors of the modern Rohingya. Besides, the Rohingya benefited from British colonialization and used World War II to strengthen their position further, claims this narrative; Islam had only a marginal presence in Rakhine during the Mrauk-U dynasty's rule, which was Buddhist, not Muslim (Ibid, n.d.). Therefore, we have seen that there are two theories that exist regarding the Rohingya's origin. One theory suggests that Rohingyas are a mixed group of people with many ethnic and racial connections. Rohingya leaders as well as academics who support their cause largely take this stance. The second theory proposes that Rohingyas are the descendants from illegal immigrants who fled East Pakistan, now Bangladesh and India, during the British era. The government and the majority of the population of Myanmar adopted this idea, which also argues that the dialect of the Rohingyas is remarkably close to that of Chittagong and Bangladesh (Ahmed, 2009).

4 Rohingya Life in Rakhine State

Muslims in Myanmar are a diverse group; they can be roughly sub-divided into four groups: Rohingya, Bamar, Zerbadees, and Indians. The majority of them, nearly a million, are Rohingyas, also known as Arakenese Muslims. Bamar Muslims are Burmese who converted to Islam, while Indian Muslims, those with Indian ancestry, come from Indian parents, and the Zerbadees are the offspring of mixed-race parents, for example, Indian fathers and Burman mothers (Yin, 2005). On the other hand, Storai (2018) asserted that Myanmar is home to five distinct Muslim groups. They are "Zerbadees," "Indians," "Panthy-Chinese," "Malay or Pashu," and "Rohingya." Zerbadees have assimilated into Burmese society on a linguistic and cultural level, while Indians also have social ties to the majority Burmese, and Panthy-Chinese, who migrated from China's Yunnan province during the nineteenth century, are primarily traders who live in Mandaly. Malaya or Pashu Muslims reside in southern Burma, and the largest Muslim group, the Rohingya, live in Arakan (Storai, 2018). Myanmar is a non-secular nation with a majority of Buddhists, around 88% of the total population, 6.2% Christians, 4.3% Muslims, 0.5% Hindus, and 2% adherents of other religions (Devi, 2019). At least two million Muslims live in Myanmar as of the 2014 census, with Rohingya Muslims accounting for roughly half of all Muslims in the nation (Kyaw, 2015). However, the majority of Rohingya Muslims live particularly in Maungdaw, Buthidaung, and Rathedaung of Northern Rakhine State, though cities like Yangon, Mandalya, and Mawlamyine also have Muslims populations (Yusuf, 2018).

Since the seventh and eighth centuries, Islam and Buddhism have coexisted peacefully. Muslim scholars of comparative religion and world history produced works on Buddhism during the eleventh to fifteenth centuries, which helped advance the scholarly study of Buddhism relative to other monotheistic religions (Storai, 2017). However, during World War II, when the British withdrew to India and the Japanese forces made progress in Arakan, the tension between Buddhists and Muslims reached a breaking point (Bhattacharya, 2012). The Rakhine Buddhists formed alliances primarily with the Japanese and Aung San's Burmese Independence Army. When the war first began, the Buddhists drove the Muslims from the Japanese-controlled areas of Southern Arakan, killing many of them in the process. Muslims in Northern Arakan were provided firearms by the British before they were forced to flee the regions they controlled. However, an armed conflict between Muslims and Buddhists subsequently broke out, with the north being predominately Muslim and the south predominately Buddhist and the communal divide reaching an impasse (Galache, 2014). Additionally, the Rohingya was not included in the 1931 classification of Burma's population, which included 15 indigenous races and 135 sub-races. This is despite the fact that some Rohingya received national registration cards after the country gained independence in 1948, and that after the military coup in 1962, the Rohingya's civil and political rights began to erode, as evidenced by the 1974 national elections held under a new constitution (Mahmood et al., 2017). However, from 1978 to 2017, Buddhist radicals and the state's security forces persecuted the Rohingya, forcing them to flee their home country. Subsequently, more than 773,000 Rohingya, including 400,000 children, crossed the border of Bangladesh, and the Bangladeshi government accommodated them in several refugee camps in Cox's Bazar on humanitarian grounds (Rohingya Refugee Crisis, 2017).

The above discussion underlines that the life of the Rohingya people in Rakhine state is full of ups and down, contested and a struggle to establish their right as a citizen in Myanmar. The politics of Myanmar, long-standing conflicts, and interaction between the Rohingyas and Buddhist people have determined the identity and citizenship rights of the Rohingyas.

5 Citizenship Status of the Rohingya People in Myanmar

A citizen is a person who belongs to a political or national community and has the same rights and obligations as other citizens, while citizenship is the legally acknowledged membership of a state, is not optional, and brings a sense of democratic inclusion or belonging (Bosniak, 2008; Macfoy, 2014). However, in the case of Rohingya, their citizenship status in Myanmar could be described as ambiguous (Brett & Hlaing, 2020). In Myanmar, there are almost 135 recognized ethnic minorities divided into eight major ethnicities, but the Rohingya was excluded from these clusters, despite the fact that many of them can trace their ancestry to millennia ago in Myanmar (Albert & Maizland, 2017). There are three types of citizens in Myanmar—full citizen, associate citizen, and naturalized citizen—as per the county's 1982 Citizenship Law. Full citizens are those who come from one of the 135 ethnic minorities and migrated in Burma prior to 1823, while associate citizens are people whose descendants were born in the country after 1823, and naturalized citizens are those whose parents hold one of the three forms of citizenships; whereas Rohingyas are considered "residential foreigners" (Sohel, 2017). Due to the lack of full citizenship rights, Rohingyas became victims of severe discrimination including limits on their freedom of movement, unfair barriers to accessing education, and arbitrary property expropriation.

Nevertheless, according to Panglong Agreement, the Union Constitution was formed 1947, and citizens in Myanmar are defined as those people who are of an "indigenous race," have a grandparent who is of an "indigenous race" or is the offspring of citizens, or those who resided British Burma prior to 1942. However, the Rohingya people were, unfortunately, not considered to be an indigenous group and were therefore disqualified from being citizens of the country (Hung, 2022). In establishing a long-term solution to the refugee flows, this refusal of citizenship and the rights that go along with it invariably presents significant barriers (Human Rights Watch, 2000). In addition, the Myanmar government introduced three different types of color-coded citizens security cards (CRCs) in 1989. For example, pink-colored cards are issued to full citizens, blue-colored cards for associate citizens, and green-colored cards for naturalized citizens. However, the Rohingya was excluded again in this process—although, following UNHCR's recommendations on the Rohingya in 1995, the authorities issued white-colored temporary registration card, but the cardholder's place of birth is not indicated on the document, making it impossible to claim citizenship (Khan & Tasneem, 2021). Moreover, according to a report of the UNHCR Myanmar authorities issued white cards for just 35,000 Rohingya refugees of the 230,000 who were brought back to Rakhine State from Bangladesh between 1992 and 1997 as a preliminary step to re-establishing one of largest communities of stateless people in Asia (McKinsey, 2007).

However, under the white card system, the Rohingya people's freedom-of-movement restrictions started in Sittwe, the capital city of the Rakhine State, and quickly spread throughout the entire state. Almost no Rohingyas were permitted to leave the state without permission from the authorities. Additionally, travel within the state was difficult and limited to two weeks; for example, moving within the same municipality required a "departure certificate," and sleeping over in others' houses needed police permission. Francis Wade in his book describes the issue in this way:

> Along the east-west road between Maungdaw and Buthidaung in the north are a series of checkpoints were police inspect the identity papers and travel documents of passing Rohingya. On the side of the road, for all to see, they are pulled from their buses and ordered inside police booths, and when a Rohingya wanted to leave their village in northern Maungdaw township and visit a relative in Buthidaung, thereby crossing the township line, they must apply at the local immigration office for the permit, paying fee of anywhere up to eight dollars each time (Wade, 2019).

Wade also states that the authorities even imposed restrictions on the marriage and reproduction of the Rohingya population by releasing an order in 2005 which read that those who are allowed to marry must keep their number of children to a minimum. The ruling powers thought this threatened the region's Buddhist population. Additionally, the Na Sa Ka personnel, the border security forces of the country that is a feared authority in the state, often invaded the private space of the Rohingya, to entering their houses and forcing mothers to breastfeed their children in front of the personnel. It is worth mentioning that, historically, the Rohingya people were issued National Registration Cards (NRCs) along with everyone else in the country; but when the Ne Win government implemented discriminatory policies toward the Rohingya in the 1970s, the NRCs of the Rohingya people were confiscated by the authorities using various means. Ridiculously, these same Rohingya citizens were then told to register themselves to prove their citizenship, but most of them now could not provide any citizenship documents, resulting in their being identified as "Bengalis" or immigrants by the junta government (Lewin, 2012). Even though the government confiscated Rohingya IDs and other government-issued documents and implemented systematic discriminatory measures, they were still considered Burmese nationals up until 1982. However, the Citizenship Act promulgated in 1982 is the official document that stripped the citizenship of the Rohingya (Alam, 2019; Cheesman, 2017).

Furthermore, Rohingyas were not included in Myanmar's first nationwide census in 2014. According to a report from Reuters, Myanmar made public the findings of its first census in 2014, but the survey excluded the country's Muslim Rohingya minority, who complained at the time of deep state-sanctioned discrimination (Reuters, 2017). In a different report, the Guardian revealed that in the violent Rakhine State, when the census was being conducted, the census-takers went to people's homes to register them, but as soon as they learned they were Rohingya, they went away from the house without doing so (The Guardian, 2014). The report also added that Ye Htut, a spokesperson for Myanmar's president, stated that only those who identified as Bengalis would be counted in the official tally, and that anyone identifying as a Rohingya would not be included (Zarni & Cowley, 2014). This contravened the government's own promises, as Myanmar had previously made a commitment in an agreement with the UNHCR that it would follow international census standards and human rights principles. The Muslim minority had been permitted to identify as Rohingya prior to the census, but after Buddhist fanatics instituted a boycott, the government decided that Rohingyas could not register as Rohingyas but must register themselves as Bengalis instead (Kipgen, 2020). But the Rohingya who declined to enroll themselves as Bengali, left without satisfactory documents, was subject to relocation to the internally displaced camps. American professor of International Relations Lindsey L. Kingston believes that the Myanmar government adopted this strategy to discriminate against the Rohingya so that later it would be easier for the government to exclude them from naturalized citizenship and subject them to deportation (Kingston, 2015).

In addition, the 1982 Citizenship Law created a hierarchy between those who have full citizenship and the others who are given a lesser rights, which is fundamentally discriminatory on the basis of ethnicity, race, or religion against the long-term inhabitants of the country (*UN Universal Periodic Review*, 2020). Due to the systematic inequality, the country has suffered through a number of internal ethnic armed conflicts including the recent Rohingya and Rakhine conflict (Jabeen, 2018). According to Hla Min, among the official number of national races the majority are Burman, consisting of 65%, while the minority groups including Kachin, Kaya, Kayin, Chin, Mon, Shan, and Rakhine share only 35% of the total population (Min, 2000). Additionally, Matthews (2001) notes that there are significant numbers of undocumented ethnic minorities including Chinese, Anglo-Burmese, and Rohingya, resulting in the longstanding internal ethnic armed conflicts that have raged since Myanmar's independence (Matthews, 2001). The 1962 military takeover resulted in the process of "Burmanization," which can best be described as the creation of a majoritarian national identity, and this effort replaced all other ethnicities, languages, and faiths of the country. The Rohingya has faced many difficulties following the military coup and has been labeled as "outsiders" or "illegals" in their own nation as well as having been subject to persecution (Ahmed, 2021).

In sum, it can be argued that the exclusion of the Rohingyas from citizenship rights is a political agenda of the military-backed Myanmar government. The supremacy of Buddhism and Burmese culture recognize the Rohingyas as a threat to their national integration and cultural supremacy. This kind of feeling has come from ultra-nationalism sentiment which is the main cause of persecution and displacement of the Rohingyas from their place of origin.

6 Conclusion

This chapter has sketched the history of Rohingya identity, the meaning of Rohingya, and their living in the Rakhine state in Myanmar. Different contesting ideas have been presented in this chapter based on diverse literature. Literature supports that Rohingya is a recognized term in the international lexicon, and the Rohingyas are a recognized community of people having their distinctive characteristics. History indicates that Rohingyas have been living in Myanmar for many centuries, but they are not considered citizens since they do not have a formal claim to one of the country's eight major ethnic groups—which are further divided into 135 sub-groups. Their ancestry is also a subject of debate, as some historians argue that they are from Arab, Persian, Moghul, Turk, Pathan, and Bengali origin, while others assert that they are illegal immigrants from what was then-East Pakistan during the British rule—also the viewpoint of the majority of the population and the government of Myanmar. As a result, since Burma's independence, the Rohingya has been subjected to regular and organized persecution by the government as well as by Buddhist nationalists. Even the country's 1982 Citizenship Law classified them as residential foreigners, which restricted their basic rights and other privileges. This citizenship law not only curtailed the rights of the Rohingyas but also pushed millions of people as stateless. Due to the repeated targets of killings and persecution, Rohingyas are forced to seek refuge in Bangladesh and other nearby countries. Approximately 1.3 million Rohingyas are now being hosted by Bangladesh. Despite international pressure on Myanmar the repatriation process is yet to start, and the stateless Rohingya population waits for the Myanmar government to recognize their ethnicity and restore their citizenship rights. The international community must work accordingly to ensure the existence of the Rohingyas as a distinct community and integral citizens of Myanmar.

References

Ahmed, I. (2009). *The Rohingya: From stateless to refugee.* Retrieved August 24, 2023, from http://www.netipr.org/policy/downloads/20100101_FromStatelessToRefugees_ImtiazAhmed.pdf

Ahmed, I., & Biswas, N. R. (2022). Rohingyas in Myanmar and Bangladesh: The violence-protection dialectic and the narratives of certain unsafety/uncertain safety. *Zenodo.* https://doi.org/10.5281/zenodo.6672039

Ahmed, M. (2021). It's not so simple: The Rohingya and Burma's complicated relationship. *Restless Beings.* Retrieved February 23, 2023, from https://restlessbeings.org/articles/its-not-so-simple-the-rohingya-and-burma-s-complicated-relationship

Akhanda, M. R. (2018). *Rohingya problem and Bangladesh.* Parilekh Prakashani.

Alam, J. (2018). The Rohingya of Myanmar: Theoretical significance of the minority status. *Asian Ethnicity, 19*(2), 180–210.
Alam, J. (2019). The current Rohingya crisis in Myanmar in historical perspective. *Journal of Muslim Minority Affairs, 39*(1), 1–25.
Alam, M. A. (1999). *A short historical background of Arakan* (pp. 27–28). Arakan Historical Society.
Alam, M. F. (2021). Role of civil society and NGOS in the Rohingya refugee crisis in Bangladesh: An overview (Chapter 5). In *The Rohingya crisis: Mapping the conundrum and challenges of peace building: Selective South Asian perspectives*. Lulu Publications.
Albert, E., & Maizland, L. (2017). *The Rohingya crisis*. Council on Foreign Relations
Bhattacharya, S. (2012). *Islam in Arakan: An interpretation from the Indian perspective: History and the present*. Rohingya League for Democracy (Burma) RLDB, 1. https://kaladanpress.com/wp-content/uploads/2022/12/Islam-in-Arakan-An-interpretation-from-the-Indian-perspective.pdf
Bhonsale, M. S. (2015). Evolution of the Arakan 'problem' in Burma. *Indian History Congress, 76*, 1.
Bosniak, L. (2008). *The citizen and the alien*. Princeton University Press.
Brett, P., & Hlaing, K. Y. (2020). Myanmar's 1982 citizenship law in context. *TOAEP Policy Brief Series, 122*, 1. https://www.toaep.org/pbs-pdf/122-brett-kyh/
Buchanan, F. (1799) A comparative vocabulary of some of the languages spoken in the Burma Empire. Asiatic Researches 5, 219–240. Rpt. in *SOAS Bulletin of Burma Research, 1*(1). Ed. M. W. Charney (2003). https://eprints.soas.ac.uk/8050/1/BuchananComparativeVocabulary.pdf
Chan, A. (2005). The development of a Muslim enclave in Arakan (Rakhine) state of Burma (Myanmar). *SOAS Bulletin of Burma Research, 3*(2), 396–420. https://citeseerx.ist.psu.edu/document?repid=rep1&type=pdf&doi=25d0efc054f99ebb7955071bbfa54dad6018025d.
Chan, E. (n.d.). Rohingya people. *Encyclopaedia Britannica*. Retrieved January 5, 2023, from https://www.britannica.com/topic/Rohingya
Charney, M. W. (2005). Buddhism in Arakan: Theories and historiography of the religious basis of ethnonyms. *SOAS*. http://eprints.soas.ac.uk/6148/1/Charney%202005%20Religious%20Basis%20of%20Ethnonyms%20-%20Rakhaing,%20Arakan,%20Burma,%20Myanmar,%20Muslims,%20Buddhists,%20Ethnology,%20Ethnicity.pdf
Cheesman, N. (2017). How in Myanmar "national races" came to surpass citizenship and exclude Rohingya. *Journal of Contemporary Asia, 47*(3), 461–483.
Devi, H. O. (2019, September 17). The vulnerability of the Rohingya refugees. *Café Dissensus*. https://cafedissensus.com/2019/09/17/the-vulnerability-of-the-rohingya-refugees/
Ebbighausen, R. (2017, June 6). The gray area in Rohingya conflict. *Deutsche Welle (DW) commentary*. https://www.dw.com/en/opinion-the-gray-area-in-myanmars-rohingya-conflict/a-40384101
Galache, C. S. (2014). Rohingya and national identities in Burma. *New Mandala*, 151–178.
Habibullah. 2015. (1995). *The history of Rohingyas*. Chittagong: Bangladesh Co-operative Society.
Habibullah. M. N. (2017). *History of the Rohingya nation* (p. 29). Bangladesh Co-Operative Book Society Ltd.
Hamilton, W. (1820). *A geographical, statistical, and historical description of Hindostan and the adjacent countries* (Vol. 2).
Human Rights Watch. (2000). Burma/Bangladesh Burmese refugees in Bangladesh: Still no durable solution. *Human Rights Watch* 12(3[C]). https://www.hrw.org/reports/2000/burma/index.htm
Hung, A. H. C. (2022). Exploring the root causes of the persecution policy against Rohingya people: A study based on three constitutions of Burma/Myanmar. *Asian Journal of Law and Policy, 2*(2), 75–97.
Hussain, S. (2018). *Burma's Rohingya: A history of genocide*. Palok Publishers.
International Christian Concern. (2021, February 1). Myanmar's persecution Rohingya Christians minority of minorities. *Persecution.org*. https://www.persecution.org/2021/04/02/myanmars-persecuted-rohingya-christians-minority-minorities/

Islam, N. (2018). Rohingya and nationality status in Myanmar. In *Citizenship in Myanmar: Ways of being in and from Burma* (p. 267).
Jabeen, M. (2018). Identity crisis: citizenship and Myanmar's Muslim ethnic group. *Journal of the Punjab University Historical Society, 31*(2).
Karim, D. A. (2016). *The Rohingyas: A short account of their history and culture*. Jatiya Sahitya Prakash.
Khan, M. S., & Tasneem, R. (2021). *How does the social structure of the Rakhine state shape the fertility behavior of Rohingyas?*
Kingston, L. N. (2015). Protecting the world's most persecuted: the responsibility to protect and Burma's Rohingya minority. *The International Journal of Human Rights, 19*(8), 1163–1175. https://doi.org/10.1080/13642987.2015.1082831
Kipgen, N. (2020). Myanmar's perspective on the Rohingya crisis. *International Journal on World Peace, 37*(1), 43–70.
Kipgen, N. (2014). Addressing the Rohingya problem. *Journal of Asian and African Studies, 49*(2), 234–247. https://doi.org/10.1177/0021909613505269
Kyaw, N. N. (2015). Alienation, discrimination, and securitization: Legal personhood and cultural personhood of Muslims in Myanmar. *The Review of Faith & International Affairs, 13*(4), 50–59. https://doi.org/10.1080/15570274.2015.1104971
Leider, J. (2018). *Rohingya—The Name and its living archive*. ISEAS. https://hal.archives-ouvertes.fr/hal-02325206
Lewin, N. S. (2012). Making Rohingya statelessness. *New Mandala*. https://www.newmandala.org/making-rohingya-statelessness
Macfoy, M. K. (2014). Introduction. In R. Bellamy, & M. K. Macfoy, (Eds.), *Citizenship Vol. II: Who is a citizen? Feminism, multiculturalism and immigration* (pp. 1–4). Routledge.
Mahmood, S. S., Wroe, E., Fuller, A., & Leaning, J. (2017). The Rohingya people of Myanmar: Health, human rights, and identity. *The Lancet, 389*(10081), 1841–1850. https://doi.org/10.1016/S0140-6736(16)00646-2
Matthews, B. (2001). *Ethnic and religious diversity: Myanmar's unfolding nemesis*. Institute of Southeast Asian Studies.
McKinsey, K. (2007, July 23). *Myanmar: UNHCR promotes first significant steps toward citizenship for disenfranchised minority*. UNHCR. https://www.unhcr.org/news/latest/2007/7/46a4c9f82/myanmar-unhcr-promotes-first-significant-steps-toward-citizenship-disenfranchised.html
Min, H. (2000). *Political situation of Myanmar and its role in the region*. Office of Strategic Studies, Ministry of Defence, Union of Myanmar.
Minahan, J. B. (2016). *Encyclopedia of stateless nations: Ethnic and national groups around the world* (2nd ed). ABC-CLIO.
Mohajan, H. (2018). History of Rakhine state and the origin of the Rohingya Muslims. *IKAT: The Indonesian Journal of Southeast Asian Studies, 2*(1), 19–46.
Nursyazwani & Freeman, P. E. (2020, June 12). The hidden heterogeneity of Rohingya refugees. *New Mandala*. https://www.newmandala.org/the-hidden-heterogeneity-of-rohingya-refugees/
Razzaq, A., & Haque, M. (1995). A tale of Rohingyas in Bangladesh. *The Centre for Human Rights, 15*.
Reuters. (2017). *Rohingya exodus: How a two-week army crackdown reignited Myanmar's Rohingya crisis*. Retrived from: https://www.reuters.com/investigates/special-report/myanmar-rohingya-crisis2/.
Rohingya Refugee Crisis. (2017, September 21). OCHA. https://www.unocha.org/rohingya-refugee-crisis
Sohel, M. S. (2017). The Rohingya crisis in Myanmar: Origin and emergence. *Saudi Journal of Humanities and Social Sciences, 2*(11A), 1007–1018. https://doi.org/10.21276/sjhss.2017.2.11.1
Storai, Y. (2017). Systematic ethnic cleansing: the case study of Rohingya community in Myanmar. *Journal of South Asian Studies, 5*(3), 157–168.

Storai, Y. (2018). Systematic ethnic cleansing: The case study of Rohingya. *Arts and Social Sciences Journal, 9*(4), 4.
Sudheer, N., & Banerjee, D. (2021). The Rohingya refugees: A conceptual framework of their psychosocial adversities, cultural idioms of distress and social suffering. *Global Mental Health, 8*, e46. https://doi.org/10.1017/gmh.2021.43
Tanenbaum Center for Interreligious Understanding. (n.d.) *The Rohingya origin story: Two narratives, one conflict*. Retrieved January 6, 2023, from https://tanenbaum.org/wp-content/uploads/2017/11/Rohingya-Origin-Fact-Sheet-.pdf.
The Guardian. (2014). *Burma census is not counting Rohingya Muslims, says UN agency*. https://www.theguardian.com/world/2014/apr/02/burma-census-rohingya-muslims-un-agency
Uddin Md Zahed, I., & Jenkins, B. (2022). The politics of Rohingya ethnicity: Understanding the debates on Rohingya in Myanmar. *Journal of Muslim Minority Affairs, 42*(1), 117–135. https://doi.org/10.1080/13602004.2022.2064054
Uddin, N. (2015). Chapter 4: State of stateless people: The plight of Rohingya refugees in Bangladesh. In *The human right to citizenship* (pp. 62–77). University of Pennsylvania Press. https://doi.org/10.9783/9780812291421-005
Uddin, N. (2020). *The Rohingya: An ethnography of 'subhuman' life*. Oxford University Press.
Uddin, N. (2022). *Voices of the Rohingya people: A case of genocide, ethnocide and 'subhuman' life*. Springer Nature.
Ullah, A. (n.d.). *Etymology of Arakan & Rohingya*. International Organization for Migration, Rohingya Cultural Memory Centre. https://rohingyaculturalmemorycentre.iom.int/multimedia/files/pdf/donwload_area/Etymology_of_Arakan_and_Rohingya.pdf
Ullah, A. A. (2011). Rohingya refugees to Bangladesh: Historical exclusions and contemporary marginalization. *Journal of Immigrant & Refugee Studies, 9*(2), 139–161.
Ullah, A. A. (2017). *Rohingya migration: Is it a function of persecution* (pp. 1–4). Bandar Seri Begawan: Universiti Brunei Darussalam.
Ullah, A. A., & Chattoraj, D. (2018). Roots of discrimination against Rohingya minorities: Society, ethnicity and international relations. *Intellectual Discourse, 26*(2), 541–565.
UN Universal Periodic Review. (1982). *37th session of The Working Group, The 1982 Citizenship Law and Right to Citizenship of Minorities and Freedom of Movement, July 2020*. https://progressivevoicemyanmar.org/2020/07/09/the-1982-citizenship-law-and-right-to-citizenship-of-minorities-and-freedom-of-movement/
Wade, F. (2019). *Myanmar's enemy within: Buddhist violence and the making of a Muslim 'other'* (pp. 92–95). Bloomsbury Publishing.
Washaly, N. (2019). *Rohingya: The identity crisis*. Ecos de la Academia. https://www.researchgate.net/publication/331286962_Rohingya_The_Identity_Crisis
Yegar, M. (1972). *The Muslims of Burma: A study of a minority group*. Harrassowitz.
Yin, K. M. (2005). Salience of ethnicity among Burman Muslims: A study in identity formation. *Intellectual Discourse, 13*(2), 161–179. https://journals.iium.edu.my/intdiscourse/index.php/id/article/view/108
Yunus, M. (1994). *A history of Arakan: Past and present*. University of Chittagong.
Yusuf, I. (2017). Three faces of the Rohingya crisis: Religious nationalism, Asian Islamophobia, and delegitimizing citizenship. *Studia Islamika, 25*(3), 503–542.
Zahed, I. U. M., & Jenkins, B. (2022). Aung San Suu Kyi and ethnic cleansing: The dark side of 'Myanmar way' democracy. *South East Asia Research, 30*(2), 202–218.
Zarni, M., & Cowley, A. (2014). The slow-burning genocide of Myanmar's Rohingya. *Pacific Rim Law & Policy Journal, 23*, 683.

Chapter 3
The Continuing History of Rohingya Settlement in Bangladesh

Md. Rafiqul Islam

Abstract This chapter provides an analytical discussion concerning the formation of the Rohingya settlement in Bangladesh. The Rohingya settlement was a phenomenon which took place due to the population's displacement from their land of origin to escape from persecution and human rights violations. After touching upon the history behind the arrival of Rohingya refugees in Bangladesh, the discussion sequentially moves on to the present scenario of post-2017, which has seen a dramatic increase of this population in host country Bangladesh. The discussion involves the measures and initiatives taken by the government of Bangladesh and other national and international agencies and organizations to properly accommodate the Rohingya refugees in the host state.

1 Introduction

The Rohingya people principally reside in the Arakan province of the state of Myanmar. The province is known in modern times as the Rakhine State (Rahman, 2010). While the people themselves have a long ancestral heritage in the land, the introduction of the term "Rohingya" is relatively recent. The people now called Rohingyas have been living in Rakhine since the period from 788 to 810 CE, as predominantly Muslim descendants of immigrants from the Middle East and later of Bengalis during the fifteenth to the seventeenth centuries (Milton et al., 2017). The Myanmar government is largely controlled by Myanmar's military junta of predominantly Burmese people, and they used their legislative authority to fully remove the citizenship rights of the Rohingya minority people in 1982. The infamous Myanmar Citizenship Act of that year officially recognizes 135 ethnic groups as part of Myanmar's ethnic population, and this list does not include the Rohingyas (Parashar & Alam, 2019). This has led to the apparent stateless status of the Rohingya

Md. R. Islam (✉)
University of Dhaka, Dhaka, Bangladesh
e-mail: rislampacs@du.ac.bd

K. Ahmed and Md. R. Islam (eds.), *Understanding the Rohingya Displacement*, International Perspectives on Migration, https://doi.org/10.1007/978-981-97-1424-7_3

population, and has given Myanmar's military apparatus free rein to violently persecute this community in their own ancestral lands. The Rohingyas faced persecution at levels seen in systematic genocides, with first their movements restricted by laws and legal obstructions, and soon their identity compromised via mandatory identification checks at designated checkpoints in the Rakhine region. Rohingyas faced harsh penalties, with fines and property confiscation on the basis of their now-compromised identification papers (Uddin, 2019). This led to the Rohingya people eventually being forcefully displaced from their homes. Forceful displacement refers to coerced and/or involuntary movement of a person or population away from their home or home region (Faye, 2021; Verme & Schuettler, 2021). The majority of the displaced Rohingya people took refuge in Bangladesh.

In the proceeding sections, this chapter discusses the history of the Rohingya settlement in Bangladesh across two time periods, which are pre-2017 and post-2017. The notable measures taken by the government in conjunction with local and international organizations are discussed within their relevant time frames.

2 History of Rohingya Settlement in Bangladesh

The history of Rohingya settlement in Bangladesh started long before the year 2000—around the 1970s—and the issue continues to be one of great concern for the host country. The discussion concerning this settlement can be divided into two time frames: pre-2017 and post-2017.

2.1 *Pre-2017 Period*

The flow of Rohingya refugees into Bangladesh started in the 1970s, predating their arrival in larger groups in the early 1990s. The cause behind the first influx of Rohingya refugees that led to around 200,000 coming into Bangladesh (Ullah, 2011) has been described thus:

> It is said that oppression, discrimination, violence and forced labour practices by the Myanmar authorities triggered an exodus of more than 250 thousand Rohingya Muslims to cross the border between 1991 and 1992. Since then the flow of this migration to the Bangladesh territory continued which contributed to shape a big figure living as 'refugees' in this country. (Uddin, 2019, p. 77)

The Rohingya exodus began around 1962 with the growing persecution of Rohingyas by the law enforcement and military organs of Myanmar, organs which are largely under the control of Myanmar's Burmese military regime (Sohel, 2017). It has been argued that the British occupation before Myanmar's independence in 1948 was the precursor to the Rohingya crisis that is so prevalent in Bangladesh and some other parts of the world today. With the "divide-and-rule" policy of the British colonial powers, seeds of dissent were sown in Myanmar's fragmented ethnic diaspora of predominantly Buddhist Burmese populations (i.e., over 87%). The colonial powers preferred to recruit the Muslim populations that make up the present Rohingya population, and the support of these powers toward resistance fighters in Arakan and in the Mon rebellion has been said to have further fueled the resentment of the majority Burmese population in the long run, leading to the focused persecution of the minority Rohingya community observed today (Ansar, 2020).

The inclusion of 135 Burmese ethnic communities as part of Myanmar's list of communities eligible for citizenship, while excluding the Rohingyas, indicates a clear systematic exclusion of this community. The results of this exclusion are quite apparent in the present timeline. The population has been reduced from around 3.6 million in the 1970s (Alam, 2019), to around 1 million in late 2020 (Reid, 2021) in Myanmar, with well over 1 million total in Bangladesh and other neighboring countries including Cambodia, Indonesia, Laos, Malaysia, and Thailand (Hamzah & Belford, 2015; Hookway, 2015). Systematic targeting of ethnic groups, even besides the Rohingya community, has been ongoing since the 1990s when a government composed of military generals was in power. Since that time, abuse and oppression have been ongoing against the ethnic Kachin, Karen, Rakhine, Rohingya, and Shan minority populations, while the government's military force, named the Tatmadaw, cracks down harshly on their insurgencies and resistances (Grundy-Warr & Dean, 2011). For the Rohingyas specifically, however, the legislative move that stripped away their citizenship rights makes them a particularly unique target among the other oppressed ethnic minority communities, with some of their history impacting how the ruling militaristic government sees them as well. The results include a persecution similar to historical accounts of systematic genocide seen throughout human history that continues to this day—for there are still Rohingyas in Myanmar. The post-2020 pandemic situation has given the authorities even more opportunities to harass the Rohingyas in Myanmar and restrict their lives further in the name of mandatory regulations, the discussion of which still barely scratches the surface of this ongoing crisis (Roth, 2020).

2.2 *Post-2017 Period: Ukhia and Tekhnaf*

In 2017, around 600,000 Rohingya refugee people were living in Bangladesh (Milton et al., 2017), but the number swelled up to an estimated 800,000 Rohingyas (or more) in the following year (Martin et al., 2018). The Prime Minister of Bangladesh, Sheikh Hasina, in a meeting with Lord Ahmad of Wimbledon, was quoted as saying regarding the Rohingya population living within the country that "Giving shelter to such a large number of Rohingyas is a big burden for us...we want to resolve the issue through discussions" (The Daily Star, 2019).

The Prime Minister continues to indicate that taking care of over 1.1 million Rohingyas is a significant burden for the country, which gives a picture of how much the Rohingya population within the country has expanded over the decades. The explosion of the population within the last decade has a lot to do with the latest

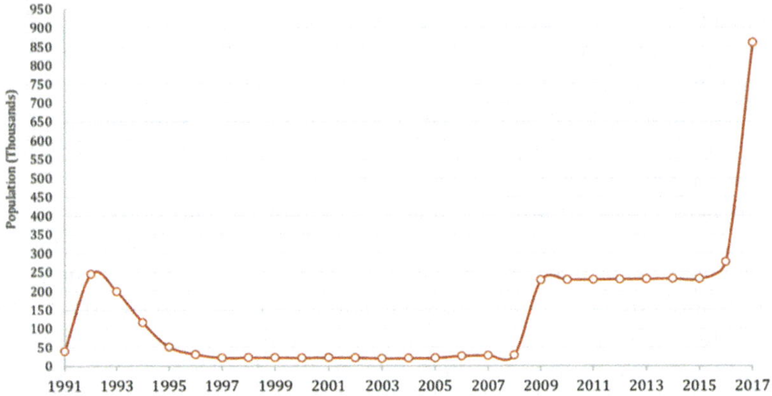

Fig. 1 Number of Rohingya refugees entering Bangladesh from 1991 to 2017 (representing the cumulative number of refugees, including pre-influx population) (Reproduced from Hassan et al., 2018)

exodus in 2017, with the addition of around 700,000 to the Rohingya population since that time (Rahman et al., 2020).

The overwhelming majority of these fleeing Rohingya people have taken up shelter in Bangladesh, where they had been slowly trickling in over the decades after the community's first exodus (Mahmood et al., 2017). The latest large-scale exodus of Rohingya people to Bangladesh that began on August 25, 2017 and brought the 600,000 additional Rohingyas to the country put a mountainous logistical dilemma upon the government of Bangladesh regarding urgent humanitarian assistance (Cook & Ne, 2018). A chronology of the forceful displacement of the Rohingya people, and their subsequent entry into Bangladesh, is illustrated in Fig. 1.

With over 1.1 million Rohingyas taking refuge in Bangladesh as of 2020, it has become increasingly difficult for the country to assist this growing population, as the country tackles issues the complexity of which are only rising (Islam et al., 2020).

The largest refugee camp, commonly referred to as the Rohingya Camp or the Kutupalong-Balukhali camp, is situated in the Ukhia and Teknaf sub-districts of Cox's Bazar. The camps located in the two areas are all situated in the southeast corner of the country near the border (Ahmed, 2018). The current population in Bangladesh is around 1.1 million (Bakali & Wasty, 2020). Within the camp area, the Kutupalong-Balukhali camp is further divided into several zones, each accommodating different groups of Rohingya refugees. These zones include Kutupalong, Balukhali, Thangkhali, Jamtoli, and other smaller sections (Hassan et al., 2018). The camp spans a vast area, comprising densely populated makeshift shelters made of bamboo, tarpaulin, and other locally available materials. The camp's infrastructure has evolved over time, with aid organizations and the Bangladeshi government working to provide essential services and support to the displaced population. Basic amenities such as water, sanitation facilities, healthcare centers, and education facilities have been established to address the immediate needs of the Rohingya refugees.

The camp also has communal spaces, markets, and various community centers to promote social interaction and engagement (Ahmed, 2018).

3 Bhasan Char: A Temporary Destination

The Bangladeshi government has constructed a temporary shelter center in Bhasan Char (Fig. 2) in the Noakhali district to relocate some of the Rohingya people in order to reduce population pressures in Cox's Bazar (Banerjee, 2020).

This government initiative to ease the population pressure in the Cox's Bazar region has, as of 2021, resulted in over 19,000 Rohingyas being relocated to the location (Nguyen & Lewis, 2022). The Rohingya population in Bangladesh has not been given any official refugee status, since Bangladesh is not an official signatory to the international instruments that protect the rights of refugees. Instead, their official status as stated by the government of Bangladesh is Forcefully Displaced Myanmar Nationals (FDMN) (Roy, 2020). Despite not being directly affiliated with the international legal instruments such as the UN Convention Relating to the Status of Refugees or its protocols, Bangladesh has been heavily involved in properly sheltering this large Rohingya population within its borders and seeing to their necessities with assistance from international and local NGOs (Milton et al., 2017). With cramped and congested camps and unsanitary conditions, the Rohingya population in the country lives with significant health risks. The health and sanitation facilities

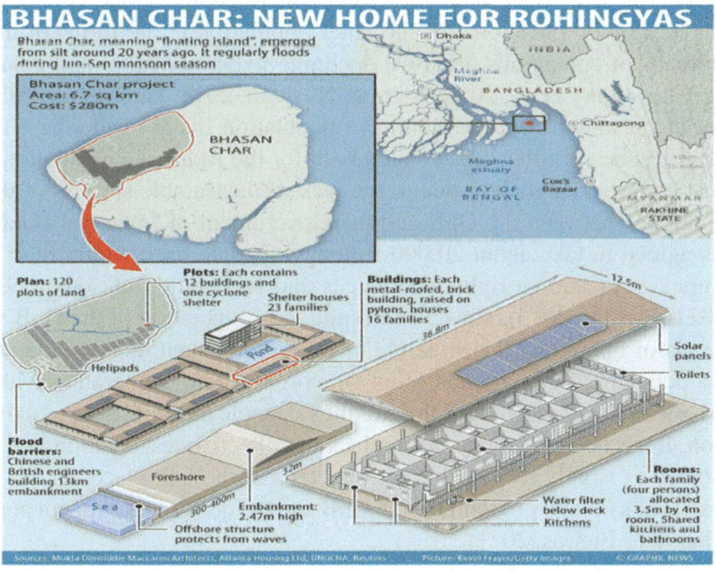

Fig. 2 Location of Bhasan Char Island (Reproduced from Islam et al., 2021)

available to this community in the camp areas are very limited, leading to disease outbreaks lasting for much longer than what is considered natural for common infectious diseases such as diphtheria, diarrhea, and the covid-19 virus, among others (Islam & Nuzhath, 2018). Their housing conditions are dire, as the available housing space cannot cope with their booming birth rates—which currently sit at around 50,000 childbirths per year (Chowdhury et al., 2018; Uddin, 2015). This situation is a direct result of the 2017 mass exodus of the Rohingyas from Myanmar. The host community of Bangladesh has been welcoming to the fleeing Rohingya population who has sought shelter inside the country, and the government has since been collaborating with local and international organizations to help shelter them (Mia et al., 2021).

The Rohingya refugees in Bangladesh are not officially recognized by the Government of Bangladesh (GoB) as refugees, but as FDMN (Rashid et al., 2021). The management of these FDMN in Bangladesh has thus far been done on a short-term basis, relying on the eventual repatriation of the Rohingya people in the country back to their home country of Myanmar while keeping the Rohingya population supported via aid and relief mechanisms with the help of NGOs, donor organizations, and UN assistance (Cook & Ne, 2018). The Rohingya refugees have been given shelter and humanitarian assistance through the aforementioned coordination between the GoB and these organizations via land allotted specifically for the Rohingyas in the two designated camp areas: Kutupalong in the Ukhia (also spelled "Ukhiya") sub-district, and Nayapara in the Teknaf sub-district (Milton et al., 2017). This has led to many security complications for the GoB and the Rohingya population in the form of human rights violations by organized crime groups and a thriving black-market economy of narcotics, contrabands, and Small Arms and Light Weapons (SALW) (Taufiq, 2019), as well as health complications for the latter population in the forms of malnutrition, outbreaks of contagious diseases, declining material health, and poor family planning (Chowdhury et al., 2018; Islam & Nuzhath, 2018; Islam et al., 2020). The crisis that has resulted from the Rohingya population living inside the borders of Bangladesh has been further exacerbated both for the Rohingya population as well as the host country Bangladesh due to the lack of measurable success of the bilateral negotiations between the GoB and the Government of Myanmar (GoM). The GoM has agreed to take about 20,000 Rohingya people back within their borders with assurances of human rights guarantees and recognition of some civil rights (Faye, 2021; Parnini, 2013). However, despite the cooperation of the GoB with the UN in terms of upholding the principle of non-refoulement, hosting the returning Rohingya population with aid and relief support via joint cooperation with NGOs and International NGOs (INGOs), the Rohingya people are still living as a displaced population. It has been mentioned that a lack of collective responsibility on the part of the GoM was largely responsible for the crisis in the first place, and is why the issue persists as a crucial problem for the GoB and the destitute Rohingya population (Bhattacharya & Biswas, 2021).

4 Conclusion

The history of the Rohingya settlement in Bangladesh and the conflict arising out of the Rohingya crisis is a complex and multifaceted issue that has been shaped by a range of historical, political, and social factors. The settlement of over one million refugees in Bangladesh has created a range of economic, environmental, and social challenges, including competition for resources, strained infrastructure, and the risk of conflict. Throughout this chapter, we have explored the history of the Rohingya settlement in Bangladesh, from the first wave of refugees in the 1970s to the current crisis. We have seen how the settlement has grown over time, and how it has created economic opportunities and challenges for both the refugee and host communities. The crisis remains far from resolved, however, with ongoing challenges and risks to both the refugees and the host community. It is critical that the response to the crisis continues to prioritize the protection of human rights, the provision of basic services, and the establishment of a sustainable approach to managing the settlement. Overall, the history of the Rohingya settlement in Bangladesh and the conflict arising out of the Rohingya crisis presents a significant challenge to Bangladesh and the international community. However, with continued cooperation and commitment to addressing the root causes of the crisis, we can work toward a sustainable and just future for all those affected by the conflict. It is essential that the international community continues to engage with this issue and support the Bangladeshi government in providing essential services to the Rohingya refugees, while also addressing the needs of the host communities to ensure a peaceful coexistence. Only through a coordinated and sustained approach can we hope to achieve lasting peace and security for all those affected by this crisis.

References

Ahmed, I. (2020). Special issue on the Rohingya crisis: From the guest editor's desk. *Asian Journal of Comparative Politics, 5*(2), 85–88.

Alam, J. (2019). The current Rohingya crisis in Myanmar in historical perspective. *Journal of Muslim Minority Affairs, 39*(1), 1–25. https://doi.org/10.1080/13602004.2019.1575560

Ansar, A. (2020). The unfolding of belonging, exclusion and exile: A reflection on the history of Rohingya refugee crisis in Southeast Asia. *Journal of Muslims Minority Affairs, 40*(3), 441–456. https://doi.org/10.1080/13602004.2020.1819126

Bakali, N., & Wasty, S. (2020). Identity, social mobility, and trauma: Post-conflict educational realities for survivors of the Rohingya genocide. *Religions, 11*(5), 241. https://doi.org/10.3390/rel11050241

Banerjee, S. (2020). *From Cox's Bazar to Bhasan Char: An assessment of Bangladesh's relocation plan for Rohingya refugees*. Observer Research Foundation. https://www.orfonline.org/wp-content/uploads/2020/05/ORF_IssueBrief_357_BhasanChar.pdf

Bhattacharya, S., & Biswas, B. (2021). International norms of asylum and burden-sharing: A case study of Bangladesh and the Rohingya refugee population. *Journal of Refugee Studies, 34*(4), 3734–3751. https://doi.org/10.1093/jrs/feaa122

Chowdhury, M. A., Billah, S. M., Karim, F., Khan, A. N., Islam, S., & Arifeen, S. E. (2018). *Demographic profiling and needs assessment of maternal and child health (MCH) care for the Rohingya refugee population in Cox's Bazar, Bangladesh.* Maternal and Child Health Division. Retrieved October 12, 2021, from http://dspace.icddrb.org/jspui/bitstream/123456789/9067/2/Special%20Report%20153.pdf

Cook, A. D., & Ne, F. Y. (2018). Complex humanitarian emergencies and disaster management in Bangladesh: The 2017 Rohingya exodus. *S. Rajaratnam School of International Studies.* https://css.ethz.ch/content/dam/ethz/special-interest/gess/cis/center-for-securities-studies/resources/docs/RSIS_Complex%20Humanitarian%20Emergencies%202017%20Rohingya%20Exodus.pdf

Faye, M. (2021). A forced migration from Myanmar to Bangladesh and beyond: Humanitarian response to Rohingya refugee crisis. *Journal of International Humanitarian Action, 6*(1), 13. https://doi.org/10.1186/s41018-021-00098-4

Grundy-Warr, C., & Dean, K. (2011). Not peace, not war: The myriad spaces of sovereignty, peace and conflict in Myanmar/Burma. In S. Kirsch & C. Flint (Eds.), *Reconstructing conflict: Integrating war and post-war geographies* (pp. 91–114). Routledge.

Hamzah, A. Z. A., & Belford, A. (2015, May 17). Pressure mounts on Myanmar over Asia 'boat people' crisis. *Reuters.* Retrieved October 11, 2021, from https://www.reuters.com/article/us-asia-migrants-idUSKBN0O20JB20150517

Hassan, M. M., Smith, A. C., Walker, K., Rahman, M. K., & Southworth, J. (2018). Rohingya refugee crisis and forest cover change in Teknaf, Bangladesh. *Remote Sensing, 10*(5), 689. https://doi.org/10.3390/rs10050689

Hookway, J. (2015, May 22). Rohingya refugee crisis likely to ease during monsoon, but only temporarily. *Wall Street Journal.* Retrieved October 12, 2021, from https://www.wsj.com/articles/rohingya-refugee-crisis-likely-to-ease-during-monsoon-but-only-temporarily-1432283124

Islam, M. M., & Nuzhath, T. (2018). Health risks of Rohingya refugee population in Bangladesh: A call for global attention. *Journal of Global Health, 8*(2), 020309. https://doi.org/10.7189/jogh.08.020309

Islam, M. N., Inan, T. T., & Islam, A. K. M. N. (2020). COVID-19 and the Rohingya refugees in Bangladesh: The challenges and recommendations. *Asia Pacific Journal of Public Health, 32*(5), 283–284. https://doi.org/10.1177/1010539520932707

Islam, M. R., Islam, M. T., Alam, M. S., Hussain, M., & Haque, M. M. (2021). Is Bhasan Char Island, Noakhali district in Bangladesh a sustainable place for the relocated Rohingya displaced people? An empirical study. *SN Social Sciences, 1*, 1–24.

Mahmood, S. S., Wroe, E., Fuller, A., & Leaning, J. (2017). The Rohingya people of Myanmar: Health, human rights, and identity. *The Lancet, 389*(10081), 1841–1850. https://doi.org/10.1016/S0140-6736(16)00646-2

Martin, M. F., Margesson, R., & Vaughn, B. (2018). The rohingya crises in Bangladesh and Burma. *Current Politics and Economics of South, Southeastern, and Central Asia, 27*(3/4), 333–375.

Mia, M. J., Hossain, M. K., Biswas, R. N., & Khan, M. R. (2021). Risk acceptance for humanitarian crisis response: Evidence from Rohingya influx into Bangladesh. *International Journal of Disaster Response and Emergency Management, 4*(1), 14–30. https://doi.org/10.4018/IJDREM.2021010102

Milton, A. H., Rahman, M., Hussain, S., Jindal, C., Choudhury, S., Akter, S., Ferdousi, S., Mouly, T. A., Hall, J., & Efird, J. T. (2017). Trapped in statelessness: Rohingya refugees in Bangladesh. *International Journal of Environmental Research and Public Health, 14*(8), 942. https://doi.org/10.3390/ijerph14080942

Nguyen, H., & Lewis, T. (2022, February 8). Bhasan Char and refugee 'warehousing'. *The Diplomat.* Retrieved June 20, 2022, from https://thediplomat.com/2022/02/bhasan-char-and-refugee-warehousing/

Parashar, A., & Alam, J. (2019). The national laws of Myanmar: Making of statelessness for the Rohingya. *International Migration, 57*(1), 94–108. https://doi.org/10.1111/imig.12532

Parnini, S. N. (2013). The crisis of the Rohingya as a Muslim minority in Myanmar and bilateral relations with Bangladesh. *Journal of Muslim Minority Affairs, 33*(2), 281–297. https://doi.org/10.1080/13602004.2013.826453

Rahman, M. R., Faiz, M. A., Nu, M. Y., Hassan, M. R., Chakrabarty, A. K., Kabir, I., Islam, K., Jafarullah, A. K. M., Alakabawy, M., Khatami, A., & Rashid, H. (2020). A rapid assessment of health literacy and health status of Rohingya refugees living in Cox's Bazar, Bangladesh following the august 2017 exodus from Myanmar: A cross-sectional study. *Tropical Medicine and Infectious Disease, 5*(3), 110. https://doi.org/10.3390/tropicalmed5030110

Rahman, U. (2010). The Rohingya refugee: A security dilemma for Bangladesh. *Journal of Immigrant & Refugee Studies, 8*(2), 233–239. https://doi.org/10.1080/15562941003792135

Rashid, R., Uddin, A. M. S., Nu, P. C., Salam, A., Barua, S., Mannan, A., Shahjahan, M., Ahmed, M. U., Rahman, R., Dondorp, A., Maude, R. J., Deen, J., von Seidlein, L., & Faiz, M. A. (2021). A descriptive study of forcefully displaced Myanmar nationals (FDMN) presenting for care at public health sector hospitals in Bangladesh. *Global Health Action, 14*(1), 1968124. https://doi.org/10.1080/16549716.2021.1968124

Reid, K. (2021, March 25). Rohingya refugee crisis: Facts, FAQs, and how to help. *World Vision*. Retrieved 10 October, 2022, from https://www.worldvision.org/refugees-news-stories/rohingya-refugees-bangladesh-facts.

Roth, K. (2020, November 8). Myanmar: Events of 2020. *Human Rights Watch*. Retrieved October 11, 2021, from https://www.hrw.org/world-report/2021/country-chapters/myanmar-burma

Roy, S. (2020). The archaeological and historical validation of Rohingya citizenship in Burma. *International Journal on World Peace, 37*(1), 7–22. https://www.proquest.com/openview/cd826087a26d369628a6463c98c309a2/1?pq-origsite=gscholar&cbl=30293

Sohel, M. S. (2017). The Rohingya crisis in Myanmar: Origin and emergence. *Saudi Journal of Humanities and Social Sciences, 2*(11A), 1007–1018. https://doi.org/10.21276/sjhss.2017.2.11.1

Taufiq, H. A. (2019). Rohingya refugee crisis and the state of insecurity in Bangladesh. In I. Ahmed (Ed.), *Genocide and mass violence: Politics of singularity* (pp.145–180). Centre for Genocide Studies, University of Dhaka. https://papers.ssrn.com/sol3/papers.cfm?abstract_id=3891359

The Daily Star. (2019, July 31). *Hosting 1.1m Rohingyas a big burden*. Retrieved January 19, 2022, from https://www.thedailystar.net/frontpage/bangladesh-pm-sheikh-hasina-says-11-million-rohingyas-big-burden-1779535

Uddin, N. (2015). State of stateless people: The plight of Rohingya refugees in Bangladesh. In R. E. Howard-Hassmann, & M. Walton-Roberts (Eds.), *The human right to citizenship: A slippery concept* (pp. 62–77). University of Pennsylvania Press. https://doi.org/10.9783/9780812291421-005

Uddin, N. (2019). The state, vulnerability, and transborder movements: The Rohingya people in Myanmar and Bangladesh. In N. Uddin, & N. Chowdhory (Eds.), *Deterritorialized identity and transborder movement in South Asia* (pp. 73–90). Springer. https://doi.org/10.1007/978-981-13-2778-0_5

Ullah, A. A. (2011). Rohingya refugees to Bangladesh: Historical exclusions and contemporary marginalization. *Journal of Immigrant & Refugee Studies, 9*(2), 139–161. https://doi.org/10.1080/15562948.2011.567149

Verme, P., & Schuettler, K. (2021). The impact of forced displacement on host communities: A review of the empirical literature in economics. *Journal of Development Economics, 150*, 102606. https://doi.org/10.1016/j.jdeveco.2020.102606

Part II
Conflict Dynamics and Security Implications

Chapter 4
Exploring Post-settlement Social Dynamics and Conflict Between the Host Community and Rohingyas

Lamia Islam

Abstract The forced displacement of Rohingyas continues to receive significant global attention due to its politico-religious and ethnic dimensions. Public and academic discussions and debates have primarily focused on citizenship crises, including genocide and security concerns. However, this chapter explores the social dynamics between the Bangladeshi host community and Rohingya people in Bangladesh, moving beyond these established frameworks. Drawing from in-depth interviews, secondary literature, and observations, this chapter reveals that the social composition in the Ukhiya and Teknaf sub-districts of Cox's Bazar has undergone significant changes, with the Rohingya people outnumbering that of the Bangladeshi host community. Initially, the Bangladeshi host community displayed sympathy, but social tensions have been increasing, especially as the socioeconomic impacts on the host community become evident. A significant portion of the host community perceives the Rohingyas as uneducated, rude, potential drug dealers, prone to criminal activities, and a security threat. The term "Rohingya" has become a social stigma and a derogatory term within Cox's Bazar and beyond. These social tensions often escalate into conflicts, posing a potential risk for future ethnic conflicts. Subsequently, minimizing these tensions between the communities is a challenging task that requires immediate attention, both theoretically and empirically.

1 Introduction

Bangladesh has been faced with several challenges because of hosting the Rohingyas, the second-largest displaced population in South and Southeast Asia (Xchange Foundation, 2018). Since the end of the 1970s, the Rohingya people have been forcibly driven from Myanmar to Bangladesh due to harsh military repression (Noor et al., 2017, p. 1192; Ullah, 2011 as cited in Siddiqui, 2022, p. 334). Among these displacements, the largest and fastest displacement influx occurred in 2017 when an estimated

L. Islam (✉)
Jagannath University, Dhaka, Bangladesh
e-mail: lamianitu@gmail.com

K. Ahmed and Md. R. Islam (eds.), *Understanding the Rohingya Displacement*, International Perspectives on Migration, https://doi.org/10.1007/978-981-97-1424-7_4

1,000,000 Rohingya, including more than 400,000 children, fled into the Cox's Bazar district, an already overpopulated coastal area of Bangladesh (Hossain et al., 2022; United News of Bangladesh, 2018). Although some Rohingyas have been repatriated in the past, that number is small in light of the widespread nature of the ethnic group's forced displacement from Myanmar (Azad & Jasmin, 2013, as cited in Siddiqi, 2022, p. 334).

Notably, the ethnic cleansing in Myanmar in August 2017 was a planned incident involving the government and military. Different local and foreign companies assisted financially in executing the plan (Fortify Rights, 2018a; Mallick, 2020, p. 204). According to the UN fact-finding mission's (2019) claim, 45 local companies and 15 foreign organizations spent USD 10 million to support the state-sponsored violence against Rohingyas across the three districts, including Maungdaw, Buthidaung, and Rathedaung, in Rakhine State (Mallick, 2020, p. 204). Further, as the Myanmar government has already approved 48 new trade projects in Rakhine State, the government is using forced displacements to strengthen economic ties with neighboring countries (Mallick, 2020, p. 205). On the other hand, Bangladesh did not sign the 1951 Refugee Convention, and it has no domestic law to differentiate between an asylum seeker and a refugee (Mallick, 2020, p. 206). In failing to do so, the Government of Bangladesh does not recognize Rohingyas as refugees (Siddiqi, 2022). Subsequently, only 33,131 people are registered as refugees, living in two camps in Cox's Bazar (Milton et al., 2017).

An agreement was previously signed by the governments of Myanmar and Bangladesh to accelerate the Rohingya repatriation process, on November 23, 2017. The basis of the agreement was a deal signed in 1992. The Bangladeshi government was obligated to abide by that earlier agreement, despite its many flaws, which include classifying Rohingyas as internally displaced people and requiring Myanmar-issued proof of residency, and allowing the Myanmar government to repatriate anyone, settle repatriates in a restricted area, and take the initiative to repatriate those Rohingyas who fled after October 2016 ("Rohingya Repatriation Deal", 2017). Meanwhile, several attempts were taken by the Government of Bangladesh to repatriate Rohingyas according to the agreement, but Rohingyas were only willing to return to Myanmar if a series of long-standing demands were met (Mallick, 2020, p. 213; Rahman, 2021). Another concern is that the repatriation process may slow down due to the military coup held in Myanmar on February 1, 2021 (Palma, 2021; Tiezzi, 2021). Given that Rohingyas are stateless as a result of the controversial citizenship law that the military government put in place in 1982 and that the army-backed government is relying on the extreme nationalist ideology of certain Buddhists to get through its current legitimacy crisis, it is absurd to think that the government will take action to resolve the issue (Khan, 2021). The Bangladeshi government offered shelter to the refugees on humanitarian grounds, believing they would be repatriated soon. But such a process was not followed due to these many different issues ("Delaying the Rohingya Repatriation", 2018; Kawser, 2018; United News of Bangladesh, 2018). As a result, the local communities of Cox's Bazar continue to experience economic, social, political, environmental, and security challenges due to the refugee influx (United News of Bangladesh, 2018; Xchange Foundation, 2018).

The tensions between the Rohingya and the host population have also increased simultaneously. It has been observed that the host community holds mixed and sensitive attitudes toward the Rohingya. They find the Rohingya a threat and the source of many social problems (Siddiqi, 2022, p. 340). The social tensions between these two communities often eventually became social conflicts (Ansar & Khaled, 2021). In this respect, the present chapter attempts to illustrate how to minimize the tensions between the communities, tensions which need to be addressed immediately. This report sheds light on the tensions between Rohingya refugees and the host community of Bangladesh through the lens of the challenges derived from economic, social, and environmental dimensions.

The chapter's Sect. 1 highlights methods and the theoretical framework of the study. Section 2 focuses on the social, economic, and environmental challenges that adversely impact the relations between Rohingya refugees and host communities. The paper's Sect. 3 explains some suggestions to reduce the tensions between the host community and Rohingya—particularly tensions that lead to violence.

2 Theoretical Framework

In recent decades, the increased attention to citizenship is well documented in many distinct but interconnected disciplines in the social sciences, including geography, anthropology, and political science (Studemeyer, 2015, p. 566). In a narrow sense, "citizenship" refers to the legal relationship between the individual and polity. Polity took the form of the city both in ancient and medieval times in Europe. Subsequently, the evolution of polities along with the lines of the formation of state gave citizenship its full institutionalized and formalized character in the West, which made nationality an essential component of citizenship (Sassen, 2002, p. 7). However, today citizenship refers to the national state that identifies the legal status of an individual in terms of state membership (Sassen, 2002, p. 7).

It is noteworthy that although citizenship has often been referred as a single concept and a unitary institution, studies of contemporary modalities recognize citizenship as a multifaceted concept construed in dynamic terms (Studemeyer, 2015, p. 567). The term is typically seen as an essential and inevitable step that paves the way to greater integration, inclusion, and recognition by the "host" country, whereas it is perceived by a new generation of hyper-mobile migrants as "flexible" (Waters, 2009, p. 637). In the same vein, Marston and Mitchell (2004, pp. 96, 101) claim that the institution of citizenship is a non-static, nonlinear, social, political, cultural, economic, and legal construction. In doing so, they recognize the concept for its flexibility rather than rigidity, as an ongoing process rather than a "finished product," and as relational rather than standardized. Sassen (2002, p. 7) explains that as the national state has been transformed, practices of citizenship have extended to international arenas. Citizen actors thus express it as "post-national citizenship," which is partly outside the national realm, or "denationalized citizenship," which is predicated on a transformation of the nation itself. However, both terms exist together as the nation-state continues to be significant (Maira, 2008, p. 703; Sassen, 2002). In this regard, Maria (2008, p. 704) defines flexible citizenship as a manifestation of both post-national and denationalized citizenship. The term emerges due to the changes in the institution of citizenship within nation-states and the shifting of power on national and global scales. However, the concept of flexible citizenship is different from the concept of dual citizenship. The former is a response to the conditions of globalization, and leaves open questions of national loyalty or strategic uses of citizenship status for legal and economic purposes, while the latter implies an actual legal status as citizen of two nation-states.

Two themes within the literature on flexible citizenship can be identified. The more established theme acknowledges that approaches including flexible accumulation of economic, political, cultural, and social capital influence the flexible attitudes toward citizenship (Harvey, 1990, as cited in Studemeyer, 2015, p. 566). On the other hand, the less developed theme explains that the basis of flexible attitudes toward citizenship involves fewer quantifiable motivations like financial security; rather, for instance, it cites personal fulfillment of life goals, establishment of identity and belonging, or simple easing of everyday routines (Marston & Mitchell, 2004, as cited in Studemeyer, 2015, p. 566). Maira (2008, p. 703) defines flexible citizenship as a form of cultural citizenship which is used to describe the emergence of new uses of citizenship by migrants. This kind of citizenship is a response to the conditions of transnationalism. Specifically, flexible citizenship is the use of transnational links to provide political or material resources which are not available within a single nation-state. Ong (1999, p. 6) asserts that the flexible notion of citizenship and sovereignty is increasingly being developed by individuals (and governments) as strategies for accumulating capital and power. Studemeyer (2015, p. 568) also defines flexible citizenship as strategies to collect different types of capital, and intending to mitigate uncertainty for oneself and/or one's family in different political, historical, cultural, and social contexts, a notion which is called a transnational safety net. Capital is defined in this context as an asset or bundle of assets that belong to an individual, a group, or an institutionalized body (e.g., a nation-state). Capital is also defined in terms of cultural and social characteristics (Bourdieu, 2002; Mohan & Mohan, 2002; Portes, 1998, as cited in Studemeyer, 2015, p. 568). In this regard, cultural capital is the cultivation of the "right" characteristics that translate into "symbolic power" within society (Bourdieu, 2002, pp. 281–282; Ong, 1999, p. 91; Studemeyer, 2015, p. 568). Education is one of the main embodiments of cultural capital. In the same vein, academic fields, foreign languages, and socioculturally appropriate etiquette and behavior also become sources of cultural capital by shaping education as knowledge (Bourdieu, 2002, p. 281–282; Studemeyer, 2015, p. 568). Still further, social capital is understood as a collection of resources derived from particular social networks and relationships (Studemeyer, 2015, p. 568). Notably, the practices of flexible citizenship are not only intertwined with labor and education, but are also embedded in larger global conflicts and questions of international human rights (Maria, 2008, pp. 710–711). Flexible citizenship has emerged along with the flow of labor across national borders that benefits one country's economy. In some cases, it facilitates labor migration, while in other cases, it paves the way for migrants strategically to move between labor markets (Maria, 2008, p. 704). In some cases, religious identity is also connected with the practices of flexible citizenship (Maria, 2008, p. 711).

From the above understanding of flexible citizenship, this study tries to comprehend the social dynamics between the displaced Rohingyas and the host communities through the theoretical framework of flexible citizenship. The purpose of the study is to address the ways to minimize the tensions between the communities by analyzing the impact of delaying the repatriation process of the Rohingyas, as well as the perception both the Rohingyas and the host communities hold of each other.

3 Methods

Focus Group Discussions (FGDs), in-depth interviews, a literature review, and casual meetings with the host community and forcibly displaced Rohingya refugees in Cox's Bazar were among the methods used to collect qualitative data for the research. The core data was compiled in three stages to provide a better understanding of the nature and progression of conflicts between the host community and the Rohingya people. Significantly, all three data collection periods took place in Cox's Bazar's Ukhia Upazila. The following criteria were used to select Ukhia Upazila as a field area: First, the Rohingya camp that is run by the government is in Kutupalong, Ukhia. Kutupalong is the largest refugee camp in the world (UNHCR, 2019). Focusing on it will help us to understand its social, economic, and environmental effects on the local community, and how the community interacts with the Rohingyas. Second, the regional and national offices of the Bangladesh Rural Advancement Committee (BRAC) gave the researcher permission to talk to Rohingya people in informal sessions, focus groups, and interviews in the temporary learning centers in Camps 4 and 17, which are in this region. Because of this, the author elected to gather data there.

The first phase involved 40 formal interviews (of 20 men and 20 women), five FGDs, and many unplanned contacts with both groups in the third and fourth weeks of October 2018 and the first week of January 2019. Local Bangladeshi civil society members (college teachers, NGO officials and activists, chair people and members of local government bodies, volunteer activists), local government officials, and the population at large who claimed to be vulnerable owing to the Rohingya camps also participated in data collection. On the other hand, camp leaders, known as Majhi by the locals, educated Rohingyas who began receiving BRAC training to work as teachers in BRAC learning centers, parents of children enrolled in BRAC learning centers, and general Rohingya people comprised the Rohingya respondents. Open-ended questionnaires were created for these structured interviews. The survey method was developed through extensive literature review and brainstorming. To round out the assessment, subjective factors were also considered. Some of the open-ended questions asked of both the host community and the Rohingya community were similar; however, topics pertaining to human security and the repatriation procedure were added to the list specifically for the Rohingya community. The interviewer asked each interviewee the same questions in the same order, and the responses were recorded. Before collecting data, the author obtained informed consent from respondents in accordance with ethical research standards. In the case of a few interviewees—particularly worried government officials—refusing to allow recording of the interviews, the interviewer was forced to merely take notes in those circumstances. While speaking with Rohingya interviewees, the author occasionally assisted the interpreter. As a result, while all of the respondents from the Rohingya population understood Bangla, some needed assistance speaking the language fluently. In this context, BRAC Education Program (BEP) staff in Cox's Bazar acted as interpreters for the interviewer. The interviewer, on the other hand, was always aware of the meaning of the interviews that the interpreter interpreted; thus the researcher double-checked the logical meaning of the translated interviews multiple times. Because of the respondents' usually difficult vocabulary, the author frequently requested assistance from BEP staff members when transcribing and cleaning the data. To ensure respondent participation, the researcher created a "balanced rapport" (Fontana & Frey, 2000) with the interviewees and used the approach of "engaged listening" (Converse & Schuman, 1974). Although respondents from the Rohingya community first indicated satisfaction with their decision to remain in the camps, as the discourse progressed, they expressed anxiety about the risk of inciting conflict with the host population. The BRAC education program's higher officials and regional leaders were similarly flexible in selecting respondents. BRAC education program regional officials in Cox's Bazar provided logistical and infrastructural support for all interviews and informal sessions.

The second data collection phase took place from the third the fourth weeks of May 2020.

The researcher purposefully chose 50 (25 male, 25 female) respondents for the research's unstructured interviews and informal conversations. Unfortunately, due to the pandemic, conducting interviews and informal face-to-face discussions was impossible. The interviewer interviewed all the respondents over the phone. Subsequently, most of the interviewees did not allow the researcher to record the interviews in this format.

In the third phase, the researcher conducted interviews and informal discussions in the last weeks of January and February 2023. As a "universal form of systematic investigation," the author again used interviews to access data (Fontana & Frey, 2000; Holstein & Gubrium, 1995, p. 1). Unstructured interviews were conducted with 20 respondents from the host community and 20 from the Rohingya community during this data-gathering phase. All respondents were purposively selected, but Rohingya respondents snowballed. The host community helped the interviewer choose the Rohingya respondents, whom they hired as a day laborer or met in the market or other public gatherings. The Rohingya community relies on the host community for food, as they are restricted within the camp. Many respondents refused to let the author record their interviews, even though the author promised not to reveal their identities.

4 Data Collection

Initially, the researcher cleaned up the data by masking the names and other personal information of the respondents. To identify key findings, all of the records and notes from the in-depth interviews and casual talks were meticulously transcribed. Because there were some issues in interpreting the Rohingya community's language, the researcher double-checked the transcribed interviews with the translator. By comparing the data, the general, new, and exceptional data trends were determined.

4.1 Limitations

Although a substantial population was available for study, the researcher faced challenges due to the shortage of time and lack of financial assistance and other resources to facilitate the interview and analysis processes. Moreover, the researcher depended on the officials of BRAC Education Program (BEP) and the host community for selecting the respondents, as both the field area and respondents were less known to the researcher. All these limitations may influence the scale of the research work by impacting the data collection and analysis depth.

5 Social Dynamics Between the Host Communities and the Rohingyas

The Rohingya are an ethnic, linguistic, and religious minority group in Myanmar's Northern Rakhine State (NRS) (Azad & Jasmin, 2013, p. 25). Historically, they have been deprived of their rights (Siddiqui, 2022; Ullah, 2011). Their exclusions from the mainstream occur due to political and economic interests rather than religious and ethnic tensions (Bepler, 2018, p. 8). Subsequently, the people of this ethnic group have been compelled to migrate to neighboring countries, especially Bangladesh (Ullah, 2011, pp. 151, 156). Over a million Rohingya live in the 34 refugee camps in the Cox's Bazaar districts (Strategic Executive Group, 2019). United News of Bangladesh (2018) explains the various challenges Bangladesh has faced due to the Rohingya influx. She (2018) mentions that from August 2017 to March 25, 2018, international donor agencies donated $322 million to Rohingyas. The government of Bangladesh estimated that $434 million had been spent on some 1 million Rohingyas during that period. Later, external agencies provided 74% of those expenses, whereas the Bangladesh government contributed the rest. Furthermore, some sources estimate that the annual cost to Bangladesh for sheltering and feeding Rohingyas refugees is $1.21 billion (Rahman, 2023). Although national and international humanitarian agencies continue to provide humanitarian assistance, the livelihood of the communities is adversely affected due to the gap between needs and resources (Jerin &

Mozumder, 2019, p. 169). The Joint Response Plan of 2019 also described the negative impact of the Rohingya influx on the Cox's Bazar host community (Jerin & Mozumder, 2019; Strategic Executive Group, 2019).

As of March 1st, 2023, the World Food Programme reported a 17% decrease in food supplies for the Rohingya refugees in Bangladesh. Due to financial limitations, the cost of food per person has dropped from $12 to $10 (1224–1070 Bangladeshi Taka [Tk]) (Karobi, 2023).

During a phone interview, an NGO worker discussing the covid-19 situation in the Rohingya camps emphasized the need to enhance local capacity and promote integration within the Rohingya community to address the challenges posed by the pandemic and its aftermath. The worker also stressed the importance of coordination between international, national, and local levels to handle the crisis of providing shelter to the Rohingya. The development worker mentioned that

> Providing door-to-door service delivery poses a significant challenge in the Rohingya camps. Nevertheless, it is crucial to persevere with this work. However, the reduction in funding from international organizations could present a hurdle. It is essential to enhance local capacity and distribute responsibilities among local actors. To achieve optimal results, close monitoring of all service delivery processes is necessary. (Interview with an NGO worker on May 21, 2020 over telephone/mobile)

In another interview, a Majhi from the Rohingya community (the community leader of a Rohingya camp is called a Majhi) said that

> Our family consists of eight members, and the assistance we are currently receiving is insufficient for our needs. We are experiencing a gradual decline not only in the availability of natural resources but also in the support provided by international organizations. Some of us who are educated have sought employment in various NGOs, while others work as day laborers. The older members of our family resort to begging in local markets. Unfortunately, conflicts occasionally arise between the local community and the Rohingya community when we venture into the host community's areas for survival purposes. However, it is extremely challenging to rely solely on the development aid provided by international organizations as it is insufficient to meet our needs. (Interview with a camp leader of the Rohingya community on January 1, 2019)

The host community also expressed their concern about the high population density and high birth rate of Rohingyas in the settlement areas, as these factors adversely affect the livelihoods of local people (Dhaka Tribune, 2017). The Bangladeshi government is also worried about the rapid population growth in the Rohingya camps. It is reported that every year an average of 35,000 newborn babies are registered to the forcibly displaced Myanmar nationals taking shelter in Bangladesh (Rahman, 2022). In an in-depth interview, a school teacher of the host community expressed his grievance in following way:

> The Myanmar government has denied the Rohingya population access to essential services such as family planning and healthcare. The military-backed government has made concerted efforts to isolate them from mainstream society. If the Rohingya people are unable to return to their home country and the high birthrate in the camps persists over the next decade, it will undoubtedly lead to socioeconomic devastation for both the local community and future generations. (Interview with a school teacher of the host community on October 19, 2018)

The Rohingya community faces numerous challenges within the Rohingya camps, primarily due to the burden of sustaining large families and the high population density. During an in-depth interview, a woman from the Rohingya community expressed her experiences to the interviewer:

> In my family, there are seven members, and over time, the assistance we receive has been decreasing. The situation has become more challenging as we no longer receive financial support from international organizations. As a result, we often visit the local market in the host community to sell the goods we receive from international organizations. We sell these items because sometimes we need to purchase necessary items by exchanging or selling extra or non-essential goods like shampoo or infant food. To support our large family, my husband also takes on daily labor jobs within the local community. Although it comes with risks, he is determined to work in the host community to ensure our family's survival. It has become one of our means of earning a living. (Interview with a housewife of the Rohingya community on October 19, 2018)

Another man from the Rohingya community expressed his concerns regarding the upcoming monsoon season. He highlighted how the densely populated camps put them at a significant disadvantage during rainy days. He said,

> Living in the camps during the monsoon seasons is an immense challenge and burden for the camp residents. The absence of a proper drainage system, exacerbated by the high population density, leads to water entering our homes. I implore the authorities to provide us with essential assistance to ensure our safety and well-being during this difficult time. (Interview with a resident of the Rohingya camps on January 5, 2019)

Furthermore, the densely populated Rohingya camps have brought about a shift in the sociodemographic composition of the Ukhiya and Teknaf sub-districts in Cox's Bazar, posing a challenge in maintaining and practicing comprehensive health and hygiene measures during the covid-19 pandemic. Shedding light on this issue, a local NGO activist shared the following insights during an interview:

> Given that approximately 40,000 people reside within every 1 square kilometer of the Rohingya camps, ensuring social distancing within the camp becomes an arduous task. The failure to maintain social distancing in the region has put both the Rohingya and host community's lives at risk. Despite numerous efforts, such as the provision of health services, raising awareness about social distancing, and distributing hygiene materials by development workers, these endeavors have had limited effectiveness in preventing the spread of covid-19 due to the high population density. Additionally, the Rohingya community's superstitious beliefs and lack of health knowledge present significant barriers to the implementation of effective health services. (Interview with a local NGO activist working in the Rohingya camps during the covid-19 pandemic on May 19, 2020, over mobile)

Simultaneously, the once-renowned tourist town of Cox's Bazar, known for its long sea beach, has been transformed into a Refugee Bazar. It now accommodates a significant number of NGOs, development experts, relief and rehabilitation providers, journalists, foreigners, and security agencies. This influx has led to certain roads becoming unusable, as they are constantly occupied by the movement of numerous relief trucks from international and domestic NGOs and donor agencies. As a consequence, the local population often endures severe traffic congestion for hours on end. A primary school teacher shared the following perspective on the situation:

> The road infrastructure has become highly vulnerable due to the influx of Rohingya refugees. The local population regularly experiences the consequences of traffic congestion, which has become a common occurrence. Just last week, my family and I had to visit the hospital for my child's illness. Despite the hospital being a 45-minute journey from our home, we arrived there 2.5 hours later. During this prolonged delay, my baby's health deteriorated. I firmly believe that the influx of Rohingya refugees is the sole reason behind the miserable condition of the roads. (Interview with a female primary school teacher in January, 2023)

In the midst of these challenges, the Roads and Highways Department has observed a significant increase of 2.5 times in traffic on its roads. This excessive load of traffic has resulted in severe damage to the road infrastructure. As a result, the department has identified the need for a reconstruction budget of approximately $100 million to rebuild the highway connecting Cox's Bazar and Teknaf. Additionally, the Local Government Engineering Department (LGED) has estimated another $100 million for the construction of roads within the camps and those connecting the camps to the highways. The Cox's Bazar Development Authority has also reevaluated its medium-term development plan in response to the influx of Rohingya refugees (Sattar, 2019).

The people of the Cox's Bazar district have directly felt the negative economic consequences of the Rohingya influx. Local food and transportation prices have surged, and there have been shortages of food grains, impacting the tourism industry and livelihoods of the local population (Dhaka Tribune, 2017). Moreover, the destruction of seasonal vegetables, crops, and paddy fields, along with the disruption of irrigation facilities and the scarcity of seeds has had a severe impact on local agriculture. As a result, people in the affected areas have struggled to repay their loans, exacerbating their economic turmoil (IC Net Limited, 2018). A farmer expressed his distressing economic situation in the following manner:

> I am currently burdened with a massive financial debt because I lost my mango garden due to the Rohingya settlement in 2017. The garden used to be my primary source of income, generating 1 lakh 65 thousand taka annually. Losing it has had a significant impact on my financial situation. (Interview with a farmer of the host community in October, 2018)

The Ministry of Environment and Forests (MoEF) of Bangladesh, UNDP, and UN Women have operated a Rapid Environment Assessment Study to identify the environmental impact of the Rohingya influx. The report describes eleven ecological impacts, including five ecosystems and five physical effects. The report says,

> Some of the problems associated with the physical environmental effects include high groundwater depletion, groundwater contamination, poor indoor air quality, incorrect management of sewer sludge, removal of soils and topography, and changes in terrain. Impacts on ecosystems with high associated risks include deforestation and forest degradation, intrusion into and resource extraction from protected areas, changes in land cover, rapid biomass reduction, species extinction, loss of wildlife habitat and narrowing of wildlife corridors, and risks of wildlife mortality. (United Nations Development Programme Bangladesh, 2018)

The deforestation occurring in the area has not only put animals at risk, particularly elephants, but has also had detrimental effects on the environment in general. Additionally, the installation of 2614 shallow tube wells to provide water for the refugees has resulted in a significant decrease of 40 to 60 feet in water levels in the affected area. The presence of 5000 unsanitary latrines and a dysfunctional sewer system has further contributed to severe environmental damage (IC Net Limited, 2018). Moreover, the settlement of Rohingyas has intensified the grievances of the local community who depend on forests and hills for their livelihoods. This has led to tensions between the host community and the Rohingyas. A forest officer from the Upazilla Forest Department explained the reasons behind this tension in the following manner:

> The initial settlement of Rohingyas resulted in the damage of 6,162.02 acres of reserved forest and 2,017.50 acres of social forests. As a consequence, the local people who were engaged in social forestry activities suffered severe economic consequences. Many individuals in the area relied on social forestry as their livelihood, often taking loans from banks or wealthy individuals at high interest rates. With the settlement of Rohingyas, they have lost their means of living, plunging them into a deep economic crisis. The biodiversity within the reserved area has been completely destroyed, with trees uprooted from their roots. Additionally, the cutting of hills has caused soil erosion, leading to the flow of soil into water bodies. This poses a significant risk to houses located near water bodies, as they may become submerged during the monsoon season. (Interview with a forest officer from the Upazilla Forest Department in January 2019)

6 Conclusion

The Rohingya community faced marginalization as a result of the actions taken by the Myanmar government. Through the use of coercion and the implementation of discriminatory laws, the government systematically discriminated against them. The Rohingya people were deprived of essential rights, such as access to education, health care, employment opportunities, and even citizenship within their own country. Regarding the displaced Rohingya in Bangladesh, a significant portion of the host community also perceives them as uneducated, rude, and a security threat, attitudes that ultimately aggravate tension between the host community and the Rohingya people. Enabling the Rohingya people to access education and various skill-training initiatives can bring about a transformative effect in reducing conflicts. Subsequently, emphasizing the importance of education and different skills within the Rohingya population can bring about numerous advantages. Through the acquisition of knowledge and skills, Rohingya individuals can actively contribute to the academic realm, bringing fresh perspectives and insights to various fields of study. Furthermore, education provides opportunities for Rohingya individuals to learn foreign languages, enabling them to improve their communication abilities and expand their horizons by engaging with a broader range of cultures and communities. This linguistic proficiency can facilitate better integration into society and enhance their prospects for economic and personal growth. Education also plays a crucial role in fostering an understanding of social norms and cultural sensitivities between the two communities. By equipping Rohingya individuals with this knowledge, they can navigate diverse social contexts more effectively, facilitating positive interactions with others and promoting mutual understanding and respect. However, although the Government of Bangladesh and various national and international organizations are providing short-term support to the Rohingya to allow access to education, primary health care, and various skills/capacity-building activities, it is insufficient to fully meet their long-term needs. The challenges arising from the influx of Rohingya refugees are substantial, making it difficult for Bangladesh, despite its progress in poverty reduction, gender equality, health, and education, to handle the situation alone. While it is essential for the international community to continue supporting Bangladesh's humanitarian efforts, a sustainable resolution ultimately depends on the Myanmar government's commitment to ensuring the safety and rights of the Rohingya population (Siddiqi & Kamruzzaman, 2021).

Initially, the local host population in Bangladesh showed support and solidarity with the displaced Rohingya refugees due to religious similarities and on humanitarian grounds. The religiously inspired moral imperative of the local hosts and institutions played a significant role in help offered to the Rohingya refugees. The displaced community also appreciated the support they received from the locals to freely practice their religion, as it provided them a sense of comfort and belonging. However, various factors have negatively impacted the attitude of the local population toward the Rohingya people over time. Economic instability, such as wage falls and price hikes, unequal access to humanitarian aid, and uneven distribution of resources have created tensions. Additionally, uncertainty about the future of the Rohingya crisis may further contribute to the strained relationship between the host community and the Rohingya refugees (Ansar & Khaled, 2021). Given this context, it is suggested that religious identity can play a crucial role in mitigating tensions between the Rohingya people and the host community. By emphasizing the shared religious values and promoting understanding, dialog, and cooperation, it may be possible to foster better relations and reduce the negative impacts caused by economic instability and uncertainty. Recognizing and respecting the religious beliefs and practices of both the Rohingya and the host community can help create an environment of mutual respect and harmony.

Moreover, the relief and rehabilitation programs for the refugees have left the poorer section of the host community feeling marginalized. At the onset of the crisis, various local entities such as host communities, faith-based groups, and local NGOs played a vital role in supporting refugees, with assistance from the local government. However, the arrival of foreign funding resulted in a shift in leadership dynamics. Eventually, the UN agencies and other international organizations assumed control, displacing the local actors from their leadership positions. The local actors perceive a lack of adequate involvement in the decision-making process by these international organizations (Khaled, 2021). Hence, it is crucial to establish stronger networks and foster relationships between the local actors and international agencies to bolster their capacity. Furthermore, given the detrimental environmental impact of the Rohingya influx, which has significantly affected the host community's livelihoods, effective coordination, and communication among various groups are also imperative to formulate sustainable solutions.

In conclusion, the escalation of social tensions frequently gives rise to conflicts, creating a potential risk for future ethnic disputes. Consequently, effectively reducing these tensions among the Rohingya and the host communities is a formidable undertaking that demands prompt attention by the government of Bangladesh and also the international agencies.

Acknowledgements The author would like to extend her appreciation to Debasish Kundu, Associate Professor in the Department of Sociology at the University of Dhaka, for his help in the conception of the research. I am also indebted to Nirjhor Anjum, Assistant Professor at Daffodil International University and Chief Technology Officer of Ollyo, for his assistance with data collection and analysis. The author also extends her gratitude to Nazrul Islam, Ex-Senior Manager, BRAC Education Program, Mr. Ehsan and Kamruzzaman, regional officials of BRAC Education Program, Cox's Bazar, for providing assistance throughout the selection of respondents and data collection procedure. The author would finally like to recognize Sohel Rana's (Executive Editor, The Morning Times) efforts in editing the chapter.

References

Ansar, A., & Khaled, A. F. M. (2021). From solidarity to resistance: Host communities' evolving response to the Rohingya refugees in Bangladesh. *Journal of International Humanitarian Action, 6*(1), 16. https://doi.org/10.1186/s41018-021-00104-9

Atim, G. (2013). The impact of refugees on conflicts in Africa. *IOSR Journal of Humanities and Social Science, 14*(2), 4–9. https://www.academia.edu/download/32109784/B01420409.pdf

Azad, A., & Jasmin, F. (2013). Durable solutions to the protracted refugee situation: The case of Rohingyas in Bangladesh. *Journal of Indian Research, 1*(4), 25–35. https://www.academia.edu/5886047/Durable_Solutions_to_the_Protracted_Refugee_Situation_the_Case_of_Rohingyas_in_Bangladesh

Bepler, S. (2018). The Rohingya conflict: Genesis, current situation and geopolitical aspects. *Pacific Geographies, 28*(50), 4–10. https://doi.org/10.23791/500410

Boamah-Gyah, K. (2008). *The socio-cultural and economic impact of refugees on the host indigenous communities in West Africa: A case study of Liberian refugees at Buduburam Community in Ghana* [Master's Thesis, University of Tromso]. https://munin.uit.no/bitstream/handle/10037/1538/thesis.pdf?sequence=1

Bourdieu, P. (2002). The forms of capital. In N. W. Biggart (Ed.), *Readings in economic sociology* (pp. 280–290). Blackwell Publishing. https://doi.org/10.1002/9780470755679.ch15

Chambers, P. (2015). The Rohingyas' trail of tears: Continuing persecution of an ethnic minority in Myanmar. *South Asia Democratic Forum.* https://www.sadf.eu/sadf-focus-nr-9-the-rohingyas-trail-of-tears-continuing-persecution-of-an-ethnic-minority-in-myanmar/

Emran, M. Z. (2018, August 28). Delaying the Rohingya repatriation. *The Daily Star*. https://www.thedailystar.net/news/letters/delaying-the-rohingya-repatriation-1625275

Farishta, A. (2014). *The impact of Syrian refugees on Jordan's water resources and water management planning* [Master's Thesis, Columbia University]. Columbia Academic Commons.https://doi.org/10.7916/D80K26P3

Hossain, M. A., Ullah, A. K. M. A., & Mohiuddin, Md. (2022). Rohingya refugees in the pandemic: Crisis and policy responses. *Global Policy*. https://doi.org/10.1111/1758-5899.13156

IC Net Limited. (2018). The survey on host communities in Cox's Bazar affected by the Rohingya crisis. *IC Net Limited*. https://www.icnetlimited.com/wp-content/uploads/2018/03/Second-Survey-on-Host-Communities.pdf

Jerin, M. I., & Mozumder, M. K. (2019). Exploring host community attitudes towards Rohingya refugees in Bangladesh. *Intervention, 17*(2), 169–173. https://journals.lww.com/invn/fulltext/2019/17020/exploring_host_community_attitudes_towards.7.aspx

Karobi, A. S. (2023, March 19). Declining funds, food for Rohingyas. *The NewAge Bangladesh*. https://www.newagebd.net/article/197176/declining-funds-food-for-rohingyas

Kawser, R. (2018, August 3). Rohingyas blamed for repatriation delay. *The Dhaka Tribune*. https://www.dhakatribune.com/bangladesh/2018/08/03/rohingyas-blamed-for-repatriation-delay

Khaled, A. F. M. (2021). Do No Harm in refugee humanitarian aid: The case of the Rohingya humanitarian response. *Journal of International Humanitarian Action, 6*, 7. https://doi.org/10.1186/s41018-021-00093-9

Kumssa, A., Jones, J. F., & Herbert Williams, J. (2009). Conflict and human security in the North Rift and North Eastern Kenya. *International Journal of Social Economics, 36*(10), 1008–1020. https://doi.org/10.1108/03068290910984786

Maira, S. (2008). Flexible citizenship/flexible empire: South Asian Muslim youth in post-9/11 America. *American Quarterly, 60*(3), 697–720. https://www.jstor.org/stable/40068521?seq=1

Mallick, A. H. (2020). Rohingya refugee repatriation from Bangladesh: A far cry from reality. *Journal of Asian Security and International Affairs, 7*(2), 202–226. https://doi.org/10.1177/2347797020938983

Manik, A. S. (2020, September 5). Rohingya influx blamed for dilapidated Cox's Bazaar-Teknaf road condition. *Bangladesh Post*. https://bangladeshpost.net/posts/rohingya-influx-blamed-for-dilapidated-cox-s-bazaar-teknaf-road-condition-13207

Marston, S., & Mitchell, K. (2004). Citizens and the state: Citizenship formations in space and time. In C. Barnett & M. Low (Eds.), *Spaces of democracy: Geographical perspectives on citizenship, participation and representation* (pp. 93–112). Sage Publications. https://doi.org/10.4135/9781446216309

Martin, A. (2005). Environmental conflict between refugee and host communities. *Journal of Peace Research, 42*(3), 329–346. https://doi.org/10.1177/0022343305052015

Milton, A. H., Rahman, M., Hussain, S., et al. (2017). Trapped in statelessness: Rohingya refugees in Bangladesh. *International Journal of Environmental Research and Public Health, 14*(8), 942. https://doi.org/10.3390/ijerph14080942

Noor, M. T., Islam, M. S., & Forid, S. (2017). Rohingya crisis and the concerns for Bangladesh. *International Journal of Scientific & Engineering Research, 8*(12), 1192–1196. https://www.academia.edu/download/55559490/Rohingya-Crisis-and-The-Concerns-for-Bangladesh.pdf

Ong, A. (1999). *Flexible citizenship: The cultural logics of transnationality*. Duke University Press.

Palma, P. (2021, February 2). Rohingya refugees: Is repatriation now up in the air? *The Daily Star*. https://www.thedailystar.net/frontpage/news/rohingya-refugees-repatriation-now-the-air-2037573

Rahman, M. (2022, April 11). Govt worried as Rohingya population grows fast in Bangladesh camps. *The NewAge Bangladesh*. https://www.newagebd.net/article/167807/govt-worried-as-rohingya-population-grows-fast-in-bangladesh-camps

Rahman, S. A. (2021, January 20). Bangladesh expects to start Rohingya repatriation to Myanmar in June. *Voice of America*. https://www.voanews.com/a/east-asia-pacific_bangladesh-expects-start-rohingya-repatriation-myanmar-june/6200978.html

Rahman, S. A. (2023). Rohingya crisis: The picture of fund crisis and its impacts. *Le Centre Tricontinental*. https://www.cetri.be/Rohingya-Crisis-The-Picture-of?lang=fr#:~:text=Every%20year%2C%20the%20plan%20is,the%20Rohingya%20refugees%20since%202017

Rohingya repatriation deal: What we know. (2017, November 26). *The Dhaka Tribune*. https://www.dhakatribune.com/bangladesh/2017/11/26/rohingya-repatriation-deal-know

Salehyan, I., & Gleditsch, K. S. (2006). Refugees and the spread of civil war. *International Organization, 60*(2), 335–366. https://doi.org/10.1017/S0020818306060103

Sassen, S. (2002). The repositioning of citizenship: Emergent subjects and spaces for politics. *Berkeley Journal of Sociology, 46*, 4–26. https://www.jstor.org/stable/41035566

Sattar, Z. (2019, July 30). Rohingya crisis and the host community. *The Financial Express*. https://thefinancialexpress.com.bd/views/reviews/rohingya-crisis-and-the-host-community-1564498784

Siddiqi, B., & Kamruzzaman, P. (2021). Policy challenges towards Rohingya crisis in Bangladesh: The role of national development experts. Center for Peace Studies. https://doi.org/10.13140/RG.2.2.22060.18566

Siddiqui, B. (2022). The 'myth' of repatriation: The prolonged sufferings of the Rohingya in Bangladesh. In N. Uddin (Ed.), *The Rohingya Crisis: Human rights issues, policy concerns and burden sharing* (pp. 334–357). SAGE India. https://www.researchgate.net/publication/355983175_The_'Myth'_of_Repatriation_The_Prolonged_Sufferings_of_the_Rohingya_in_Bangladesh

Sohel, I. M., & Siddiqui, P. (2019, April 4). Tensions and potential conflict between host communities and Rohingya refugees. *The Independent*. https://m.theindependentbd.com/printversion/details/194317

Strategic Executive Group. (2019). *Joint response plan for Rohingya humanitarian crisis January–December 2019*. https://www.humanitarianresponse.info/sites/www.humanitarianresponse.info/files/documents/files/2019_jrp_for_rohingya_humanitarian_crisis_compressed.pdf

Studemeyer, C. C. (2015). Geographies of flexible citizenship. *Geography compass, 9*(10), 565–576. https://doi.org/10.1111/gec3.12247

Tiezzi, S. (2021, February 3). What the Myanmar coup means for China. *The Diplomat*. https://thediplomat.com/2021/02/what-the-myanmar-coup-means-for-china/

Ullah, A. A. (2011). Rohingya refugees to Bangladesh: Historical exclusions and contemporary marginalization. *Journal of Immigrant and Refugee Studies, 9*(2), 139–161. https://doi.org/10.1080/15562948.2011.567149

UNHCR Population Statistics Database—At a Glance. (2019). *United Nations High Commissioner for Refugees*. https://www.unhcr.org/figures-at-a-glance.html

UNHCR Standing Committee (2004). "*Economic and social impact of massive refugee populations on host developing countries, as well as other countries*." 29th Meeting. https://www.unhcr.org/media/economic-and-social-impact-massive-refugee-populations-host-developing-countries-well-other-0

United Nations Development Programme Bangladesh. (2018). *Report on environmental impact of Rohingya influx*. Ministry of Environment and Forests, Government of the People's Republic of Bangladesh, UN Women. https://www.humanitarianresponse.info/sites/www.humanitarianresponse.info/files/documents/files/mar_2018_report_on_environmental_impact_of_rohingya_influx_un_women_undp.pdf

United News of Bangladesh (2018, May 14). CPD: Rohingya crisis affecting Bangladesh society, economy adversely. *The Dhaka Tribune*. https://www.dhakatribune.com/bangladesh/2018/05/14/cpd-rohingya-crisis-affecting-bangladesh-society-economy-adversely

Waters, J. L. (2009). Immigration, transnationalism and 'flexible citizenship' in Canada: Ong's thesis ten years on. *Tijdschrift Voor Economische en Sociale Geografie, 100*(5), 635–645. https://doi.org/10.1111/j.1467-9663.2009.00569x

Xchange Foundation. (2018). *Bangladeshi host community perspectives on the Rohingya crisis, June–July 2018*. https://data.humdata.org/dataset/2803bb47-ba07-4387-9ee6-edbbcd49f541

Chapter 5
Rohingyas in Bangladesh: Economic and Environmental Conflict Potential

Md. Rafiqul Islam

Abstract This chapter elaborates upon the economic and environmental conflict potential of the Rohingya conflict in Bangladesh. The economic and environmental situation within the host country of Bangladesh has taken a significant detrimental turn after the increased pressure exerted by the growing Rohingya refugee population on its resources. The areas of economic and environmental conflict potential of the Rohingya crisis in the host state have been assessed across four areas. These areas are unmet demand for commodities, livelihood competition, price hikes, and environmental degradation. The discussion then moves to focusing on the key areas of this dimension of conflict potential in Bangladesh.

1 Introduction

The impact of the Rohingya crisis on Bangladesh has been significant, particularly in terms of the country's economy and environment (Ahmad & Naeem, 2020). This chapter will explore the various economic and environmental challenges posed by the Rohingya crisis in Bangladesh and its conflict potential in the host country. From an economic perspective, the Rohingya crisis has had a significant impact on Bangladesh. The influx of refugees has placed a significant burden on the country's finances, as the government has had to provide basic necessities such as food, water, and shelter for the refugees (Rahman, 2018). This has strained the country's resources, particularly in terms of health care, education, and social services. The presence of the refugees has also had an impact on the job market in Bangladesh. The large number of Rohingya refugees has led to increased competition for jobs, particularly in low-skilled sectors such as agriculture and construction (Dey, 2017). This has had a negative impact on the employment prospects of local Bangladeshi workers, particularly those living in the areas surrounding the refugee camps. In addition to its economic impact, the Rohingya crisis has also had significant environmental consequences in Bangladesh. The large number of refugees has placed

Md. R. Islam (✉)
University of Dhaka, Dhaka, Bangladesh
e-mail: rislampacs@du.ac.bd

K. Ahmed and Md. R. Islam (eds.), *Understanding the Rohingya Displacement*, International Perspectives on Migration, https://doi.org/10.1007/978-981-97-1424-7_5

a strain on the country's fragile ecosystem, particularly in the Cox's Bazar region where most of the refugees are located. Deforestation, soil erosion, and water pollution are all major concerns, as the refugee population puts pressure on the limited resources of the area (Hoque et al., 2021). The use of firewood and other biomass by the refugees has also contributed to air pollution in the region, further exacerbating environmental problems. The impact of the crisis on the environment is not limited to the immediate area around the refugee camps, but also has implications for the wider region. This chapter tends to analyze the impacts of Rohingyas on the overall environment in Bangladesh. The impacts have been assessed based on the perception of the local people as well as published literature. First, an analytical lens has been presented on economic and environmental conflict potential. After presenting the analytical lens, the methodology for data collection, data analysis, and presentation of data has been presented in this chapter. Lastly, this chapter presents the overall impacts on economy and environment in Bangladesh.

2 Economic and Environmental Conflict Potential: An Analytical Lens

Economic and environmental conflict that stems from refugees and displaced populations in host communities can influence various facets of people's lives. These influences can range from competition in wage-earning activities and a drop in overall minimum wage and unwanted changes in the local ecosystem, to the deterioration of the tourism industry and wide-scale deforestations that can make the area less suitable for habitation, with entire ecosystems being eliminated in the process. Such a varied manifestation requires a number of variables to be considered. This chapter first discusses how refugee and displaced populations can lead to economic and environmental conflict in host societies. The discussion then moves on to the variables of economic conflict and those that have been incorporated into this study. The findings related to these variables of economic conflict from the host-community participants have been discussed in detail. Afterwards, the findings of this study are then compared to the findings gathered from the in-depth interviews of the Rohingya population, and the results are presented in a detailed section. Necessary details and reasoning behind certain research design decisions are detailed in appropriate sections of this chapter. Finally, the comparisons are supplemented with data from expert interviews to give an appropriate picture of the economic and environmental conflict in the host community of Bangladesh involving its Rohingya refugee population. In each of the sections, relevant theories and information from existing literature have been used to supplement the findings and to solidify or contrast with the data where appropriate.

The economic theory of conflict indicates that shifts in economic conditions within a society can lead to a shift in economic opportunities for the communities involved. This can in turn lead to struggles by communities based on the advantages they have lost or gained in the process of such economic shifts (Sandler, 2000). In Bangladesh, which hosts a sizeable number of refugees that now outnumber the local population by a significant margin of 2 to 1 (Alam et al., 2022), economic issues have already taken shape. The rise in prices of daily commodities coupled with rising unemployment in the region has led to growing unrest among the host population in Cox's Bazar (Ahmad & Naeem, 2020). Food prices have impacted the host populations significantly, while even Rohingya refugees who have had the opportunity to earn some subsidiary income have found it hard to purchase additional foodstuffs to fulfill their monthly needs (Alam et al., 2022). Wage opportunities have decreased for host-community Bengalis as well as Rohingya refugees who seek to obtain a source of income to fulfill some of their basic needs (Ahmad & Naeem, 2020). Such economic changes are part of a wide array of influences that started with the Rohingya influx within the previous decade (Babu, 2020). As such, there are grounds for significant economic conflicts to manifest.

The environmental conflict theory presupposes that destruction or degradation of the environment can lead to resource constraints among groups and can lead to violent confrontations and conflict due to communities striving for increasingly scarce resources as a result of environmental degradation (Atkins, 2016; Martin, 2005). In that respect, environmental degradation has been especially severe in Cox's Bazar following the latest large exodus of Rohingya refugees to the area. Substantial losses are represented by over 3000 ha of forest having been converted. As one study by Hasan et al. (2020) emphasizes,

> To support Rohingyas' livelihoods, fuelwood collection and illegal logging have become widespread since their arrival, causing severe environmental degradation, including loss of a vast amount of forest cover. To devise conservation and protection strategies for a highly sensitive ecosystem, it is imperative to understand the degree of forest cover deterioration and associated impacts related to Rohingya emigration. (Hasan et al., 2020)

Moreover, when the economic interests of the host community are not fulfilled in the face of environmental degradation contributed to by refugee populations, there can be higher chances of conflicts erupting (Agblortia & Grant, 2021). This is why discussing economic and environmental conflict potentials can be beneficial in supporting each aspect (i.e., economic and environmental) of the relationship between these two communities. Such conditions can be volatile potential sources of conflict between the host and Rohingya refugee communities.

The variables of economic conflict potential involve issues of conflict that have an inherently economic dimension to them. Of these factors, "unmet demand for commodities" is a variable that is tied to the market's ability to maintain the necessary supply to meet public demand for such goods. It is related to the public's purchasing power, but does not necessarily directly influence the purchasing power of the general public, in this case, the host community. When an increase in demand due to a country hosting a refugee population leads to pressure on the local market's ability to meet such demands, it can lead to price increases of commodities across the board, which in turn creates dissatisfaction among both host and refugee populations (Taylor et al., 2016). Whether or not a community recognizes such unmet demands determines how they connect the economic situation to other factors in an economic conflict.

In situations of economic conflict, the question of "livelihood competition" is a significant one. Host populations are generally averse to letting refugee populations have their own independent and self-sustained sources of income to prevent possibilities of these populations restricting the sometimes-existing labor and livelihood shortages (Porter et al., 2008; Teye & Yebleh, 2015). Although proponents have suggested cooperative participation of both host and refugee populations in income-generating activities for the pursuit of a more cohesive society, as seen in pilot projects of integration in Uganda (Schmitz-Pranghe & Vollmer, 2019), issues remain when there is high competition for livelihood options. In Bangladesh, reports show that the Rohingya influx has created new avenues of work for Bangladeshis in the aid and relief sector (MacGregor, 2018). However, local availability of income-generating activities and related shortages can lead to a reduction in general wages where refugee populations are involved (Francis, 2015). In Cox's Bazar, this situation is coupled with a negative impact on the tourism industry as a result of the environmental degradation in the region after the Rohingya mass influx (Dey, 2018); this too can create grounds for conflict between the host and refugee communities.

The factor of livelihood competition then leads to the inflated price of goods in host societies as a result of increased demand from a refugee population influx. As such, "price hikes" have been considered as a variable for conflict potential to develop. This is already a significant factor in Cox's Bazar, where the price hike of local goods has led to general dissatisfaction of the local host population as well as Rohingya refugees who try to make ends meet with extra income (Uddin & Nesa, 2021). For environmental conflict potential, "environmental degradation" connected to any of the parties involved can be decisive in gauging how one party sees the other as being responsible for degradation of their shared environment (Atkins, 2016).

3 Economic and Environmental Context in Cox's Bazar

The Rohingyas have settled in the city of Cox's Bazar a town in the southern part of Bangladesh. This area is famous for its economic, environmental, and tourism value. This area has its distinctive value for its very long, sandy beachfront, stretching from Sea Beach. This area is also known for containing the tropical rainforest of Himchari National Park where bio-diversity exists. Different kinds of birds and sea turtles breed in this distinct area. This area is important for its reserve forest, where local and indigenous people depend on the resources for their livelihood. Different types of animals especially elephants live in the reserve forest area. However, the settlement of 75,000 Rohingya refugees in this area significantly damaged the environment of this area. It is estimated that approximately 2000 ha of the forest after the arrival of the Rohingyas have been damaged (Mukul et al., 2019). Immediately after the arrival of the Rohingyas they constructed their house, cleared forests, and used other resources for their survival. In another study, it has been stated that Bangladesh lost BDT 741.31 billion (c. US$86.67 million) in 2018 which is equivalent to the land they have occupied (Hosen & Shahria, 2020; UNDP, 2018).

Besides the immediate impacts, the area has been affected by serious environmental changes such as deforestation, landslides, and the destruction of wildlife (Hossain et al., 2023). A study shows that clearing reserve forests has caused deforestation in the area which is causing negative impacts on the environment and human living. Local people are highly impacted by the environmental destruction. Among the most far-reaching consequences of the living of the Rohingya people are the destruction of the wildlife habitat, soil erosion, desertification, and disruption of the water cycle (Imtiaz, 2018). The environmental destruction is also causing an economic slowdown and loss of traditional livelihoods. Among other environmental concerns are huge pollution, depletion of subsurface water supplies, habitat loss, and fragmentation (Hossain et al., 2023).

Rohingya settlement in Cox's Bazar has also changed the land cover and function of the ecosystem. More than one million people have already put tremendous pressure on water, biomass, socioeconomic and environmental conditions, and land surface temperature (Hossain et al., 2023). The increasing Rohingya population is thus causing more pressure on the existing environmental resources. An imbalance between human and animal living has been generated. For example, elephants have lost their habitat; thus, elephants often come to the human habited areas and generate human–elephant conflicts.

The economic cost of the Rohingya settlement in this area is far-reaching and detrimental to the economy and livelihood of the local people (Ahmad & Naeem, 2020). Although the presence of Rohingya people has resulted in employment opportunities for the local people, the food prices and house rent have doubled. Jobs have been scarce as Rohingyas are putting pressure on the existing jobs. Even, local people exploit the Rohingyas by employing them with low wages. This is creating competition with the local people. In sum, it can be argued that the settlement of the Rohingyas has tremendous impacts on the environment and economy in Cox's Bazar that demand systematic study to explore.

4 Methodology

To examine the economic and environmental conflict potential related to the Rohingya conflict in Bangladesh, a research methodology was employed which combined qualitative and quantitative approaches. The primary data collection for this study relied on three key methods: key informant interviews (KIIs), focus group discussions (FGDs), and surveys. These methods were selected to ensure a comprehensive and nuanced understanding of the multifaceted aspects and perspectives surrounding the conflict.

KIIs played a pivotal role in this research methodology, allowing for in-depth conversations with individuals possessing significant knowledge and expertise in relevant domains. The selection of key informants was guided by their direct involvement or expertise in matters related to the Rohingya conflict, economic implications, and environmental factors. Through these interviews, insights were obtained regarding the underlying economic drivers, environmental consequences, policy implications, and community perspectives surrounding the conflict. The KIIs followed a semi-structured approach, enabling flexibility and the exploration of emergent themes. The data derived from KIIs provided rich qualitative insights, augmenting the overall analysis.

In addition to KIIs, FGDs were conducted to capture diverse viewpoints and facilitate interactive exchanges among participants from various stakeholder groups. The FGDs included representatives from governmental agencies, nongovernmental organizations, community leaders, environmental experts, and members of the Rohingya community. The discussions were conducted in a facilitated group setting, creating a platform for participants to share their experiences, perceptions, and concerns regarding the economic and environmental dimensions of the conflict. Guided by predetermined themes, the FGDs facilitated comparative analysis and the identification of commonalities and divergences among participants' perspectives. FGDs yielded valuable qualitative data, enabling a deeper exploration of the economic and environmental factors associated with the conflict.

Complementing the qualitative insights from KIIs and FGDs, surveys were employed to gather quantitative data. The survey was designed in alignment with the research objectives and relevant literature, tailored specifically to assess economic and environmental dimensions. The survey targeted a diverse range of participants, including local residents, policymakers, and members of the Rohingya community. The questionnaire encompassed a mix of closed-ended and open-ended questions, enabling both quantitative analysis and qualitative responses. The survey responses yielded quantitative data on various aspects, such as economic impacts, environmental challenges, and social dynamics, which were analyzed using appropriate statistical methods.

Ethical considerations were of paramount importance throughout the research process. Informed consent was obtained from all participants, ensuring confidentiality and anonymity. The research design and data collection instruments adhered to established ethical guidelines and principles. By employing a combination of KIIs, FGDs, and surveys, this research methodology facilitated a comprehensive exploration of the economic and environmental conflict potential related to the Rohingya conflict in Bangladesh. Triangulating data from multiple sources enhanced the credibility and validity of the research findings, fostering a comprehensive understanding of the intricate dynamics at play.

5 Major Areas of Economic and Environmental Conflict Potentials

This study assesses the economic and environmental conflict potential involving the host and the Rohingya community in Cox's Bazar in the following areas:

1. Unmet demand for commodities

2. Livelihood competition
3. Price hikes
4. Environmental degradation.

Each of these areas of economic conflict have a respective variable that describes the findings from the host society. The analyses of these economic areas and their resulting effects, as a part of the overarching economic conflict in the Cox's Bazar region surrounding the camps, have been done with the help of existing literature on related topics.

5.1 Unmet Demand for Commodities

When refugee populations inhabit a country in large numbers and for long periods, it can lead to pressures on a host country's resources. This is especially the case when the resources of the host country are already limited (Hansen, 2018). Long-term refugee settlements within a host country tend to put more pressure on the host country's resources as time progresses and the refugee situation remains unresolved. This pressure on resources in the host country extends to the host country's market. Such extended pressure can lead to the markets consistently being unable to meet the demands of both the host and the refugee population. This can take acute forms near refugee settlements. Refugee settlements are often not that far from host population localities, which leads to the market's unmet demands extending to host populations significantly (Taylor et al., 2016).

The benefits of the expanding market due to the influx of refugees have been prominent in Cox's Bazar, including the rise of nongovernmental sectors and growth of small business and emerging new living opportunities. However, the negative impacts of the refugee influx on the economy of Bangladesh, as has been seen in studies, outweigh the positive sides of the issue (Alam et al., 2022; Uddin & Nesa, 2021).

Where there is unmet demand for commodities, especially the commodities which a population considers basic to their needs, there is dissatisfaction among potential consumers who are willing to pay for a good that is in short supply. The set of basic commodities considered here comprises an essential set of goods that a population generally needs in their everyday lives, involving basic food, clothing, and utensils, among other such fundamental items. The unmet demand for such commodities can lead a conflict to manifest if the dissatisfied population identifies the unmet demand with a specific issue, which in the case of Cox's Bazar is the presence of the refugee population. If the host population thus identifies the refugee issue with an ongoing market deficit of supplying basic commodities, then this can be a potential source of conflict between the host and refugee communities. This relates to the findings among the host community regarding the market's inability to meet the increased demand for basic commodities of the Rohingyas. If the host population identifies that the market is unable to keep up with demands for basic commodities from the

Rohingya population, then this can translate to—at least in the local market—being generally unable to meet the demand for the host population as well, even when it is restricted to the regions proximal to refugee settlements.

The support from the host population in this case is overwhelming compared to those that do not agree with the statement (Fig. 1). This illustrates that the host population sees the local market at minimum as being unable to meet the needs of the Rohingya refugee population in terms of basic commodities. The factor of unmet demand for commodities thus has significant conflict potential among the host and Rohingya refugee communities.

The Rohingya population has been questioned regarding the economic and environmental issues in the Cox's Bazar region, and the findings reveal that the Rohingya population experience significant economic and environmental issues in their own lives. However, they do not necessarily associate it with the local host population. When asked about the unmet demand for commodities, participants have mentioned in the focus group discussions how they are instead unable to buy their commodities because of not having much scope for work. This led to the question of livelihood competition, a topic to which the conversation was eventually directed while discussing unmet demand for commodities and issues of price hikes. One of the participants elaborated in this regard:

> We don't have a lot of scope for work, and when we do find it, it is temporary. A lot of us then stay without work for months until we can find work again. This is a big problem for a lot of us, as the rations and relief we get do not get us through the full month. (FGD outcome; FGD conducted in Teknaf in May 2022)

In order to achieve deeper understanding about the increasing demand of the communities, this study interviewed several key informants. The unmet demand for commodities as the market struggled to provide adequate supplies to both the host

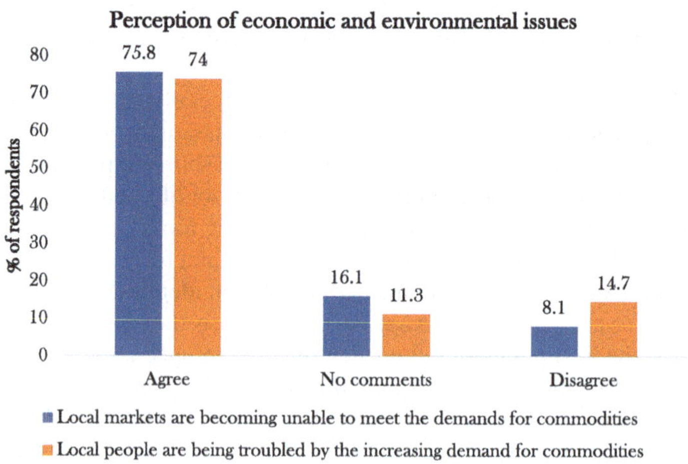

Fig. 1 Economic and environmental conflict: unmet demand for commodities. *Source* Developed by the author based on data collected from the field

and the refugee community has long been evident. The reason behind this unmet demand for commodities and the resulting scarcity of resources has been identified by a key informant, a development expert working closely with the Rohingya issue in Cox's Bazar, thus:

> There is a record that says that every day the forests were destroyed in huge swaths, so what happened is that the dependence of the host community on the forest has been going down drastically. Because now there's hardly any forest anymore. So, the community that was dependent on the forest is now depending on the market to buy those products. (KII conducted in May 2022)

The demand for commodities will only increase in the future because of declining interest on the part of donor organizations toward the Rohingya people. The global scenario has drastically changed after the outbreak of the pandemic and the war between Russia and Ukraine. Many countries are already facing crises to mitigate the increasing demand of the people. In such a context, the Rohingya crisis can become a serious burden and source of conflict if donors divert their funding toward other areas of the world. A director of an international organization argued,

> If the Rohingyas do not go back to Myanmar, the ultimate burden will fall on the government of Bangladesh. And the donor agencies will gradually cut their support because they will have other priorities. (Expert Interview conducted in June 2022)

Indeed, economic competition and resource scarcity will be the major source of conflict in the host country, because the international community is gradually lessening its interest toward the Rohingyas. The pressures of the future will rest on the shoulders of Bangladesh. The local people have already become furious and frustrated, and they want the Rohingyas back in their home country.

5.2 Livelihood Competition

Livelihood competition caused by refugee influx can lead to a significant drop in wages and income-generating opportunities for the host population (Teye & Yebleh, 2015). While this can lead to positive outcomes of new avenues of wage-earning activities, potential for conflict remains when the host population faces the negative impacts on their livelihoods.

Whether the host population identifies the refugee influx with a drop in minimum wages or the available number of wage-earning opportunities, the potential for conflict can either be viable or nonexistent regarding this issue. The host population was thus asked whether or not they directly connect the issue of available employment opportunities to the Rohingya refugee issue (Fig. 2). The host population was also asked if they are aware of a general drop in wages for daily labor for workers within the host community in the area. The perception regarding the impact of the Rohingya influx on the tourism industry was also assessed along with the perception regarding the rise in unlawful income-generating activities in the region concerning catching shrimp fries from the Bay of Bengal. Compared to the change in available

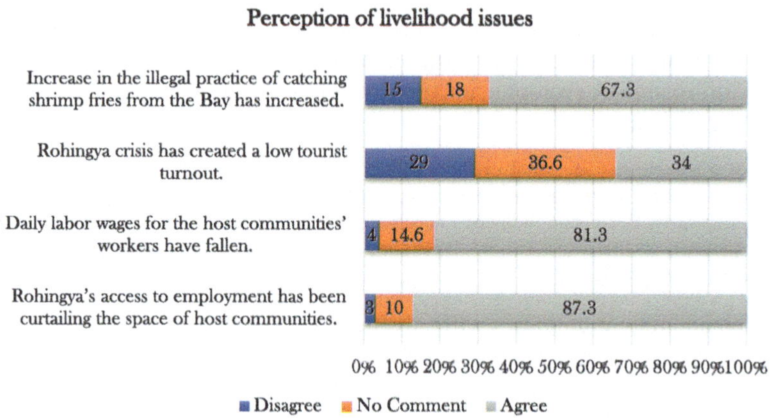

Fig. 2 Economic and environmental conflict: livelihood competition. *Source* Developed by the author based on field data

employment, participants were not asked directly whether they equate the change in daily labor wages and the rise in the illegal practice of catching shrimp fries at the Bay of Bengal to the Rohingya refugee issue. However, if the host population near the Rohingya refugee camps have a perception of a change in these areas, then this can still have significant conflict potential among the two communities.

The findings from the host community indicate an overwhelming perception of equating the Rohingya refugee issue to the decreasing employment opportunities. Additionally, the host population has perceived an overall drop in daily labor wages in the area and a rise in the illegal catching of shrimp fries at the Bay of Bengal in equally overwhelming numbers. However, the host population was divided on whether the Rohingya influx has indeed resulted in a lower tourist turnout, even though the overall perception of the sampled population trended toward supporting this notion.

Another participant elaborated on the question of livelihood competition, opining that competition is significant within the Rohingya community compared with the host population:

> When we go find work like daily labor, we have to do it for very cheap when we are even able to find any. A lot of us are very desperate for some money. Even after we sell some of our rations, we often need money. So, we try to take whatever cheap work we find or else someone else from here (i.e., the Rohingya camps) will take it instead. That is how it goes here for finding labor work. (FGD outcome; FGD conducted in Ukhiya in May, 2022)

It needs to be noted that Rohingyas have no formal right to work in Bangladesh. Thus, their work is mainly informal in the form of low-cost, low-skill manual labor (Zetter & Ruaudel, 2016). The Rohingya participants have emphasized the constraints upon findings opportunities for livelihood and the competition they face while doing so, which often come from their own people.

The key informants also provided valuable information about the livelihood issues, scarcity, and competition between the communities. The key informants who closely experience this in their daily life have shed light on how the livelihood competition that the local host population has been embroiled in with the Rohingya community in Cox's Bazar is skewed in the favor of the Rohingyas due to how low their minimum acceptable wages are. Due to how the local population have significantly more expenses, the livelihood competition is proving to be a difficult challenge for them. This is doubly so because of how the rapid rise in demand for commodities has led to price hikes that the local population is now increasingly unable to substantially afford. This does not discredit the issues the Rohingya community is facing in their struggle to find the balance of a proper life amid truncated legal status in Bangladesh, but the issue for conflict potential remains a concern. A KI argued that

> The Rohingya people have become desperate for income and engage in activities that are unlawful for some quick money. The possibility is there even though we are not completely certain of it happening. (KII conducted in May 2022)

The global pandemic, world economic recession, and climate change have adversely affected many countries, including Bangladesh. Moreover, the refugee crisis has also influenced the price of food, fuel, and fertilizer, which has been a source of instability and unrest in the country. Now, the local people blame the Rohingyas as the source of all their suffering in Cox's Bazar. Before the arrival of INGOS, the locals mainly depended on income from the forest, such as wood-cutting and land cultivation. However, the Rohingyas and the presence of INGOS have diminished the income source from forest resources. The hospitality of the local population has been worn thin. Now, local people are complaining about the encroachments on their lives, livelihoods, and environment. These complaints are getting louder and progressively more threatening.

5.3 Price Hikes

Economic issues that result in price hikes of basic commodities have been reported to cause civil unrest in many societies (Bazzi, 2014). The connection between refugee issues and price hikes has been similarly observed (Getmansky et al., 2018; Taylor et al., 2016). Especially in Bangladesh's case, the economic impact of the Rohingya refugees has been an increase in demand for basic commodities for an additional population with a high birth rate. The resulting price hikes have impacted people across the board, as basic commodities have become increasingly more and more expensive for the host population as well as part of the Rohingya refugee population, the latter seeking to make ends meet with additional income. There is significant conflict potential in the area if the host population perceives the refugee issue to be connected to the price hikes in the area concerning basic staples. The study asked the host population about the market dynamism and price issues in the post-Rohingya settlement (Fig. 3).

The findings from the host community point toward an overwhelming support for the notion that increases in the prices of basic staples have taken place due to the

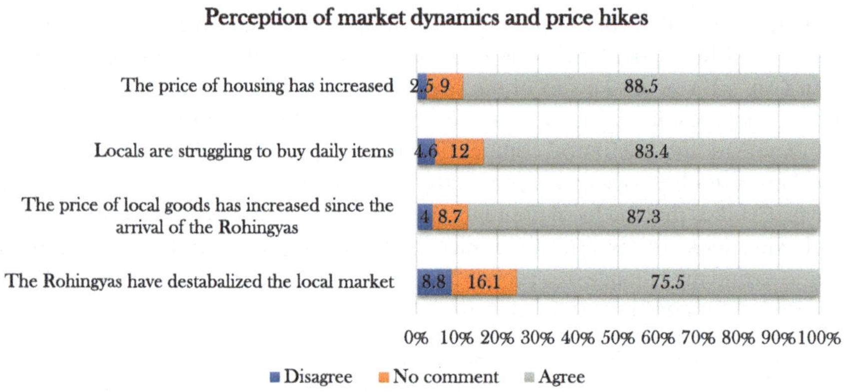

Fig. 3 Economic and environmental conflict: price hikes. *Source* Developed by the author based on field data

Rohingya influx. Support for this exceeds 80% of the respondents (i.e., over 80% of the sampled participants from the host population). This factor thus has significant potential for manifesting a conflict between the two communities.

Increasing population and price hikes have a causal relationship. If we now look at the commodities market, which is to say the established market system, we see it catering to around 400,000 to half a million people. But all of a sudden, you have the same market, same infrastructure, same supply chain, but the number of buyers suddenly increases dramatically. What naturally happens is that the price of the commodities all of a sudden goes up. An expert who is working in the region explains:

> We did a study around bamboo, which is one of the materials used by everybody for the construction of houses, and the price of it all of sudden becomes doubled, because of the huge demand and supply gap. Same happened with other commodities also. So, who is feeling the pinch? Suppose, the vegetable, which was sold at a certain price before the crisis. Now there is all of a sudden there is inflation or appreciation by 2 or 3 times. (Expert interview conducted in June 2022)

The people of the host community are highly affected by this sudden price hike, as they are forced to buy commodities from the same market. A study by the World Food Program in Cox's Bazar shows that:

> The cost of a typical food basket in June 2022 (BDT 1,181) was 3 percent higher than in May 2022 (BDT 1,147) and 15 percent higher than in June 2021 (BDT 1,023). When compared to the post-COVID-19 level (BDT 891, June 2020), the June 2022 basket was significantly higher (+33 percent), putting a strain on a household's purchasing capacities in Cox's Bazar. (WFP-VAM Market Monitor, 2022)

Moreover, a growing population, particularly among the Rohingyas, is putting pressure on existing jobs and services. Under this situation, the price of labor goes down because more people are searching for jobs; Rohingyas are preferred for their cheap labor, and the price of the labor-driven commodity goes up. As result, the income of the community is all of a sudden decreasing at the same time as their expenses are going up. A key informant argues that:

> All of a sudden you will see issues around poverty, issues around hunger because we are talking about laborers over here, and laborers are the poorest. Or we are talking about the small marginal farmers. (KII 12 conducted in March 2022)

There was also a study indicating that during the pandemic, the rate of poverty increased all over Bangladesh. It was around 22–23%, and acute poverty was around 12%. But there are some studies that say that it has actually doubled (Gjerløw et al., 2021). This scenario of price hikes was more pronounced in Cox's Bazar, especially in Teknaf and Ukhiya, because of the unique pressures on the market.

5.4 Environmental Degradation

As environmental degradation can be the basis of conflict erupting between a host and refugee community, it is imperative to explore this aspect of the relationship between the two communities (Atkins, 2016). How much one of these communities perceives the other to be responsible for environmental degradation can provide insights into the conflict potential between the two communities. The host community's perception is first explored via survey questions pertaining to environmental degradation in the Cox's Bazar region as well as the Rohingya camps specifically. The results show that an overwhelming majority of the host respondents consider the increasing number of landslide occurrences to be an impact of the Rohingya crisis in the region (Fig. 4). Similar results were found in how the host population considers the plastic containers supplied to the Rohingya population as a significant threat to the local environment. The host population largely sees the high number of latrines that do not have proper soak pits in the Rohingya camps as responsible for the water contamination within the refugee camps. Additionally, the host population recognizes that vegetation in the hills in the region have been depleted, and that the forests are all in the process of being turned into agricultural land. The results of these inquiries signify that the host population is aware of the overall environmental degradation that is taking place within the Cox's Bazar region, and not just focusing on what harm to the environment the Rohingya refugee population might be responsible for.

These results indicate that the host population strongly identifies the Rohingya refugee community as being responsible for a significant portion of the environmental degradation in the Cox's Bazar region. This provides an overall high economic and environmental conflict potential between the two communities from the side of the host population.

Regarding environmental degradation, the Rohingya refugee population has primarily mentioned how landslides and storm surges have made them more and more vulnerable. One participant notes that,

> The plastic covers we often use for our roofs are often blown far away during storms, while landslides cause houses to break down. I don't really know if cutting more and more trees

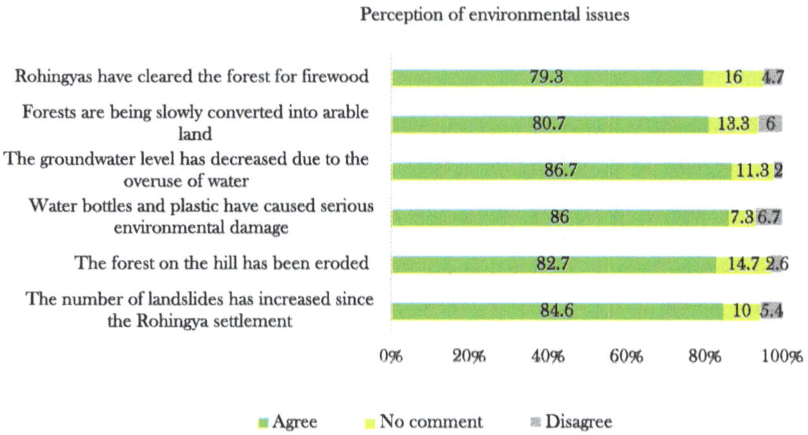

Fig. 4 Economic and environmental conflict: environmental degradation. *Source* Developed by the author based on field data

> is why these keep happening, but our houses are too weak to handle these disasters. (FGD outcome; FGD conducted in Ukhiya in May 2022)

The environmental degradation, even when considered apart from its link to habitation issues and related social and economic concerns, is a risk for the entire region due to the devastating effects it has already had. However, the local people perceive the environmental resources differently than the Rohingyas, as poor local people are highly dependent on environmental resources for their livelihood. A key informant mentions that,

> His family did not face food crisis before the arrival of the Rohingyas in 2017. He used to grow fruits and earned a good amount of money yearly. The settlement of the Rohingyas has abolished his livelihood as the forest has been turned into Rohingya settlement. (KII conducted in March 2022)

The story is the same for many other farmers in Teknaf and Ukhiya in Cox's Bazar. This environmental resource plundering has already generated resource conflict in Cox's Bazar between the locals and the Rohingyas.

A security expert explained the potential for environmental conflict within the context of resource competition between the communities. The expert highlighted part of the issue like this:

> Yes, we are certainly seeing a clearly emerging environmental conflict tied with resource scarcity in the area due to the Rohingya crisis...but also a humanitarian and security crisis in the area alongside an economic risk. It is not only limited to a resource or environmental conflict. We try to understand this issue in terms repatriation measures, but by doing that we are overlooking a macro-level impact in the region. (Expert interview conducted at Dhaka in March 2022)

As the environmental issues remain tied to the economic concerns of the host and refugee communities in Cox's Bazar, the situation becomes increasingly detrimental for the local ecosystem and forest resources that allow the area to maintain its natural condition. This poses a conflict potential in the region that may be increasingly harder to recover from once a threshold is passed and the environment is irreparably damaged alongside the resultant devastating economic repercussions.

6 Conclusion

This chapter has explored the various ways in which the influx of Rohingya refugees has affected Bangladesh, particularly in terms of the strain it has placed on the country's economy and environment. From an economic perspective, the Rohingya crisis has resulted in significant costs for Bangladesh, particularly in terms of the resources needed to support the refugees. The government has had to spend considerable amounts of money on providing basic necessities such as food, water, and shelter for the refugees, and this has placed a significant burden on the country's finances. Furthermore, the presence of the refugees has had a negative impact on the job market, as many Bangladeshis have been displaced from their jobs due to the influx of cheap labor from the refugee population. In addition to its economic impact, the Rohingya crisis has also had significant environmental consequences. The large number of refugees has placed a strain on Bangladesh's already fragile ecosystem, with deforestation, soil erosion, and water pollution all being major concerns. The use of firewood and other biomass by the refugees has also led to increased levels of air pollution, further exacerbating environmental problems in the region.

Overall, the Rohingya crisis in Bangladesh is a complex and multifaceted issue that requires a coordinated and sustained response from both the international community and the Bangladeshi government. While efforts are being made to address the various economic and environmental challenges posed by the crisis, much more needs to be done in order to ensure that the needs of both the refugees and the host community are met. In conclusion, the Rohingya crisis in Bangladesh is a stark reminder of the immense human cost of conflict and displacement. While the economic and environmental impacts of the crisis are significant, it is important to remember that these are just symptoms of a much larger problem.

References

Agblortia, S. K., & Grant, M. (2021). Revisiting the host–refugee environmental conflict debate: Perspectives from Ghana's refugee camps. *Canadian Journal of African Studies, 55*(1), 141–159. https://doi.org/10.1080/00083968.2020.1799830

Ahmad, S. M., & Naeem, N. (2020). Adverse economic impact by Rohingya refugees on Bangladesh: Some way forwards. *International Journal of Social, Political and Economic Research, 7*(1), 1–14. https://doi.org/10.5281/zenodo.3698176

Alam, A., Dutta, I., Haque, M. E., & Nogales, R. (2022). Impact of Rohingya refugees on food prices in Bangladesh: Evidence from a natural experiment. *World Development, 154*, 105873. https://doi.org/10.1016/j.worlddev.2022.105873

Atkins, E. (2016). Environmental conflict: A misnomer? In G. Sosa-Nunez & E. Atkins (Eds.), *Environment, climate change and international relations* (pp. 99–113). E-International Relations Publishing.

Babu, K. E. K. (2020). The impacts and challenges to host country Bangladesh due to sheltering the Rohingya refugees. *Cogent Social Sciences, 6*(1), 1770943. https://doi.org/10.1080/23311886.2020.1770943

Bazzi, S. (2014). Economic shocks and conflict: Evidence from commodity prices. *American Economic Journal: Macroeconomics, 6*(4), 1–38. https://doi.org/10.1257/mac.6.4.1

Dey, S. (2017). Adverse Rohingya impacts on Bangladeshi economy and its solutions. *American Journal of Trade and Policy, 4*(3), 129-32.

Dey, S. (2018). Adverse Rohingya impacts on Bangladeshi economy and its solutions. *American Journal of Trade and Policy, 5*(2), 81–84. https://doi.org/10.18034/ajtp.v5i2.438

Francis, A. (2015). *Jordan's refugee crisis*. Carnegie Endowment for International Peace. https://www.jstor.org/stable/resrep12890?seq=1

Getmansky, A., Sınmazdemir, T., & Zeitzoff, T. (2018). Refugees, xenophobia, and domestic conflict: Evidence from a survey experiment in Turkey. *Journal of Peace Research, 55*(4), 491–507. https://doi.org/10.1177/0022343317748719

Gjerløw, H., Karim, S., & Østby, G. (2021). When governments and international organizations shut down: The impact of COVID-19 on refugees' and host community's use of educational services in Cox's Bazar. *Frontiers in Education, 6*, 696176. https://doi.org/10.3389/feduc.2021.696176

Hansen, R. (2018). The comprehensive refugee response framework: A commentary. *Journal of Refugee Studies, 31*(2), 131–151. https://doi.org/10.1093/jrs/fey020

Hasan, M. E., Zhang, L., Dewan, A., Guo, H., & Mahmood, R. (2020). Spatiotemporal pattern of forest degradation and loss of ecosystem function associated with Rohingya influx: A geospatial approach. *Land Degradation and Development, 32*(13), 3666–3683. https://doi.org/10.1002/ldr.3821

Hoque, M. M. M., Rehnuma, M., Uddin, S., Ahmed, S., Sarker, M. E., & Biswas, G. K. (2021). Impacts of Rohingya migration on surrounding environment of Ukhiya, Bangladesh. *American Journal of Pure and Applied Biosciences, 3*(4), 106–112.

Hosen, S., & Shahria, G. (2020). Economic challenges of Rohingya peoples: A study on displacement (Rohingya) peoples on Myanmar in Cox's bazar. *International Journal of Social, Political and Economic Research, 7*(3), 415–436.

Hossain, F., Kamal, A. M., Sadeak, S., & Gazi, M. Y. (2023). Quantitative soil erosion risk assessment due to rapid urbanization in the Cox's Bazar district and Rohingya refugee camps in Bangladesh. *Stochastic Environmental Research and Risk Assessment, 37*(3), 989–1006.

Imtiaz, S. (2018). Ecological impact of Rohingya refugees on forest resources: Remote sensing analysis of vegetation cover change in Teknaf Peninsula in Bangladesh. *Ecocycles, 4*(1), 16–19.

MacGregor, F. (2018, January 30). Rohingya refugee crisis creates new generation of Bangladeshi aid workers. *IOM*. Retrieved August 28, 2023, from https://www.iom.int/news/rohingya-refugee-crisis-creates-new-generation-bangladeshi-aid-workers-iom

Mukul, S. A., Huq, S., Herbohn, J., Nishat, A., Rahman, A. A., Amin, R., & Ahmed, F. U. (2019). Rohingya refugees and the environment. *Science, 364*(6436), 138–138.

Porter, G., Hampshire, K., Kyei, P., Adjaloo, M., Rapoo, G., & Kilpatrick, K. (2008). Linkages between livelihood opportunities and refugee–host relations: Learning from the experiences of Liberian camp-based refugees in Ghana. *Journal of Refugee Studies, 21*(2), 230–252. https://doi.org/10.1093/jrs/fen015

Rahman, M.Z. (2018). Livelihoods of Rohingyas and Their Impacts on Deforestation. In: Tani, M., Rahman, M. (eds) *Deforestation in the Teknaf Peninsula of Bangladesh. Springer*, (pp. 113–125). Singapore. https://doi.org/10.1007/978-981-10-5475-4_9

Sandler, T. (2000). Economic analysis of conflict. *Journal of Conflict Resolution, 44*(6), 723–729. https://doi.org/10.1177/0022002700044006001

Schmitz-Pranghe, C., & Vollmer, R. (2019). Breaking Cycles: conference documentation. In *Breaking Cycles of Displacement* (Vol. 2, p. 30). DEU.

Taylor, J. E., Filipski, M. J., Alloush, M., Gupta, A., Valdes, R. I., & Gonzalez-Estrada, E. (2016). Economic impact of refugees. *Proceedings of the National Academy of Sciences, 113*(27), 7449–7453. https://doi.org/10.1073/pnas.1604566113

Teye, J. K., & Yebleh, M. K. (2015). Living without economic assets: Livelihoods of Liberian refugees in the Buduburam Camp, Ghana. *Journal of International Migration and Integration, 16*(3), 557–574. https://doi.org/10.1007/12134-014-0352-6

Uddin, M. R., & Nesa, F. (2021). The Rohingya refugee crisis: Socio-economic, and environmental impacts on local community in Bangladesh. *Journal of Asia Pacific Studies, 6*(2), 275–288.

UNDP. (2018). *Impacts of the Rohingya refugee influx on host communities*. United Nations Development Programme.

Zetter, R., & Ruaudel, H. (2016). Refugees' right to work and access to labor markets–An assessment. World Bank Global Program on Forced Displacement (GPFD) and the Global Knowledge Partnership on Migration and Development (KNOMAD) Thematic Working Group on Forced Migration. *KNOMAD Working Paper*. Washington, DC: World Bank Group.

Chapter 6
Rohingyas in Bangladesh: Regional and International Conflict Potential

Md. Rafiqul Islam and Maria Hussain

Abstract This chapter highlights the regional and international conflict potential of the Rohingya conflict in host country Bangladesh. The situation in South Asia has continually worsened due to the increasing complexity in bilateral and multilateral relations introduced by the Rohingya issue. The areas of regional and international conflict potential of the Rohingya conflict have thus far been assessed across areas of regional and international spheres of conflict. The regional sphere includes areas of mutual distrust and threat perception, insurgent activities and bilateral relationships, hampering regional cooperation, the vulnerability of Bangladesh, and illicit businesses and trafficking of women; while the sphere of international conflict involves multilateral relationships across various areas. The discussion then moves to focusing on the key areas of this dimension of conflict potential.

1 Introduction

The Rohingya refugee crisis has had significant regional implications, with Bangladesh bearing the brunt of the crisis. The large number of refugees has placed a significant burden on the country's resources and infrastructure, with many refugees living in deplorable conditions with inadequate access to basic necessities. The crisis has also had political implications, with the influx of refugees leading to tensions between Bangladesh and Myanmar, as well as straining relations between Bangladesh and other neighboring countries. Finally, the crisis has also had significant international implications, with the international community condemning Myanmar's military for its actions and imposing sanctions and other measures in response. The United Nations has been heavily involved in the crisis, with multiple reports and investigations into the violence and persecution of the Rohingya. Furthermore, the

Md. R. Islam (✉) · M. Hussain
University of Dhaka, Dhaka, Bangladesh
e-mail: rislampacs@du.ac.bd

M. Hussain
e-mail: maria.hussain@du.ac.bd

K. Ahmed and Md. R. Islam (eds.), *Understanding the Rohingya Displacement*, International Perspectives on Migration, https://doi.org/10.1007/978-981-97-1424-7_6

crisis has raised important questions about international law and the responsibility of the international community to protect vulnerable populations. Myanmar has been accused of committing genocide against the Rohingya, which has sparked debates about the use of international legal mechanisms to hold perpetrators accountable. The economic impact of the crisis has been felt across the region, with the large number of refugees placing a significant burden on resources and infrastructure in Bangladesh, and affecting trade and investment in the region. The crisis has also had cultural implications, particularly for the Rohingya people themselves, as the violence and persecution they have faced has threatened their cultural identity and forced many to flee their homes and abandon their traditions. This chapter aims to explore the regional and international effects and potential for conflict of the Rohingya refugee crisis in those areas, highlighting its complex and multifaceted nature, as well as the urgent need for a coordinated response from the international community to address the root causes of the conflict, protect the rights of refugees, and promote sustainable solutions that will help ensure the safety and well-being of all those affected.

2 Regional Security Issues: Analytical Lens

Bilateral relationships between sovereign countries are formed when the two countries in question recognize one another as being sovereign states. This establishes bilateral ties, which progress via an exchange of diplomatic agents between the states such as ambassadors, who then help in arranging dialog and cooperation between both parties (Thompson & Verdier, 2013). Recognition of sovereignty is thus a precondition of bilateral relationship between states. Bangladesh's bilateral relations with countries such as India and Myanmar have several facets to them, as is pertinent to all interstate relationships. The Bangladesh-India bilateral relationship began from Bangladesh's independence in 1971, and has been a generally positive relationship since its inception, with strong economic ties (Pant & Bhattacharjee, 2020). The two countries have been successful in resolving a border dispute that had been ongoing for several decades with the land boundary agreement in 2015 (Quadir, 2015). This is despite ongoing water disputes with Bangladesh that India has been generally reluctant to resolve despite negotiations (Sarker, 2019). With Bangladesh and Myanmar's bilateral relations on the other hand, a tenuous relationship began to deteriorate after the Rohingya genocide and the resulting crisis began in late 2016 and early 2017 (Banerjee, 2020). This is exemplified in the tendency of Myanmar's military forces to fire openly on Bangladeshi fishermen on the grounds of ambiguous suspicions in the area near the coastal seas around St. Martin's Island of Bangladesh (Ahamed & Chowdhury, 2020).

The debate over refugees and displaced people is also pertinent in the context of Bangladesh because the country does not recognize the displaced people as refugees. Although a large number of displaced Rohingya people are living in Bangladesh, the country has yet to signal that it is a receiving state of refugees, given that it is not a state party to the 1951 Convention Relating to the Status of Refugees or its 1967 protocol and the Convention Relating to the Status of Stateless Persons of 1954 and 1961 (Hossain, 2021). Bangladesh received refugees on the basis of "good practice of the Government of Bangladesh" (Guhathakurta, 2017). The UNHCR's legal status in the country is based on a memorandum of understanding and its yearly extension. Bangladesh's position is that no refugee would be allowed to settle in Bangladesh permanently. The UNHCR's agreement with the Bangladeshi government has a special focus on repatriation, and then third-country resettlement (Kiragu et al., 2011).

The Myanmar and Bangladeshi governments have agreed to a procedural framework for repatriation, which was supposed to start on January, 23 2018 and be completed preferably within two years. The bilateral framework consists of three key documents. These are: "Arrangement on Return of Displaced Persons from Rakhine State" by November 23, 2017, terms of reference for a "Joint Working Group" by December 19, 2017, and "Physical Arrangement for Repatriation" by January 16, 2018, including a verification form that the prospective returnees must fill out in advance (Hoang, 2020). The Myanmar Government and military continued to perform their displacement operations and human rights violations, and the overall situation has not improved enough for the forced migrants to return home to Myanmar.

A series of bilateral negotiations between the GoB and the GoM has not yielded fruitful results regarding the resettlement, repatriation, and reintegration of the Rohingya displaced people to their home country of Myanmar. This has led to a further deterioration of bilateral relations between the two countries (Banerjee, 2020; Jacob, 2017). In turn, this has resulted in tensions in border control and trade, as narcotic traffic through the borders near Myanmar and Bangladesh is causing major security and public safety concerns in coastal areas of Bangladesh. Such issues raise glaring security concerns regarding bilateral relations between Bangladesh and Myanmar and in turn between Bangladesh and India and between Bangladesh and China. This is especially so because India and China hold amicable bilateral relations with Myanmar despite the tensions Bangladesh is facing with the country regarding Rohingya repatriation (Banerjee, 2020; Bashar, 2018).

India is currently supporting Myanmar on the Rohingya issue despite its initial support toward Bangladesh. Due to India having significant stakes in Myanmar—with energy deals concerning the Shwe gas field in Rakhine and the interstate pipeline project between the countries—maintaining positive relations has become a necessity for India (Yhome, 2018). This has resulted in various criticisms toward the Indian government, and the country continues to refrain from addressing them to any significant capacity (Hazra, 2021).

3 Methodology

The research methodology employed here focused primarily on Key Informant Interviews (KIIs) to gain valuable insights into the regional and international dimensions of the Rohingya conflict. KIIs served as the main data collection method for this study, providing a platform to engage with individuals possessing relevant expertise and experience in the regional and international dynamics surrounding the conflict.

The selection of key informants was guided by their direct involvement in regional and international organizations, diplomatic agencies, academic institutions, and NGOs dealing with conflict resolution and human rights issues. These informants played a crucial role in shedding light on the geopolitical factors, regional power dynamics, international interventions, and diplomatic initiatives related to the Rohingya conflict.

Semi-structured interviews were conducted with the key informants to allow for flexibility and the exploration of emergent themes. The interview questions were designed to elicit detailed responses regarding the regional and international implications of the conflict. The interviews covered a wide range of topics, including regional political interests, international humanitarian responses, diplomatic efforts, and the role of international organizations. Through these interviews, valuable qualitative data was obtained, offering nuanced insights into the complex regional and international dimensions of the Rohingya conflict.

Ethical considerations were diligently addressed throughout the research process. Informed consent was obtained from all participants, and measures were taken to ensure the confidentiality and anonymity of the information shared. The research design and interview protocols adhered to established ethical guidelines and principles.

By employing KIIs as the primary data collection method, this research methodology facilitated a comprehensive exploration of the regional and international conflict potential associated with the Rohingya conflict in Bangladesh. The insights gained from the key informants provided a deeper understanding of the geopolitical landscape, diplomatic challenges, and regional dynamics that influence the conflict.

4 Major Areas of Regional and International Conflict Potentials

The conflict potential of the Rohingya people in their regional context is a "high politics" issue. Thus, the perception of the local people may not be enough to draw conclusions about how the relationship between and among the countries in the South Asian region is being framed and redefined. The views of experts are more pertinent in exploring the conflict potential of the Rohingya people in the region. Experts have repeatedly pointed to how the regional conflict potentials have been exacerbated due to the Rohingya issue.

4.1 Mutual Distrust and Threat Perception

On Bangladesh-Myanmar bilateral relations, a security expert who was interviewed for the purpose of this study has pointed out in this respect that,

> …we have observed that the sensitive Rohingya issue has created considerable distance, mutual distrust, and a threat perception between Bangladesh and Myanmar. This has led to a deterioration of the military relationship between these two countries. (Expert interview conducted at Dhaka in May 2022)

As previously mentioned in the above sections, Myanmar's military has not been cooperative in dealing with the Rohingya repatriation issue (Banerjee, 2020). Moreover, the border forces have over the years been unnecessarily hostile to Bengali fishermen near the coastal areas (Ahamed & Chowdhury, 2020). All this taken together raises the issue of Myanmar explicitly appearing to be uncooperative with efforts to resolve Bangladesh's Rohingya crisis while being the country responsible for initiating it. Expert data has pointed toward this degradation of bilateral relations between the countries, and this observation is an extension of the data that already point toward this direction. What experts have additionally pointed out is how this can limit the two countries from extending future cooperative endeavors between their respective militaries in other avenues of military cooperation.

What this points toward is a mutual distrust between the two countries at the military level, which can limit future progress toward bilateral relationships to the detriment of Bangladesh following the advent of the Rohingya crisis. Moreover, continuing this trend, seeing Myanmar as a neighboring country posing an emerging threat to the national security and sovereignty of Bangladesh can be a natural continuation of the existing relationship between the two countries, as security experts interviewed for this study have succinctly pointed out.

4.2 Insurgent Activities and Bilateral Relationships

The insurgent activities that have previously caused significant concern in the Chittagong Hill Tracts (CHT) region for the host government of Bangladesh may be revitalized in a new and more concerning form because of the now increasingly alarming Rohingya presence in the area. As one of the security experts interviewed for the study pointed out,

> We know that there is significant inter-ethnic and inter-tribal connectivity alongside the border areas of India and Myanmar, and that can lead to possible risks in the future for a territorially small country like Bangladesh. Such risks are already starting to emerge. We are already observing an increase in unlawful activities in the area by the locals and they are being influenced by the Rohingya population there. This has led to vulnerability in the age of globalization. (Expert interview conducted at Dhaka in May 2022)

This interconnectedness has the potential to facilitate the transfer of ideas, influences, and even unlawful activities between different groups residing in the region.

The expert noted that the presence of the Rohingya population has already started to impact the local dynamics, leading to an increase in unlawful activities by certain segments of the local population. These activities are influenced and driven by the interactions and influence of the Rohingya population residing in the area.

The expert's observations serve as a cautionary reminder that the presence of the Rohingya community, with its unique political, social, and economic circumstances, has the capacity to significantly impact the security environment in Bangladesh. Consequently, this necessitates a deeper understanding of the interplay between the Rohingya crisis, regional dynamics, and local security concerns to effectively address and mitigate the potential risks associated with these evolving dynamics.

This can open up several issues in the bilateral relationships of Bangladesh with neighboring states India and Myanmar. With India, this can lead to an undermining of relationships, as India starts assessing the CHT region as a source of instability for the national security and sovereignty of Bangladesh, and might even lead to less-than-fruitful bilateral relations with a country having an emergent regional instability. On other hand, bilateral relations with Myanmar may suffer a significant degradation as a growing Rohingya population and resulting lawlessness leads to regional instability near its borders for Myanmar to potentially capitalize upon. As data from experts interviewed for this study has pointed toward, this is already taking shape, as several organized criminal groups have begun exploiting the region. This occurs by extending the existing black-market economy in the Cox's Bazar region to the CHT region through the Rohingya population and related organized criminal groups of Bangladesh, as security experts have explained.

4.3 Hampering Regional Cooperation

The capabilities of regional cooperation enabling the host country Bangladesh to resolve this issue have been a source of skepticism for the respondents, as one of the experts working on the economic and intercommunal development of the Cox's Bazar region has pointed out:

> So far, I do not see many international agencies talking about this issue at the international level. I do not see the seriousness of this issue among the UN agencies or other governments from the region to address this crisis. Again, we need to be very critical of the extent to which we succeed diplomatically with this issue, to ensure that our crisis becomes their crisis also. (Expert interview conducted at Cox's Bazar in May 2022)

The hampering of regional cooperation can lead to Bangladesh eventually being solely responsible for bearing the entire burden of the Rohingya population within its borders. This is becoming more and more evident, as resources from international agencies and organizations are being reduced amid stagnation of the repatriation process of the Rohingya population of Bangladesh to Myanmar. As an expert working on a large-scale development project in the Cox's Bazar region argued,

> International support for this issue will dry up if proper attention is not generated toward accelerating the need to repatriate this Rohingya population. Otherwise, Bangladesh will be left to support this entire population on its own, while the international community will look elsewhere. (Expert interview conducted at Cox's Bazar in May 2022)

The skepticism surrounding the capabilities of regional cooperation to effectively address the Rohingya crisis has raised concerns among the respondents, particularly in relation to the engagement of international agencies and neighboring governments. A key expert, specializing in the economic and intercommunal development of the Cox's Bazar region, highlighted the lack of prominence given to the issue at the international level. The expert noted the absence of seriousness and active engagement from UN agencies and regional governments in addressing the crisis. This lack of attention raises doubts about the extent to which diplomatic efforts can effectively resolve the Rohingya crisis and emphasizes the need for a critical assessment of the situation, ensuring that the crisis is acknowledged as a shared concern.

The reduction in international cooperation for ameliorating the Rohingya crisis, coupled with the protracted negotiation process with Myanmar, poses a significant risk of overburdening Bangladesh in the near future. This risk can only be mitigated if substantial international attention is generated to address the Rohingya crisis within its borders. Without renewed focus and support from the international community, Bangladesh faces the daunting task of shouldering the humanitarian and socioeconomic consequences of the crisis on its own. It is imperative that global awareness and concerted efforts be directed toward resolving the Rohingya crisis to prevent Bangladesh from shouldering this burden disproportionately. It is crucial to consider that the reduction of international cooperation for the Rohingya crisis amid stagnating negotiation with Myanmar can put Bangladesh at significant risk of overburdening itself in the near future unless international attention is significantly generated toward the Rohingya crisis within its borders.

4.4 Vulnerability of Bangladesh

This all serves to shed light on how vulnerable the position of Bangladesh is as a host country in dealing with the Rohingya crisis, and how vulnerable the local host community is becoming. Such vulnerability is exemplified in the declining chance of support, both at regional and global levels, for their increasingly concerning situation and for the repatriation of the Rohingyas to their country of origin. Our respondents have also commented on how the Rohingya issue can be put aside and fruitful bilateral relations can still be established between Bangladesh and Myanmar through other avenues such as economic and military areas. Similar instances have been noted between other countries, such as between India and China, where trade relations prosper amid military tensions in contentious regions. However, the desire for initiatives of such cooperative considerations, as respondents have pointed out, does not seem apparent from the military government of Myanmar. Regardless, the Rohingya presence in the host country near the border regions continues to become increasingly concerning for bilateral relations for the host community and the host government of Bangladesh.

4.5 Illicit Businesses and Trafficking of Women

Increasingly concerning for Bangladesh as a result of the Rohingya crisis is the increase of the human security issue in the Cox's Bazar region. Drug trade and human trafficking, particularly of women and children, have been a cause of major concern for authorities in the region (Ahamed & Chowdhury, 2020; Banerjee, 2020). Experts interviewed for this study have argued that this poses both a threat to the traditional as well as the human security dimension of Bangladesh. Experts point toward how drug abuse has been rampant among civilian populations in the Cox's Bazar region and has impacted the youth population greatly in terms of making progress in careers and relationships, and the secondary literature clearly points toward this trend in the region (Banerjee, 2020). Moreover, the data points toward how this can compromise regional security, with the continued introduction of narcotics, small arms, and light weapons amid insurgent initiatives of organized groups among the Rohingya population. With both traditional and human security being put at risk, the data points toward how Bangladesh will be in a significantly vulnerable position if it is unable to appropriately deal with the Rohingya issue and its resulting compromises to both areas of security in due time. This can further contribute to regional conflict potential, as national vulnerability provides avenues for neighboring states and interest groups to utilize and exploit the situation to their benefit.

4.6 International Conflict

There are quite a number of ways in which the crisis has impacted the international community. This Rohingya crisis has resulted in a massive humanitarian crisis, with over 1 million Rohingya refugees currently residing in overcrowded camps in Bangladesh. The refugees are in dire need of food, water, shelter, and medical care. The international community has responded with aid and donations, but the situation remains precarious. Moreover, Myanmar's handling of the crisis has led to significant diplomatic fallout with other countries.

The Rohingya crisis has contributed to a larger global refugee crisis, with many Rohingya refugees attempting to flee to other countries in the region, including Malaysia and Indonesia. The crisis has highlighted the need for a more comprehensive approach to refugee protection and resettlement. Furthermore, the crisis has contributed to regional instability in South Asia. Bangladesh, which has taken in the majority of Rohingya refugees, has been strained by the influx of people and has had to work with the international community to manage the situation. The crisis has also had an impact on neighboring countries, which have been forced to deal with the spillover effects of the conflict. The crisis has had an economic impact on the region. The large number of refugees has put a strain on resources and infrastructure, particularly in Bangladesh. The crisis has also affected trade and investment in the region, with some countries imposing sanctions on Myanmar in response to the situation as has been already mentioned. The important human rights concerns this crisis had raised are also of significant importance, particularly around the treatment of refugees and the responsibility of the international community to protect them. The situation has sparked debates about the role of human rights in international relations and the need for greater accountability for human rights violations (Adams, 2019). An additional and significant part of this crisis is the cultural impact on the Rohingya people themselves. The violence and persecution they have faced has threatened their cultural identity, and many have been forced to flee their homes and abandon their traditions. The crisis has highlighted the importance of cultural preservation and the need to protect the rights of minority groups. Overall, the Rohingya crisis has had a significant impact on the international community, highlighting the need for greater cooperation and coordination in addressing humanitarian and human rights issues.

5 Conclusion

In conclusion, the Rohingya refugee crisis has had a profound regional and international impact, highlighting the urgent need for a coordinated response from the international community. The crisis has resulted in a massive displacement of Rohingya refugees, who have faced unimaginable violence and persecution at the hands of Myanmar's military. The humanitarian crisis that has emerged as a result of the conflict has seen over one million Rohingya refugees fleeing to Bangladesh, where they continue to face significant challenges in accessing basic necessities such as food, water, shelter, and medical care.

The crisis has also had significant implications for regional stability, with the strain on resources and infrastructure in Bangladesh leading to an increased risk of political and social instability in the region. The economic impact of the crisis has been felt across the region, with burdens on resources and related infrastructure seemingly inevitable given the large number of refugees involved. The crisis has also affected trade and investment, with some countries imposing sanctions on Myanmar in response to the situation.

The crisis has also had profound human rights implications, with the treatment of the Rohingya refugees raising important concerns about the responsibility of the international community to protect vulnerable populations. The situation has sparked debates about the role of human rights in international relations, and the need for greater accountability for human rights violations. Furthermore, the crisis has highlighted the importance of cultural preservation and the need to protect the rights of minority groups.

The international community can take several actions to address the Rohingya crisis in Bangladesh, including providing humanitarian aid, advocating for the rights of refugees, supporting efforts to hold perpetrators accountable for human rights abuses, and working toward a political resolution to the conflict. Specifically, countries and international organizations can provide financial and material aid to support the basic needs of Rohingya refugees, as well as support education and healthcare initiatives to improve living conditions in the refugee camps. They can also pressure Myanmar's government to end the violence and persecution against the Rohingya, and support efforts to bring perpetrators to justice. Finally, they can support diplomatic efforts to find a political solution to the conflict, including promoting dialog between Myanmar and Bangladesh to resolve the issue of repatriation of Rohingya refugees to Myanmar.

Moving forward, it is imperative that the international community works together to address the root causes of the conflict, protect the rights of refugees, and promote sustainable solutions that will help ensure the safety and well-being of all those affected. This will require a coordinated response from the international community, working in partnership with the governments of Myanmar and Bangladesh to address the underlying issues that have contributed to the crisis. Ultimately, the Rohingya refugee crisis serves as a powerful reminder of the urgent need for greater cooperation and coordination in addressing humanitarian and human rights issues on a global scale.

References

Adams, S. (2019). 'If not now, when?': The responsibility to protect, the fate of the Rohingya, and the future of human rights. *Global Centre for the Responsibility to Protect*. https://doi.org/10.2139/ssrn.3319491

Ahamed, A., & Chowdhury, M. A. (2020). Bangladesh-Myanmar border relations: A study of some geopolitical and economic issues. *European Scientific Journal, 16*(22), 320–351. https://doi.org/10.19044/esj.2020.v16n22p320

Banerjee, S. (2020). The Rohingya crisis and its impact on Bangladesh-Myanmar relations. *Observer Research Foundation*. Retrieved January 20, 2021, from https://www.orfonline.org/wp-content/uploads/2020/08/ORF_IssueBrief_396_Bangladesh-Myanmar.pdf

Bashar, I. (2018). Impact of the Rohingya crisis on the threat landscape of the Myanmar-Bangladesh border. In C. Echle, R. Gunaratna, P. Rueppel, & M. Sarmah (Eds.), *Combatting violent extremism and terrorism in Asia and Europe: From cooperation to collaboration* (pp. 29–42). Konrad-Adenauer-Stiftung.

Guhathakurta, M. (2017). Understanding violence, strategising protection: Perspectives from Rohingya refugees in Bangladesh. *Asian Journal of Social Science, 45*(6), 639–665. https://brill.com/view/journals/ajss/45/6/article-p639_3.xml?casa_token=urBKAbXsyA8AAAAA:qk6SHIo2MrH-k8qc65pcgvLh2kXIpfRj5nrFjZsjcOlfwtzCBjucoFmv7sBz4T_UfSb_Tb7vZug

Hazra, A. (2021, May 19). Rohingya crisis: India's actions must match its words. *The Rohingya Post*. https://www.rohingyapost.com/rohingya-crisis-indias-actions-must-match-its-words/

Hoang, M. T. (2020). *Crimes against humanity and the responsibility to protect: The case of the Rohingya crisis in Myanmar* (Master's thesis, Norwegian University of Life Sciences, Ås).

Hossain, M. S. (2021). Bangladesh's judicial encounter with the 1951 refugee convention. *Forced Migration Review* (67), 59–61. Retrieved August 28, 2023, from https://ora.ox.ac.uk/objects/uuid:dbe4b5d1-04d1-4d99-b2fa-735442904e38/files/s3f462670q

Jacob, H. (2017, January 23). The nowhere people next door: New Delhi should use creative diplomacy to persuade Myanmar to resolve the Rohingya crisis. *The Hindu*. https://www.thehindu.com/opinion/lead/The-nowhere-people-next-door/article17078540.ece

Kiragu, E., Rosi, A. L., & Morris, T. (2011). *States of denial: A review of UNHCR's response to the protracted situation of stateless Rohingya refugees in Bangladesh*. Policy Development and Evaluation Service, United Nations High Commissioner for Refugees. Accessed August 28, 2023, from https://www.unhcr.org/media/states-denial-review-unhcrs-response-protracted-situation-stateless-rohingya-refugees

Pant, H. V., & Bhattacharjee, J. (2020, July 29). The enduring logic of India-Bangladesh ties. *Observer Research Foundation*. https://www.orfonline.org/expert-speak/the-enduring-logic-of-india-bangladesh-ties/

Quadir, S. (2015, June 6). India, Bangladesh sign historic land boundary agreement. *Reuters*. https://www.reuters.com/article/bangladesh-india-land-treaty-idINKBN0OM0IV20150606?edition-redirect=in

Sarker, S. (2019, December 18). Impact of CAA on Bangladesh: Despite Dhaka's efforts, anti-India sentiment on the rise among its citizens. *First Post*. https://www.firstpost.com/india/impact-of-caa-on-bangladesh-despite-dhakas-efforts-anti-india-sentiment-on-the-rise-among-its-citizens-7796251.html

Thompson, A., & Verdier, D. (2013, September 23). *Multilateralism, bilateralism and regime design*. Department of Political Science, Ohio State University. https://politicalscience.osu.edu/faculty/athompson/Lateralisms.pdf

Yhome, K. (2018). *Examining India's stance on the Rohingya crisis*. Observer Research Foundation. https://www.orfonline.org/research/examining-indias-stance-on-the-rohingya-crisis/

Chapter 7
Rohingyas in Bangladesh: Sociopolitical Conflict Potential

Md. Rafiqul Islam and Umme Wara

Abstract This chapter discusses the sociopolitical conflict potential of the Rohingya conflict in host country Bangladesh. The sociopolitical landscape of Bangladesh has taken a drastic turn due to the involvement of the Rohingya refugee population, and it has significantly impacted the host community in often negative ways. The areas of sociopolitical conflict potential of the Rohingya conflict in the host state are divided across seven areas of assessment. These areas are population, resource scarcity, health care, education, public goods, gender issues, and political issues, and they are first considered individually. The conflict potential across these areas is then discussed as a whole to paint a more concise picture of the host country's situation.

1 Introduction

The Rohingya crisis in Bangladesh has had a profound sociopolitical impact on the country, with far-reaching consequences for both the Rohingya refugees and the local Bangladeshi population. This chapter examines the various ways in which the crisis has impacted the sociopolitical climate of Bangladesh and explores the conflict potential that it poses for Bangladesh. The crisis has put significant strain on the social and political structures of Bangladesh. The presence of over one million Rohingya refugees has led to increased competition for limited resources, including jobs, land, and basic services. This has resulted in tensions between the refugees and the host community, with incidents of violence and discrimination reported in some areas. Furthermore, the Rohingya crisis has created a complex legal and political situation in Bangladesh. The government has been faced with the challenge of providing for the needs of the refugees while also maintaining the rights and interests of the local population. This has led to a range of policy responses, including the establishment

Md. R. Islam (✉) · U. Wara
University of Dhaka, Dhaka, Bangladesh
e-mail: rislampacs@du.ac.bd

U. Wara
e-mail: wara.criminology@du.ac.bd

K. Ahmed and Md. R. Islam (eds.), *Understanding the Rohingya Displacement*, International Perspectives on Migration, https://doi.org/10.1007/978-981-97-1424-7_7

of refugee camps, the provision of aid and services, and attempts to repatriate the refugees to Myanmar. The crisis has also had significant implications for the human rights of both the refugees and the local population. The Rohingya refugees have faced widespread discrimination and violence, both in Myanmar and in Bangladesh, while the local population has expressed concerns about the impact of the refugee influx on their own rights and freedoms. These sociopolitical challenges have the potential to escalate into conflict within Bangladesh. Tensions between the refugee and host communities have already led to instances of violence and unrest, and there are concerns that further tensions could arise in the future. The complex legal and political situation surrounding the crisis also presents a risk of conflict, with different groups advocating for different approaches to managing the crisis. Given the complex nature of the crisis and the potential for conflict, it is important to understand the sociopolitical impacts of the Rohingya crisis in Bangladesh. This chapter particularly examines the sociopolitical conflict potential of this crisis faced by both the refugees and the host community, including issues of demographic change, access to basic services, health care, education, scarcity of public goods, and gender issues alongside sociopolitical issues; these are illustrated across seven key areas. The discussion then moves on to the key aspects of the sociopolitical conflict potential within the host state.

2 Sociopolitical Conflict Potential: Analytical Lens

Studies show that refugees and displaced communities leave their homes for a variety of reasons, but these two types of populations are fundamentally different. Displaced communities are displaced within their own state borders, while refugee populations cross international borders into other countries or lands outside of their origin state. The very definition of a refugee as per the international Refugee Convention mentions the factor of being forced to leave one's country as a prerequisite. Displaced communities are at risk of being vulnerable to an oppressive government when the government is responsible for their displacement. Although displaced populations have some protection via the Geneva Convention, this is quite limited. Forced displacement is seen as a war crime according to these instruments, and this does not directly lead to how displaced people would be treated as a result of their displacement (Jacques, 2012). Refugees, on the other hand, are at risk of having no identity and becoming stateless as a result, while being at the mercy of the host community (Kyaw, 2017). Although this risk is mitigated via international conventions which many states of the globe are a party to, not all states fully accept this obligation to protect these populations (Janmyr, 2021). Such is the case for Bangladesh, which is not a party to these conventions that see to the protection of the refugees while providing basic necessities and protection for them during their refuge. Moreover, while states designate such populations within their borders with "refugee" or other restricted statuses which limit their rights and opportunities, refugees struggle for obtaining those very same rights and opportunities (Murshid, 2013). This leads to the question of sociopolitical conflict between the refugees and the host community.

The variables of social conflict potential that have been considered in this study involve the factors that influence the relationships of communities in a society. The first of these factors is the "management of population" as described by Parajuli (2020). This independent variable determines how effectively the lives of civilians within a society can be regulated (Garry & Checchi, 2019). Population management is again inherently related to family planning, birth rates, and the supply of necessary goods in proportion to a population's growth (Parajuli, 2020). Next, we examine "resource scarcity," which can lead to a reduced standard of living for both the refugee and host populations. The larger a refugee population becomes, the greater their need for resources; as resources become scarce, the potential for social unrest and conflict grows (Islam & Wara, 2022). A third variable that has been considered here is "access to health care." Conflicts can overload and undermine healthcare systems and facilities (Kirschnera & Finaret, 2021). Access to health care is necessary for healthy populations, and when this is connected to a conflicting situation, it can become a decisive factor in exacerbating a conflict (Garry & Checchi, 2019). A fourth variable is "access to education," which can quickly become one of the sources influencing a conflict's trajectory. Access to education can be seen as a source of conflict when one community in a society sees itself being deprived of its benefits by another community which is receiving them (Pherali, 2019). This becomes less of a concern when the effects of a lack of access to education are seen to be equally widespread across communities in a social conflict.

The fifth variable is "access to public goods." This can influence a social conflict significantly when one community starts to benefit from proper access to public goods at the expense of another community. The effects are exacerbated when this shift is apparent to the latter community, which is suffering from a lack of access to public goods that had not been the case before the conflict started to take shape (Whitt, 2021). The sixth variable involves "gender issues," which include instances where women are subjected to adverse experiences or violence, and how that is reflected within communities of a society (Christou, 2018). The instances of violence (or adverse experiences) against women and the perception of those instances are of course deeply related to each other, but the perception is what determines how it changes communal relationships and thus influences a social conflict. This leads to the seventh variable, "political pressure," which involves the range of political influence a refugee population is able to exert on the host population. Refugee populations strive to obtain political rights and influence in adverse conditions, even in host countries, and this variable encompasses how such influence translates onto the case of Rohingya refugees in Bangladesh.

3 Methodology

To investigate the sociopolitical conflict potential surrounding the Rohingyas and the conflict in Bangladesh, the study employed a research methodology which drew upon a combination of qualitative and quantitative approaches. The primary data collection for this study relied on three key methods: key informant interviews (KIIs), focus group discussions (FGDs), and surveys. These methods were chosen to ensure a robust and nuanced understanding of the complex dynamics and perspectives involved in the conflict.

Key informant interviews (KIIs) constituted a crucial component of this research methodology. KIIs allowed for in-depth conversations with individuals who possessed significant knowledge and expertise in various relevant domains. The selection of key informants was guided by their direct involvement or expertise in matters related to the Rohingyas and the sociopolitical context in Bangladesh. Through these interviews, insights were gained into the underlying factors, historical background, policy implications, and community perspectives surrounding the conflict. The interviews were conducted in a semi-structured manner, allowing for flexibility and exploration of emerging themes. The data obtained from KIIs provided valuable qualitative insights and perspectives, enriching the overall analysis.

In addition to KIIs, FGDs were employed to capture diverse viewpoints and facilitate interactive exchanges among individuals from different stakeholder groups. FGDs were conducted with carefully selected participants, including representatives from governmental organizations, nongovernmental organizations, community leaders, academic experts, and members of the Rohingya community. The FGDs were conducted in a facilitated group setting, providing a platform for participants to share their experiences, perceptions, and concerns regarding the conflict. The discussions were guided by a predetermined set of themes, allowing for a comparative analysis of different perspectives and the identification of commonalities and divergences. FGDs offered valuable qualitative data, enabling a deeper exploration of the social, political, and cultural dimensions of the conflict.

To complement the qualitative insights gathered through KIIs and FGDs, surveys were conducted to obtain quantitative data. The surveys were designed based on the identified research objectives and relevant literature. The survey targeted a diverse range of participants, including local residents, policymakers, and members of the Rohingya community. The questionnaire included a mix of closed-ended and open-ended questions, allowing for both quantitative analysis and qualitative responses. The survey responses provided quantitative data on various aspects of the conflict, including perceptions, attitudes, and socioeconomic factors, which were analyzed using appropriate statistical methods.

It is important to note that ethical considerations were carefully addressed throughout the research process. Informed consent was obtained from all participants, ensuring confidentiality and anonymity. The research design and data collection instruments were developed in accordance with established ethical guidelines and principles.

By utilizing a combination of KIIs, FGDs, and surveys, this research methodology facilitated a comprehensive exploration of the sociopolitical conflict potential surrounding the Rohingyas and the conflict in Bangladesh. The triangulation of data from multiple sources enhanced the credibility and validity of the research findings, enabling a more comprehensive understanding of the complex dynamics at play.

4 Major Areas in Sociopolitical Conflict Potential

The sociopolitical conflict and its effects are reflected among the host community in a myriad of ways. Refugees and displaced populations change the landscape as well as the composition of the host society, and the situation in Cox's Bazar is a case in point. The majority of the changes have taken place after the Rohingya exodus reached a point where this population was too large for any social change to go unnoticed. Instead, the social effects of the Rohingya population impacted the host society in several areas, among which, seven areas are assessed here. These are as follows:

1. Population
2. Resource scarcity
3. Health care
4. Education
5. Public goods
6. Gender issues
7. Political pressure.

Each of these areas has a respective variable that describes the findings from the collected data for that area of social effect in the host society. The perceptions of the Rohingya people have been incorporated into this section to see how the Rohingya people perceive the sociopolitical changes in the region as well. The information from experts has been added to substantiate the discussion and explore how the changes have been contributing to conflict and violence in the region. The analysis of these social effects, as a part of the overarching social conflict in the Cox's Bazar region surrounding the camps, has been done with the help of existing literature on related topics.

4.1 Population

The population of a host community experiences a drastic change when it has to accommodate a large number of refugees or displaced people arriving in their area. The population dynamic of the host then has to shift to accommodate this new group of people. This is more so when the population is a refugee population with a different ethnicity than the host population, such as the Rohingyas. Moreover, when the displaced population is also composed of refugees from a neighboring country, then many additional factors come into play. These factors involve international conventions relating to the protection and the rights of refugees (i.e., the Refugee Convention and its protocols) and isolating the population in such a way that this new group of people does not immediately integrate with the host community and give rise to various issues of identity politics and national security (Babu, 2020). Alongside ensuring this new group's safety and security while keeping the host country's security concerns in mind, the new groups and/or communities still have to be accommodated in the host country's territory. This accommodation, however, can be pushed to its limits when the population is too large for the host to properly manage. Herein lie the issues related to population management in the host country of Bangladesh regarding refugees. The Rohingya people have been welcomed by the Bangladesh government and the host society in Cox's Bazar during the decades of sequential exoduses from Myanmar. Now, with over a million Rohingya people inside Bangladesh's border, some obvious issues related to population have arisen for both the host government and the host community. However, the process of Rohingya population management has generated multiple social problems and challenges which have strong conflict potential. While asking the local people about the social issues, the respondents mentioned multiple issues in their social life (Fig. 1).

The findings from the host community survey show the position of an overwhelming majority of the respondents is that the Rohingyas lack proper knowledge regarding family planning, and the subsequent pressure on the food supply for this refugee community itself is the result of it. Associating the population growth of the Rohingya community with social conflict within the host community comes to the fore when the findings reveal that respondents mostly point toward how the increasing birth rate is having a negative impact on the areas within and nearby the camps. These

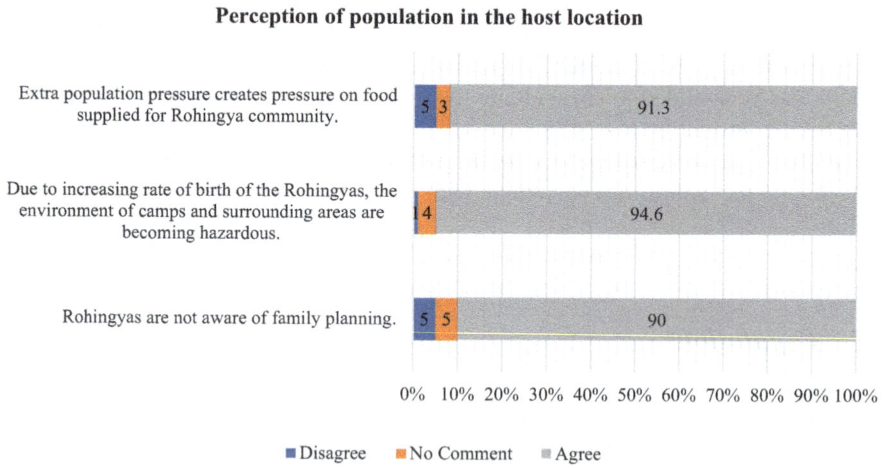

Fig. 1 Sociopolitical conflict: population management. *Source* Developed by the authors based on field data

results show how issue of population management of the diaspora as seen by the host community is skewed against the Rohingyas, which has thus become a potential source of conflict within the Cox's Bazar region. The respondents opine that population pressure has positive correlation with the food shortage and scarcity of the resources. Both communities are competing for these resources for their survival in the region. Environmental hazards are also a result of the increasing Rohingya population as they put pressure on the existing resources which are in scarce supply.

When social conflict is discussed in terms of population management and how it affects the dynamics among the communities within it, family planning and a sufficient food supply to sustain that population become significant factors. These two factors can influence the shift of the demographic composition of a population, i.e., the rates of birth and the demands for basic nutrition by the different communities. This is significant for Bangladesh as its demographic composition in its Cox's Bazar region has now shifted due to the very high birth rates of the Rohingya population compared to the host community. This has been associated with the lack of knowledge of family planning within Rohingya families in the refugee camps, alongside the inability of the Rohingya women to influence such decisions (Azad et al., 2021).

If the host community associates the lack of family planning within the refugee and/or displaced communities with its rapid birth rates and the subsequent pressures on the local food supply, there is the possibility of it being linked to social conflict within these two sets of communities.

The Rohingya refugee population has increased in numbers over the years, and this has led to an increase in accommodation problems for the host country as reserve forests have been uprooted and made into new arable land and housing areas for the new and increasing number of Rohingya refugees (Milton et al., 2017). The limited land resources of Bangladesh (more so in the coastal areas) are now being stressed as the mountainous ecosystem is being changed to house the Rohingyas. The population dynamic has also shifted from a purely demographic perspective, and as in Cox's Bazar, Rohingya refugees now outnumber local Bengali people by nearly 5 times (Yasmin & Akther, 2019). This shift, alongside the other issues including pressures of land resources, food, and other necessities, leads to a manifestation of conflict in the host society. This shift of a conflict from the origin country to the host country can be seen as a conflict being displaced from the origin to the host country as a result of the new issues the host country faces. This leads to social conflict stemming from various issues, population management being just one of them.

However, the Rohingya people perceive the issue of social conflict differently. They hardly acknowledge that the presence of a large number of people is causing social conflict in the region. The FGD participants provided their opinion about the social issues, mentioning many issues regarding their livelihood and economic situations. However, with regards to primarily social issues, the problems have not surfaced nearly as much. When the issue of population was put forward among the participants, they responded as to how their allocated housing spaces did not accommodate their numbers. A participant elaborated in one of the focus groups that

> The housing spaces we are given are often too little to support our families. Rooms for four people are used to house eight or more, and that is without counting new daughters-in-law when they move in with their husbands. (FGD outcome; conducted in Ukhiya in May 2022)

The Rohingya people interviewed in these discussions did not explicitly see the population as directly impacting the food supply or that they should be more knowledgeable about family planning. When asked about whether the population was a factor in creating pressure on the food supply for the Rohingyas, participants pointed out that their ends could be met with only a little more support from the authorities:

> We are given food to last the month, but the rations only last about 20 days. We have to look for some extra work to get the money to make to the end of the month each time. Only a little bit more support from the government and NGOs can get our families enough rations. (FGD outcome; conducted in Ukhiya in May 2022)

Indeed, the Rohingya people rarely consider themselves the source of social conflict in the host society. This study then turned to information from the experts about the social conflict potential of the Rohingya people. Expert findings shed light upon the sociopolitical aspect of the Rohingya refugee crisis in Bangladesh. Regarding population growth, experts interviewed for this study touched upon several facets of the Rohingya crisis and provided several reliable predictions based on the present trends and outcomes. Similarly, for other aspects of the Rohingya crisis, reliable data have been obtained from the interviewed experts.

The genocide and persecution of the Rohingya people have forced all groups of people (ultranationalist, fanatic, moderate, and progressive) to settle in Cox's Bazar and live in these congested camps. After the settlement they remain divided, with their different ideologies and beliefs, and equally engaged in conflict as those in Bangladesh (Islam et al., 2022).

The mass exodus has increased the population significantly in the area. Equally, the explosive population growth has led to various sociopolitical issues, and the resulting impact on other aspects has been explained in previous sections.

4.2 Resource Scarcity

The increasing population has inevitably impacted the existing resources. Along with the resources, the commodity and labor markets have become highly competitive (Fig. 2).

A director of an international NGO explained how the national resources are at stake and how the resource scarcity is being generated:

> Let us talk about the natural resources over here, about the forest, and about the water that is being drawn from the inside, from the aquifers. All of a sudden, three times the population is drawing the same water. So there was a study by WASA that says that the water level of those areas are going down drastically. Same is with the forest. Because this used to be one of the most popular reserves of Bangladesh. There are 2 or 4 national parks in the Teknaf and Ukhiya area. It is a good habitat for wild animals. But what happened when the Rohingyas

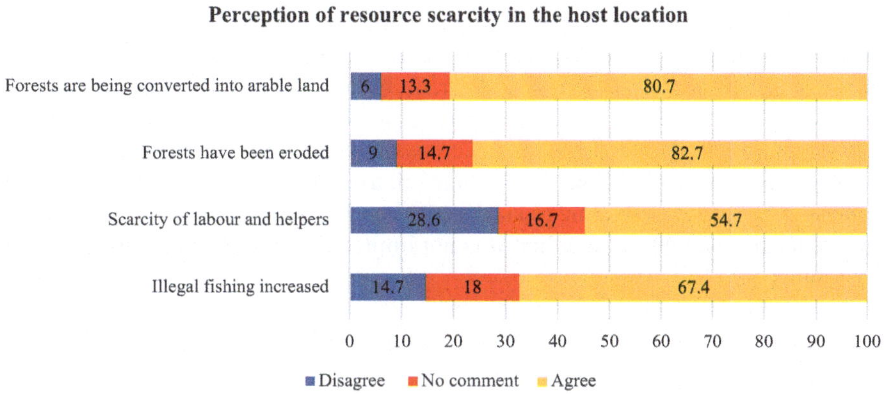

Fig. 2 Sociopolitical conflict: resource scarcity. *Source* Developed by the authors based on field data

> came is that they had to be settled somewhere, so these entire forests were cut. There is a record that says that everyday the forests were destroyed in huge swaths, so what happened is that the dependence of the host community on the forest has been going down drastically. Because now there's hardly any forest anymore. So the community that was dependent on the forest is now depending on the market to buy those products. Again, this is one of the issues here. (Expert interview conducted at Dhaka in June 2022)

The Rohingya influxes led to a large increase in freshwater consumption from underground freshwater aquifer reserves and wood usage from forest reserves in Cox's Bazar. This then led to a sharp decrease in underground water levels and rapid deforestation in the area.

One expert interviewee, a director of a research organization and academician working on refugee issues, explained how this has affected the habitability of the Cox's Bazar region:

> Over four thousand acres of forests and hills were cut down to facilitate habitation for the Rohingyas and more than half of all natural forests there have been cleared out of vegetation. With diminishing cultivable lands and fishing and water bodies alongside diminishing spaces for rearing livestock, resources are diminishing in the area. This poses a significant concern for the Rohingya and Bengali populations in the region. (Expert interview conducted at Dhaka in July 2022)

The large Rohingya presence has thus led to rapid environmental degradation with visible changes to the landscape and quality of life for the populations in the area. With underground freshwater aquifers and forests being ever more rapidly diminished, the changing landscape from cutting up the hills for settlement space has led to drastic changes to the landscape at the expense of the local ecosystem and quality of life in Cox's Bazar.

The people of Bangladesh, particularly the local host community in Cox's Bazar who has been very cooperative with the Rohingya people—and it is hoped that they will continue to be—are now suffering significantly because of the increasing constraints on the limited resources in the area as the Rohingya population increases in size. Their intercommunal relationship has suffered as a result. And at the national level, Bangladesh's economy, its environment, its governance, its politics, and even its security have suffered a significant crisis because of the Rohingya issue. The country is certainly seeing a clearly emerging environmental conflict tied to resource scarcity in the area due to the Rohingya crisis. Resource scarcity is causing not only an environmental conflict, but also a humanitarian and security crisis in the area alongside the related economic risks. As a result, this issue is now moving toward a comprehensive and all-out conflict. It is not limited to a conflict of resources or the environment.

4.3 Health Care

A functioning system of health care within populations is vital for communities to develop and prosper. Access to healthcare facilities is thus a crucial indicator as to how prosperous a community is. This indicator changes when access to such facilities shift due to the addition of a displaced community to the host population. In the survey process, local people were asked about how the presence of Rohingya people is affecting their healthcare access and consequently generating social problems. The majority of the local people argue that the Rohingya presence in their area has negatively affected their services and health facilities (Fig. 3).

The findings from the host community suggest that the local people mostly agree that the spread of contagious diseases within and around the camp areas is on the rise. This is supported by previous studies on the spread of contagious diseases in

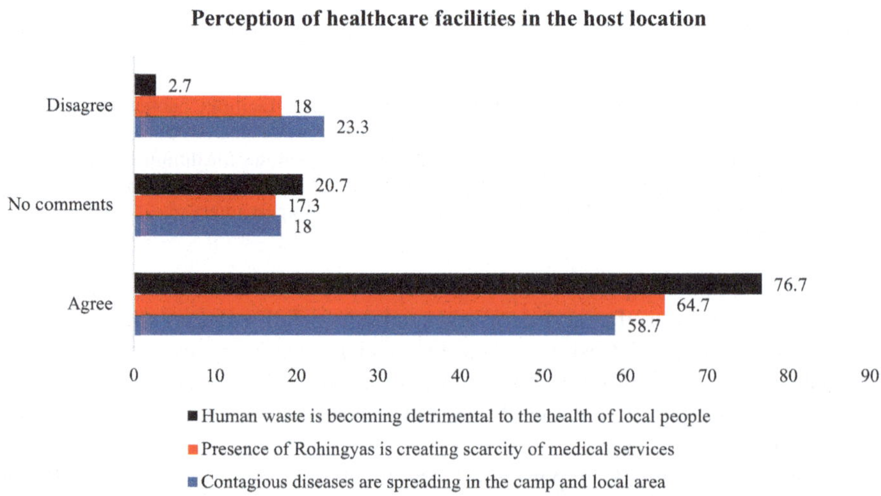

Fig. 3 Sociopolitical conflict: access to health care. *Source* Developed by authors based on field data

the area indicating a rise in respiratory and intestinal diseases (Faruque et al., 2021; Summers et al., 2018). However, the respondents from the host community were of the position that the medical care (i.e., healthcare) facilities being available for the Rohingyas in the area are causing the locals to have less access to such facilities. The local people also perceive that pressure on the healthcare services by the Rohingyas is diminishing such services for the local people.

This shows that access to healthcare facilities is another potential source of conflict for the host community. The Rohingya community has benefitted from access to healthcare facilities from a variety of healthcare organizations from both government and nongovernment sectors at national and international levels. This can lead to an improvement in living conditions for this displaced community, and the host community can also benefit if this leads to an increase in employment opportunities and access to healthcare facilities for the locals. However, if such opportunities for the host community shift in a way that the locals subsequently have fewer income opportunities or fewer healthcare facilities, then it becomes a detriment for the host community to accommodate this new population. For the host community, income opportunities can decrease or remain unchanged for a variety of reasons, including skilled workers from other areas of the host country taking up the newly available jobs, among others. Access to healthcare facilities can decrease as well for the host community for reasons such as the increasing demand for health care and the available facilities being used by the displaced community. Whatever the reasons, if the host community identifies such changes and links them to the displaced and/or refugee community, then it can become a potential source of social conflict for the host community.

However, this study asked the Rohingya respondents through FGDs how they have perceived the healthcare facilities in the region and how they have been provided with the healthcare facilities. With regards to the health services provided to the Rohingya community, the participants in the discussion pointed out that although the number of available healthcare centers in the camps was satisfactory, their quality of service was far from being the same. A participant in one of the focus groups elaborated:

> There are a good number of centers but none of them have doctors ready most of the time. When they are there, the lines are so long that a lot of us leave after a few hours of standing at them. It's tedious and causes many ill people to avoid going to them later on. Other times, the nurses just give us some basic tablets like paracetamol and saline packets for most of our problems. (FGD outcome; conducted in Teknaf in May 2022)

However, with regards to the spread of contagious diseases within the camp and surrounding areas, the participants were unwilling to elaborate on how serious they felt the issue was. Indeed, the Rohingyas hardly perceived that their presence in the region was the cause of diminishing the healthcare facilities and spreading of contagious diseases. Thus, the study sought expert opinions from the appropriate authorities.

Different sources purport that the Rohingyas are responsible for spreading of contagious diseases such as HIV/AIDS (Rahman et al., 2020).

Regarding health issues, a key informant pointed to how the Rohingya presence has significantly contributed to the deterioration of the health condition of people in the area:

> The Rohingyas in the camps at Cox's Bazar have generally unclean conditions in their huts and their attires. Moreover, the Rohingyas have been responsible for spreading some of the contagious diseases to our local areas from time to time. They are not safe people to be around due to their generally unkempt way of life. (KII conducted at Cox's Bazar in May 2022)

Some reports support this argument about the spreading of contagious diseases by the Rohingya people. A study suggests that "in 2017, soon after these Rohingya people had arrived in Bangladesh, the health authorities carried out diagnostic tests and identified 85 cases of HIV. The cumulative number has risen steadily since then, 273 in August 2018, 319 in March 2019, and 395 in the recent estimate in 2020" (Khan et al., 2021). Besides the HIV affected, women and girls are also infected by other sexually transmitted diseases in increasing numbers every year. In order to get more information about the health issues, this study interviewed health experts who are working in the Rohingya camps. One employee of an international organization argued,

> Health issues and the spreading of contagious diseases really matter in Cox's Bazar. Since 2017 population is increasing and services and resources are diminishing. Women and girls are getting involved in prostitution and any form of illegal business. This is the real danger for the region. (Expert interview conducted in June 2022)

Indeed, congested places, compromising living conditions, and uncertainty are the main causes for the health issues in Cox's Bazar. These conditions may widen the difference between the Rohingya people and local people. Local people are already frightened by the increasing population and contagious diseases. Such negative perceptions may generate conflict and violence in the region if proper policies are not undertaken. The presence of a large number of Rohingya people, supporting staff needs, logistics, and infrastructure have also complicated the entire healthcare system of the local people. Once reaching the healthcare center the local people face difficulties and financial costs. For example, one key informant narrated a pathetic story of her daughter's death. She spoke with great anger and anguish toward the Rohingyas:

> One afternoon my daughter got in an accident. Our healthcare center is located 2 kilometers away from our house. We started to take her to the hospital, but the road was congested with a traffic jam. Many vehicles of the UN organizations and local NGOs were returning to Cox's Bazar that made the huge traffic jam. We waited and waited. Unfortunately, my daughter died. This was happened for the traffic jam. (KII conducted in Ukhiya in March 2022)

The increasing population in the area due to the large influx and subsequent growth of the Rohingya population has led to a decrease in the quality of life across various areas, including a significant increase in traffic congestion (Biswas et al., 2022). The recent study by Biswas et al. (2022) highlights this and shows how the local residents have suffered in terms of the ability to reach their workplaces and destinations and the environmental degradation negatively affecting all populations as a result.

4.4 Education

Educational facilities for displaced communities are essential when planning their repatriation to their country of origin in the long term. This is primarily required to prepare the current and future generation of the displaced population for when they are eventually repatriated to live new lives in their country of origin. However, while that process is in progress, issues can arise when these facilities hamper the existing educational facilities for the host community, particularly the host community's children. The influence might be a net positive one, as was the case in Florida, USA, with the influx of Haitian migrants, but that may not be the case for states that are less developed in comparison (Figlio & Özek, 2019). Aside from the resulting problems such as the reduction of educational facilities for host community children, decreasing interest of the local children in completing mandatory or higher education in favor of new employment or other opportunities can also hamper their education. When this is identified by the host community, a potential for conflict is created which is centered around the change in the access to education for host community children (Fig. 4).

The findings here point toward how participants from the host community view the changes in access to education for the host community children (i.e., local children) given the influx of Rohingya refugees. The local people were also asked whether the presence of the Rohingyas are affecting the education of the local children. More than half of the respondents (60%) opined that presence of the Rohingyas is affecting the educational environment and opportunities of the local people.

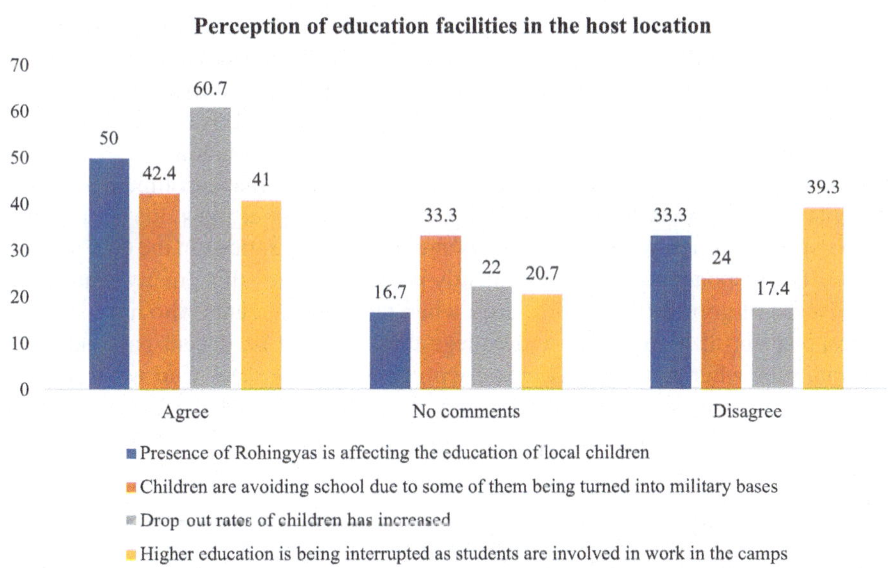

Fig. 4 Sociopolitical conflict: access to education. *Source* Developed by authors based on field data

The host community's perception points toward how local children have less access to religious education in maktabs (i.e., schools where education is provided on Islamic teachings and principles) due to these facilities being used by Rohingya children in increasing numbers. With regards to many of the local educational institutions in Cox's Bazar being used to house military personnel and equipment (Ahmed, 2022), the host participants have mostly agreed upon how this has resulted in the local children avoiding going to these institutions for education afterward. Although participants agree that Rohingya children do not have proper educational facilities in the camps, they have linked the associated changes from the Rohingya influx to decreasing participation in educational institutions of local children. This is indicated by the general statement that the local children are facing problems in receiving education due the arrival of the Rohingyas. Although not as strong of a point compared to the other social aspects of the situation, access to education still has significant potential to be a source of conflict for Cox's Bazar's host community.

Through FGDs this study explored the opinion of the Rohingya people. This study also asked questions about how they have been accessing education. Regarding education, most of the participants in the focus groups expressed their frustration about the education facilities in the current camps. There were statements such as "There are many schools in the camps, but with very less facilities. The children just play all day," and "many schools have no students in them, and classes are not really taking place due to the corona." One participant elaborated:

> We have learning schools and Madrasas here. But these schools are not adequate in providing education. Our children mainly play games there. There is no future of our children in the camp. (KII conducted in April 2022)

The Rohingyas are also frustrated about the system and policy of the government of Bangladesh, as they have only been given scope to be educated in English and the language of Myanmar. Reports suggest that NGOs and international organizations intend to educate the Rohingya children in Bengali (Bakali & Wasty, 2020), which has caused some division and is a strong source of conflict potential.

Regarding education, experts have highlighted how the enrollment of local students has continued to decrease alongside rising dropout rates due to lucrative job prospects through working for NGOs and relief organizations in the Cox's Bazar region. The respondents have consequently pointed out how this greatly diminishes the chances of good work opportunities when the same students who have skipped or dropped out of high school and college then lose out on decent pay and work opportunities when having to compete with Rohingya workers who work for less than desirable wages. An education expert and professor of Dhaka University who worked as team leader education project in Cox's Bazar described many effects of this. He argues,

> The influx of large numbers of the Rohingyas has firstly reduced the capacity of the local authority and generated a capacity cap to manage the education system in the region. The host community students have been affected seriously. Many of the students after their HSC have stopped their study and started working in the NGO based learning centers Rohingya camps. Local educational institution are not getting students for the higher studies. Moreover,

> the behavior of the primary and high school students has been negatively affected by the Rohingya children as they mix and play frequently with the Rohingya children. (Expert interview conducted in Dhaka in July 2022)

Indeed, the presence of more than one million Rohingyas has greatly affected the education system and facilities in the greater Cox's Bazar region. The local students who drop out for prospective NGO work then become permanent dropouts when the cheaper Rohingya labor makes their income unsustainable. This contributes significantly to the nationwide unemployment problems.

4.5 *Public Goods*

The influx of a large number of refugees into a country can lead to a change in the accessibility of public goods for both the refugee and the host community. The refugee community's tendency to receive a less than optimal level of public goods is linked to their status as refugees and being outside of their country of origin. This limits their rights due to their lack of citizenship, which restricts their freedoms and opportunities (Omata & Sterck, 2020). For the host community, the pressure on the available supply of public goods can be significant when the demand for such goods is high for both the host community and the sizeable refugee population. Such has been the case in Jordan (Alshoubaki & Harris, 2018) and Germany (Thielemann, 2018), with the influx of Syrian refugees following the civil war in Syria that began in 2011. This pressure, created by a large refugee influx, on access to public goods for host and refugee communities has also been observed in Cox's Bazar, Bangladesh. Several government and international programs centered on the supply of public goods to the Rohingya people have closed down due to unsustainable supply and demand. This led to the entry of local organizations to fill the gap left by these programs, which in the end was helpful but limited in alleviating the demand of the Rohingya population. The host community also suffered as a result of rising commodity prices and a general lack of supply of public goods (Gjerløw et al., 2021). If this issue becomes identified by the host community as being linked to the refugee situation, then this can lead to a potential source of conflict in the region.

Our findings show that respondents strongly attribute the diminished supply of public goods, namely food and clothing, to the demand for those goods by the Rohingya refugee population (Fig. 5).

The participants also strongly associated feelings of deprivation on the part of the host community to the relief and aid received by the Rohingya refugee population from agencies, in spite of how these have improved lives in the camps. This finding from the random sampling done on the host population surrounding the Rohingya camps is a crucial indicator that a source of conflict is on the rise with regards to access to public goods. This leads to the access of public goods being a potential source of conflict between the refugee and host community in Cox's Bazar.

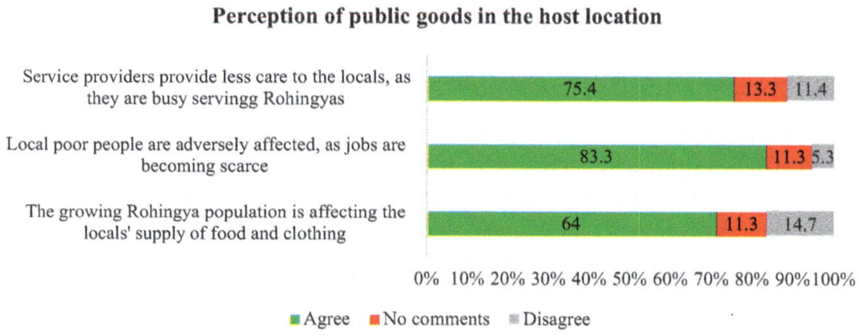

Fig. 5 Sociopolitical conflict: access to public goods. *Source* Developed by authors based on field data

With regards to public goods, the Rohingya focus groups interviewed gave mixed responses. Regarding food and utensils, Rohingya participants expressed their concerns about how short in supply they always seem to be. On the other hand, with regards to clothing supplies and the overall aid and relief programs, Rohingya participants gave positive responses. Participants were more inclined to specifically mention shortages in food supplies than any other factors.

Regarding public goods, an expert working as a journalist and activist in the Cox's Bazar region illustrated how the supply-and-demand issue has negatively affected the local population due to the influx of Rohingyas after the precipitating crisis:

> Initially before the crisis, the host community used to get around 400-500 taka. The women used to get around 300 taka. But because of the sudden influx of labor through the Rohingyas, the price went down drastically. So who is feeling the pinch? It is the host community, because they are not getting the employment nor the labor anymore. A sudden inflation or appreciation by 2 or 3 times led the income of the host community to go further down, while at same time their expenses have gone up. (Expert interview conducted at Dhaka in May 2022)

The increasing population has tremendously affected the supply and demand of public goods in Cox's Bazar. The local people have become the minority and are struggling to manage their families. Their income has been reduced due to heavy competition from the Rohingyas. Subsequently, their purchasing power has been drastically reduced through heavy inflation, putting them in a difficult situation in trying to sustain their families with their reduced wages and livelihood prospects.

4.6 *Gender Issues*

The studies undertaken on this aspect of the social situation on Cox's Bazar point toward the potential for a gender-based dimension to the social conflict between the host and Rohingya community to develop. This study explores this aspect of social conflict by focusing on the perceptions of the host community and how they perceive issues related to sexual harassment of host as well as Rohingya women.

Issues related to gender can arise when refugee populations are hosted by another country due to how vulnerable women can become in such situations. Compared to men, women and children are particularly vulnerable to displacement and situations of humanitarian crisis following a civil war (Hilhorst et al., 2017). With regards to decision-making dynamics in families that remain intact after such humanitarian-crisis-induced displacements, women in particular have little say in making and undertaking major decisions within the household in economic and income-generating activities. Their safety and security, as well as privacy, also become compromised as facilities in refugee camps and settlements are often not up to par with high standards of living, despite large-scale efforts of governments and organizations to assist them (Nyabvudzi & Chinyamurindi, 2020). With regards to incidents of gender-based violence (GBV), women have been very vulnerable, especially in the context of the Rohingya refugee crisis. Reports have shown that GBV affects women and girls disproportionately in both host and Rohingya communities in Cox's Bazar, Bangladesh, with the detrimental social practice of child marriages being prevalent in these two communities (Toma, 2018). Reports of women and child trafficking are widespread in the area, putting Rohingya women and children at a constant risk of being victims of such organized criminal activities (Goodman & Mahmood, 2019). Rohingya women are subjected to sexual violence often, and their opportunities for independence remain limited as refugees.

A particular report on this humanitarian crisis makes an alarming find regarding this aspect of the social situation in Cox's Bazar; domestic violence is seen as an acceptable social norm, and since the crisis it has increased in both communities, due to the difficult environment and the lack of opportunities for productive livelihoods (Toma, 2018). In the Rohingya camps, GBV, trafficking of women, and prostitution have been reported in the local and international media, which underpins a distinct problem for social cohesion and security in the region. This study asked the local respondents about some of these social issues, and a majority of these respondents believed that poverty-stricken Rohingya women are involved in various activities which are of concern for the country (Fig. 6).

The findings were particularly surprising in that the perception of the host community points toward the host population being more responsible for incidents of sexual harassment of Rohingya women than the Rohingya community is for sexual harassment of women from the host community. The difference is slight, but nonetheless significant in showing how sensitive the host community is toward incidents of GBV against women. This aspect of social conflict is thus more dependent on the perception regarding this issue of the Rohingya community in Cox's Bazar. This is because, unlike the other issues discussed above, the gender dimension of social conflict does not show nearly as much conflict potential between the host and the Rohingya community in Cox's Bazar.

On gender issues, the Rohingya population within the focus groups did not hint at a specific community outside of the Rohingya population in the camps. However, many mentioned instances of vulnerable Rohingya women being victims of trafficking in foreign countries. One participant noted,

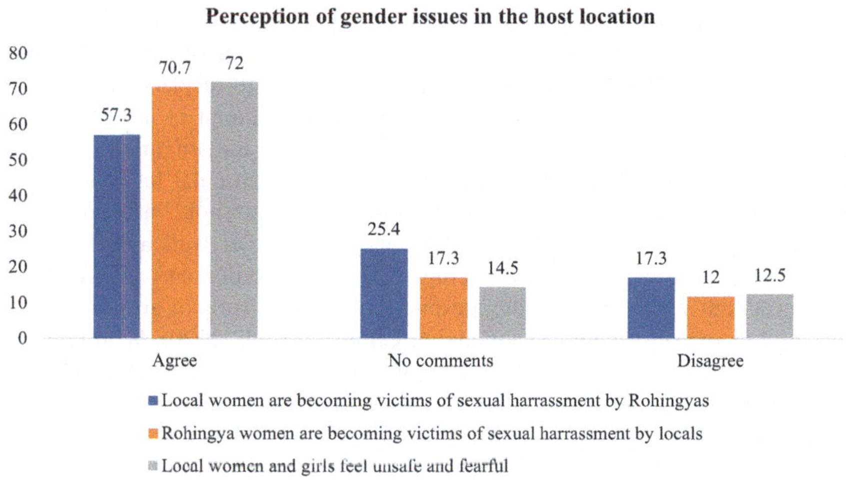

Fig. 6 Sociopolitical conflict: gender issues. Developed by authors based on field data

> Women are being regularly trafficked out of here. Allah knows what happens to them, even though they sometimes go with a smile saying that they are getting good husbands. Some do not seem happy to leave but we do notice many disappearing without a trace and no one really feels safe about these things here. (FGD outcome; FGD conducted in Teknaf in May 2022)

Regarding gender issues, experts have pointed out how women, especially Rohingya women, have been vulnerable to trafficking and involvement with organized criminal groups in the area. The involvement of such organized groups with members from both the Rohingya and the Bengali community has not only led to these women being put in danger—a situation that is now significantly harder to combat due to this "collaboration"—but this also raised concerns for gender issues at the host community level as well. A police officer in Cox's Bazar mentioned that

> Incidents of harassment of Bengali women by Rohingya men have become increasingly more common, and the local population have become increasingly wary around Rohingya camp areas. This growing tension can, as respondents have argued, lead to conflict escalation at significant levels. (Expert interview conducted in Cox's Bazar in June 2022)

As the Rohingyas are living in inhuman conditions, they seek an improvement of their lifestyles outside of their camps, sometimes to the detriment of the local host population. This has led to women from the host society being placed in precarious situations by men from the Rohingya refugee population.

Gender-based violence is also increasing in the camps and host places. The study asked the Jailor of Cox's Bazar about the extent of the GBV, as he works specifically in the field of handling criminals. The Jailor mentioned,

> Most of the Rohingya criminals are accused for Yaba business and harassing their partners. Women are treated as highly inferior and tortured by the husbands. We normally find the case of domestic violence in the form of battery, mental torture, verbal abuse, intimidation,

sexual abuse by relatives and extended family, and abduction, rape and torture. And the rate of the gender-based violence is increasing in number. (Expert interview conducted in Cox's Bazar in June 2022)

The data above point toward how Rohingya men have become heavily involved in committing domestic violence within their own families. The extension of such cases, tied with how the cases also frequently involve the illegal drug trade, indicates that the Rohingya population constitutes a significant security risk for the host community at the expense of Rohingya women in the refugee camps.

4.7 Political Issues

Political pressure is often put upon the refugees and displaced people that take refuge in the host country. The very label they are given, be it refugee or displaced people, or in the case of Bangladesh's Rohingya refugees, Forcefully Displaced Myanmar Nationals (FDMN), has political intent behind it. The government utilizes the label put upon refugees and displaced people to manage them or to restrict certain rights of these populations as it deems necessary for both serving their interests and serving the interests of the host state (Sajjad, 2018). On the other hand, refugees and displaced people in host countries strive to obtain a modicum of the rights that they have lost by their displacement. This is not in the form of direct participation in the political system, as refugees around the globe are usually barred from direct political participation in host states. Instead, protests, diplomacy, and engaging with the media become their method of being connected with external stakeholders (Bekaj & Antara, 2018). If the host population thus sees the political influence of the refugee population as detrimental to their own collective social lives, then there is potential for conflict to manifest. In order to explore the conflict potential in the context of political issues, the local respondents were asked about the involvement of the Rohingya people in the political process, in managing voter ID cards, and in other political activities. A majority of the respondents supported the arguments that the Rohingya people have potential for generating conflict in a political context (Fig. 7).

The findings from the host community indicate that participants overwhelmingly are supportive of the notion that not only is allocating influence to the Rohingya population a threat to the political stability of their locality, but the Rohingya population is using political influence to take over agricultural and forest resources. The majority of the participants also agree that Rohingya refugees are attempting to exert influence (i.e., dominate) local people using a political framework. This signifies that there is a significant conflict potential when the host population's perception of political pressure from refugees is taken into consideration.

As far as political pressure of the host and local populations are concerned, participants among the Rohingya population expressed their concerns over how they are at the receiving end of harmful political pressure from other Rohingya people within the camps. Mentions of the host community population did not come up when answering

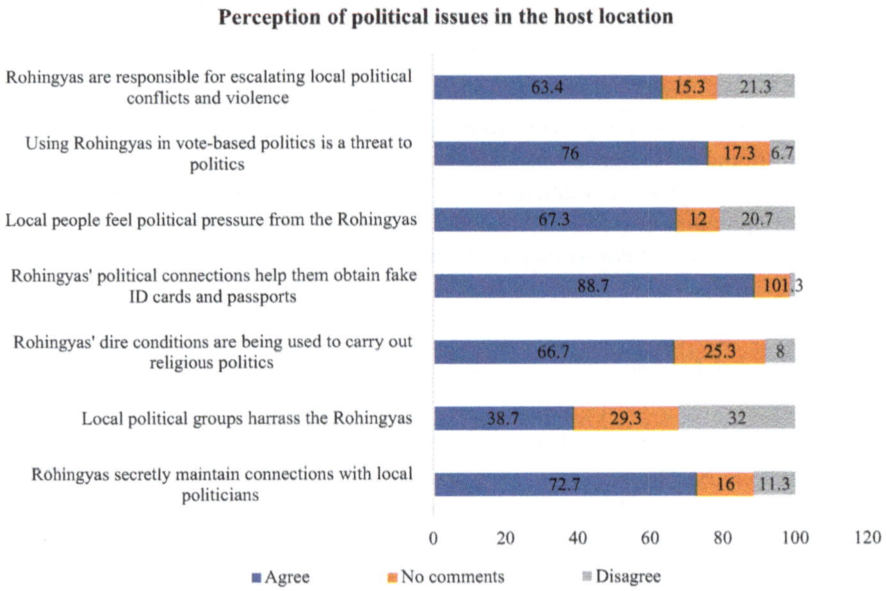

Fig. 7 Sociopolitical conflict: political pressure. *Source* Developed by authors based on field data

questions on whether they are experiencing political pressure from any particular political leader or group. One participant mentioned in this regard,

> There are some people here who prevent us from speaking out loud. We generally do not find much issue with the Bengali people we talk with. But the problems that these (i.e., aforementioned) people are causing is both making us look bad and extorting us for their own gain. (KII conducted in May 2022)

Such findings indicate that the social conflict potential may not be as strong from the side of the Rohingya population as it is from the side of the host population.

Regarding political pressure, a professor of international relations and security expert working on this issue highlighted that although the issue is present and has caused some concern for the overall security and politics of the region, the issue has not escalated significantly yet. He pointed out that

> Whenever there is a refugee community in a host country, the political leaders have tried to take advantage of them, either using them as vote banks, or exploiting them for labor, or using them for criminal activities and such....Such attempts are already being made, but since there is also a law and order situation involved, the government of Bangladesh is heavily employing its security apparatus to keep such issues under control thus far. (Expert interview conducted in March 2022)

The findings from the respondents show that the situation of political destabilization of the Cox's Bazar region—and to some extent, the entire host country of Bangladesh—due to the Rohingya presence is something that is a cause for concern. Moreover, respondents' speculations point to how this can become a major issue in the near future if not kept in check through rigorous measures or if not resolved altogether through the repatriation of the refugees. Another expert highlighted the issues of the young people who might be targeted by extremist groups, which would inevitably complicate the political environment of Bangladesh. The expert said,

> The international community is not rightly addressing the young Rohingya people who are constantly trying to escape this life. The group of people can be targeted by the transnational extremist groups in order to destabilize the region, which may have strong negative impacts in the political arena. Bangladesh may emerge as the hub of terrorist extremism. (Expert interview conducted in Dhaka in June 2022)

Local political parties communicate with Rohingya groups for various purposes. When such micro-level considerations are expanded to the macro-level, there are greater opportunities for these refugee communities to be exploited for political gains. The potential for contributing to conflict in the host place through political exploitation of the Rohingya refugee population is significant among the host population. This can have serious ramifications as Rohingyas become involved with the political activities of the host as a result of such exploitation by special-interest groups.

5 Conclusion

The Rohingya crisis in Bangladesh has had a significant sociopolitical impact on the country, with far-reaching implications for both the Rohingya refugees and the local Bangladeshi population. The crisis has strained social and political structures within the country, creating tensions and challenges that could potentially escalate into conflict. The sociopolitical impact of the crisis has been felt in a variety of ways, including competition for limited resources, discrimination, and violence and complex legal and political challenges. The presence of over one million refugees has created a significant strain on resources and services in Bangladesh, leading to increased competition and tensions between the refugee and host communities. The complex legal and political situation surrounding the crisis has also presented a risk of conflict, with different groups advocating for different approaches to managing the crisis. In fact, one of the most pressing challenges facing Bangladesh is the potential for conflict arising from the crisis. Tensions between the refugee and host communities, as well as the complex legal and political situation surrounding the crisis, present a risk of escalation into violence and unrest. To mitigate this risk, it is critical that the Bangladeshi government and the international community work together to address the root causes of the crisis and promote greater stability and security within the country. To this end, a coordinated and sustained response is needed, focusing on the protection of human rights, the provision of basic services, and the establishment of a sustainable approach to managing the crisis. By prioritizing the needs and rights of both the refugees and the host community, we can help to build a more peaceful and just future for Bangladesh and the region as a whole.

Overall, the sociopolitical impact of the Rohingya crisis in Bangladesh highlights the urgent need for action to address the complex challenges posed by the crisis.

References

Ahmed, H. U. (2022, February 13). Need for holistic growth of Cox's Bazar. *The Financial Express*. https://thefinancialexpress.com.bd/views/views/need-for-holistic-growth-of-coxs-bazar-1644246023

Alshoubaki, W. E., & Harris, M. (2018). The impact of Syrian refugees on Jordan: A framework for analysis. Journal of International Studies, 11(2)

Azad, M. A., Zakaria, M., Nachrin, T., Das, M. C., Cheng, F., & Xu, J. (2021). *Family planning knowledge, attitudes and practices among Rohingya women living in refugee camps in Bangladesh: A cross-sectional study*. Research Square. https://doi.org/10.21203/rs.3.rs-1163154/v1

Babu, K. E. K. (2020). The impacts and challenges to host country Bangladesh due to sheltering the Rohingya refugees. *Cogent Social Sciences, 6*(1), 1770943. https://doi.org/10.1080/23311886.2020.1770943

Bakali, N., & Wasty, S. (2020). Identity, social mobility, and trauma: Post-conflict educational realities for survivors of the Rohingya genocide. *Religions, 11*(5), 241. https://doi.org/10.3390/rel11050241

Bekaj, A., & Antara, L. (2018). *Political participation of refugees: Bridging the gaps*. Robert Bosch Stiftung. https://www.idea.int/sites/default/files/publications/political-participation-of-refugees-bridging-the-gaps.pdf

Biswas, B., Mallick, B., Ahsan, N., & Priodarshini, R. (2022). How does the Rohingya influx influence the residential satisfaction and mobility intentions of the host communities in Bangladesh? *Journal of International Migration and Integration, 23*(3), 1311–1340.

Christou, A. (2018). Introduction: Mapping gendered violence—Contemplating conflict and crisis in contemporary societal struggles. *Frontiers: A Journal of Women Studies, 39*(2), vii–xii. https://doi.org/10.5250/fronjwomestud.39.2.0vii

Faruque, A. S., Khan, A. I., Islam, S. M., Nahar, B., Hossain, M. N., Widiati, Y., Hasan, A. M., Prajapati, M., Kim, M., Vandenent, M., & Ahmed, T. (2021). Diarrhea treatment center (DTC) based diarrheal disease surveillance in settlements in the wake of the mass influx of forcibly displaced Myanmar national (FDMN) in Cox's Bazar, Bangladesh, 2018. *PLOS One, 16*(8), e0254473. https://doi.org/10.1371/journal.pone.0254473

Figlio, D., & Özek, U. (2019). Unwelcome guests? The effects of refugees on the educational outcomes of incumbent students. *Journal of Labor Economics, 37*(4), 1061–1096. https://doi.org/10.1086/703116

Garry, S., & Checchi, F. (2019). Armed conflict and public health: Into the 21st century. *Journal of Public Health, 42*(3), e287–e298. https://doi.org/10.1093/pubmed/fdz095

Goodman, A., & Mahmood, I. (2019). The Rohingya refugee crisis of Bangladesh: Gender based violence and the humanitarian response. *Open Journal of Political Science, 9*, 490–501. https://doi.org/10.4236/ojps.2019.93027

Gjerløw, H., Karim, S., & Østby, G. (2021). When governments and international organizations shut down: The impact of COVID-19 on refugees' and host community's use of educational services in cox's bazar. In Frontiers in Education (Vol. 6, p. 696176). Frontiers Media SA.

Hilhorst, D., Porter, H., & Gordon, R. (2017). Gender, sexuality, and violence in humanitarian crises. *Disasters, 42*(S1), S3–S16. https://doi.org/10.1111/disa.12276

Islam, M. R., & Wara, U. (2022). Conflict potential of the Rohingya people in Bangladesh and beyond. *Journal of Asean Studies, 10*(1), 107–127. https://doi.org/10.21512/jas.v10i1.8215

Islam, M. R., Islam, M. T., Alam, M. S., Hussain, M., & Haque, M. M. (2022). An assessment of the sustainability of living for Rohingya displaced people in cox's bazar camps in Bangladesh. *Journal of Human Rights and Social Work, 7*(3), 331–345.

Jacques, M. (2012). *Armed conflict and displacement: The protection of refugees and displaced persons under international humanitarian law*. Cambridge University Press.

Janmyr, M. (2021). Non-signatory states and the international refugee regime. *Forced Migration Review, 67*, 39–42. https://ora.ox.ac.uk/objects/uuid:75a26b3a-59b7-4c8d-bd9b-c225b3b4dd3e/files/scf95jc82s

Khan, M. N., Rahman, M. M., Rahman, M. M., & Islam, M. M. (2021). HIV transmission knowledge among Rohingya refugee women in Bangladesh: A cross-sectional survey. *British Medical Journal Open, 11*(10), e047516. https://doi.org/10.1136/bmjopen-2020-047516

Kirschnera, S. A., & Finaret, A. B. (2021). Conflict and health: Building on the role of infrastructure. *World Development, 146*, 105570. https://doi.org/10.1016/j.worlddev.2021.105570

Kyaw, N. N. (2017). Unpacking the presumed statelessness of Rohingyas. *Journal of Immigrant and Refugee Studies, 15*(3), 269–286. https://doi.org/10.1080/15562948.2017.1330981

Milton, A. H., Rahman, M., Hussain, S., Jindal, C., Choudhury, S., Akter, S., Ferdousi, S., Mouly, T. A., Hall, J., & Efird, J. T. (2017). Trapped in statelessness: Rohingya refugees in Bangladesh. *International Journal of Environmental Research and Public Health, 14*(8), 942. https://doi.org/10.3390/ijerph14080942

Murshid, N. (2013). *The politics of refugees in South Asia: Identity, resistance, manipulation*. Routledge.

Nyabvudzi, T. G., & Chinyamurindi, W. T. (2020). Career development barriers in the post-settlement phase amongst women refugees: Implications for human capital development. *Gender Questions, 8*(1), 1–26. https://hdl.handle.net/10520/EJC-1e3e68e63c

Omata, A. B., & Sterck, O. (2020). The Kalobeyei Settlement: A self-reliance model for refugees? *Journal of Refugee Studies, 33*(1), 189–223. https://doi.org/10.1093/jrs/fez063

Parajuli, K. R. (2020). Rethinking population policies from family planning to population management. *Rupantaran: A Multidisciplinary Journal, 3*, 51–61. https://doi.org/10.3126/rupantaran.v3i0.31741

Pherali, T. (2019). Education and conflict: Emergence, growth and diversification of the field. *Education and Conflict Review, 2*, 7–14. https://discovery.ucl.ac.uk/id/eprint/10081478/.

Rahman, M. R., Faiz, M. A., Nu, M. Y., Hassan, M. R., Chakrabarty, A. K., Kabir, I., Islam, K., Jafarullah, A. K. M., Alakabawy, M., Khatami, A., & Rashid, H. (2020). A rapid assessment of health literacy and health status of Rohingya refugees living in Cox's Bazar, Bangladesh following the August 2017 exodus from Myanmar: A cross-sectional study. *Tropical Medicine and Infectious Disease, 5*(3), 110. https://doi.org/10.3390/tropicalmed5030110

Sajjad, T. (2018). What's in a name? 'Refugees', 'migrants' and the politics of labelling. *Race & Class, 60*(2), 40–62. https://doi.org/10.1177/0306396818793582

Summers, A., Humphreys, A., Leidman, E., Mil, L. T., Wilkinson, C., Narayan, A., Miah, M. L., Cramer, B. G., & Bilukha, O. (2018). Notes from the field: Diarrhea and acute respiratory infection, oral cholera vaccination coverage, and care-seeking behaviors of Rohingya refugees—Cox's Bazar, Bangladesh, October–November 2017. *Morbidity and Mortality Weekly Report, 67*(18), 533–535. https://doi.org/10.15585/mmwr.mm6718a6

Thielemann, E. (2018). Why refugee burden-sharing initiatives fail: Public goods, free-riding and symbolic solidarity in the EU. *Journal of Common Market Studies, 56*(1), 63–82. https://doi.org/10.1111/jcms.12662

Toma, I. A. (2018). *Rohingya refugee response: Gender analysis*. Oxfam. Retrieved August 28, 20203, from https://oxfamilibrary.openrepository.com/bitstream/handle/10546/620528/rr-rohingya-refugee-response-gender-analysis-010818-en.pdf?sequence=1&isAllowed=y

Whitt, S. (2021). Ethnic trust, minority status, and public goods in post-conflict societies. *Journal of Peace Research, 58*(6), Sam Whitt. https://doi.org/10.1177/0022343320984211.

Yasmin, L., & Akther, S. (2019). The locals and the Rohingyas: Trapped with an uncertain future. *Asian Journal of Comparative Politics, 5*(2), 104–120. https://doi.org/10.1177/2057891119865021

Chapter 8
The Rohingya Crisis: Its Geopolitical Context and Security Ramifications

Mahfuzur Rahman

Abstract The Rohingya crisis cannot be properly comprehended without a thorough understanding of the perennial military rule and associated power structures present in Myanmar and the way these structures led to the massive clearing operation against Rohingya civilians in 2017 in Rakhine State. An in-depth analysis of these structures and their historical bases is offered by way of providing a contextual understanding of the current geopolitical situation in Southeast Asia. Though the region's political sphere includes such regional powers as China and India, as well as relational maneuvering between Myanmar and Bangladesh, the scope of the crisis is such that it has substantial implications for all of these parties. The sources of these implications are discussed, along with their various forms, before a brief sketch of possible futures and hoped-for solutions.

1 Historical Perspective

It is important to understand the historical connotations of the Rohingya issue; otherwise, one can be swayed by various narratives. Arakan (now Rakhine) was detached from the Irrawaddy Valley (central Burma) due to the presence of hills (Arakan Yama), jungle terrain, and poor communication infrastructure and was politically independent or self-ruled for most of its history (Bahar, 2010). Commercially and socially, the region was more connected with the southeast of Bengal (present-day Bangladesh). When the Pagan Kingdom was established around 800 CE, it was powerful enough to push east and west of the Irrawaddy Valley (Aung-Thwin, 1986). During this period, the Rakhine people crossed into Arakan and settled there (Gutman, 2001). The kingdom collapsed after a Mongol invasion in 1286, and Arakan broke away from Burma as the region became fragmented. However, in the 1750s, the Burmese Kingdom again acquired strength and became a powerful kingdom. In the process, it conquered Arakan in 1784 (Ibrahim, 2016, p. 5). "It has been estimated that around 30,000 Muslims fled Arakan during the brief forty years of Burmese

M. Rahman (✉)
Dhaka, Bangladesh
e-mail: mahfuzba2172@gmail.com

K. Ahmed and Md. R. Islam (eds.), *Understanding the Rohingya Displacement*,
International Perspectives on Migration, https://doi.org/10.1007/978-981-97-1424-7_8

rule." Meanwhile, this annexation of Arakan brought Burmese rule to the border of British India. Eventually, in 1826, after the first Anglo-Burmese War, Arakan was annexed by the British, and by 1886, the whole of Burma came under British India (Ibrahim, 2016). In 1937, it was made a full colony in its own right (on the basis of the pre-1824 borders), and it became independent in that particular geographical form in 1948 (Ibrahim, 2016).

From the thirteenth to the end of the seventeenth centuries, there were periods of Burmese dominance, periods when Arakan was independent, and even when regional kings were powerful enough to conquer part of modern-day Bangladesh (Ibrahim, 2016). During the rule of the Mrauk-U dynasty, Arakan experienced the confluence of multicultural and multi-ethnoreligious groups of people (Ibrahim, 2016). The Afghan Muslims, known as "Kaman," arrived in the 1660s as recruited mercenaries of the Arakan Kingdom and, over time, settled there (ÇAKMAK, 2022). They have been accepted as one of the official ethnic groups in Myanmar. However, the Rohingyas, who have lived in Arakan since 1000 CE, have not been recognized as an official ethnic group. The Myanmar establishment's narrative holds that this group of people arrived in Burma during British rule and even as late as the War of Liberation of Bangladesh in 1971 (Steinberg, 2021). Nonetheless, multiple nineteenth-century British reports recorded the name of local Muslims as "Rooinga" (Ibrahim, 2016). As Ibrahim (2016) records, "Francis Buchanan suggested in 1799 that there were two groups of communities native to Arakan, one who called themselves 'Rooinga' and Muslims, and the other is 'Rakhing,' who are Buddhists" (p. 24). Yet Kaplan (2010) observes that "the Rohingyas were part of a beautiful hybrid Buddhist Hindu-Muslim civilization in Arakan where the influence of Persia and India cross-hatched with those of Siam and the rest of Southeast Asia" (p. 179). Islam (2022) explains in his book that the Arab Muslims first came into contact with Arakan through trade and commerce during the eighth century CE, and some of them settled in Arakan villages. Islam (2022) also confirms that Rohingyas have been living in Arakan for more than 1000 years. The famous historic mosque built in 1433 at Kawalon, named "Sandi Khan Mosque," was demolished by the Myanmar military in September 1996 under the orders of former Prime Minister General Khin Nyunt (Islam, 2022). These are only some of the references that suggest the Muslims have been residing in Arakan (Rakhine) for a considerable period of time throughout history. Burmese authorities may term them Bengali (or Kalar; that is, black), but the greater community of Muslims living in Rakhine call themselves Rohingya.

Rohingyas have long been part of Rakhine society and have contributed to economics as well as the social and political life of Myanmar. They have been members of Parliament and ministers (Islam, 2022). The first parliamentary government of Myanmar (1948–1962) officially declared Rohingya as one of the indigenous ethnic groups of Burma. The declaration made by then-Prime Minister U Nu reads: "The people living in Maungdaw and Buthidaung regions are our national brethren. They are called Rohingyas. They are on the same level of nationality as Kachin, Karen, Mon, Rakhine, and Shan. They are one of the ethnic races of Burma" (Radio speech by prime minister U Nu, September 25, 1954, at 8:00 p.m.). In the failure of people's collective memory, they forget how dangerous the distortion of history is and that they distort history at their own peril.

However, from time to time, Rohingyas faced organized massacres that are sometimes called Rohingya Pogroms; the most notable ones were in the 1780s (1784), 1940s, 1978, 1991–92, 2012, 2016, and 2017 (Saber, 2022). Recently, the persecution took on an institutional shape when Rohingyas were denied citizenship under the 1982 Myanmar Citizenship Act. The 2017 pogrom on Rohingyas by the Burmese Military has been viewed as a textbook example of ethnic cleansing by the UN (Samad, 2023). Rohingyas have also been identified by this organization as the most persecuted minority group in the world (Blackmore, 2019). The genocide of 2017 compelled about a million Rohingyas to flee their homes to seek refuge in neighboring Bangladesh. This has been termed a genocide as well as a crime against humanity by the US ("Myanmar Rohingya Violence Is Genocide, US Says," 2022). The Rohingya refugee population has become a challenge for Bangladesh and the world community and has taken the shape of a global crisis. This chapter will highlight the actors who are responsible for the crisis that precipitated in August 2017 and consider how this event was orchestrated to such a magnitude. The study also focuses on the geopolitical context as well as relevant security ramifications. Finally, a way forward will be suggested at the conclusion.

2 The Actors Responsible for the Crisis of August 2017[1]

Senior General Min Aung Hlaing. He is a Bamar (the majority ethnic group in Myanmar) who grew up in the military with mediocre performance but became known as a tenacious, composed soldier and a pursuer of lofty aims. His personality has been described as egoistical ("Myanmar Spirit," 2018). He enjoys immense power granted by the 2008 constitution (orchestrated by the military) to the extent that he actually granted himself a five-year extension, which would have expired in 2021. After becoming commander-in-chief of the Defense Services in 2011, he said, "We have an unfinished job to be done" (Rahman, 2021a, 2021b). Following this, a heightened persecution of Rohingyas in Myanmar was observed. After the ethnic cleansing of the Rohingya from Rakhine in 2017, when the West and the world community were pursuing repatriation of the Rohingya, his comment to the media was, "There are no options to bring them back" (Rahman, 2021a, 2021b). This powerful man in Myanmar leads a military organization—possibly more than just the armed forces—called the Tatmadaw.

The Tatmadaw. Directly or indirectly, the Tatmadaw has ruled Myanmar for seven decades (Myoe, 2014). A military under a military over time turns into a monster, and the Tatmadaw is no exception. It is a meritocratic organization with immense institutional strength, possibly the only institution that outshines all others in the country. When a monstrous organization is combined with a meritocracy, the mix is very dangerous. They maintain huge business interests, control the economy to a great extent, and look after the ministries of the Interior, Defense and Security, and Immigration (i.e., the border), having influence also in external ministries. The constitution allocates 25% of seats in Myanmar's parliament to the military, besides their supported political party. The National Defense and Security Council is the highest executive body in the country and has the power to dissolve the parliament if situation demands; this council is led by a military majority. Myanmar's generals were canny in the way they handled the Rohingya issue and took both the regional powers on their side as well as two permanent members of the UN Security Council (UNSC), so that UNSC could not condemn the crackdown on the Rohingya. Their manipulation of geopolitics and geostrategy is praiseworthy. As Kaplan (2010) suggests, "China, India, and other Asian nations are jockeying for position with one of the world's worst, weirdest, wealthiest, and most strategically placed rogue regimes" (p. 257). When someone is sitting across the table from a Tatmadaw general, he is not sitting across from a mere security official but also an intellectual, a diplomat, a businessman, a politician, and a leader of a meritocratic organization (all in one) who has institutional knowledge of having run the country for several decades. They talk less and listen more, and their expressions seldom reveal their conclusions. In the case of the Rohingya issue, one needs to understand that they are dealing with a smart set of cunning professionals.

Aung San Suu Kyi. She became world-famous for leading campaigns for the restoration of democracy in the'90s. She spent almost 15 years under house arrest between 1987 and 2010 and was awarded the Nobel Peace Prize in 1991. In the 2015 election, her party, the National League for Democracy (NLD), was victorious for the first time in 25 years in a contested election in Myanmar. She fell from grace when she failed to condemn the military atrocities against the Rohingyas in August 2017. Her background and connection with the West and her apparent heroism in fighting for democracy and peace influenced the West to put her on a high pedestal. It may be suggested that she is just a racist, power-hungry politician, and the rationales are as follows:

(i) In 2013, BBC presenter Mishal Husain interviewed Suu Kyi, pressing her with questions about political challenges she was not handling well and specifically mentioning the Rohingya persecution issue. Suu Kyi came up with her baffling "Both sides in fear" stance and became defensive, and she rarely fared worse in public than in her interview with Husain. After the interview, Suu Kyi did not realize that the microphone was on and expressed her anger to an aide: "No one told me I was going to be interviewed by a Muslim" (Fisher, 2016). This is not the attitude of a mother of democracy, an icon of humanity, or a bona fide Nobel laureate on peace. This is purely racist. Afflicted by Bamar supremacy, she showed no sympathy toward the Rohingyas. However, she may be a smart politician, but Tatmadaw is smarter. At the end, she failed to recognize the "no-go areas" of the Tatmadaw.

(ii) In 2014, members of England's Royal College of Defence Studies went to listen to her talk at Sandhurst Military Academy, UK. After her address, a Bangladeshi participant, Captain Mohammad Musa, asked her position on the persecution of minorities in her country—specifically Rohingyas. She answered that "both the majority and the minority are in fear," and this situation is a ramification of fear, so she has no comments about it (Md. Musa, personal communication, May 22, 2023). This "both in fear" arithmetic is not difficult to understand. She is just a politician, and the election was coming up in 2015; she could not afford to annoy her majority or the Tatmadaw by speaking in support of the Rohingyas.

(iii) In December 2019, she went to The Hague's International Court of Justice (ICJ) to defend Tatmadaw against allegations of genocide and ethnic cleansing. Her decision to attend the ICJ had won her huge popularity back home. There were billboards in every corner of Myanmar with Suu Kyi in front and the Tatmadaw generals' pictures behind her, and the caption read, "We are with you" (Rahman, 2021a, 2021b). She was ready to compromise her fame as a hero of democracy and peace in favor of power-hungry politics. An election was again upcoming in 2020. In that ICJ courtroom, the present author was sitting some 20 feet away from her. She was calm and indifferent to the evidence of genocide displayed by the Gambian side. When a Gambian lawyer showed pictures of genocide at "Inn Din" village (no less terrible than Mai Lai of Vietnam) on the screen in which kneeling Rohingya men were grouped together in one picture and all were beheaded in the next, it touched almost everyone in the courtroom. Some Rohingya widows were in the courtroom too, their sobbing adding to the somber atmosphere of the room, but it was clear that Suu Kyi, the so-called "mother of democracy and peace," was unmoved. She was wearing a smile of indifference on her face.

3 How Was the Rohingya Massacre of 2017 Orchestrated?[2]

In answering this, it is very pertinent to discuss Myanmar's strategic culture in relation to the Rohingyas. Here, an attempt has been made to analyze their strategic culture from the viewpoint of Jack Snyder and Colin Grey (who brought this vocabulary into the security lexicon) (Gray, 1999; Neumann & Heikka, 2005).

Myanmar Strategic Culture constitute (Selth, 2021) of their (*national strategic community, dominant elite in polity*) shared belief (*Rohingyas are non-ethnic to Myanmar*), their assumptions (*Rohingyas have migrated in recent past*), and modes of behavior (*hostile to Rohingyas*) derived from common experiences (*growth rate of Rohingya population is high and inter-marriages with ethnic locals are on the rise*) and accepted narratives (*there will be Islamization from the western border*) that shapes collective identity (*collective security anxiety*) in relationship to other groups (*Rohingyas*) and which determines their appropriate end (*goal*), ways (*method of military operations*) and means (*resources in the hands of government: military*) for achieving security objectives (*Myanmar free of Rohingyas*). Now, let us examine some facts about the orchestration of the 2017 Rohingya genocide. In doing this, a few dots would be put at the discretion of the readers to connect.

In 2011, Senior General Min Aung Hlaing took over as Myanmar's Chief of Defense. In one of his strategic directives, he categorically mentioned that "there is an unfinished job." Following his takeover, it was observed that hate speeches against Rohingyas intensified. Myanmar's media started demonizing the Rohingyas and building aggressive public opinion that Rohingyas are basically Bengali and have migrated to Rakhine State in the recent past. Some militant Buddhist monks under the leadership of Ashin Wirathu and his anti-Muslim 969 Movement kindled further upheaval (Islam, 2022) by professing that in future there would be an Islamization of Myanmar from the west (Rakhine/Bangladesh).

In 2014, a group of senior Bangladeshi military officers attended an international strategic-level course in Beijing. In one of the discussions, a very senior Chinese general asked one of the course participants about the importance of the Rohingya in Bangladesh's domestic politics. The Chinese general wanted to know whether, if a serious situation developed, Bangladesh was determined enough to enter into armed conflict with its neighbors on the Rohingya issue (participant officer's personal communication, October 28, 2017).

In 2013/14, a Myanmar–China gas pipeline was commissioned from Kyaukphyu (Sittwe, a Rohingya-dominated area in Rakhine) to Kunming (China). China has spent a lot of resources and effort on this project. Energy is the "center of gravity" for China. Energy security is very important for rising China. There was a similar situation with the Yadana gas pipeline from offshore Myanmar in the south overland to Thailand (Bulletin 36, 2000). In that episode, thousands of Karens were tortured and expelled by the Myanmar military from around the gas pipeline—either internally displaced or compelled to take shelter in refugee camps in Thailand (Human Rights Watch, 2007). Along with the gas pipeline, a multi-billion-dollar oil pipeline project in Rakhine was under construction and completed in 2014/15 and is awaiting commission.

In 2016, in the name of a "clearing operation" in the hills of Rakhine, Myanmar Security Forces carried out various brutalities against Rohingya civilians, and around 90,000 Rohingyas took shelter in Bangladesh (Behrens & Henham, 2013). In retrospect, we understand that this was a preliminary operation to observe the global reaction and study the pulse of world bodies (and specifically Bangladesh) prior to the broader 2017 Rohingya atrocities.

In May 2017, the oil pipeline was commissioned (running parallel to the gas pipeline), considered the more important of the two pipelines. In July 2017, information reached the Bangladeshi intelligence community that a military buildup was in process in Rakhine State. Bangladesh's security concerns were expressed to their Myanmar intelligence counterpart (Defense Attaché Brigadier General Aung Zaw Ooa at the Myanmar Embassy, Dhaka). The 2016 incident was also mentioned, particularly how, in the name of a clearing operation, Rohingya civilians were targeted, and there was an influx of refugees. However, the Myanmar counterparts confirmed that there would be a security forces operation on Mayu Range against insurgents and dissident groups in the second week of August 2017. It was explicitly stated that this had nothing to do with civilians and there would be no repetitions of the 2016 situation (Ooa, personal communication, August, 2017).

In June 2017 and July 2017, Senior General Min Aung Hlaing visited Russia and India, respectively, and met with strategic leaders for discussions.

Myanmar's military buildup was completed by the third week of August 2017. The Kofi Annan Commission Report, charged the previous year with recommending solutions for the unrest in Rakhine State, was published on August 24, 2017 ("Kofi Annan Foundation," n.d.). A number of issues relating to the Rohingyas were addressed in the report. This was what the Rohingyas had been waiting decades for—finally, their civil and political rights might be recognized. Despite this positive development, Myanmar claimed that the Arakan Rohingya Salvation Army (ARSA) carried out attacks at over 30 security forces camps simultaneously in the early morning of August 25, 2017, in which some members of their security forces were killed. (Wade, 2017) Following this, Myanmar's forces—who were already concentrated there—carried out a massive ethnic cleansing operation against Rohingya civilians in the name of an operation against Islamist terrorists. There are four questions about this so-called ARSA attack that raise serious doubt as to the official explanation:

(i) ARSA did not attack thinly held and less equipped Myanmar Security Forces camps held by paramilitary forces, but ostensibly waited to attack Myanmar Security Forces camps until their full buildup had been completed with regular forces.
(ii) ARSA allegedly waged its attack against these well-prepared camps, augmented by regular forces, with only machetes and locally made guns (ARSA weapons were exhibited by Myanmar Security Forces in the media).
(iii) Myanmar claimed they suffered a number of casualties. However, there was never a military funeral service after this announcement. In April 2021, a Karen group killed and injured some members of the Myanmar Security Forces at the Thailand border, and the Myanmar media reported on the customary military funeral ceremony.
(iv) ARSA conducted its attack in the very early morning of August 25, 2017, and Myanmar's military conducted their large-scale coordinated operation in the morning of August 25, 2017 (in the military, such a large-scale operation takes quite some time for planning, preparation, and logistics buildup). After this so-called ARSA attack on the morning of August 25, Myanmar was very quick to come on record, saying that since the situation is unstable in Rakhine, the recommendations of the Kofi Annan Report now cannot be followed. At the same time, they convened a national committee, co-opting some members of ASEAN to prepare their own report.

In the first week of September 2017, Prime Minister Modi of India visited Myanmar. He spoke of his appreciation to Myanmar for the measures taken toward peace and national reconciliation. He also expressed concern about various incidents of terrorism and extremist-inspired violence (Pulipaka et al., 2017).

In November 2017, Senior General Min Aung Hlaing visited China. During discussions with President Xi Jinping, the general thanked China for standing at the forefront of Myanmar's side on the Rakhine issue (i.e., the Rohingya issue).

Discussing historical events is important for learning lessons, but equally important is anticipating what is coming next. Senior General Min Aung Hlaing reiterated in an international media interview in May 2021 that there is no option for taking back the Rohingyas ("Myanmar Junta Leader," 2021). Meanwhile, the NLD (Aung Sun Suu Kyi's Party)-led National Unity Government (NUG) continues to express that once democracy is restored and they are back in power, they are willing to absorb the Rohingyas into their society and even take legal action on the atrocities committed against the Rohingyas. This is a positive gesture, but one has to remember that the NUG is offering this under certain circumstances and in exchange for support from Muslim countries as well as the egalitarian community of the world.

It should be remembered who is calling the shots in Myanmar. The understanding is that, as long as the two permanent members of the UN Security Council support the military junta in Myanmar, it will remain in power there. A case in point is Bashar al-Assad in Syria. We can foresee an unfolding of events when the dust settles in Myanmar and the junta is stable, whereby the remaining Rohingyas (possibly 400–600,000 people) in Myanmar, especially in Rakhine State, could be expelled in due course.

4 Geopolitical Context

In this part of the world, big power relationships and regional power rivalries dominate geopolitics, and this has ramifications for many world events. A brief example is found in the headline "Indian Ocean relationship between US and China in the Pacific interlocks with the regional rivalry between China and India" (Kaplan, 2010, p. 21).

Both India and China are energy-hungry powers for whom energy security plays a key role. In particular, China's energy security is their central focus for economic development. China needs Myanmar as a vassal state for its energy security, for the oil and gas pipelines where it has spent billions of dollars in energy infrastructure, essentially to avoid the Malacca Strait and the precarious South China Sea (Church, 2017). India also invested almost a billion dollars in the Kaladan Multi-Modal Transit Transport Project, which is strategic for its connectivity to the eastern states through the Bay of Bengal and Myanmar (Pattanaik, 2018). India, including her allies, does not want Myanmar to totally fall into the fold of China, for clear geostrategic reasons.

In the Indian Ocean region, China is vertically expanding and India is horizontally expanding (Kaplan, 2010). This is a kind of geopolitical and geostrategic "Tectonic Plate" movement in different directions, causing geopolitical and geostrategic tremors, in which Bangladesh is trying to balance its relationship with all. This has caused it to be a kind of buffer state that has built-in side effects. Besides, it is easier to tame smaller countries with security anxiety, instability, and the absence or deficiency of democracy, and Bangladesh is no exception. For the Indo-Pacific idea and appearance of Quad (the Quadrilateral Security Dialogue between Australia, India, Japan, and the US), the presence of China in the Indian Ocean and the issue of containing China could create a tense situation even in the Bay of Bengal. Here, issues like the Rohingya crisis have seemingly been sucked into the vortex of global and regional geopolitics, where finding a solution could be complex. It is already being linked to the global and regional geopolitical landscape.

On the global stage, China and Russia have sided with Myanmar on the Rohingya issue, whereas the West has a different position. At a regional level, both China and India have taken the side of Myanmar that is also for geostrategic purposes. However, the future may turn out differently, as the junta in Myanmar seems more and more likely to enter the fold of China due to international pressure. At the local level, the dynamics are a little different. The National Unity Government (NUG) (after the military coup in Myanmar in February 2021, Aung San Suu Kyi's party gathered all dissident ethnic organizations together to form NUG) would like to resolve the Rohingya issue at the union level under present circumstances. However, the United League of Arakan (ULA) and the Arakan Army (an armed ethnic organization in the Rakhine State of Myanmar; the ULA is the political wing of the AA) practice internal politics that are not so welcoming to the idea of Rohingya repatriation (Lintner, 2019). AA, though quite powerful and controlling 60–70% of Rakhine (where ultimately the Rohingyas will return), relies on China as their source of power. So the repatriation of the Rohingyas does not depend entirely on AA alone. Lately, some drama has occurred regarding the repatriation initiative with Chinese mediation. China wants to show Bangladesh who is calling the shots. If Bangladesh wants to resolve the Rohingya refugee issue, it would be difficult without China. In the big picture, by tilting more toward India, Bangladesh is likely to face an arm twist with the Rohingya repatriation issue.

5 Security Ramifications of the Conflict: An Analysis[3]

In the southeastern part of Bangladesh, bordering India and Myanmar, where the Rohingya refugees are staying, there are perfect geophysical conditions for insurgency. The insurgents and separatists can melt away quickly, while it is a nightmare for regular forces. Though India claims to have a peace deal with separatist groups in Mizoram and Tripura states, having borders with the Chittagong Hill Tracks (CHT) of Bangladesh means it is not all that peaceful. There are movements by separatist groups. The same holds true in the case of Bangladesh. Though a peace deal has been in place in the CHT since December'97 with the insurgent groups, there are now four political groups whose armed wings are active. In the Chin and Rakhine states of Myanmar bordering Bangladesh, there are ethnic armed groups like the Chin National Army and the Arakan Army (AA). A peace deal was signed in Myanmar too, but now AA has become enormously powerful, causing serious headaches for the junta (Rahman, 2022). Then, there are other complex issues; for example, there are differences between the central government and outlying states on particular issues in the case of India. On some issues, there is organizational inertia, and the outlook of "intelligence organizations" may not fully tally with the center or the states. In the case of Myanmar, the situation is a little different. The AA runs a parallel administration in most parts of Rakhine, whereas the junta mostly controls the cities. Having relations with one may antagonize the other. Add to this conundrum, the Arakan Rohingya Salvation Army, an armed Rohingya Islamist group, which the Myanmar junta claims, is destabilizing Rakhine. About the Rohingya repatriation issue, Myanmar's Chief of Defense, General Min Aung Hlaing, and the Arakan Army Chief at Rakhine, Major General Tun Myat Naing, have opposing and dubious viewpoints. Above all, there is the geopolitics of regional and global powers. So how Bangladesh should navigate in this murky water is a complex question.

What is obvious now is a complicated combination of risks. Bandarban (located in the southeast adjacent to the Rohingya camps) is the only district of Bangladesh that has a border with two countries (India and Myanmar). This is also possibly the only district where drugs (opium and marijuana) are cultivated, with the cooperation of exotic groups operating there. Teknaf (close to the Rohingya refugee camps) is the transit hub for drugs. Drugs are the mother of all other evils, like arms smuggling and human trafficking (Rohingya refugees are a readily available target group). Of late, Rohingya involvement in drug proliferation and related violence has greatly increased. There is a potential that this community may be sucked into "Narco Terrorism" in future if this situation is not addressed. In addition, there is the specter of violent extremism and terrorism. However, these kinds of non-traditional security issues do not take place in a vacuum. Interestingly, they have the potential to destabilize bilateral relations with neighbors and turn into more traditional security concerns. Separatist and exotic groups themselves are sources of non-traditional security threats.

The traditional and non-traditional threats to Bangladesh emanating from the security environment in the southeast are fairly easy to comprehend, and as such, various agencies are preparing for the future to avoid being surprised. It can be said they are preparing based on what is happening now, possibly not what is lurking around the corner. When the Islamic States of Iraq and the Levant (ISIL) surfaced in the Middle East, the foreign fighters became a headache not only to the West but almost to the entire world. The question is, how many of them were there? Maybe 10,000, 20,000, or 30,000 created havoc, but they mostly came from a pretty decent background. They or their families did not suffer; they experienced only feelings of injustice before adventurism drew them there, and the world has experienced what monsters they became. Now, we need to fathom that there are more than 400,000 children growing up in the Rohingya camps inside Bangladesh without proper education, hopes, or dreams. They have seen horrors all their lives. In 2017, many of them saw their mothers being violated; for them, there is no rock bottom. By 2030, most of them will be adults. Homeless, with trauma in their minds and hatred in their hearts, and without proper education, hopes, and dreams, it is unthinkable what monsters they might turn into if they are exploited and if this issue is not addressed. There are two options: We can address it now or wait for it to be addressed later when it turns into a full-blown security situation. The choice is with us and the global community. Students of security studies would understand that it is coming, and it is not going to affect Bangladesh alone. It will have regional and global ramifications. It is going to be too much of a burden for Bangladesh to handle in a situation where it is just a victim of geopolitical circumstances.

6 The Way Forward

The Rohingya issue cannot be reconstructed on a bilateral basis. It has to be considered on a global basis. This is a political problem created by Myanmar, and it has been militarily perpetrated by the junta. Bangladesh is not a party to it; she is just a prisoner of geography. It is recommended that the Rohingya issue be addressed in three tiers within the ambit of global governance and international legal frameworks and principles to arrive at a political solution. At a regional level, the involvement of regional organizations (i.e., ASEAN, BIMSTEC) would provide dividends far out of proportion to the effort expended. The involvement of China, India, Japan, and Korea (all major investment partners of Myanmar) could be instrumental. At the bilateral level, Dhaka should maintain engagement with Naypyidaw, however traumatic it may be. Meanwhile, for sustainable peace in this part of the world, addressing non-traditional security concerns (i.e., drug trafficking, arms smuggling, and human trafficking) should also be addressed simultaneously. Since they are transnational phenomena, a single-country solution will fall far short of the desired result. India, Bangladesh, and Myanmar must work together to address it.

Notes

1. Material in this section originally appeared in an article by the author in Bangladesh's *Daily Sun*. See Rahman, Md. M. (2021, May 12). Myanmar coup and Bangladesh perspective. *Daily Sun*. https://www.daily-sun.com/post/552356/Myanmar-Coup-and-Bangladesh-Perspective. ↑
2. Material in this section originally appeared in an article by the author in Bangladesh's *The Daily Star*. See Rahman, Md. M. (2021, July 7). Rohingya refugee crisis: putting the pieces of the puzzle together. *The Daily Star*. https://www.thedailystar.net/views/opinion/news/rohingya-refugee-crisis-putting-the-pieces-the-puzzle-together-2124331. ↑
3. Material in this section originally appeared in an article by the author in Bangladesh's *The Daily Star*. See Rahman, Md. M. (2022, March 6). Watch out for trouble in southeast Bangladesh. *The Daily Star*. https://www.thedailystar.net/views/opinion/news/watch-out-trouble-southeast-bangladesh-2976326. ↑

References

Aung-Thwin, M. (1986). *Pagan: The origins of modern Burma*. University of Hawaii Press.

Bahar, A. (2010). *Burma's missing dots*. Xlibris Corporation.

Behrens, P., & Henham, R. (2013). *Elements of genocide*. Routledge.

Blackmore, E. (2019, April 9). The Rohingya people. *National Geographic*. https://nationalgeographicco.uk/2019/2/therohingyapeople

Bulletin 36, WRM (2000, July 17). Burma: gas dictatorship and multinationals at Yadana. *WRM*. https://wrm.org.my/bulletin-articles/Burma-gas-dictatorship-and-multinationals-at-Yadana

Çakmak, S. (2022). Asylum seeker and refugee problem: the case of Arakan Muslims. *Nevşehir Hacı Bektaş Veli Üniversitesi SBE Dergisi*, *12*(3), 1887–1896. https://doi.org/10.30783/nevsosbilen.1141047

Church, P. (2017). *A short history of south-east Asia*. John Wiley & Sons.
Fisher, M. (2016, March 25). "No one told me I was going to be interviewed by a Muslim": Aung San Suu Kyi's Rohingya Problem. *Vox*. https://www.vox.com/2016/3/28/11306856/aung-san-suu-kyi-muslim-rohingya-bbc
Gray, C. S. (1999). Strategic culture as context: The first generation of theory strikes back. *Review of International Studies, 25*(1), 49–69. https://www.jstor.org/stable/20097575
Gutman, P. (2001). *Burma's lost kingdom: Splendors of Arakan*. Boulder Co.
Human Rights Watch. (2007). *Burma: Army attacks displace hundreds of thousands*. Retrieved August 28, 2023, from https://www.hrw.org/news/2007/10/25/burma-army-attacks-displace-hundreds-thousands
Ibrahim, A. (2016). *The Rohingyas: Inside Myanmar's hidden genocide*. Oxford University Press.
Islam, N. (2022). *The Rohingya of the Arakan: Conflict, crisis, and solution*. The Other Press.
Kaplan, R. D. (2010). *Monsoon: The Indian Ocean and the future of American*. Power Random House.
Kofi Annan Foundation. (n.d.). Retrieved December 6, 2023, from https://www.kofiannanfoundation.org/app/uploads/2017/08/FinalReport_Eng.pdf
Lintner, B. (2019). *The United Wa State Army and Burma's peace process*.
Myanmar Junta Leader. (2021, May 24). Retrieved December 6, 2023, from https://www.reuters.com/world/asia-pacific/myanmar-junta-leader-casts-doubt-return-rohingya-2021-05-24/
Myanmar Rohingya Violence Is Genocide, US Says. (2022, March 21). Retrieved December 6, 2023, from https://www.bbc.com/news/world-asia-60820215
"Myanmar Spirit." (2018, March 28). Retrieved December 6, 2023, from https://www.seniorgeneralminaunghlaing.com.mm/en/6258/people-bear-mind-myanmar-spirit-without-racial-religious-discrimination-strive-countrys-development-cohesive-union/
Myoe, M. A. (2014). The soldier and the state: The Tatmadaw and political liberalization in Myanmar since 2011. *South East Asia Research, 22*(2), 233–249. https://doi.org/10.5367/sear.2014.0205
Rahman, Md. M. (2021a, May 12). Myanmar coup and Bangladesh perspective. *Daily Sun*. https://www.daily-sun.com/post/552356/Myanmar-Coup-and-Bangladesh-Perspective
Rahman, Md. M. (2021b, July 7). Rohingya refugee crisis: putting the pieces of the puzzle together. *The Daily Star*. https://www.thedailystar.net/views/opinion/news/rohingya-refugee-crisis-putting-the-pieces-the-puzzle-together-2124331
Rahman, Md. M. (2022, March 6). Watch out for trouble in southeast Bangladesh. *The Daily Star*. https://www.thedailystar.net/views/opinion/news/watch-out-trouble-southeast-bangladesh-2976326
Neumann, I. B., & Heikka, H. (2005). Grand strategy, strategic culture, and practice: The social roots of Nordic defense. *Cooperation and Conflict, 40*(1), 5–23. https://doi.org/10.1177/0010836705049731
Pattanaik, S. S. (2018). Geo-strategic significance of Bay of Bengal and Andaman Sea: Leveraging maritime, energy and transport connectivity for regional cooperation. *South Asian Survey, 25*(1–2), 84–101. https://doi.org/10.1177/0971523119835045
Pulipaka, S., Singh, A. G., & Sircar, S. (2017). *India and connectivity frameworks*.
Saber, M. (2022). *Ballad of Rohingya: Conflictual past, exiled present, uncertain future*. Patakh Shamabesh.
Samad, M. A. (2023). Ethnic cleansing of the Rohingyas: A historical analysis. *Paramita: Historical Studies Journal, 33*(2). https://doi.org/10.15294/paramita.v33i2.46697
Selth, A. (2021). Myanmar's Military Mindset: An Exploratory Survey. Griffith Asia Institute, Griffith University.
Steinberg, D. I. (2021). *The Military in Burma/Myanmar*. ISEAS-Yusof Ishak Institute.
Wade, F. (2017). *Myanmar's enemy within*. Zed Books Ltd.

Chapter 9
Military Coup D'état, State of Anarchy, and the Future of Ethnic Armed Resistance Vis-à-Vis Reconciliation in Myanmar

Abu Salah Md. Yousuf

Abstract After decades of catastrophic economic and political repression under military rule, the people of Myanmar were expecting normalcy in 2011, as the quasi-civilian democratic government made headway toward peace and reconciliation. However, this did not last long, as the military once again staged a coup against the newly elected NLD government on February 1, 2021. Since then, Myanmar has been mired in chaos and violence, and people across the nation are fighting to restore democracy. Mass protests and civil disobedience have deadlocked the country on the brink of civil war. Thus, the hopes and dreams of an inclusive and democratic Myanmar have been imprisoned and sealed away once more, and the future of the ethnic reconciliation process following the coup seems bleak. Against this backdrop, our study examines the Myanmar military's long-standing ambitions to rule the country and its prejudices against ethnic minorities, which culminated in a military coup against Myanmar's elected government in 2021, jeopardizing the ongoing peace processes that had been a ray of hope after years of ethnic conflict. The chapter sketches the primary factors contributing to this failed ethnic reconciliation process, such as the Burmanization of Myanmar, radical Buddhism, military hegemonic attitudes, constitutional alienation of minorities, and relentless violence and discrimination against different ethnic groups.

1 Introduction

Since the birth of nation-states, these institutions have been using people's nationalist sentiments to defend territory and win wars. Today, this approach has proven to be Myanmar's doom. The "failed nation-building process" of this Southeast Asian country has led to a protracted civil war between military regimes and ethnic minorities since its independence in 1948 (International Crisis Group, 2022). Following the

A. S. Md. Yousuf (✉)
Bangladesh Institute of International and Strategic Studies, Dhaka, Bangladesh
e-mail: abuyousuf167@gmail.com

K. Ahmed and Md. R. Islam (eds.), *Understanding the Rohingya Displacement*, International Perspectives on Migration, https://doi.org/10.1007/978-981-97-1424-7_9

infamous military coup in 1962, the military of Myanmar, known as the Tatmadaw, assumed the role of protector of the country while attempting to bring a false sense of unity to the conflict-ridden territory in the name of "Burman-Buddhist nationalism." Ignoring the diverse ethnic groups with their distinct identities and forcing them into assimilation for the sake of Burmese pride were never answers to the question of a united Myanmar in any true sense. Instead, Tatmadaw-sponsored "Burmese nationalism" has only served to establish ethnic hierarchies in which Burman-Buddhist culture became regarded as superior to the other 135 ethnic groups who live in the frontier and borderlands of Myanmar.

The sense of Burmese-Buddhist supremacy was first "legally" established in Burma by the U Nu government's "divide and rule scheme" between 1948 and 1962. The state forced ethnic groups into assimilation through legalistic quashing of their rights to practice their cultures and traditions, while denying them participation in the agreed-upon federal-state system in the first Panglong conference led by Aung San. The overbearing policies against ethnic minorities only reached new heights when U Nu's government was pushed down from the pedestal by Ne Win's military coup seizing control of the country in 1962. In Win's 26 years of rule, the government employed force and brutality to push ethnic groups into submission, while ethnic groups responded with armed insurgency which resulted in decades of violent conflict. His hardline policies of ethnic assimilation, estrangement, and repression coerced ethnic groups into forming their own armed resistance against the military's ruthless control over every aspect of their lives. Due to this, discrimination and the repressive military strategies of Burmanization have been at the heart of ethnic tensions in Myanmar. Therefore, in 2011, the establishment of the Union Solidarity and Development Party (USDP) as a semi-democratic government foreshadowed a glimmer of optimism for Myanmar and a possible opportunity for peace negotiations in future. The military-instructed government of USDP took the very first steps in reforming the country when it attempted to create political accommodation for the prominent stakeholders in the political arena by introducing the Nationwide Ceasefire Agreement (NCA) for Ethnic Armed Organizations (EAOs) and holding the first democratic election (won by The National League for Democracy, or NLD) in Myanmar after decades of limited public participation in the election process. The NLD government, led by Aung Sang Suu Kyi and elected twice in the general elections of 2015 and 2020, also prioritized solving the ethnic crisis in the country and garnered both national and international support for its cohesive policies.

However, this did not last long, as the military once again staged a coup on February 1, 2021, against the newly elected NLD government. A year after the coup, Myanmar became mired in chaos and violence, as people across the nation were fighting for the restoration of democracy in the country. A significant group of them fled across the border to save their lives, and the rest remained engaged in mass protests and civil disobedience. The situation ultimately deadlocked the country on the brink of a civil war. Things further deteriorated because of the COVID-19 pandemic's effect on the economy and healthcare system (Hossain et al., 2022b; Ullah & Chattoraj, 2022). Thus, the dreams of an inclusive and democratic Myanmar have been imprisoned and sealed away once more. Today, the future of the ethnic reconciliation process following the coup depicts nothing but a bleak picture.

Against this backdrop, our research examines the Myanmar military's long-standing ambitions to rule the country and its prejudices against ethnic minorities. The situation culminated in a military coup against Myanmar's elected government in 2021 and jeopardized the ongoing peace processes that had been a ray of hope for the country's future after years of ethnic conflict. The present chapter sketches the primary factors contributing to this failed ethnic reconciliation process, such as the Burmanization of Myanmar, radical Buddhism, the military's hegemonic attitudes, constitutional alienation of minorities, and relentless violence and discrimination faced by different ethnic groups. The study unravels how the military intentionally propagated Burmese-Buddhist nationalism to foil ethnic reconciliation processes and perpetuate their dominance over the country.

The chapter is divided into six sections, including the introduction and conclusion. Section 2 deals with the policies of the military regimes of Myanmar and depicts how the reconciliation process became so complicated. Section 3 highlights the reconciliation initiatives. It discusses the time period when the NLD government was talking about the Twenty-First Century Panglong, and also focuses on the differences between the Bamar community and the EAOs. After the military coup of 2021, the situation changed drastically and tensions between the military and EAOs have escalated. This escalation is highlighted in Sect. 4 along with the argument that, at present, the military is not only confronted by the EAOs but also by many of the Bamar people. Against this backdrop, Sect. 5 tries to understand the ongoing challenges for any reconciliation between the military and the EAOs of Myanmar. The final section summarizes how the consecutive military regimes complicated the negotiation process and identifies the deep-rooted problems between the military and the EAOs.

2 The Military Regimes and Ethnic Policies of Myanmar

During British colonial rule in Myanmar, the term "ethnic groups" was coined, a term which continued to play a crucial role in defining Myanmar's "national races" in the following years of the country's independence (Clarke et al., 2019). Post-colonial independent states frequently end up with weak state structures learned from and introduced by the colonial empires for the sake of better, broader, and more easily controlled administration. However, following the method of creating a Westphalian nationalistic state in Myanmar is extremely difficult due to the fact that the country is ethnically heterogeneous, with a diverse mix of cultures and cross-breeding among people from different regions, each of which has its own language, customs, and traditions. The Tatmadaw, Myanmar's self-declared defenders who have dominated the country for more than 60 years, has repeatedly failed to grasp this fundamental truth about Myanmar's population and culture. At the root of Myanmar's nearly 60-year-old ethnic strife are the ideologically biased policies of "Burmese-Buddhist supremacy" propagated by the Tatmadaw through the use of perilous violent, structural repression of the ethnic minority groups (Soundararajan et al., 2023). Ethnic groups, their armed wings, and the transitioning state authorities of either military dictatorships or pseudo-democratic governments have been at loggerheads in discussions around establishing peace and creating a federal union of Myanmar—which was promised to them before the independence of then Burma.

Since the country's inception, the essence of Myanmar's administrative and cultural history has been defined by tutelary military regimes and ethnic conflicts. This has brought decades of structural discrimination, human rights violations, and political alienation against the diverse minority groups living in Myanmar (Zaw, 2018). Nevertheless, the grand saga of military regimes and ethnic policies began 70 years ago with the assassination of Aung San. Due to the tactful leadership of General Aung San, aided by the Burma National Army and people from the frontier areas, Myanmar became a sovereign state after being freed from the British Empire in 1948 (Devi, 2014, pp. 46–50). General Aung San's ethnic policies were intended to provide due credit to the people living in the frontier areas for their contribution to the state's independence. The free Union of Burma was also built with the intention of respecting their rights and individualism. To advance his aspirations, Aung San attempted to bring leaders from ethnic minorities such as Chin, Kachin, and Shan, as well as the Burmese government, together at a meeting at Panglong in Shan State in February 1947, gathered at the same table so they could work together for a federal Union of Burma. Ethnic minority groups joined with the purpose of achieving total autonomy for their regions at that time, as they wanted to preserve their culture and identity, which could only be achieved through a federal system of government (Schmidt-Leukel et al., 2021, p. 313). However, Aung San was unable to keep his promises, as he was assassinated six months before Burma's independence. Following his demise, U Nu took over as Prime Minister, becoming the country's first independent prime minister. He did not abide by the Panglong agreement, and his version of the Burmese Constitution at the Burma Assembly upheld a nation-building process focusing on the Bamar-Buddhist majority vis-à-vis General Aung San's vision that preached pluralism and celebration of diversity so that people from all walks of life might live in harmony. U Nu's erroneous perception of Buddhist-Burman ethnic and religious superiority led him to declare Buddhism the state religion of Burma in 1961, which was in direct opposition to the policies of the Panglong Conference (Sakhong, 2012, p. 323). However, his administration was put to an end when General Ne Win seized control of the government in 1962. The military coup led by General Ne Win was officially recognized as the Revolutionary Council (RC), which systematically destroyed democracy in Myanmar and established a long-standing military dictatorship.

By adopting the national ideology known as "The Burmese Way to Socialism" to steer the country, Ne Win's Revolutionary Council indirectly admitted that the ethnic policies of the regime would not be desirable for the minorities. The Tatmadaw leader saw ethnic divisions as a barrier, and would go to any length to guarantee a united Burma, which was more conducive to his idea of regional domination (Taylor, 2009, p. 588). Violent ethnic policies of assimilation were implemented under the rule of

Ne Win's dictatorial and socialist administration. His forceful regulations destroyed cultural practices such as performing ethnic songs, and prohibited the publication of ethnic languages, including teaching materials (Sakhong, 2012, p. 323). Even the ethnic council, which had been in existence since 1947, was dismantled, demonstrating that the socialist administration had no intention of safeguarding ethnic diversity. The Buddhist supremacist outlook of the regime led to the vilification of other religions, such as Christianity, Islam, and Hinduism. Pagodas were built all over the country, even in Christian-majority areas, for the promotion of Buddhism—the latter now considered dominant among the religions (Schmidt-Leukel et al., 2021).

Ne Win's exclusionary policies also included an agenda of ethnic alienation. During his reign, the 1982 citizenship legislation stated that true citizens of the country were members of ethnic groups in Myanmar that had lived in the territory prior to 1823. This effectively obliterated any opportunity for minorities such as the Rohingya (Ullah, 2011), the Indians, and the Chinese to obtain their ethnic rights as citizens because they became classified as third-class citizens by this constitution (International Crisis Group, 2021). Political engagement of minorities and their representations was also effectively restricted by the fact that only the Burma Socialist Program Party (BSPP), which was affiliated with the military, was permitted to participate in parliamentary proceedings (Zaw, 2018, pp. 121–38). Recognizing this uncertainty, ethnic groups demanded the establishment of the federal administrative system promised before the nation's independence. However, they had to contend with a brutal onslaught by the military, as General Ne Win implemented the "four-cut" strategy on the minority regions in 1966. The strategy was designed to counter the ethnic-identity-fueled insurgent groups that were forming their own armies for protection: Karen National Union (KNU), Kachin Independent Organisation (KIO), Shan State Army (SSA), New Mon State Party (NMSP), Karenni National Progressive Party (KNPP), Arakan Liberation Party (ALP), and Chin Democracy Party (CDP).

The four-cut strategy was based on the ideology of "one voice, one blood, and one nation" (Zaw, 2018). The military focused on fragmenting four main points of cooperation (food, funds, intelligence, and recruits) among the insurgency groups and civilians in conflicted areas. The insurgents were attacked by cutting off their food supply, their protection money from the villagers, their contacts (information and intelligence) with the locals, and then by enlisting the villagers against them in the conflict.

The socialist government further demonetized banknotes to halt black-market transactions that provided resources to insurgent groups. This had a severe impact on the civilian minority population, which was also reliant on black markets for supplies due to Myanmar's poor economic distribution; thus, many became penniless. The entire country was divided into "black, brown, and white" zones, respectively, denoting areas under complete control of insurgent groups, areas under partial control of insurgent groups, and areas under complete military control. Ethnic civilians were forced to relocate as their villages were burned down, and anyone resisting the relocation would be shot to death. A brutal campaign of torture, rape, and abuse was exercised against anyone suspected of aiding insurgency groups. Free-fire was allowed in brown and black zones where civilians lived. This operation resulted in the deaths of countless people and the destruction of thousands of communities in ethnic areas. The military was successful in instilling fear in civilians who aided the rebel groups and weakening those groups into submission. Although the military government denied the existence of the "four-cut strategy," it was again exercised in 2012, 2016, and 2017 to suppress ethnic and religious minorities (Rohingya, Kachin, Chin and others) even after the Ne Win and military eras had supposedly ended. The four-cut strategy has again returned after the 2021 coup, but the target is the whole population of Myanmar, both Burman and non-Burman.

Nevertheless, during the early 1970s, Ne Win's socialist model of state began to crumble as the country faced severe food scarcity and growth in black markets and corruption. Riots broke out due to food shortages, corruption, declining economies, and deteriorating standards and conditions at universities. Myanmar had already been classified as a Least Developed Country (LDC) by the year 1987 (Devi, 2014, pp. 46–50). Eventually, after one of the biggest mass demonstrations Myanmar has ever seen, Ne Win resigned in July 1988 after his 23 years of rule. The protests were viewed as a threat by the military authority, which feared losing its dominant position. Hence, the Tatmadaw resorted to killing thousands of protesters in the demonstrations to tame the revolution. The military, led by Saw Maung, once again consolidated a coup. On September 18, 1988, Saw Maung organized the State Law and Order Restoration Council (SLORC) with the help of 19 senior military officers, and the military authority was reinstated in Myanmar for a second time on September 18, 1988, which lasted until March 30, 2011. His military regime continued to exert power as the state authority, announcing a seven-step plan to achieve a so-called "discipline-flourishing democracy" in 2003. Power was then passed to the NLD, led by Aung Sang Suu Kyi, who won the 1990 general election fair and square, showing the pathways toward drafting a new constitution. Despite numerous attempts, this government also failed to solve the ethnic conflict and instead chose to ignore the plight of ethnic people. Borderland inhabitants were left without security and human rights (Ullah, 2014), while insurgent armed organizations were tamed through illusory ceasefires that had no political basis (Ullah & Ferdous, 2023). In the name of taking steps toward establishing democracy, the government urged EAOs to join the Border Guard Force (BGF), which was commanded by the Myanmar army, in order to participate in the 2010 elections (Sakhong, 2012). They were also told to create their own new political parties with no connection to the EAO groups. The military party, SPDC, was renamed the State Peace and Development Council as the new military representative party reached a ceasefire with the majority of ethnic armed groups in the country.

Because of these ceasefires, after years of conflict, the ethnic groups in these regions saw some stability as the government granted them economic autonomy to run businesses (Sakhong, 2012). While other ethnic groups observed a truce in anticipation of a fairly elected parliament, the Karen National Union (KNU) and the Restoration Council for Shan State (RCSS) defied the ceasefire agreement and continued fighting during this period. Some ethnic groups, such as Shan and Mon, were finally given a chance to vote for representatives of their own communities in

2010. In contrast to the previous SPDC military party, the new Union Solidarity and Development Party (USDP), led by President Thein Sein, put forward positive efforts for ethnic reconciliation after winning the 2010 election by holding talks with ethnic armed groups without any preconditions. This paved the way for the establishment of a quasi-democratic government in Myanmar, thereby bringing an end to the country's more than 60-year-old military regime.

With its calculated assimilation, alienation, and repression strategies, the military regime perpetuated ethnic chaos. The Bamar-Buddhist nation-building process was never going to fit into Myanmar. However, the regime persisted in using violence to establish it by force, if not political dialogue. The 60-year military regime included persecutions such as unlawful killings, forced labor, sexual and physical violence, and forced relocation of minority people (Amnesty International, 1997). These violent conflicts and brutal military assaults have compelled thousands of minority people to take refuge in neighboring countries such as Bangladesh, Thailand, China, and India, and many of them are internally displaced, having no way to go back to their homes (Hossain et al., 2022a). Many ethnic people hold grudges, mistrust, and hatred for the Tatmadaw and even Bamar majority civilians, which has been evident in every peace negotiation attempt since 2011.

3 Negotiations and the Twenty-First Century Panglong

In a multi-ethnic society like Myanmar, with varied stakeholders having their own agendas, social reconciliation is incredibly challenging to say the least. Due to decades of military institutionalization over Myanmar's economy and society, efforts to bring the country back together have been jeopardized, making progress toward peace all around the country far more complex. For too long, the country has only seen blood and violence. Therefore, establishing a comprehensive and non-discriminatory peaceful reconciliation strategy was undoubtedly the first and most important step. The transition from military dictatorship to quasi-democracy in the hands of the USDP government echoed this notion of "reconciliation through free participation." After assuming power, the USDP government immediately began peace negotiations. It took the Thein Sein government two years and countless discussions to finally sign a ceasefire with eight ethnic armed factions on October 15, 2015, called the Nationwide Ceasefire Agreement (NCA) (Schmidt-Leukel et al., 2021, p. 313). The NLD government carried on the spirit of the USDP government as it aimed to forge a peace initiative with the ethnic armed groups.

Bringing peace back to Myanmar was the declared agenda of the NLD government and Aung San Suu Kyi, who took office on March 30, 2016, after winning the historic 2015 general election. After decades of pursuing the wrong agenda for state security, Myanmar's authorities decided to change course, focusing on the human-security side of violent conflicts. The Union Peace Conference—Twenty-First Century Panglong was one of the most significant moves toward peace reconciliation made by the NLD government. The Conference succeeded the original

Panglong Conference of 1947, which historically united ethnic minority groups and the Bamar majority in support of Myanmar's independence. However, the 1947 conference's legacy is weighty and extremely difficult to match, since in that conference, Aung San sought to promote minority autonomy while upholding Myanmar's unity as a symbol; there has never been another successful peace negotiation of this magnitude since Myanmar's independence. The inaugural session of the Twenty-First Century Conference, held in 2016, was attended by over 1,800 delegates from EAO-NCA signatories, governments, political parties, non-signatories, civil society organizations, and the international community. Even though bringing together so many of the conflict's stakeholders was a major accomplishment, the conference's final outcome was not particularly fruitful. The "Northern Alliance," consisting of the Arakan Army (AA), Ta'ang National Liberation Army (TNLA), and Myanmar National Democratic Alliance Army (MNDAA), were not included in the process, which made inclusivity a major issue (Transnational Institute, 2017).

As the conference progressed, it became clear that there was a conflict of interests, as the government-power-sharing military avoided discussing a federal union and instead focused on adhering to the 2008 military-drafted constitution, while EAO leaders and ethnic political parties pushed for a federal union and self-determination to exercise economic and political rights. EAO groups such as the United Wa State Army (UWSA) and the Tai-Leng (Shanni) Nationalities Development Party (TNDP) demanded their own autonomous states. The second session of the conference successfully included the non-participants from the first session, the "Northern Alliance," which was undoubtedly a significant step in moving the peace negotiations forward. However, the process again fell behind on the political contention of self-determination and non-secession ('*Secession*', 2017). The military insisted that, in order to obtain self-determination and the right to draft their own constitution, minority groups must sign a non-secession clause. Minority groups maintained that such conditions demonstrated the government's suspicion of their intentions, which was never the proper way to proceed with the peace process. This only prolonged the political struggle between the parties in the negotiations, even after peace had been established. Although the groups intended to discuss these issues during the following session, the third iteration of the conference in 2018 entirely avoided this discussion in favor of progressing other dialogues (Choudhury, 2018). This deliberate ruse enraged the EAOs more, evinced when the session began amid fighting between the Tatmadaw and the EAOs, as well as between various ethnic armies in Kachin, Shan, Karen, and Mon states, all of which were in direct violation of the spirit of the ongoing peace process. At this point, the negotiations began to feel more like a political settlement to disarm and contain the EAO groups rather than an attempt to advance the conflict resolution process as a whole. On the one hand, agreements were signed between NCA signatory EAOs, indicating headway; on the other hand, non-NCA northern groups were approached once again to disarm, which would effectively put them at risk, casting doubt on their capability among their supporters.

The discussions should have focused on the escalation of the northern conflict. Instead, this session concluded with Tatmadaw Commander-in-Chief Senior General

Min Aung Hlaing's hegemonic speech to the ethnic population, in which he directly threatened them to remain in line, effectively diminishing the equal platform for cooperation as the military implicitly declared itself in charge, despite the country's democratically elected government (Choudhury, 2018). The last session in 2020 also failed to resolve the major stalemate issues of the federal union, federal army, non-secession clause, and self-determination. Major EAOs such as the Kachin Independence Organisation (KIO) and the United Wa State Army (UWSA) abstained from signing the NCA, with demands for fairer political dialogue. A ceasefire between these groups thus became necessary, as they constitute more troops than most of the NCA signatory groups (Wansai, 2018). Now that the 2021 coup has occurred, there is no way to tell whether the Panglong Conference would have succeeded in bringing overall peace and reconciliation to the conflict-torn nation.

The stagnant peace negotiations of the Panglong Conference of the Twenty-First Century may have failed for various reasons. However, the primary reason was that the NLD government and military failed to comprehend the primary reason for ethnic instability in the country over such a long period. Much instability is due to the relative deprivation ethnic groups have experienced since independence because they had no say in the political arena. The military's consistent preference for centralized security in the peace process and minority groups' desire for decentralized systems indicate that peace will only come when they can begin living their cultures and customs on their own terms, which will be impossible under a security and administrative system that prioritizes the Bamar majority (Thawng, 2018).

4 The Return of Military Rule and the Ethnic Groups

The Tatmadaw, as an institution, has had the taste of power for too long, and its aspirations to control the country are now inexorably linked to its very survival. The military's fear of losing autonomy and control led to the adoption of the 2008 constitution, which ensured that they retain authority even if they are not in charge of the country's administration. It was on February 1, 2021, that their delusional matrix was once again exposed when they staged a military coup against the democratic NLD administration, declaring a nationwide emergency in accordance with the 2008 constitution, which gave them political authority over state decisions. However, the Tatmadaw is having a difficult time justifying their actions this time around, as the public has condemned them since the first day of the coup. They have taken to the streets, peacefully protesting for the restoration of their hard-won democracy, demonstrating complete disobedience to the regime, as civil servants walked out on their jobs and the public refused to pay bills. The military used force to crush people and tamp them down through torturous assaults. As of April 2, 2022, the Tatmadaw has burned villages, shut down the internet to prevent the spread of information, tortured prisoners, detained up to 10,000 people, and killed at least 1723 people in its struggle for power ('Daily Briefing', 2022). While the international community has imposed sanctions to halt military operations, violence appears to be spreading throughout the country, including into areas where people have lived in relative peace since Myanmar's independence.

Myanmar's military has been in charge of the country for many years, with no accountability for its actions against the state and its people. Even after the introduction of a democratic government, the military continued to have ardent supporters who believed in their ideology of Burmanization. So, why was the coup seemingly inevitable, in the name of a fictitious "national emergency," when the country was finally set on a path of democratic transition? Perhaps the military coup was the result of Min Aung Hlaing's presidential ambitions and the fear of the military losing political influence over the state. It has once again enslaved the state, and the institution seems only concerned with preserving its own control. The events leading up to the coup demonstrate how the military realized that the democratic government had begun to show its backbone, which obviously did not bode well for the military agenda. First, the military's request for an inquiry into the 2020 general election was denied. The NLD won the election with more than 80% of the vote and a clear majority in Parliament, despite the military automatically receiving 25% of the available seats (Fawthrop, 2021). This occurred in both democratic general elections, the first of which was held in 2015. Without providing evidence, the military-backed USDP claimed that its own investigation had discovered 10.5 million suspect votes (Schmidt-Leukel et al., 2021).

The military accused the NLD-controlled Union Election Commission (UEC) of malfeasance. It was determined that the claims of the military came from a place of frustration and had no merit, and therefore, Aung San Suu Kyi rejected an investigation into the elections. The NLD government's second blow came in the shape of the president's unwillingness to proclaim a national emergency, as the military had asked, under the 2008 constitution. The military began to experience an existential crisis at this point, as they saw themselves losing control over both the state and the public, as evidenced by the elections and subsequent actions of the democratic government. Apparently, the time bomb of democracy was ticking. The military coup was initiated to achieve what they wanted while pushing the country back in every way possible. If these explanations are believed to be the actual motivations behind these military actions, the stakes are high this time, and violence may become prolonged.

Ethnic communities in Myanmar have historically formed armed groups to protect themselves from the deprivation they have experienced under military rule. Today, Burmese civilians are finally compelled to face what minorities have experienced since the country's independence. Even more than one year into the coup, Myanmar's civil disobedience movements are still ongoing and ethnic groups have participated fiercely in the resistance, which created a nationwide ethnic solidarity, as now the whole state faces the same grievance of military suppression. Ethnic armed groups' prior experience in dealing with the Tatmadaw has made them unquestionably critical political actors in the country following the democratic peace processes under the NLD government. Their role has been vital in sustaining the resistance of the majority of civilians in urban areas. EAOs' responses are divided, as some have come forward to help the disobedience movement by providing shelter to the displaced people and weapons to the grassroots fighters, while others have maintained their distance from the conflict (Martin, 2021). The chain of events leading to the ethnic minority's participation in the civil resistance started with the major EAOs breaking ceasefire agreements. EAO groups such as the Restoration Council of Shan State (RCSS), Karen National Union (KNU), Kachin Independence Army (KIA), Karenni National Progressive Party (KNPP), and Chin National Front (CNF) have taken a stand against the junta, which has effectively shattered the country's peace process (Martin, 2021).

However, there are ethnic armed groups who have remained outside of the conflict. Northern state groups such as the United Wa State Army (UWSA) and the National Democratic Alliance Army (NDAA) have stayed out of the fighting. These groups enjoy political autonomy in their regions due to their geographical distance from Myanmar's political propaganda. Non-signatories of the NCA, such as the Arakan Army, the Ta'ang National Liberation Army, and the Myanmar National Democratic Alliance Army, keep their distance too, as they were excluded from the negotiation process in 2011 (International Crisis Group, 2022).

The ethnic groups that have refrained from clashing with the military have a point. The NLD government, in the end, too, has Bamar-centric agendas, which was one of the reasons why the Panglong Conference concluded with intangible results. The junta has a majority of Bamar members, which ultimately shapes this coup as an intra-Bamar power struggle (Sun, 2022). The battle will not end with ethnic interests at the forefront in any context. The shadow government, named the National Unity Government (NUG), which emerged as the representative of the NLD administration, reflects this lack of ethnic inclusivity as well; its cabinet shuffling has ignored Shan state, which constitutes one of the largest ethnic groups.

Nevertheless, these groups are entangled with the country's emergency, as this might be their one chance to abolish the 2008 constitution and build a federal government, which the NUG promoted when it asked for the EAOs' assistance. Due to this, the People's Defence Force (PDF) was established as the armed wing of NUG in May 2021. The EAOs provided training to the young civilians who are fighting to retain democracy in Myanmar. Though the EAOs have been in close connection with them in different forms, the NUG or PDF do not have any central command over them, which has made the resistance scattered (International Crisis Group, 2022). Bamar civilians and anti-coup politicians have gone so far as to apologize to ethnic militias for previously believing military propaganda that the ethnic groups were attempting to destabilize the country, in the hopes of gaining their cooperation. However, it will be extremely difficult for NUG to win the trust of the EAOs, because their skepticism is deeply ingrained toward both the military and the NLD government (Win, 2021). Leading all of the EAOs to develop a strategic attack would be a dilemma for the military, as it fears unity, but it is nearly impossible for NUG to accomplish this, as the representative government clearly lacks the authority and legitimacy to do so.

Social cohesion is a point of contention in ethnically heterogeneous cultures. The greater a community's cultural diversity is, the more threatened each group feels, as they regard other groups as "outgroups" (Laurence et al., 2018, pp. 295–418). Social solidarity becomes more difficult to build in these communities as people compete for the same economic and social resources while trying to retain their cultural and ethnic identities. This much-needed cohesion between ethnic minorities and the Bamar majority was established following the February 1 coup. Ethnic groups became a part of the ongoing civil strife by arming the PDF and freeing civilians, activists, politicians, and members of the Committee Representing Pyidaungsu Hluttaw (CRPH) from the junta's detention. Additionally, activists and civilians have relocated to areas of the Kayin, Mon, and Shan states that are controlled by their EAOs (Martin, 2021). While the military has concentrated its efforts in urban areas, ethnic armed groups have coordinated actions in the borderlands, forcing the military to fight on multiple fronts, which will benefit the PDF strategically. The assistance of EAOs has shifted the majority Burmans' empathy for ethnic minorities, including the Rohingya, particularly among the youth (Ozturk et al., 2021). As they face the same oppressions that ethnic groups have faced for decades while being deluded by military propaganda and Burman-supremacist ideology, they have come to understand that there is no hope for a united and democratic Myanmar until the grievances of the minorities are resolved. Urban youth now view the military as a common enemy, uniting with ethnic minorities in their struggle against the regime, as the EAOs take the lead in protecting escaping dissidents and resisting the military dictatorship (Cabot, 2021). This solidarity was demonstrated last March, when protestors demanded a federal democracy and constitutional amendments that reflected the ethnic nation's pre-military aspirations.

5 The Challenges of Reconciliation

Reconciliation is difficult to achieve in the aftermath of war, as survivors of war require time to emerge from the wreckage of death, horror, and loss they have been left to contend with. In the case of ethnic conflicts, the challenges to reconciliation are more complex because the causes of these conflicts generally include violations of human rights, as well as deliberate economic and social negligence, which, if not addressed properly, leaves a society vulnerable to relapse into violent conflict in the post-war stage (Brounéus, 2008). Consolidation and reconciliation efforts between the Tatmadaw, ethnic communities, and the democratic government pre-2021 coup show the same picture of conflicting interests in its hierarchical structure of "national races." The following section elucidates some of the challenges in the process of reconciliation.

5.1 The Tatmadaw's Self-preserving Agendas

Under the banner of Bamar-Buddhist nationalism, the Tatmadaw ruled Myanmar with propaganda as a means to unify the state and uphold the puritan roots of ethnicity and religion. However, the junta's approach began to change following two of Myanmar's most significant revolutionary uprisings: the "8888 uprising" in 1988 for democratization and the Saffron Revolution of 2007. The military government's persecution of protesters during both uprisings drew international condemnation of the regime. Throughout that time, the junta's fear of losing authority was on display on several occasions (Schmidt-Leukel et al., 2021).

The Tatmadaw was well aware that even if a democratic administration were to form, the military would always retain supreme power under the constitution. In addition, Suu Kyi's international image was ruptured due to her infamous defense of the Rohingya genocide issue in The Hague. The landslide win of the NLD in 2020 was the last straw for the military, as the NLD government dared to decline their demand to investigate the general election results (Schmidt-Leukel et al., 2021). Therefore, in the name of establishing democracy, they staged the February coup. The military know that as long as the country's political and regional arenas remain chaotic, they will never lose control. Therefore, it can be argued that the Tatmadaw will not back down easily this time.

5.2 *Incompatible Aspirations of the Ethnic Groups*

The varied aspirations of ethnic minority groups are one of the underlying impediments to the reconciliation process. The 135 ethnic minority groups living in Myanmar fought alongside the Bamar majority for Myanmar's independence, with Aung Sang promising that their culture and traditions would be celebrated under a unified Burma. Yet, they had to endure decades of severe repression and violations of human rights at the hands of military regimes. Year after year, peace processes were initiated and ceasefires were signed, but the discrimination and plight of minorities and the accountability of their perpetrators were rarely addressed in any adequate manner (Ullah & Chattoraj, 2023). The primary assurance given to them in the 1947 Panglong Agreement was that Myanmar would have a federal government system, ensuring regional autonomy for the groups (Devi, 2014). However, no government has been able to keep that promise to this day. As a result, minorities developed disparate survival strategies over time.

Across the border, minority groups from Kachin, Karen, and Rakhine states seek a federal government in their respective regions, though some Karen people doubt this proposition (Hein, 2021). Additionally, the United Wa State Army (UWSA) in the northeast Burma state seeks recognition as an autonomous state ('UWSA Leader', 2019). At one point, minorities in the Shan and Chin states desired autonomy as well. While the EAO leaders united in the Twenty-First Century Panglong in the hopes of establishing a federal system, which desire was repeatedly denied, it became clear that they had conflicting interests among themselves. Chit Thu's Karen BGF and other smaller EAO factions have remained loyal to the military in post-coup conflicts for mutual advantage (Ong, 2021). With all these complex goals in the context of the 2021 coup, the democratic system has been shattered, and the ceasefires have been tainted. Therefore, there is a little room for knowing whether ethnic groups will ever trust any government again regarding a federal system, or if they will be willing to cast off their respective interests to pursue mutually beneficial goals for all of them.

5.3 *Weak Leadership of the NLD*

Both ethnic minorities and the international community regarded the NLD as Myanmar's sole hope for democracy. The NLD administration, led by Nobel Peace Prize laureate Suu Kyi, swept the 2015 elections, in which support from minorities was a significant factor. From this government, the expectations had also been high. The minority's and the NLD government's objectives were to some extent identical: to create a united Myanmar with a federal government structure that promotes peace while granting ethnic minorities long-overdue ethnic and political rights. However, minorities have been disappointed by the government's actions (Ebbighausen, 2021). The governing body seemed comprised of inept members who lacked necessary experience to conduct a meaningful peace dialogue. Loyalty to the party's CEO was regarded as more important than the ability to obtain high-ranking positions (Barany, 2018). Even the post-coup NUG administration of 2021 lacked ethnic diversity. Aside from that, the administration has been wary of upsetting its power-sharing arrangement with the military. The military's ruthless suppression of the EAOs was rarely acknowledged; on the other hand, EAOs' armed resistance was highlighted. Despite the ongoing national peace process, the government remained silent during the brutal military campaign in Kachin State, northern Shan State, and Rakhine State (Weng, 2018). It even supported the genocide against the Rohingya community on an international platform, claiming that it was necessary to save the Rakhine Bamars from Muslim oppression (Burrett, 2021). The NLD government was caught flat-footed in each of these occurrences. Despite losing faith in the government, minorities realized that anything is better than military dictatorship; thus, they had no choice but to support the NLD again in 2020. However, now that the coup has taken place, it may become a difficult issue as to whether the NLD government is genuinely qualified to rule and guide the country through a democratic transition.

5.4 *Bamar Nationalism and Buddhist Supremacy*

Myanmar started on the wrong foot when it endorsed a nation-building process using the doctrines of Bamar nationalism and Buddhist supremacy to oppress minorities. The doctrines automatically stipulate that any reconciliation process that excludes Myanmar's ingrained chauvinism and xenophobia would fail. The military utilized "Burmanization" propaganda to assert that because Burmans make up the majority of Myanmar's population and claim a lineage in the territory, they are the country's legitimate leaders. Buddhism was a state-sponsored religion, while religious diversity was viewed with skepticism, and other religions as "foreign" to the land of Burma. The Ne

Win era's idea of "The Burmese-Buddhist Way to Socialism" ended up splitting the majority and minority in a protracted ethnic conflict as the military attempted to incorporate frontier cultures into the majority Burmans by forcing students to convert to Buddhism, removing crosses, and erecting pagodas in the Christian-majority Kachin state (Gray, 2018). The Tatmadaw's agenda was to readily exploit Burman nationalism by garnering majority support for Burman cultural promotion in order to maintain its authority. This profound hostility instilled hatred in the minds of the minorities against the Burmans, even against those with do not have ties to the government or the army. As a result of "Burmanization," many ethnic minorities in Burma have had their distinct cultural identities erased over the course of several decades through the implementation of repressive laws, compulsory religious conversions, economic deprivation, and, in some cases, violent assault.

In addition, expeditiously increasing Buddhist supremacy after 2011, particularly the use of anti-Islamic rhetoric, resulted in the Rohingya genocide (Gunasingham, 2021). There also exist constitutional laws that specifically target Muslims, such as the "race and religion protection" bill proposed by the Ma Ba Tha, a group of prominent Buddhist abbots (Gunasingham, 2021). While Aung Sang Suu Kyi preached in favor of Buddhism in her speeches, it is critical to recognize that Buddhism as a religion and Buddhism as a state-sponsored ideology may not be similar. It can be extremely dangerous for ethnic and religious minorities, as this version of the religion now espouses militant Buddhism, which justifies atrocities against anyone who might or might not endanger the religion's supremacy (Fuller, 2017).

5.5 *Constitutional Challenges*

The 1974 Constitution's motto of "one ethnicity, one language, one religion" telegraphed the state's inability to tolerate minorities (Kuppuswamy, 2013). The 1982 ethnocentric citizenship law created a partisan sense of citizenship status by classifying groups that were in Burma prior to 1823 as Myanmar's sole true inhabitants. Due to the law, various ethnic groups, particularly the Rohingyas (Ullah & Chattoraj, 2018), faced difficulties claiming citizenship, which resulted in the expulsion of their full citizenship rights despite generations of familial ties to Myanmar (Chow & Easley, 2019; Ullah, 2016). On the other hand, the 2008 constitution can easily be described as military enshrinement. Here are some of its controversial laws that stagnate the reconciliation process between the government and ethnic minorities:

- The 2008 constitution vote gives the military 25% of parliamentary seats and the "veto" button, which it has repeatedly used to stop any discussion of the 1947 Panglong Agreement's federal government structure. As a result of this provision, the military retains the authority to veto any constitutional amendment (Chow & Easley, 2019).
- Some of the 2008 constitution carries instances of Islamophobia, such as the "Race and Religion Protection Law", which sought to regulate the Muslim population

in Rakhine State, barred the inter-religious marriage of Buddhist women, and authorized the government to handle religious conversions (Mathieson, 2015).

- The 2008 constitution made the president a potential military puppet. With the majority of the electoral council comprised of military personnel, the Tatmadaw received leeway to gravely influence the electoral council of presidentship.
- Finally, the 2008 constitution empowered the military to declare a state of emergency, which it eventually used to depose the NLD government on February 1, 2021.

6 Conclusion

Ethnic discrimination and a coercive military strategy of Burmanization have been at the heart of the ethnic tensions in Myanmar since the country's independence in 1948. When Burma gained independence in 1948, the military was one of the first obstacles to establishing peaceful co-existence. The Tatmadaw, for their part, views the federal system as a threat to Myanmar's unity and a silent perpetrator against their goal of a united Myanmar. On the other hand, ethnic minorities envision Myanmar as a federal state, with sovereignty over their respective regions, allowing them to practice and preserve their cultural traditions. In action, the military regimes have deployed force and violence to push the ethnic groups into submission, while these groups responded with insurgency and armed resistance.

The military also refused to relinquish its legacy as protector, or more accurately, their assumption of themselves as Myanmar's rightful rulers. Due to these enduring differences, ethnic minorities have been subjected to unrelenting repression in every facet of life for more than 60 years, and the political turmoil is still ongoing. This leaves a big question mark as to whether peace will ever be established. The protracted civil war may continue to rage, as will the repression by the juntas. The military has again failed to understand that it simply cannot protect Myanmar by regarding anyone as an enemy of Myanmar if s/he opposes the junta. As the chapter has discussed, apart from the Tatmadaw's agenda, incompatible aspirations of the ethnic groups, the NLD's weak leadership, and constitutional challenges also play critical roles. To understand the future of the peace negotiations, all these issues have to be taken into account. It is quite difficult to predict the exact future of the situation; however, by addressing the root causes of the issue, we can help the country remodel its ineffective tools of state administration and counterproductive ideologies.

References

Amnesty International. (1997, July 21). *Myanmar: Ethnic minority rights under attack*. https://www.amnesty.org/en/documents/asa16/020/1997/en/

Barany, Z. (2018, January). Burma: Suu Kyi's missteps. *Journal of Democracy, 29*(1), 5–19. https://www.journalofdemocracy.org/articles/burma-suu-kyis-missteps/

Brounéus, B. (2008). *Reconciliation: Theory and practice for development cooperation.* Swedish International Development Cooperation Agency.

Burrett, T. (2021, February 16). *Why the coup is bad news for Myanmar's ethnic minorities.* New Internationalist. https://newint.org/features/2021/02/16/why-coup-bad-news-myanmar-ethnic-minorities

Cabot, C. (2021, April 14). *Myanmar ethnic groups unite in fight against army, sights set on federal rights.* France 24. https://www.france24.com/en/asia-pacific/20210414-myanmar-ethnic-groups-unite-in-fight-against-army-sights-set-on-federal-rights

Choudhury, A. (2018, August 2). *The third 21st century Panglong Conference: A review.* Institute of Peace and Conflict Studies. http://www.ipcs.org/comm_select.php?articleNo=5499

Chow, J., & Easley, L. (2019, June 25). *Myanmar's democratic backsliding in the struggle for national identity and independence.* The Asan Forum. https://theasanforum.org/introduction-35/

Clarke, S. L., Myint, S. A. S., & Siwa, Z. Y. (2019). *Re-examining ethnic identity in Myanmar.* Centre for Peace and Conflict Studies. https://reliefweb.int/attachments/4ab984fa-7971-362a-ac06-92561e2eb979/Ethnic-Identity-in-Myanmar.pdf

Daily briefing in relation to the military coup. (2022, April 1). Assistance Association for Political Prisoners. https://aappb.org/?p=20885

Devi, K. (2014). Myanmar under the military rule 1962–1988. *International Research Journal of Social Sciences, 3*(10), 46–50. https://www.academia.edu/download/44797405/8.ISCA-IRJSS-2014-173.pdf

Ebbighausen, R. (2021, February 25). *Myanmar coup: Ethnic minorities, pro-democracy protesters warily united.* Deutsche Welle. https://www.dw.com/en/myanmar-coup-ethnic-minorities-pro-democracy-protesters-warily-united/a-56685579

Fawthrop, T. (2021, February 27). *Myanmar's ethnic groups join together to reject military rule.* The Diplomat. https://thediplomat.com/2021/02/myanmars-ethnic-groups-join-together-to-reject-military-rule/

Fuller, P. (2017, November 14). *Myanmar and Buddhist extremism.* The Conversation. https://theconversation.com/myanmar-and-buddhist-extremism-86125

Gray, D. (2018, March 16). *Myanmar forces Burman culture on minorities, erases identity.* Associated Press. https://apnews.com/article/249d72db491a47a79886c43b6085b6d2

Gunasingham, A. (2021, September 21). *Myanmar's extreme Buddhist nationalists.* The Interpreter. https://www.lowyinstitute.org/the-interpreter/myanmar-s-extreme-buddhist-nationalists

Hein, Y. (2021, September 2). *Visions of a federal future for Myanmar are fading fast-Part II.* The Irrawaddy. https://www.irrawaddy.com/opinion/guest-column/visions-of-a-federal-future-for-myanmar-are-fading-fast-part-ii.html

Hossain, M. A., Huda, M. N., Ullah, A. K. M. A., & Renzaho, A. (2022a). Risk factors, challenges, and psychological well-being of the Rohingya refugees in Bangladesh: Policy implications. *International Journal of Health Planning and Management, 37*(4), 1912–1917.

Hossain, M. A., Ullah, A. K. M. A., & Mohiuddin, M. (2022b). Rohingya Refugee in the pandemic: Crisis and policy responses. *Global Policy, 14*(1), 183–191. https://doi.org/10.1111/1758-5899.13156

International Crisis Group. (2021, January 22). *Identity crisis: Ethnicity and conflict in Myanmar.* Report No. 312. Retrieved from https://www.crisisgroup.org/asia/south-east-asia/myanmar/312-identity-crisis-ethnicity-and-conflict-myanmar

International Crisis Group. (2022, January 12). *Myanmar's coup shakes up its ethnic conflicts.* Report No. 319. Retrieved from https://www.crisisgroup.org/asia/south-east-asia/myanmar/myanmars-coup-shakes-its-ethnic-conflicts

Kuppuswamy, C. S. (2013, June 1). *Challenging the reconciliation process: Myanmar's ethnic divide and conflicts.* Institute of Peace and Conflict Studies. https://www.files.ethz.ch/isn/165111/IB221-Kuppusamy-Myanmar.pdf

Laurence, J., Schmid, K., & Hewstone, M. (2018). Ethnic diversity, ethnic threat, and social cohesion: (Re)-evaluating the role of perceived out-group threat and prejudice in the relationship between community ethnic diversity and intra-community cohesion. *Journal of Ethnic and Migration Studies, 45*(3), 395–418. https://doi.org/10.1080/1369183X.2018.1490638

Martin, M. (2021, June 3). *The importance of ethnic minorities to Myanmar's future*. Stimson Center. https://www.stimson.org/2021/the-importance-of-ethnic-minorities-to-myanmars-future/

Mathieson, D. (2015, June 16). *Religious extremism looms over Myanmar*. Human Rights Watch. https://www.hrw.org/news/2015/06/16/religious-extremism-looms-over-myanmar

Ong, A. (2021, June 11). *Ethnic armed organisations in post-coup Myanmar: New conversations needed*. Institute of Southeast Asian Studies—Yusof Ishak Institute. https://www.iseas.edu.sg/articles-commentaries/iseas-perspective/2021-79-ethnic-armed-organisations-in-post-coup-myanmar-new-conversations-needed-by-andrew-ong/

Ozturk, M., Gilani, I., & Khaliq, R. U. (2021, March 20). *Myanmar: 'Military coup triggers shift in national consciousness*. Anadolu Agency. https://www.aa.com.tr/en/asia-pacific/myanmar-military-coup-triggers-shift-in-national-consciousness/2182486

Sakhong, L. (2012). *In defence of identity: The ethnic nationalities' struggle for democracy, human rights and federalism in Burma, a collection of writings and speeches, 2001–2010*. Orchid Press.

Schmidt-Leukel, P., Grosshans, H., & Krueger, M. (Eds.). (2021). *Ethnic and religious diversity in Myanmar: Contested identities*. Bloomsbury Publishing.

Secession, self-determination haunt second round of Panglong Conference. (2017, May 29). The Myanmar Times. https://www.burmalink.org/secession-self-determination-haunt-second-round-panglong-conference/

Soundararajan, M., Jaishankar, K., Bushell, M., Telford, L., & Treadwell, J. (2023). The victimization of Rohingyas in Myanmar and Bangladesh: Breaking the silence-postcolonial criminology, ethnography and genocide. *The British Journal of Criminology, azad069*.

Sun, Y. (2022, February 1). *One year after Myanmar's coup, old and new resistance is undermined by divisions*. Brookings. https://www.brookings.edu/articles/one-year-after-myanmars-coup-old-and-new-resistance-is-undermined-by-divisions/

Taylor, R. (2009). *The state in Myanmar*. NUS Press.

Thawng, C. B. (2018). Natural resource sharing: The position, perspective, and prospect of ethnic political organizations' leaders towards peace process in Myanmar. In *Graduate studies in the disruptive society: Innovation in human rights, development studies, and resource politics, 42*.

The Irrawaddy. (2019, April 17). *UWSA leader repeats demands for autonomous Wa State on 30th anniversary*. The Irrawaddy. https://www.irrawaddy.com/news/burma/uwsa-leader-repeats-demands-autonomous-wa-state-30th-anniversary.html

Transnational Institute. (2017, September 19). *Beyond Panglong: Myanmar's national peace and reform dilemma*. Transnational Institute. https://www.tni.org/en/publication/beyond-panglong-myanmars-national-peace-and-reform-dilemma

Ullah, A. K. M. A. (2011). Rohingya Refugee to Bangladesh: Historical exclusions and contemporary marginalization. *Journal of Immigrant and Refugee Studies, 9*(2), 139–168.

Ullah, A. K. M. A. (2014). *Refugee politics in the Middle East and North Africa: Human rights, safety, and identity*. Palgrave McMillan.

Ullah, A. K. M. A. (2016). Rohingya crisis in Myanmar: Seeking justice for the 'Stateless.' *Journal of Contemporary Criminal Justice, 32*(3), 285–301.

Ullah, A. K. M. A., & Chattoraj, D. (2022). *Covid-19 pandemic and the migrant population in Southeast Asia: Vaccine, diplomacy, and disparity*. World Scientific.

Ullah, A. K. M. A., & Chattoraj, D. (2018). Roots of discrimination against Rohingya minorities: Society ethnicity and international relations. *Intellectual Discourse, 26*(2), 541–565.

Ullah, A. K. M. A., & Chattoraj, D. (2023). *The untold stories of The Rohingyas: Ethnicity, diversity, and media*. Bristol University Press.

Ullah, A. K. M. A., & Ferdous, J. (Eds.). (2023). *Governance, migration and security in international relations*. Springer.

Wansai, S. (2018, September 3). *Constitution-making and peace process stagnation in Myanmar: Will a conditional clause help restore confidence in the 21st century Panglong Conference?*

Transnational Institute. https://www.tni.org/en/article/constitution-making-and-peace-process-stagnation-in-myanmar-will-a-conditional-clause-help
Weng, L. (2018, April 27). *Ethnic groups have lost faith in the NLD*. The Irrawaddy. https://www.irrawaddy.com/opinion/ethnic-groups-lost-faith-nld.html
Win, T. S. (2021, October 1). *The coup united the people of Myanmar against oppression*. Al Jazeera. https://www.aljazeera.com/opinions/2021/10/1/the-coup-united-the-people-of-myanmar-against-oppression
Zaw, H. T. (2018). Conflict resolution and peacebuilding: The long-lasting trauma of Myanmar. *Advances in Journalism and Communication, 6*(4), 121–138. https://www.scirp.org/journal/PaperInformation.aspx?PaperID=89095&#abstract

Chapter 10
Crime and Securitization Conundrums in the Rohingya Camps

Khandaker Farzana Rahman and Md. Nazmul Arefin

Abstract This chapter explores the complex relationship between the Rohingya camps, their environment, and the propensity for criminal activities. It delves into the crime and securitization challenges faced within the Rohingya camps, examining the unique dynamics and complexities that contribute to the vulnerability of the population to criminal activities. Using secondary resources, we addressed the key aspects such as the crime and securitization conundrum in the Rohingya camps, the presence of criminal gangs, illegal weapons, and abduction, gender-based violence, extremism, and insecurity, the impact of refugee populations on crime, and the overall impacts of the Rohingya camps on crime in Bangladesh. The objective of this chapter is to discuss whether there exists a correlation between Rohingya settlements and a heightened likelihood of criminal activities during the period spanning from 2017 to 2020, as is frequently documented by law enforcement agencies. We pose question on the common discourses found in different studies that there is significant impact on crime rates after the Rohingya peoples' arrival, and subsequently push boundaries for further research.

1 Introduction

> Ours [the twentieth century] has been the century of departure, of migration, of exodus—of disappearance, the century of people helplessly seeing others, who were close to them, disappear over the horizon.
>
> *John Berger (Cited in* Gatrell, 2013*)*

Today's Rohingya refugee crisis represents the culmination of a number of historical trajectories of systematic discrimination, forced migration, and targeted violence conducted by the Myanmar junta government. Myanmar is a country located in

K. F. Rahman (✉)
University of Dhaka, Dhaka, Bangladesh
e-mail: kfrahman@du.ac.bd

Md. N. Arefin
University of Alberta, Edmonton, Canada
e-mail: marefin1@ualberta.ca

K. Ahmed and Md. R. Islam (eds.), *Understanding the Rohingya Displacement*, International Perspectives on Migration, https://doi.org/10.1007/978-981-97-1424-7_10

Southeast Asia that is home to a diverse collection of ethnic groups, which has given the country an appearance of more political division than many other nations in the region. The Rohingya are a Muslim, ethnolinguistic minority group that is not recognized as "citizens" of Myanmar (Ullah, 2011). They are part of the ethnic lines that run through the northern part of the state of Rakhine. However, the Rohingyas' historical reality was ignored and erased by the Myanmar government, which tends to reject them based only on their color and religion leading to the denial of citizenship, participatory rights, historical disenfranchisement, and finally annihilation (O'Brien & Hoffstaedter, 2020; Ullah & Chattoraj, 2023). As a result of the extensive and systematic attacks, the Rohingya people are now deemed by the United Nations to be "one of the most persecuted groups in the world" (Zarni & Cowley, 2014, p. 709).

Following instances of severe state repression in 1978, 1991–1992, and 2016, a significant number of Rohingyas were compelled to migrate across the border and seek refuge in Bangladesh. The latest surge of refugees into Cox's Bazar was the result of a lethal genocidal operation carried out by the Myanmar military against the Rohingya Muslim community in August 2017. This influx comprised of 745,000 individuals, including over 400,000 children, as reported by the UN Joint Response Plan for the Rohingya Humanitarian Crisis in 2019 (p. 10). Now in Bangladesh, the Rohingyas are provided with limited access to civil identity and are settled in one of the most massive and densest[1] refugee camps in the world. Several recent studies indicate that the camps are highly susceptible to a spectrum of delinquency such as inter-partner violence, drug peddling, and violent conflicts. Along with such issues, adolescent girls are vulnerable to forced early marriage, sexual violence, and trafficking (Krehm & Shahan, 2019; Inter-Sector Coordination Group, 2018; XChange Foundation, 2018). Against this background, our section of the book aims to contribute to the literature on the criminality of the refugees by describing the crimes conducted in the camps by the Rohingya. We seek to explicate the recent criminal activities perpetrated by the Rohingya within the confines of the camps, by using content analysis of national and international media, as well as NGO reports.

The issue of refugee resettlement has become a global concern, with several countries enacting policies to restrict it due to mounting security apprehensions. To date, there is a lack of significant empirical evidence regarding the potential impact of the situation on Bangladesh. Existing research on the correlation between refugee resettlement and criminal activity has primarily concentrated on Europe and Africa. The findings of these studies suggest that the influx of refugees and asylum seekers is linked to a rise in nonviolent criminal behavior (Fisk, 2018). The objective of this chapter is to discuss whether there exists a correlation between Rohingya settlements and a heightened likelihood of criminal activities during the period spanning from 2017 to 2020, as is frequently documented by law enforcement agencies. The chapter ultimately finds the absence of substantial empirical evidence that can establish

[1] According to The United Nations (2019) (January–December) Joint Response Plan for Rohingya Humanitarian Crisis Report, as of January 2019, a staggering number of more than 900,000 stateless Rohingya refugees are living in 34 extremely congested camps inUkhiya and Teknaf Upazilas.

association between the resettlement of the Rohingya in Bangladesh and rise of criminal activity.

2 Crime and Securitization Situation in the Rohingya Camps

> We now deal with a number of these [criminal] incidents involving the Rohingyas on a daily basis.
>
> *Md.Rezaul Karim, in charge of Kutupalong Rohingya camp (Cited in* United News of Bangladesh, *2019)*

The issue of criminality among refugees is a highly politicized topic that has garnered significant attention and debate within the field of criminology (Feltes et al., 2018). Law enforcement agencies in Bangladesh have expressed concern over the rapid spread of crimes, chaos, and disorder within the Rohingya refugee camps. The matter of securitization is emerging as a significant apprehension for the host nation for various reasons. Despite the fact that Bangladesh has a lengthy record of providing refuge to Rohingya individuals since 1948, the security concerns associated with their hosting are highly intricate and tenuous due to a variety of cross-regional and political factors. According to O'Driscoll (2017), a Conflict Research Fellow at the Social Science Research Council in the United States, there are numerous concerns regarding the securitization of hosting Rohingya refugees in Bangladesh. These concerns stem from various factors, as outlined by O'Driscoll (2017, p. 2):

- The rise of Islamic extremist groups within refugee camps;
- Crossing the border in large numbers to smuggle drugs and weapons;
- Job competition in an impoverished country and region;
- Competition over an inadequate supply of resources;
- Food and housing inflation;
- The deforestation of forests and plantations;
- A political desire for Rohingya to return to Myanmar; and
- The rhetoric that denies the Rohingya's status as refugees.

According to the police, a significant number of unemployed and idle Rohingyas residing in the camps have resorted to engaging in various criminal activities for financial gain, relying on the assistance provided by nongovernmental organizations (Aziz, 2019; Molla, 2019). After the sun goes down, it becomes increasingly difficult to oversee a million jobless people while at the same time deploying a small force to control their illegal activities. In light of the current circumstances, the Bangladeshi authorities have made the decision to station an increased number of policemen in the camps (Molla, 2019). Through an examination of a substantial corpus of newspaper and nongovernmental organization reports, this chapter has distilled the most pervasive instances of deviant behavior occurring in the refugee camps of Cox's Bazar in the recent past as follows:

Table 1 Rohingyas involved in major crimes in the period 2017–2019 (Based on the reports of The Daily Star and other national dailies)

Crime	Cases filed	Number of accused
Abduction	15	79
Arms possession	36	82
Attack on police	1	8
Human trafficking	24	102
Murder	43	136
Narcotics	208	368
Rape/attempted rape	31	56
Robbery	9	32
Other crimes	46	110

- Murder and abduction
- Gender-Based Violence (GBV)
- Intimate Partner Violence (IPV) and domestic violence.
- Intra-community conflicts
- Sexual harassment, abductions, and rape attempts
- Gambling; using and selling drugs
- Robbery and theft
- Human trafficking
- Inter-community marriage-related conflicts
- Unsanctioned relationships
- Violent extremism.

Table 1 gives a glimpse of different crimes which the Rohingyas have committed since their last influx of 2017–2019:

3 Criminal Gangs, Illegal Weapons, and Abduction

> The pattern of the crimes [in the camps] changes with time. Some troublemakers [among the Rohingyas] are now more into extortion and abduction.
>
> *ABM Masud Hossain, Superintendent of Police, Cox's Bazar (Cited in* Molla, 2019*)*

Criminal gangs have gained a significant foothold in the Cox's Bazar refugee camps. According to investigative media reports, at least seven criminal gangs are responsible for severe crimes such as kidnapping, extortion, murder, Yaba[2] smuggling, human trafficking, and rape, and their influence over the camps is growing (United News of Bangladesh, 2019). The realization of camps as a conducive environment for the proliferation of illicit criminal behaviors has resulted in the emergence of a camp-based gang culture. The group known as the Abdul Hakim gang

[2] Methamphetamine (popularly named Yaba or Baba).

is considered to be the most dangerous among them (United News of Bangladesh, 2019).

Investigative reports also suggest that these gangs are purportedly involved in illicit activities such as the smuggling of arms and drugs, as well as instances of murder and abduction (Molla, 2019). It can be concluded that the Rohingya camps located in Cox's Bazar are being subjected to many instances of organized criminal activity, and are prone to potential threats from members of their own community.

4 Drug Dealing

The illicit trade of narcotics across the border between Bangladesh and Myanmar is a significant security concern for Bangladesh. The presence of Rohingya refugee camps is exacerbating the existing security predicament. The lack of employment opportunities and idleness experienced by the Rohingya population residing in camps has led to a growing involvement in the illicit trade of narcotics, particularly Yaba, utilizing the well-known pathway of Cox's Bazar. In the first two years since their influx (August 2017–August 2019), 1100 Rohingyas have been subject to accusations and arrested in 471 criminal cases, of which 208 of them were on narcotics charges (The Business Standard Report, 2019). The narcotics traffickers, according to researcher Banerjee (2019), are hiding out in the camps and using the camps as safehouses for the distribution of methamphetamine. Supporting the claims of Banerjee, media reports say that around 200 small huts are being used as Yaba warehouses in the Kutupalong and Balukhali camps alone (Mahmud, 2018). According to the Chittagong Narcotics Control Department, a total of 462 Rohingya individuals, both male and female, have been apprehended in Chittagong over the past six years spanning from 2017 to June 2022 (Rohingya involvement, 2022).

Table 2 presented below provides an overview of the major drug-related seizure operations during the period spanning from 2017 to 2020.

5 Gender-Based Violence

> In Myanmar my husband would work all day. I used to do chores and we had a good time together but, after coming here, my husband did not have anything to do and started having relationships with other women. In Myanmar, there was a law that said you could not marry twice, but here there is no such thing … Men and women are going between camps saying that they are unmarried so they can have affairs.
>
> *Anika Shama, a Team Leader with the Danish NGO DanChurchAid, Quoted in the Guardian (Cited in* Marsh, 2019*)*

Gender-based Violence (GBV) is a transgression against fundamental human rights, including the right to personal security, the right to optimal physical and

Table 2 Major drug-related seizure operations related to Rohingya Camps (Based on reports from national and international media)

Date of operation	Place of operation	Description
28 Sept., 2017	Bay of the Naf river	Four individuals, including three Rohingya men and one Bangladeshi, were apprehended while attempting to illegally transport a quantity of 800,000 methamphetamine pills across the border from Myanmar into the country
30 Sept., 2017	Teknaf upazila	Members of the Bangladesh Border Guard (BGB) have taken three Rohingya youths into custody from the Naf River after seizing 20,925 pieces of Yaba
28 Oct., 2019	Beach in Cox's Bazar	A Rohingya individual was apprehended by the Bangladesh police for possession of methamphetamine pills valued at USD 5 million. A total of 800,000 pills were found within sacks aboard the trawler
1 Dec., 2019	Teknaf upazila	A 20-year-old Rohingya individual was apprehended by law enforcement officials in possession of 200,000 Yaba tablets
11 April, 2020	Chattogram	Three Rohingya individuals were apprehended by law enforcement officials during a police operation. The individuals were found to be in possession of a significant quantity of Yaba tablets, totaling 50,000 in number

mental health, the right to be free from torture or cruel, inhuman, or degrading treatment, and the right to life (Inter-Agency Standing Committee, 2015). The Rohingya population was compelled to vacate their native territory in Myanmar and seek shelter in the refugee camps in Bangladesh.

In these extremely crowded camps, half of the one million refugees are women and children. The case studies conducted by Linda Nordby of Uppsala University make it clear that though the women are now away from the violence they faced in Myanmar, GBV continues to affect their lives in the refugee camps in several brutal ways (Nordby, 2018). In her research, Nordby (2018) identified unequal power relationships as the underpinning reason for gender-based violence.

According to Oxfam (2019), an international nongovernmental organization, approximately 29% of women residing in the camp have reported feeling unsafe, and numerous incidents of gender-based violence are reported on a weekly basis. UNICEF provided GBV support to a total of 12,876 Rohingya refugees in 2019, of which 490 were girls and 75% were female adults (Marsh, 2019). Rape is also endemic in the camp in Cox's Bazar. The camps exhibit a notable prevalence of rape, albeit largely underreported. Marsh (2019) aptly observed that sexual violence, encompassing rape, is considerably underreported owing to the existence of social stigmas and taboos associated with the subject matter.

6 Intra-community Conflicts

According to Aziz (2019), the camps frequently experience disorder and strained relations as a result of confrontations between opposing factions of Rohingya people. These conflicts are typically rooted in disagreements and internal struggles related to familial matters, kinship disputes, commercial ventures, financial wrongdoing, and the pursuit of power and control, both within the camps and in relation to the surrounding community. IRC's (2019) research similarly reveals that various groups participate in conflicts to acquire positions that are perceived as powerful, such as the status of "Majhis."[3]

7 Extremism and Insecurity

The Rohingya issues have become a significant concern in the security discourse of Bangladesh. A mass assembly of nearly 200,000 Rohingya individuals took place on August 25, 2019, commemorating the second anniversary of their displacement into Bangladesh ("Genocide Day," 2019). The Rohingya community voiced their demand for citizenship and other fundamental entitlements from Myanmar, prior to their willingness to repatriate. This significant demonstration prompted concern from authorities and irritation from the government regarding the management and operations of the Rohingya camps, as well as the insecurity within the camps. As a result, the Bangladeshi government suspended three officials, including Mohammad Abul Kalam, the Refugee Relief and Repatriation Commissioner (RRRC) in Cox's Bazar, for permitting the refugees to organize such an extensive demonstration (Human Rights Watch, 2019).

Concerns and sensitivity have been raised over the suspected presence of the extremist group Arakan Rohingya Salvation Army (ARSA) among the displaced people living in the camps. Some 3500 fighters were reportedly hiding out in the refugee camps, according to Deutsche Welle, and many of them crossed over to Myanmar to receive military training in secret (Czimmek & Islam, 2019).

8 Does the Presence of Refugee People Affect Crime?

While the interconnectedness between refugees and crime has been a subject of research in recent times, there is a more established body of literature on immigrants and crime (Amuedo-Dorantes et al., 2021). However, the available empirical studies on the connection between immigration and crime seem to be transient, because they often concentrate on the refugees hosted by developed countries and the role of

[3] Regarded as the Rohingya leaders in the camps who are assigned to help "maintain order" in the community.

voluntary migration on crime, while ignoring other regions where 85% (UNHCR, 2017) of the world's refugee population live. Theories and models are analyzed in this section to substantiate the links between refugees, immigrants, and crime. This section ends through a rigorous review of refugees' legal access to employment and wages along with their propensity to crime in their host community—a multiplicity of factors that can help us understand the connection between crime and refugees.

The topic of immigration has garnered significant attention due to its potential to impact the labor market, law and security, inter-state trade, and the political economy of both the host and home country. Heightened levels of apprehension have been attributed to the significant influx of refugees originating from Afghanistan, Syria, and Myanmar in the current global context. The influence of low-cost labor and employment prospects on the likelihood of criminal behavior among immigrant populations in a host community is a significant factor to consider. According to Card's (2001) research, the repercussions of immigration on local labor markets and wages are minimal. Foged and Peri (2016) conducted a study in Denmark which supports the notion that migration has a favorable effect on the wages and employment of unskilled natives. The study found that "the influx of refugees, who were primarily less educated people in manual-intensive jobs, prompted less skilled native workers to increase their mobility toward more complex occupations and away from manual tasks" (Foged & Peri, 2016).

Despite the absence of a consensus, there has been an unforeseen surge in criminal activity attributed to refugees and migrants. This phenomenon, however, has had a temporary effect on unemployment rates and the labor market. According to Borjas's (2003) study, immigration has notable adverse impacts on the labor economy of the local people. Endogenous issues may arise regarding effects on labor, such as a rise in the number of unemployed individuals in the domestic region. The impact in question has the potential to increase the likelihood of criminal activity, not only among refugees, but also among local workers with less skills who are confronted with reduced employment prospects (Borjas et al., 2010, cited in Akbulut-Yuksel et al., 2022). In a similar vein, different studies argue that rates of reoffending may be different among immigrants who are with and without legal employment status. Mastrobuoni and Pinotti (2015) consider immigrants' legal status to examine the rate of recidivism. Baker (2015), analyzing the case of the USA, attributes a drop-off in crimes relating to property to increased labor-market opportunities for three million immigrants who were given legal status through the 1986 Immigration Reform and Control Act. Ousey and Kubrin (2018) conclude that there is a very weak, yet negative, impact of immigration on crime. However, they acknowledge that studies positing an equivocal relation between criminal activities and immigration mostly have recourse to the comparison of authorized versus illegal immigrants, with the evidence that unauthorized immigrants have restricted work prospects and insubstantial access to different freedoms.

Furthermore, it is possible for refugees to engage in deviant behavior as a result of experiencing violence in their past, which may increase their susceptibility to engaging in violent behavior. Recent research has revealed the influence of adverse life events and traumatic experiences on individuals' risk aversion, time preferences, and subsequent conduct (Akbulut-Yuksel et al., 2022). According to Moya and Carter's (2019) findings, there is evidence to suggest that individuals who have been displaced in Colombia as a result of widespread violence are at a heightened risk of experiencing extreme poverty and financial instability in the years that follow. Couttenier et al. (2019) conducted a study on asylum seekers and found that individuals who have experienced conflicts or mass killings are 35% more prone to engaging in violent criminal activities in their host country.

The relationship between refugees and crime seems to be elusive, which is confirmed in the contemporary scholarly literature; it could be inferred that there is a potential measurement error in the number and documentation of refugee populations or a lack of reporting of crimes committed in refugee camps owing to security fears. In consequence, a significant displacement of refugees may potentially yield favorable effects on criminality within receiving communities, while the arrival of refugees may affect employment prospects and remuneration at the local level. As refugees are not entitled to the same freedoms that a native can access—which often makes them vulnerable—there might be refugees with legal status and vice versa; their level of authority also may have impacts on the crime rate of a particular settlement.

9 Impacts on Crime of the Rohingya Camps

There exists a handful of scholarly investigations on the aftereffects of refugee populations on crime rates in the United States, Europe, and the United Kingdom. As per the New York Times, an analysis of census data spanning from 1980 to 2010 consistently indicates that individuals who are immigrants exhibit a lower likelihood of engaging in criminal activities as compared to those who are natural-born citizens of the United States (Pérez-Peña, 2017). Furthermore, the incidence of criminal behavior among refugees is even lower (Rueckert, 2017). The purported correlation between the resettlement of refugees and an increase in criminal activity is often based on anecdotal evidence rather than empirical data analysis. The incidence of criminal activity among refugees residing in various nations, including Jordan, Turkey, Iran, Uganda, Lebanon, and Pakistan, does not typically exhibit a significant increase in comparison to the time before their arrival (World Bank, 2017).

The availability of dependable data on crimes that have taken place in the Rohingya refugee camps situated in Cox's Bazar is limited, and it is worth noting that not every incident is reported to the local police. Regarding Rohingya camps in Bangladesh, the information from law enforcement indicates that crimes committed in the camps and the number of Rohingya arrested in Bangladesh in 2022 were 16 times higher than that of 2017. Police arrested 2531 Rohingya and registered 1220 cases, and counted 1628 arrests and 666 cases, respectively, in the preceding year and 2021 (Reuters, 2023). Approximately 90% of the cases reported in 2022, as well as a comparable percentage of arrests made, pertained to offenses such as homicide, unlawful possession of weapons, illicit drug trade, theft, sexual assault, abduction, assault on law enforcement officials, and trafficking of human beings. Nonetheless, the number of Rohingyas who have been convicted remains unknown. According to a report by Reuters in 2023, there has been a surge in the number of Rohingya killings, with 31 cases reported that year, surpassing the previous record of 27 in 2021. Additionally, the number of arrests related to drug offenses has exhibited an upward trajectory from 2018 to 2021 (Reuters, 2023).

It must be borne in mind that in the case of the Rohingya refugees in Bangladesh, the number of refugees residing in the camps amounted to 918,910 in 2021 according to one study; in addition, many are unregistered and living outside the camps (Kameke, 2023). Both the refugees inside and outside the camps have stringent living conditions, and their opportunities for work are highly restricted. The children born inside the host countries are not given nationality and left with very minimum protection from national and international agencies. In addition to the repressive background faced by such an ethnic minority from Myanmar and their limited life and employment opportunities in Bangladesh, crime rates or reoffending might be due to other factors, i.e., those that cannot be immediately controlled.

As stated before, although Rohingyas have been living in Bangladesh for decades, they are only allocated the most basic humanitarian assistance, experience mobility restrictions, and are deprived of freedom to work. The reality is that they are forced to get involved with informal activities, working without legal status and with low remuneration. They are engaged in the labor market as unskilled workers in competition with native unskilled/skilled workers, which in consequence negatively impacts the employment opportunities of native people. In addition, evidence shows that Rohingya refugees are often subject to victimization and abuse by the existing authorities and law enforcement. Such abuse has been said to occur on apparently fabricated grounds, such as for carrying and smuggling drugs. In addition, the matter of extortion was scrutinized by Human Rights Watch (2023) with regard to the involvement of APBn (Armed Police Battalion) officers who are responsible for maintaining law and order within the camps, as well as through communication channels with Majhis, the leaders of the camp community. According to the report, law enforcement officials typically requested a sum ranging from 10,000 to 40,000 taka (equivalent to US$100–400) as a means of circumventing arrest and demanded a higher amount of 50,000 to 100,000 taka (equivalent to $500–1000) for the liberation of a detained relative. Refugee households frequently face the compulsion to liquidate their final resources in order to satisfy illicit requests from various entities, potentially leading them to engage in illicit conduct. Even the justice system exhibits greater severity toward the Rohingyas in comparison to the native population. A 28-year-old Rohingya refugee received a death sentence from a lower court in the Cox's Bazar district for the possession and smuggling of methamphetamine tablets. This marks the first instance of capital punishment being implemented under the 2018 Narcotics Control Act in Bangladesh (Anjum, 2022). True drug lords in Bangladesh hardly face punishment on this level, on the other hand.

No matter the extent of the refugee influx or its legal standing in the host country, all the studies demonstrate that crime rates may be influenced by the arrival of refugees. While many studies mentioned in the earlier section have found an increase in property crime and theft among newly settled refugees, the Rohingya refugee population in Bangladesh has been disproportionately involved in violent crimes and illegal business. Since the Rohingya have been subjected to state-sanctioned atrocities and widespread violence, it is not unreasonable to assume that the stresses they have endured in trying to gain access to basic entitlements in both their home and host countries have contributed to their criminal behavior. On the other hand, restrictions on access to the labor market and many fundamental rights, as well as a high potential to be victimized, may increase the propensity to commit crime by the Rohingyas.

Once again, the Rohingya have been utilized as mules by criminal organizations to transport contraband over international borders. These data suggest that the Rohingya have a larger propensity to commit crime than the local population, but this does not support the conclusion that the crime rate per thousand Rohingya is rising. Owing to data constraints, the above hypothesis could not be empirically tested, nor can it be firmly concluded which factors are conducive to producing a negative immigration-crime influence in the Rohingya settlements.

Thus, after more data can be generated, "future research may pin down the sensitivity of crime committed by refugees to policy changes" (Akbulut-Yuksel et al., 2022). This may also help to estimate the greater deterrence costs for refugees, such as the possibility of repatriation or resettlement or a longer prison sentence within the justice system. It is also important that more research is performed to collect the necessary data and shed light on the precise processes behind the long-term disproportionate impact of violence against Rohingya refugees, which can have links with crime rates in Bangladesh. Such data would broaden the spectrum sufficiently to test whether the later generations are more crime-prone than the earlier ones.

10 Conclusion

After decades of systemic discrimination, dehumanization, polarization, statelessness, and targeted brutality in Rakhine State, the Rohingya people were forced to seek safety in refugee camps. Myanmar's government institutions have caused them to be ranked among the most persecuted people in the world. The government of Bangladesh showed great humanitarian kindness as a host by accepting millions of Rohingya refugees when no one else would take them in. It is tragic that so many former victims have turned evil. The illicit activities they engage in have made the host communities feel unsafe. All around them, innocent Rohingyas are in a state of fear. Arrests and court cases illustrate how law and order are deteriorating in the camps. The government gradually begins to view them as a threat to national security. Bangladesh's domestic stability appears threatened by the rising crime rate. And there are bigger issues on the horizon. Several security threats and community risks may result from the long-term dispossession of this persecuted, alienated, and jobless community.

However, it has been observed in existing literature focusing on refugees in developed countries that an influx of refugees often leads to an increase in property-related criminal activities, whereas based on data obtained from police and media outlets in Bangladesh, there appears rather to be a significant rise in incidents of organized and violent criminal behavior in the areas where the Rohingya population resides. The Rohingya populace has been subjected to enduring acts of aggression and prolonged societal tensions, resulting in a surge in detentions and legal proceedings. Moreover, consistent manipulation and abuse from different local sources also influences them to be delinquent in order to protect their life and liberty. On top of that, the Armed Police Battalion (APBn) in Bangladesh has been alleged to have participated in activities such as extortion, arbitrary arrests, and harassment of Rohingya refugees. According to Human Rights Watch (2023), the situation is particularly worrisome as refugees are already subjected to violence from criminal gangs and armed groups.

The present chapter asserts that the existing studies have not established a definitive correlation between refugees and crime. Causal evidence regarding the influence of refugees on crime rates in a camp settlement specifically in the context of Bangladesh leads to the conclusion that many factors including limited access to basic demands, restrictions on local labor market opportunities and remuneration, as well as potential victimizations and abuse against them lead the Rohingya to get involved in different violent activities to protect their lives, families, and jobs. Such a situation could easily lead to the occurrence of more negative emotions for refugees, and potential insecurity in the respective areas, which must be addressed through effective deterrence mechanisms from the national and international actors. Though our work tried to add value to the scholarship on the refugee-crime nexus by advancing an analysis on the Rohingya in Bangladesh, a negative immigration-crime relationship in a scenario should not be unpropitious to the law-abiding immigrants. Thus, there remain ample opportunities for future work regarding the nexus and impact of Rohingya refugees on crime in Bangladesh. Along with this, it could also be beneficial to examine whether the second generations of Rohingya are equally as crime-prone as the original one residing in Bangladesh.

References

Akbulut-Yuksel, M., Mocan, N. H., Tumen, S., & Turan, B. (2022). *The crime effect of refugees* (No. w30070). National Bureau of Economic Research. https://doi.org/10.3386/w30070

Amuedo-Dorantes, C., Bansak, C., & Pozo, S. (2021). Refugee admissions and public safety: Are refugee settlement areas more prone to crime? *International Migration Review, 55*(1), 135–165. https://doi.org/10.1177/0197918320920192

Anjum, S. (2022, June 30). *Rohingya man sentenced to death in Bangladesh*. The Diplomat. https://thediplomat.com/2022/06/rohingya-man-sentenced-to-death-in-bangladesh/

Aziz, A. (2019, March 24). *What is behind the rising chaos in Rohingya camps?* Dhaka Tribune. https://www.dhakatribune.com/172280

Baker, S. (2015). Effects of immigrant legalization on crime. *American Economic Review, 105*(5), 210–213. https://doi.org/10.1257/aer.p20151041

Banerjee, S. (2019). *Drug trafficking and Rohingya refugees in Bangladesh.* Observer Research Foundation. https://www.orfonline.org/expert-speak/drug-trafficking-and-rohingya-refugees-in-bangladesh-49005/
Borjas, G. J. (2003). The labor demand curve is downward sloping: Reexamining the impact of immigration on the labor market. *The Quarterly Journal of Economics, 118*(4), 1335–1374. https://www.jstor.org/stable/25053941
Borjas, G. J., Grogger, J., & Hanson, G. H. (2010). Immigration and the economic status of African-American men. *Economica, 77*(306), 255–282. http://www.jstor.org/stable/27764418
Card, D. (2001). Immigrant inflows, native outflows, and the local labor market impacts of higher immigration. *Journal of Labor Economics, 19*(1), 22–64. https://doi.org/10.1086/209979
Couttenier, M., Petrencu, V., Rohner, D., & Thoenig, M. (2019). The violent legacy of conflict: Evidence on asylum seekers, crime, and public policy in Switzerland. *American Economic Review, 109*(12), 4378–4425. https://doi.org/10.1257/aer.20170263
Czimmek, S., & Islam, A. (2019, Sep, 24). *Rohingya militants active in Bangladeshi refugee camps.* Deutsche Welle. https://www.dw.com/en/rohingya-militants-active-in-bangladeshi-refugee-camps/a-50490888
Feltes, T., List, K., &Bertamini, M. (2018). More refugees, more offenders, more crime? Critical comments with data from Germany. In H. Kury & S. Redo (Eds.), *Refugees and migrants in law and policy* (pp. 599–624). Springer. https://doi.org/10.1007/978-3-319-72159-0_26
Fisk, K. (2018). One-sided violence in refugee-hosting areas. *Journal of Conflict Resolution, 62*(3), 529–556
Foged, M., & Peri, G. (2016). Immigrants' effect on native workers: New analysis on longitudinal data. *American Economic Journal: Applied Economics, 8*(2), 1–34. https://doi.org/10.1257/app.20150114
Gatrell, P. (2013). *The making of the modern refugee.* Oxford University Press.
'Genocide Day': Thousands of Rohingya rally in Bangladesh camps. (2019, August 25). Al Jazeera. https://www.aljazeera.com/news/2019/08/day-thousands-rohingya-rally-bangladesh-camps-190825055618484.html
Human Rights Watch. (2019). *Bangladesh: Clampdown on Rohingya refugees.* https://www.hrw.org/news/2019/09/07/bangladesh-clampdown-rohingya-refugees
Human Rights Watch. (2023, January 17). *Bangladesh: Rampant police abuse of Rohingya refugees.* https://www.hrw.org/news/2023/01/17/bangladesh-rampant-police-abuse-rohingya-refugees
Inter-Agency Standing Committee. (2015). *IASC guidelines for integrating gender-based violence interventions in humanitarian action.* https://interagencystandingcommittee.org/working-group/iasc-guidelines-integrating-gender-based-violence-interventions-humanitarian-action-2015
IRC's (2019). The Shadow Pandemic: Gender-Based Violence among Rohingya refugees in Cox's Bazar. Online available: https://www.rescue.org/sites/default/files/document/2247/theshadowpandemicbangladesh.pdf
ISCG (2018) *JRP for Rohingya Humanitarian Crisis: March-December 2018. Inter Sector Coordination Group.* https://reliefweb.int/report/bangladesh/j rp-rohingya-humanitarian-crisis–march-december-2018-0.
Kameke, L. V., (2023, May 12). *Refugee population Bangladesh 2012–2021.*Statista. https://www.statista.com/statistics/733986/bangladesh-refugee-population/
Krehm, E., & Shahan, D. A. (2019). *Access to justice for Rohingya and host community in Cox's Bazar.* International Rescue Committee. https://www.rescue.org/sites/default/files/document/3929/accessingjusticeassessmentexternalfinalsmall.pdf
Mahmud, T. (2018, September 1). *Crime on rise in Cox's Bazar camps.* Dhaka Tribune. https://www.dhakatribune.com/bangladesh/nation/2018/09/01/crime-on-rise-in-cox-s-bazar-camps
Marsh, S. (2019, December 3). *'My dignity is destroyed': The scourge of sexual violence in Cox's Bazar.* The Guardian. https://www.theguardian.com/global-development/2019/dec/03/my-dignity-is-destroyed-the-scourge-of-sexual-violence-in-coxs-bazar

Mastrobuoni, G., & Pinotti, P. (2015). Legal status and the criminal activity of immigrants. *American Economic Journal: Applied Economics, 7*(2), 175–206.

Molla, M. A. (2019, August 26). *Refugee camps: Crime spikes while Rohingyas despair*. The Daily Star. https://www.thedailystar.net/rohingya-crisis/news/refugee-camps-crime-spikes-while-rohingyas-despair-1744768

Moya, A., & Carter, M. R. (2019). Violence and the formation of hopelessness: Evidence from internally displaced persons in Colombia. *World Development, 113*, 100–115. https://doi.org/10.1016/j.worlddev.2018.08.015

Nordby, L. (2018). *Gender-based violence in the refugee camps in Cox Bazar: A case study of Rohingya women's and girls' exposure to gender-based violence*. [Master's thesis, Uppsala University]. https://www.diva-portal.org/smash/get/diva2:1219686/FULLTEXT01.pdf

O'Brien, M., & Hoffstaedter, G. (2020). There we are nothing, here we are nothing!"—The enduring effects of the Rohingya genocide. *Social Sciences, 9*(11), 209–225. https://doi.org/10.3390/socsci9110209

O'Driscoll, D. (2017). *Bangladesh Rohingya crisis—Managing risks in securitisation of refugees*. Evidence and Knowledge for Development (K4D) programme. http://www.gsdrc.org/wp-content/uploads/2017/11/224-Managing-risks-in-securitisation-of-refugees.pdf

Ousey, G., & Kubrin, C. (2018). Immigration and crime: Assessing a contentious issue. *Annual Review of Criminology, 1*, 63–84. https://doi.org/10.1146/annurev-criminol-032317-092026

Oxfam. (2019). *Breaking barriers for Rohingya refugee women*. https://www.oxfam.org/en/breaking-barriers-rohingya-refugee-women

Pérez-Peña, R. (2017, January 26). Contrary to Trump's claims, immigrants are less likely to commit crimes. *The New York Times*. https://www.nytimes.com/2017/01/26/us/trump-illegal-immigrants-crime.html

Reuters. (2023, January 24). Surging crime, bleak future push Rohingya in Bangladesh to risk lives at sea. *The Daily Prothom Alo*. https://en.prothomalo.com/bangladesh/bangladesh-in-world-media/kyja3qkac0

Rohingya Involvement. (2022, August 02). Rohingya involvement in smuggling, kidnapping on the rise. *Dhaka Tribune*. https://www.dhakatribune.com/bangladesh/crime/291549/rohingya-involvement-in-smuggling-kidnapping-on

Rueckert, P. (2017). Do refugees cause more crime? The facts say probably not. *Global Citizen*. https://www.globalcitizen.org/fr/content/these-are-the-facts-on-refugees-and-crime/

The Business Standard Report. (2019, August 25). *Two years in Rohingya camps: 1,100 arrested in various cases*. The Business Standard. https://tbsnews.net/bangladesh/two-years-rohingya-camps-1100-arrested-various-cases

The United Nations. (2019). *Joint response plan for Rohingya humanitarian crisis report*. https://reliefweb.int/sites/reliefweb.int/files/resources/2019%20JRP%20for%20Rohingya%20Humanitarian%20Crisis%20%28February%202019%29.compressed_0.pdf

Ullah, A. A. (2011). Rohingya refugees to Bangladesh: Historical exclusions and contemporary marginalization. *Journal of Immigrant & Refugee Studies, 9*(2), 139–161. https://doi.org/10.1080/15562948.2011.567149

Ullah, A. A., & Chattoraj, D. (2023). *The untold stories of The Rohingyas: Ethnicity, diversity, and media*. Bristol University Press.

UNHCR. (2017). *Bangladesh: Analysis of gaps in the protection of Rohingya refugees*. https://www.unhcr.org/46fa1af32.pdf

United News of Bangladesh. (2019, August 5). 2 years of Rohingya influx: 43 murdered in camps, 32 killed in gunfights. *The Daily Sun*. https://www.daily-sun.com/post/418026/2-years-of-Rohingya-influx:-43-murdered-in-camps-32-killed-in-gunfights

World Bank. (2017). *Intentional homicides (per 100,000 people)—Turkiy, Jordan, Pakistan, Lebanon, Iran, Islamic Rep., Ethiopia, Kenya, Uganda, Congo, Rep., Chad*. UN Office on Drugs and Crime's International Homicide Statistics database. https://data.worldbank.org/indicator/VC.IHR.PSRC.P5?locations=TR-JO-PK-LB-IR-ET-KE-UG-CG-TD&year=2014&year_low_desc=true

XChange Foundation. (2018, May 23). *Rohingya repatriation survey*. http://xchange.org/?p=7137
Zarni, M., & Cowley, A. (2014). The slow-burning genocide of Myanmar's Rohingya. *Pacific Rim Law & Policy Journal, 23*(3), 681–752. https://digitalcommons.law.uw.edu/wilj/vol23/iss3/8

Part III
Media Narratives and Propaganda in Conflict

Chapter 11
Media, Propaganda, and the Othering Process of the Rohingyas

Amena Khatun

Abstract The rhetoric and tactics used to attack and punish the Rohingya minority population in Myanmar are thoroughly examined in this chapter. It discusses the historical denial of these people's citizenship rights and creation of a foreign identity as a means of "othering" them. To understand how various propaganda channels form biased narratives and how structural organs have been utilized to systematically marginalize and demean the Rohingya people, the conceptual framework of propaganda as well as the propaganda model developed by Edward Herman and Noam Chomsky has been employed. It explores the sociopolitical elements that have facilitated their marginalization and the creation of an "other" identity, emphasizing the effects of these developments on their social, cultural, and political rights. The intellectual underpinnings of propaganda are explored in the second section, along with the tactics used to sway public opinion and promote particular narratives. It investigates how false information, deception, and emotive appeals are used as instruments to sway public opinion, mold attitudes, and defend laws that discriminate against the Rohingya population. It looks at how misinformation that feeds into negative stereotypes and keeps the Rohingya population marginalized is spread by state-run media, hate speech, social media, literature, and religious leaders. It comes to the conclusion that for many years, hate and justification for violence against the Rohingya community have been normalized due to a concerted misinformation effort and a lack of representation for the group in the media and in governance.

1 Introduction

One of the world's most persecuted, defenseless, and oppressed minority, the Rohingyas of Myanmar are the victims of numerous human rights violations, such as ethnic cleansing, statelessness, and potentially genocide (Hossain et al., 2022; Kingston, 2018). Hundreds of thousands of Rohingyas have been forced to escape to

A. Khatun (✉)
Department of Mass Communication and Journalism, University of Rajshahi, Rajshahi, Bangladesh
e-mail: amenakhatun@ru.ac.bd

K. Ahmed and Md. R. Islam (eds.), *Understanding the Rohingya Displacement*, International Perspectives on Migration, https://doi.org/10.1007/978-981-97-1424-7_11

neighboring countries like Bangladesh, Thailand, Malaysia, and India due to violent attacks in 1978, 1991–1992, 2016, and 2017. The majority of Rohingya people moved mostly to Bangladesh because it was closer and they shared the same faith (Albert & Maizland, 2017; Hossain et al., 2022). According to Médecins Sans Frontières (MSF), an international media humanitarian aid organization, at least 9000 members of the ethnic Rohingya minority were killed, of which 730 were children under the age of five, in the recent attack on August 25, 2017. More than 647,000 Rohingya fled to Bangladesh after the attack (Frontières, 2017). The Myanmar government has long viewed the Rohingyas as a demographic extension of Bangladesh in the Chittagong region, and sought policy accordingly to reorient the dichotomous understanding of Burmese society in order to exclude the ethnic "other" who was seen as a legacy of British colonial rule (Chowdhory & Mohanty, 2020). On the other hand, in terms of the Bangladeshi government, the Rohingya were not officially known until 1977, after they had crossed the border from Myanmar in large numbers as a result of political unrest in their land of origin (Washaly, 2019).

Rohingyas are frequently referred to in Myanmar as "illegal Bengalis," "a group of terrorists," or "illegal economic migrants" from the colonial era who constitute a threat to the security of the nation. Even local, national, and social media of the country portrayed Rohingyas as criminals, burdens, and security issues as well as spreading hate speech and negative propaganda against the Rohingya minority (Mozur, 2018; Ullah & Chattoraj, 2023). In addition, amid the most recent assault on the Rohingya in 2017, the local media in Myanmar not only did the report on Rohingya issues with bias, but also used derogatory terms to characterize the Rohingyas, such as "terrorist attack," "separatist movement," "threat to national security," "militant," and "religious extremism," while the state-run national media depicts Rohingya as a homogeneous group of perpetrators endangering the peace and stability of their country (Kironska & Peng, 2021; Soe, 2021). Social media especially Facebook was used by the Burmese military and conservative Buddhist groups to spread hatred toward the Rohingya minority, and human rights activists have charged Facebook for instigating offline violence against the Rohingya community by disseminating hate speech and nationalist propaganda online (Aziz, 2022). The majority of Burmese people have accepted this bad image of Rohingyas as true over the past five decades. And the government has successfully been able to "other" the Rohingyas as illegal immigrants or as Bengalis, invoking their sovereignty as a state to exclude the Rohingya, who are now perceived as an external threat, from the nation, and the absence of national legal structures that provide individuals with protection has made things quite unstable for them (Ahsan Ullah, 2016; Shani & Saeed, n.d.). This process of "othering" the Rohingyas actually began in the 1770s, when Arakan was seized and annexed by the Burmese King Bodawpaya in 1784, starting a protracted guerrilla war during which the Burmese allegedly killed more than 200,000 Arakanese. Two-thirds of the surviving Muslim Arakanese fled into the neighboring Chittagong region after a failed effort to overthrow Burmese sovereignty in 1786, and this was the beginning of an influx of Arakanese Muslim refugees into Bengal (Harvey, 2019; Uddin, 2015). Many refugees returned after the British incorporated Arakan into its empire in 1885, but during World War II, riots between the

Rohingya and Rakhine Buddhists started, leading approximately 22,000 Muslims to flee to nearby British Indian areas that are now part of Chittagong in Bangladesh (Karim, 2016; Uddin, 2015). However, Arakan remained a sovereign state until 1784, when it was expanded to include the Chittagong region in the southern part of modern-day Bangladesh. The Arakanese had their first encounter with Muslims when Arab traders stopped at an Arakan port on their way to China, and it is believed that the Rohingyas are descended from this first wave of Muslims, who became a mixed race composed of solders-turned-migrants from Bengal who arrived between the ninth and fifteenth centuries, married local women, and settled in the region (Uddin, 2015) (Fig. 1).

To understand the decades-long construction of the Rohingya identity as "foreigners," "outsiders," or "illegal Bengalis," it is crucial to track down and examine the conspiracy and the history of "othering" of Rohingyas in Myanmar. According to Barkun, the essence of conspiracy beliefs lies in attempts to delineate and explain evil (Barkun, 2013a; Knight, 2003). At their broadest, conspiracy theories "view history as controlled by massive, demonic forces." The locus of this evil lies outside the true community, in some "other, defined as foreign or barbarian, though often disguised as innocent and upright," The result is a worldview characterized by a sharp division between the realms of good and evil (Barkun, 2013b).

Penalties for disobeying the law in Myanmar can be severe; people were routinely imprisoned for expressing viewpoints deemed objectionable by the state (Allott, 1994; Fink, 2001). Amnesty International in its research report of 2016 and Human Rights Watch in 2017 claimed that Myanmar's legal system concurrently inhibits people who might peacefully protest nationalists' extreme speech that mirrors that of the ruling party (Lee, 2019). In this way, Myanmar's official media informs its people about the types of expression that are tolerated by the government and those that are unlikely to be suppressed. For example, Global New Light of Myanmar (GNLM), the official media, sets the bar for what is acceptable, which contributes to an environment that encourages and tolerates nationalist hate speech, particularly that

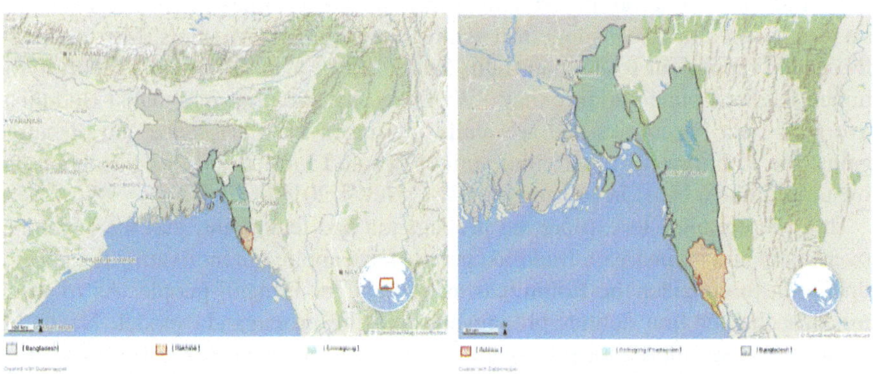

Fig. 1 Map of Rakhine, Chattogram (Chittagong) and Bangladesh. *Source* Map is reproduced by Author (Karim, 2016; Uddin, 2015) and created by Datawrapper (2023)

which targets the country's Muslim Rohingya population (Lee, 2019). Additionally, Myanmar entered the Information and Communications Technology (ICT) realm relatively late, but it enabled public access to the internet in the early 2000s (Bradley, 2022). However, the country was long considered to be an outcast in the international community during the rule of the oppressive military junta from 1962 to 2011, and the digital transformation began in the country only after the military handed over power to a civilian administration, which made the nation more accessible to the outside world (Bradley, 2022).

In 2014, the price of data consumption was significantly reduced after the government granted telecom licenses to Qatar's Ooredoo and Norwegian telecom operator Telenor, and overnight, the price of SIM cards dropped from $200 to $1.50 (Fujita, 2017). Due to the price reductions and the opening of the market to international operators, mobile phone penetration rates swiftly increased from a very low base to more than 50% by 2015 and were estimated to have topped 90% by the end of 2016 (Matsui, 2015). These changes made the internet widely accessible to the majority of people in Myanmar. According to DataReportal, in Myanmar, the internet penetration rate in January 2022 was 45.9%, whereas the number of internet users was 25.28 million of the 54.6 million total population. It also revealed that by the start of 2023, social media users in the country numbered 20.75 million and of them, 19.25 million people were Facebook users (Kemp, 2022). Facebook has become the social media platform of choice for most of Myanmar's population, with around 90% of mobile phone users relying on it to get news and other information. Many people in the country use Facebook on their smartphones rather than on a desktop computer or a search engine like Google or Yahoo for their first exposure to the internet (Gowan, 2014). However, social media has also played a considerable role in shaping the issue of the Rohingya and their identity, ancestors, and role in Myanmar. Due to the negative propaganda and circulations, the persecutions of Rohingya people have been intensified. The New York Times and a UN fact-finding mission highlighted the role of social media networks, Facebook in particular, in fuelling hate speech and negative propaganda against the Rohingya minority in Myanmar. According to a New York Times investigation, the Myanmar military has routinely exploited Facebook as a tool in its ethnic cleansing effort against the Rohingya Muslims (Mozur, 2018). UN special rapporteur for human rights Yanghee Lee also submitted a report to the Human Rights Council adding that, "We know that the ultra-nationalist Buddhists have their own Facebooks and are really inciting a lot of violence and of hatred against the Rohingya or other ethnic minorities and I am afraid that Facebook has now turned into a beast in Myanmar," (BBC News, 2018).

This chapter aims to explore the propaganda and techniques that the Myanmar government and mainstream Buddhist people have applied in motivating the general population to consider the Rohingyas as "others" or Bengali people. As to structure, this chapter first defines propaganda and the propaganda model. Next, this chapter discusses the major propaganda types that the Myanmar government used to ensure the "othering" process of the Rohingyas. Third, this chapter highlights mediums by which the Myanmar government actualizes the process of "othering" of the Rohingyas in Myanmar. And finally, this chapter will appeal to the propaganda model in order to shed light on the subject's future.

2 The Process of Rohingya "Othering"

U Nu, the first Prime Minister of independent Burma—now called Myanmar—and his government (1948–1958) recognized the Rohingya as a distinct race within the nation by saying:

> The people living in Maungdaw and Buthidaung regions are our nationals, our brethren. They are called Rohingyas. They are one of the same par in the status of Nationality with Kachin, Kyah, Karen, Mon, Rakhine and Shah and they are one of the ethnic races of Burma (U Nu, as cited in Haque, 2017).

During this time, the Rohingyas were represented in Parliament and government institutions, and a radio station was even established to broadcast programs in the Rohingya dialect. The 1961 census indicated that the Mayu district, bordering then-East Pakistan, was 75% Rohingya, a notable recognition (Ullah & Chattoraj, 2023). However, the situation dramatically worsened and questions arose regarding their ethnicity and citizenship during the tenure of the military government that began in 1962. The junta's one-party system, the Burma Socialist Programme Party, did not waste time in closing the Rohingya's social and political institutions. Many private Rohingya businesses were taken over by the government, sociocultural organizations were banned, and even the Rohingya language broadcasts from Rangoon Radio station were ended. The junta cleverly used Theravada Buddhism to bolster its rule and commenced Burmanization of the Rakhine administration. Continued persecution of the Rohingya rendered them "aliens" or "others" in their own land (Bari, 2018).

2.1 *British Colonization and Independence*

According to Turner (2017), during the British colonization period in Myanmar, Burmese Buddhists felt that knowledge of the Buddha's teachings—generally known as "sāsana"—was slipping away before their eyes, creating new fears for the future of Buddhism. Later on, various British policies were perceived by a majority of Buddhists as an attempt to undermine their religion and culture (Turner, 2017). Experts argued that British policies significantly changed the country's structure. These policies disrupted Buddhist ideology, impacted village economies, filled many government positions with Indian immigrants, and encouraged Indian and Chinese business interests; hence, Burmese Buddhists' developing anger created tension between them and other ethnic minorities (Godrej, 2008). When World War II broke out in Burma, they not only recruited the Muslims as troops, but also set them against

Buddhists who supported the Japanese. In pursuit of their own military goals, both the British and Japanese soldiers took advantage of the animosity and hatred among the local populace.

Searching for the roots of the Rohingya crisis, some specialists think that the first phase of conflict actually started during the decolonization process in 1947, although General Aung San, who is considered the founder of modern Burma, tried to unify the state through the historical Panglong Agreement with the ethnic leaders which promised that states with ethnic minorities would be given more freedom from the federal government. Aung San's famous quote was, "If Burma receives one Kyat, you will also receive one kyat," which made the promise of equitable distribution of resources between Myanmar's Bamar core and the ethnically diverse periphery. He further said,

> The dream of a unified and free Burma has always haunted me. We who are gathered here tonight are engaged in the pursuit of the same dream. We have in Burma many indigenous people; the Karen, the Kachin, the Shan, the Chin, the Burmans and others. In other countries too there are many indigenous people, many "races;" the "races" do not have rigid boundaries; religion is no barrier either, for it is a matter of individual conscience. If we want the nation to prosper, we must pool our resources, manpower, wealth, skills and work together. If we are divided, the Karen, the Shan, the Kachin, the Chin, the Burman, the Mon and the Arakanese, each pulling in a different direction, the Union will be torn, and we will come to grief. Let us unite and work together (Yawnghwe & Sakhong, 2022).

But soon after the agreement, General Aung San was assassinated, and the promise could not be fulfilled; this lies at the heart of a violent cycle of conflict which continues in the country (Pattison, 2012). On the basis of the Panglong Agreement, the Union Constitution was formed in 1947 in which citizens were defined as those people who belong to an "indigenous race," having a grandparent from an "indigenous race," or are children of citizens, or those who lived in British Burma before 1942. However, the Rohingya people were, unfortunately, not considered to be an indigenous group and were therefore disqualified from being citizens of the country (Hlaing, 2007). In terms of the classification and definition of a Burmese citizen, the 1947 constitution provided a very general description; hence, a supplemented law known as the Union Citizenship (Elective) Act of 1948 was also passed, which mandated that eligible Burmese citizens apply for and receive a "certificate of citizenship" as proof of their nationality. Many Rohingya were qualified for citizenship if they had settled in British Burma at least eight years prior to 1942. However, most Rohingya were not aware of the provision requiring such a citizenship document, and as a result of their failure to adhere to the requirement, the majority of Rohingyas became illegal immigrants. Due to this regulation, Rohingyas who fled to Myanmar during the Second World War were not allowed to return, and any who did were viewed as illegal immigrants (Yegar, 1972). According to a report of Human Rights Watch from 2000 titled "Burmese Refugees in Bangladesh: Still No Durable Solution," tensions between the Myanmar government and the Rohingya increased soon after independence with the, government's portrayal of them as "illegal immigrants" contributed to the rise in hostility. Afterwards, a group of Arakanese Muslims launched a political drive to integrate the towns of Maungdaw and Buthidaung into East Pakistan, but the proposal was rejected by the Constituent Assembly in Rangoon (Human Rights Watch, 2000). The report also described that, with a view to fulfilling their demand for the right to live in an autonomous northern part of Rakhine as full citizens of Myanmar, segments of the Rohingya community resorted to violent conflict against the government beginning in 1950. Through a series of assaults, armed organizations called Mujahids drove out residents of Maungdaw, Buthidaung, and a portion of Ratherdaung who were neither Muslims nor sympathetic to their cause, which escalated the Rohingya issue and portrayed them as a danger to Buddhists. However, the Burmese Army controlled the Arakan rebellion successfully through its counterinsurgency operations in November 1954. In connection with this, Gupta (2009) argues that the outbreak of the Mujahid insurrection in north Arakan could be attributed to the violent exactions of local militias, the dissatisfaction of local landlords, the unfair treatment of Muslims by Arakanese administrators, and murky business conflicts.

In addition, Smith (1991) points out that since independence, dissidents from virtually every ethnic and political group have taken up arms against the central government at some stage; ethnic leaders claim that their last residue of goodwill for the Panglong Agreement dissipated when Ne Win seized power in 1962 and tore up the 1947 constitution. He also mentions that many ethnic minorities still believe that no true census of the real population in Burma has ever been taken, and that Burma today has some of the most extreme citizenship laws in the world. Full citizenship is, in theory, confined to those who can prove that they had ancestors resident in Burma before the first British annexation in 1824 (Smith, 1991).

In Myanmar, non-Buddhists have always been regarded with great suspicion, and the erosion of Rohingya rights began to accelerate rapidly after the military coup in 1962 and during the 1974 national election (in which the Rohingya were denied the right to vote). In February 1978, the Burmese government launched Operation Nagamin (Dragon King) to expel "illegal foreigners," serving as a cover to target Rohingyas, and over a span of three months, 200,000–250,000 Rohingya were forcibly evicted from their homes in Rakhine State and compelled to flee to neighboring Bangladesh (Akesson & Basso, 2022). Operation Nagamin targeted the so-called illegal residents in the problematic region of northern Rakhine, leading to marginalization, displacement, and mass persecution of the Rohingyas who were arrested on arbitrary grounds, raped, and had their villages destroyed; hundreds of thousands of Rohingya subsequently left the country (Khan, 2022). Both the military and democratic regimes in Myanmar have failed to prioritize ethnic minorities' sovereignty over the political and economic resources of their states; even the military leadership from 1962 to 2011 implemented a unitary state and imposed Burman Buddhism as a strategy to unify Myanmar's multiethnic nation (Anwary, 2020). In fact, denying the legitimacy of Rohingya residency in Myanmar has enabled the authorities to place restrictions on Rohingya rights, and the politicized nature of Myanmar's legal system has allowed the authorities to weaponize laws to restrict Rohingya rights (Lee, 2019). The arbitrary application of laws, citizenship impediments, and rights restrictions consequently became the norm for the Rohingya throughout the period of military rule, and when the military stepped away from total political control and Myanmar began a move toward quasi-civilian government, the Rohingya were already the world's largest stateless group (Lee, 2019).

2.2 *The 1982 Citizenship Act*

It is notable that historically, Rohingya people were assigned National Registration Cards (NRCs) just like everyone else in the country, but when the Ne Win government implemented discriminatory policies toward the Rohingya in the 1970s, the NRCs of the Rohingya people were confiscated by the authorities by various measures. These same Rohingya citizens were subsequently told to register themselves to prove their citizenship, but most of them now had no citizenship documents to show, resulting in their being identified as "Bengalis" or immigrants by the junta government (Lwin, 2012). Even though the government confiscated Rohingya IDs and other government-issued documents and implemented systematic discriminatory measures, they were still considered Burmese nationals up until 1982. The Citizenship Act promulgated in 1982 is the official document that stripped the citizenship of the Rohingya (Lwin, 2012).

Chris Lewa, in his journal article titled "North Arakan: an open prison for the Rohingya in Burma," details how in 1982 Burma's military rulers brought a new Citizenship Law which deprived most people of Indian and Chinese descent of citizenship, though the timing of its promulgation, shortly after the refugee repatriation in 1979, strongly suggests that it was specially designed to exclude the Rohingya (Lewa, 2009). Lewa describes that the 1982 law identified three categories of citizens: full, associate, and naturalized. Full citizens are those belonging to one of 135 national races who settled in Burma before 1823, the start of the British colonization of Arakan; the Rohingyas do not appear in this list, and the government does not recognize the term "Rohingya." Associate citizenship was only granted to those whose application for citizenship under the 1948 Act was pending on the date the Act came into force. And naturalized citizenship could only be granted to those who could furnish "conclusive evidence" of entry and residence before Burma's independence on January 4, 1948, who could speak one of the national languages well, and whose children were born in Burma. Very few Rohingyas could fulfill these requirements, and most were therefore excluded from all three categories (Lewa, 2009). In spite of there being ample evidence that the history of the Rohingyas could be traced back to the eighth century CE, they were not recognized as one of the national races and the 1982 Citizenship Act functioned as no less than an instrument of oppression, categorization, and discrimination against the Rohingyas by linking ethnicity and religion with citizenship (Gupta, 2009).

2.3 Post-citizenship Act Persecution

In the 1990s, the military junta developed the State Law and Order Restoration Council (SLORC), which evolved into the National League for Democracy (NLD) party that exists today. Guided by policies enacted by the SLORC, from 1991 to 1992, the Myanmar Armed Forces undertook another military operation targeting Rohingyas in northern Rakhine State called Operation PyiThaya (Clean and Beautiful Nation), which included the tactic of setting fire to the homes of Rohingya who were unable to prove their legal ties to the land. According to a report by International Crisis Group in 2014, the junta regime began a significant military deployment to northern Rakhine State in 1991. Here, the troops confiscated Muslims' land for building camps and agricultural production, as well as imposed arbitrary taxes and used the Rohingya Muslims as forced laborers. In addition to continuous violence, the economic burden of these demands became unbearable for the Rohingya people and by the early 1992, more than 25,000 Muslims had fled to Bangladesh, where they were housed in crowded refugee camps—this was considered the second push of Rohingya from Myanmar to Bangladesh (International Crisis Group, 2014). Though under a tripartite agreement with the association of the United Nations High Commissioner for Refugees (UNHCR) a total of 236,000 Rohingya were repatriated from Bangladesh to Myanmar during 1992–1996, most of them came back later on through illegal means as Rakhine State remained unsafe for them (Uddin, 2020). For the last 20 years, state-sanctioned anti-Muslim propaganda has enraged Rakhine Buddhists toward Rohingya Muslims, which resulted in the massacre in 2012. According to a report of Human Rights Watch in 2013, with the help of local authorities, the Burmese government forcibly displaced more than 125,000 Rohingya and other Muslims in October 2012 (Human Rights Watch, 2013). The report also indicated that Burmese officials, community leaders, and Buddhist monks organized and encouraged ethnic Arakanese, backed by state security forces, to conduct coordinated attacks on Muslim neighborhoods and villages and forcibly relocate the population. Although the then-president of the country later promised that the offenders would face justice, nothing was done to put an end to the violence. Hate speech and rumors played an important role in the othering process of the Rohingyas. Early in 2012, hostility between the Rakhine and Rohingya communities grew as a result of accusations that a Rohingya Muslim man had raped and murdered a Buddhist Rakhine woman. These events led to a violent confrontation between Buddhists and Rohingyas in June that resulted in a deadly communal riot that lasted until October and killed more than 200 people, with around 150,000 people becoming homeless (Shamsuddoha, 2019). The vast majority of the victims of this riot were Rohingyas, though there have been Rakhine victims. Among the Rohingya victims, some were taking shelter in displacement camps; others tried to enter neighboring countries such as Bangladesh (Brooten et al., 2015). During this time, around 120,000 Rohingya fled across the border and sought refuge in Bangladesh, and 87,000 more did so in 2016 (Uddin, 2020).

In December 2014, the government passed an abusive anti-Muslim four-law package known as the Race and Religious Protection Act, promoted and written by Ma Ba Tha, a racist Buddhist organization allegedly working to instigate hatred and violence against Muslims in Myanmar—particularly the Rohingya in Rakhine State—to establish discriminatory measures regarding marriage, religion, and reproductive rights. Although not directly related to the Rohingya, this package of laws did give hints of a certain ethno-religious bias (González Villa, 2019).

Further, in 2015, Buddhist nationalists protested President Thein Sein's government's plan to allow temporary ID card holders to participate in a constitutional referendum. But due to heavy pressure from the Buddhist nationalists, the government of Myanmar cancelled temporary identity cards—which effectively disqualified the Rohingya from voting. No Muslim candidate was even nominated by the political parties, including the National League for Democracy (NLD), as the parties were not willing to appear sympathetic to Muslims at a time when the county was experiencing a strong anti-Muslim sentiment (Kipgen, 2021). In 2017, the Myanmar security forces launched extensive military operations in Maungdaw, Buthidaung, and Rathedaung townships that included burning villages, destroying property, and violence against civilians of the Rohingya population. This operation was in response to attacks claimed by the Arakan Rohingya Salvation Army (ARSA), a non-state armed group, against Myanmar police, Border Guard Police, and military posts in Rakhine State that killed at least 12 Myanmar security personnel on August 25 (Parmar et al., 2019). In a report, American news website TIME stated that in the weeks after attack, the government security forces started a campaign of extrajudicial killings, sexual violence, and arson that drove more than 700,000 Rohingya Muslims from the country's western Rakhine State (TIME, 2018). The report also added that top diplomats and UN Officials described the military's attack as an ethnic cleansing, which some liken to genocide. The mass exodus of Rohingya people in this particular year has been recognized as the fastest growing refugee influx in the world, and these refugees are currently living in the most densely populated camps in the world in the Cox's Bazar district of Bangladesh (Habib, 2023). From the many descriptions above, we observe that the Myanmar government has continuously taken different steps toward "othering" and ousting Rohingyas from their homeland for decades. Government hostility toward the Rohingya has fostered a long history of systematic violence and discrimination, although this was less pronounced from Burmese independence to the military coup in 1962 (Tay et al., 2019). However, the decades-long propaganda and public brainwashing campaigns have helped Myanmar's junta government to continue its persecution of the Rohingya. The military dictators have tried to create images of the Rohingya as a terrorist group, and argued that they need to be in state power to tackle these terrorist threats. Given this continuous propaganda against the Rohingya, most of the Bamar have begun to believe that the Rohingya are indeed illegal immigrants and harmful to the stability of Burmese state-building; as a result, most Burmese people have supported the previous and continuing attacks against the Rohingya (Tareque, 2021).

The Myanmar government has long been pursuing various strategies and plans to alter public perception of the Rohingyas and construct this particular image. For example, in the country's state media, official documents, and school textbooks, the Rohingyas are referred to as Bengali, a racist local reference (Tareque, 2021).

Since 1962, the Rohingyas of Rakhine State in Myanmar have been subjected to discrimination and exclusion in systematic attacks linked to their identity, and this negative propaganda intensified the situation after the brutal campaign against the Rohingya people in 2017 as Myanmar state media contributed to mis-framing the situation in Rakhine State, thereby instilling fear of the Rohingya people among the majority population and contributing to violence against the members of this ethnic group (Kironska & Peng, 2021).

3 Conceptual Ideas of Propaganda

Hadley Cantril (1938), associate professor of Psychology at Princeton University and president of the Institute for Propaganda Analysis, stated that propaganda is difficult to describe because it encompasses so many different things. It is an expression of opinion or action by individuals or groups deliberately designed to influence opinions or actions of other individuals or groups with reference to predetermined ends. This definition implies several things; first, that propaganda is a positive thing; second, it is well-planned; third, it is selfish; fourth, it is non-critical, making use of suggestion and not reason; and, finally, it may be good or harmful depending on the societal perspective of the person judging it. Cantril also stated that the history of propaganda is old. It is an ancient art, and this technique can be found in the orations of Demosthenes against the Macedonians. The early Christian missionaries were propagandists, and we find as early as 1633 Pope Gregory XV establishing a Catholic propaganda institute. But propaganda on a wholesale basis was first used during the Second World War. Newspapers, the radio, and the movies all are vehicles of propaganda (Cantril, 1938). A more neutral and general definition can be found from Neil Postman, writing in the 1990s: "Propaganda is intentionally designed communication that invites us to respond emotionally, immediately and in an either/or manner" (Postman, 1993). Cunningham (2002), meanwhile, lists numerous specific features of propaganda; for example, self-serving reports, lies, distortions, fabrications, exaggerations, disinformation, selective discourse and censorship, spin, slanted or loaded words, mass persuasion, manipulation, brainwashing, religious discourse, rumors and gossip, and more. He also describes that for the most part, "we also assume that behind the scenes controlling the message's content and its flow are groups and individuals who are cunningly adept and sufficiently powerful to wage intermittent campaigns of persuasion as in say, political elections, advertising campaigns and rumor mongering" (Cunningham, 2002).

4 The Propaganda Model

According to Edward S. Herman and Noam Chomsky (2010), a propaganda system will consistently portray people abused in enemy states as worthy victims, whereas those treated with equal or greater severity by its own government or clients will be unworthy. In 1988, Herman and Chomsky developed a propaganda model, a conceptual model in political economics, in their book *Manufacturing Consent: The Political Economy of the Mass Media.* This model is an analytical framework that attempts to explain the performance of the US media in terms of the basic institutional structures and relationships within which they operate. Herman and Chomsky viewed that among other functions, the media serves and propagandizes on behalf of the powerful societal interests that control and finance them. The representatives of these interests have important agendas and principles that they want to advance, and they are well positioned to shape and constrain media policy. They also elaborated upon some structural factors of the media such as ownership control, dependency on other major funding, and mutual interest and relationships between the media and those who make the news and have the power to define it and explain what it means. This model also incorporates other closely related factors such as the ability to complain about the media's treatment of news, to provide experts to confirm the official slant on the news, and to fix the basic principles and ideologies that are taken for granted by media personnel and the elite but are often resisted by the general population (Herman & Chomsky, 2010). According to this model, there are five factors involved: ownership, advertising, sourcing, flak, and anti-Communist ideology. These work as "filters" through which information must pass, and individually and often in additive fashion they help shape media choices (Herman, 2018).

From the perspective of ownership, Herman and Chomsky argued that since mainstream media is comprised of either large companies or is a part of conglomerates, they prioritize their own financial interests; hence, the information supplied to the public will be biased or slanted in favor of these interests, and news stories that threaten the media owners' corporate financial interests will face the greatest bias and censorship. About advertising or funding they have contended that funding generated through advertising—and most newspapers have to attract advertising in order to cover the costs of production—causes stories that conflict with funders' "buying mood" to be marginalized or excluded. An additional filter relates to the sourcing of mass media news; as the media cannot afford to place reporters everywhere, they are, for example, dependent upon the pronouncements of the Prime Minister's personal spokesperson for government news. Another filter described by Herman and Chomsky is negative responses to a media statement or program. These may take the form of letters, telegrams, phone calls, petitions, lawsuits, speeches and bills before government, and other modes of complaint, threat, or punitive action. And finally, the filter of ideology relates that anti-ideologies exploit public fear and hatred of groups that pose a potential threat, for example, communism once posed the primary threat to freedom of speech, movement, the press, and so forth, and such a portrayal was often used as means to silence voices critical of elite interests (Herman & Chomsky,

2010). A propaganda system will consistently portray people abused in enemy states as worthy victims, whereas those treated with equal or greater severity by its own government or clients will be unworthy (Herman & Chomsky, 2010).

5 Major Propaganda Used Against the Rohingyas

The following discussion delves into the pervasive tactics of disinformation and manipulation that have targeted the Rohingya community. This section uncovers the deceptive narratives employed to marginalize and dehumanize the Rohingyas, perpetuating their persecution and denying their fundamental rights. We explore the intricate web of propaganda that portrays Rohingyas as Bengalis, illegal economic migrants, and even terrorists, fueling the perception of Muslims as an internal threat. Additionally, we examine the portrayal of Rohingyas as outsiders or alien invaders and the deliberate denial of their ethnic identity. The insidious claims of impure blood and the misuse of Buddhism as the religion of the "true" Burmese people further contribute to the marginalization of the Rohingyas. Moreover, we analyze the role played by mainstream media, social media platforms, books, the MRTV App, and religious leaders or monks in disseminating and amplifying this harmful propaganda. By scrutinizing these tactics, the aim is to expose the mechanisms behind the propaganda and shed light on its devastating consequences for the Rohingya community.

5.1 State-Sponsored Conspiracies

Conspiracy theories have a long history of being associated with propaganda, prejudice, and genocide, where they are often strongly believed by the perpetrators of terrorist attacks and were used as justification by the governments, like Nazi Germany and the Soviet Union, who used such theories to justify their terrorist activities. In the case of Myanmar, especially in the early post-independence period, an anti Muslim conspiracy theory was invented as early as the 1950s (Foxeus, 2022). The Burmese "grand conspiracy theory" first appeared in three articles by the film director Shwe Done Bi Aung that were published in Thway Thauk Magazine in January, May, and August 1953. These articles were later republished in a pamphlet called "Koudaw-karun" or the "Compassion of the Monk" which served as a model for later anti-Muslim conspiracy theories by reproducing what were alleged to be secret documents intended for internal circulation among Muslims alone (Foxeus, 2022). It is a conspiracy theory about an alleged secret plan by Muslims to not only turn Myanmar into an Islamic country, but also to achieve world dominion for Islam in the twenty-first century. Under the headline of "The secret (hlyaw-hwek) Spread of Muslims," it states:

> Regarding cherishing and protecting our nation and religion daily in Myanmar, we all Muslims must all help and support each other in economic and social affairs. Therefore, we, all the Muslims, as an offensive action regarding economic and social affairs, must buy only at shops having the symbol of a star on half-moon and the symbol 786, which are Islamic symbols. The meaning is that when the three digits (786) are combined, it amounts to 21.21 as a symbol that, when the 21st century is reached, our Islam must become supreme among all races/nations in the world, including Myanmar. (Shwe Done Bi Aung, n.d., 37–38, as cited in Foxeus, 2022)

According to Iselin Frydenlund (2021), Buddhist monks have played important roles by partaking in social affairs and presenting themselves as acting as vanguards of traditions, race, and religion. For example, "969 movements" were established by a group of Buddhist monks to "protect Buddhism" to stand as the discursive antithesis to "786," a numerical presentation of the first verse of the Quran which is commonly on display in Muslims shops throughout South and Southeast Asia (Frydenlund, 2021). The 969 movement underpins another conspiracy theory to spread Islamophobia and lead anti-Muslim violence. After the military took over in 1962, a structural Islamophobia was also observed in Burma and the Rohingyas were progressively stripped of their privileges under the Ne Win's ultra-nationalist military regime (Bakali, 2021). However, 969 movements propagated the notion that Muslim men contribute to the mass Islamization of Myanmar because they marry both Muslim and non-Muslim women, convert non-Muslim women to Islam, and have many children with them. It is widely believed in Myanmar that Muslim men are more fertile than Buddhist men and they are allegedly waging a "Love Jihad" or "Romeo Jihad" against Buddhists, a conspiracy theory also popular among certain Hindu nationalist groups in India (Gupta, 2009; Rao, 2011). This has often been exaggerated to generate fear and concern. For example, Ashin Wimalar Biwuntha, a 969 leader, said, "Muslim men try to win the love of poor Buddhist women for their reproductive tactics and they produce a lot of children, they are snowplowing and we have a duty to defend ourselves if we don't want to be overwhelmed" (Kyaw, 2016).

In addition, senior government officials, establishment monks, and even some members of the NLD—the political party of Nobel Peace Prize winner Aung San Suu Kyi—have supported the 969 campaign (Marshall, 2013). In 2012, over 688,000 Rohingyas were forced to flee Rakhine for Bangladesh, a neighboring country, as a result of 969 movements instigated by Ma Ba Tha (Bilay, 2022). Additionally, due to the widespread dissemination of public narratives warning of the threat of "Islamization" or of Muslims taking over the nation (despite Muslims making up less than 5% of the population), this nationalist group was successful in persuading former president Thein Sein to approve a controversial set of four laws on race and religion, including restricting intermarriage with Muslims (Bilay, 2022; Moe, 2018).

5.2 Bengalis/Illegal Economic Migrants

The Rohingyas are referred to in Myanmar as "Bengalis" or colonial-era illegal economic migrants who pose a threat to the country's security. They are referred to as such in the country's government documents, state media, and school textbooks (Zarn & Cowley, 2014). Some radical opponents of Islam call the Rohingya "Bengalis" to indicate that the Rohingya are illegal migrants from neighboring Bangladesh (Ebbighausen, 2018). The Myanmar government and the Buddhist nationalists continue to promote this propaganda to justify the decades-long oppression of the Rohingya (Vatti, 2017). The Burmese military government claims that the Rohingya people are not native to Myanmar; rather, that they immigrated from Bangladesh. They were officially declared as being illegal in 1982 and have remained so ever since, and experienced sporadic violence over the decades (Sohel, 2017). Migrants from Bengal into Rakhine before the inception of border control are used as examples for the claim that the Rohingya are Bengalis who arrived during the British era and should be expelled from Burma. In addition, the Buddhist majority in Myanmar has long rejected the existence of the mostly Muslim Rohingya minority group, portraying them as illegal immigrants from the district of Chittagong of Bangladesh, and causing them to become victims of genocide (Siddiquee, 2019). Since genocidal actions take years to plan and are not accidental, the diabolical masterminds or ideologues inside the ruling party frequently construct justifications for committing such atrocities, aided by other prominent groups within the perpetrating community such as religions, businesses, and social and political elites, who occasionally collaborate on the heinous programs observed in Myanmar (Siddiqui, 2019).

5.3 A Terrorist Group/Muslims as Terrorists/Muslims as an Internal Threat

The kings of medieval Burma never saw Islam as a foreign religion and needed Muslims not just for military purposes but also for establishment of the state and economic stability. However, military dictators, particularly after the "8888" Burmese uprising (on August 8, 1988), exploit Islamophobia to divert the attention of the majority Buddhists away from seizing political control. It was relatively easy to spread Islamophobia and use hate speech to accuse Muslims of being terrorists (Zarni & Brinham, 2017). Aside from that, it is claimed that Saudi Arabia, Pakistan, and even the Organization of Islamic Cooperation provided funding and other forms of support to civil society organizations supported by the military that spread the narrative that Muslims pose a threat and that Rohingyas are illegal immigrants who may turn into "Jihadists" (Tareque, 2021). According to Bina D'Costa (2012), a member of Drishtipat Writers' collective and author of *Nationbuilding, Gender and War Crimes in South Asia,* stated that the military regime sought to portray itself as the protector of its citizens and strategically employed misperceptions, fear, and prejudice to portray all Rohingya as terrorists and a massive security threat. In Myanmar, the Rohingya were painted as intruders and "enemies" within from neighboring Bangladesh who needed to be killed or wiped out as a "virus" by evil, ultra-racist intellectuals like Aye Chan, Aye Kyaw, and Khin Maung Saw—who played the role of Julius Streicher, a propagandist who acted as a catalyst to expedite the "Jewish solution" in Nazi Germany. Bigoted monks like Ashin Wirathu provided the religious justification through his nationalist and anti-Muslim rhetoric for "purifying" the Buddhist motherland from the minority Muslims, who were falsely depicted as a "threat" to Buddhism and its way of life (Siddiquee, 2020).

Additionally, the military has made clear its interest in limiting media debate on sensitive topics (Brooten, 2016). The military provides little usable information for journalists and rarely offers contact information for follow-up; it has threatened media with lawsuits if they printed or aired statements against it. For example, in May 2015, the military threatened media with lawsuits if they publicized statements by the blacklisted Kokang rebels (Brooten, 2016). Rahim and Khan (2021) argue that in Myanmar, the Rohingyas are not truly represented in the state media. Because of the government's direct censorship and repression of the media in representing indigenous people like the Rohingya, there is virtually no independent media coverage of events in Rakhine State and thus the Rohingyas are not accurately reflected in the state media (Rahim & Khan, 2021).

5.4 Outsiders/Alien Invaders

Despite centuries of habitation in Myanmar, Rohingyas are not acknowledged as citizens and are typically viewed as outsiders or Bangladeshis for political and ethnolinguistic reasons. In her thesis, Ananna (2022) stated that due to their distinct religious, linguistic, ethnic, and economic positions, the Rohingya have been explicitly framed as "the other" or as aliens. Legal, social, and political structures have been developed to reinforce this otherization (Ananna, 2022). According to Marcuse, cited by Ananna, it is true that the Rohingya speak a Bengali dialect that is similar to the Bengali spoken in the southeast region of Bangladesh and that they are Muslim in their beliefs and practices, but the attempt to portray the Rohingya as outsiders or Bangladeshis, on the other hand, is unjustified in terms of truth (Marcuse, 1964, as cited in Ananna, 2022). Nonetheless, Myanmar's elites believe that the Rohingya are recent immigrants from Bangladesh and that the term "Rohingya" was coined to distinguish them from Bengali Muslims (Ibrahim, 2016). Diplomat Magazine, cited by Sohel (2017), reported that a young boy named Mohammad Rafique said, "Burmese view us simply as 'animal,' 'non-human,' or 'aliens.'".

5.5 *Not an Ethnic Group*

Rohingyas are not on the list of 135 state-recognized ethnic groups of Myanmar, and according to state and Rakhine nationalist narratives, the term "Rohingya" was created in the 1950s to promote the political demands of the Bengalis in Myanmar. Mohammad Tareque in his Ph.D. thesis titled "Is Ethnic Cleansing of Rohingya Solely for Political Power? Unfolding the Reality" (2021) explored how official Myanmar state histories and laws support this view, which claims there are no Rohingya in the history of Myanmar and exclude the Rohingya from the list of 135 state-recognized ethnic groups of Myanmar that is enshrined in the citizenship law and the constitution. Thein Sein, the then-president of Burma, stated in London in July 2013 that "we don't have the Rohingya ethnicity." Ultra-nationalist Rakhine Buddhists framed the Rohingyas as illegal immigrants who migrated from East Bengal during the British rule of Burma or after Burma and Pakistan's independence in 1948 and 1947, respectively. Aye Maung, an influential Rakhine Member of Parliament and Chairman of the Rakhine Nationalities Development Party (RNDP) spelled out his party's vision of the Rakhine State thus: "We need to rebuild the Rakhine State only for the Rakhine who alone are the indigenous on the soil." Thus, they overlook the long history of the Rohingyas in the Rakhine region and claim that "Rohingya" is a recently invented ethnicity because the term was not included in British surveys during the colonial era (Tareque, 2021). In spreading this propaganda, the Myanmar government denied the Rohingyas citizenship, as the government argued that they are not one of the ethnic communities indigenous to Myanmar and excluded from full citizenship, whereas "Full Citizenship" is restricted to nationals of specific ethnic groups who settled in Burma prior to 1823 (Chakraborty, 2021).

5.6 *Impure Blood/Kalar*

In Myanmar, Rohingyas are often accused of having impure blood or being dark-skinned "Kalar." In the eyes of Burmese people, the Rohingyas do not look like them; their skin color and culinary culture are labeled as similar to those of Bangladeshis and Pakistanis, hence, some fanatic Buddhists have called the Rohingya "Kalar" (Minahan, 2016; Yin, 2005). In Myanmar, the term "Kalar" refers to the dark-skinned "ugly" people. By referring to them as "Kalar," the Burmese authorities try to equate all Muslims with the recent migrants from India under the British, or even accuse them of being more recent illegal immigrants (Yin, 2005). It is a racist term that was widespread and colonially rooted, especially toward the dark-skinned, hard-working races who, according to stereotypes of the time, manned the British colonial administration, possessed entrepreneurial skills, sided with the British colonizers, married local Buddhist women, and created impure-blooded children (Zarni & Cowley, 2014). Mikael Gravers writes that Muslims are still called "Kalar" or "black foreigners from India" and accused of forcing Buddhist women into marriage, while Muslim women are not allowed to marry Buddhists or even to convert. Frydenlund (2021) notes that there are some narratives promoted by Buddhist nationalist monks claiming that Muslim people influenced Burmese women to convert to Islam. For example, in 2013 and 2014, Buddhist monk U Wirathu and his supporters published a story in the form of a booklet titled "The Victim's Voice who Just Escaped from Tigers (Muslims)," which is about a Burmese Buddhist woman called Ma War War Myint who has left her Muslim husband. Her story begins by explaining how she was forced to convert to Islam by a Muslim man in the name of marriage. Ma War War Myint described that

> a Muslim wedding ceremony was arranged in the mosque, forcing her to accept the Nikah and then she was informed that she had become a Muslim, but she continued to go the monastery. But when her husband found out, he began to severely punish and torture her. Even the torture also resulted in the miscarriage of their first child when seven months pregnant. And the second son was given a Muslim name by the father, but at the hospital the mother had given him a Burmese Buddhist name. Frydenlund (2021)

The word "Muslim" is explicitly used in the text as a racial category, and the husband is both an adherent of Islam and a member of the Muslim "race." The text also derides the husband by referring to him as "Muslim" with the derogatory "Kalar," and describing how Muslim men marrying Myanmar "girls" is only done to increase the Muslim population (Frydenlund, 2021). Buddhist monk sermons, lay presentations, photo shows, biweekly and weekly journals, pamphlets, pronouncements, images, songs, conferences, stories, novels, and social media have all been used to spread their message throughout the nation portraying Muslims, the Rohingya in particular, as polygamists who marry Buddhist women and convert them to Islam in order to have bigger families than Buddhists (Kyaw, 2015). In the marketplace, Muslims are also alleged to only transact with Muslims or buy from Muslim-owned shops, which makes Muslims become better-off and more able to lure Buddhist women of lower socioeconomic backgrounds. It is also alleged that those Buddhist women who marry Muslim men will be converted to Islam and raise their children as Muslims (Kyaw, 2015).

Buddhist monks have described interreligious marriage as dangerous and a serious concern for the Buddhist community. For example, U Wirathu (2013), Ashin Thawpaka (2015), and Eindasekka Bhiwuntha (2014) are three Buddhist monks who believe that marriages between Buddhist women and Muslim men are dangerous. U Wirathu contends that Muslims want to spread their religion by "swallowing" other people. As a result, he believes that unassuming, honest, and uneducated Buddhist women fall into the trap set by these "wolves." Similarly, Eindasekka Bhiwuntha urges Buddhist women to emulate a role-model drawn from a Buddhist canonical text to further an anti-Muslim agenda, while Ashin Thawpaka asserts that Buddhist women who are not devoted to religion can easily be "swallowed" by others (i.e., Muslims). And the cultural position of Myanmar's Muslims has once again declined as a result of this intense securitization, which strikes at the core of Buddhist existence. Muslims are increasingly viewed as a threat to Buddhism and Buddhists as well as being unwelcome foreign guests (Foxeus, 2019).

5.7 *Buddhism as the Religion of the "True" Burmese People*

Over the years, the military junta government in Myanmar has placed much emphasis on Buddhism as the religion of the "true" Burmese people. As a result, the Rohingya people's religious aspect began to be viewed unfavorably by the wider Burmese population (Hukil & Shaunik, 2013). The Rohingya, in particular, have become the focal point of a dangerous strain of racism and intolerance that is fueled by religious differences between Buddhist nationalists and Muslim minorities. Despite the 2008 Burmese Constitution, which supposedly provides religious freedom, there is an implicit acknowledgment of Theravada Buddhism's unique position as the religion practiced by the vast majority of the citizens (89%), giving the majority a numerical advantage that has evolved into a moral authority. The limits of religious freedom are perfectly illustrated in the oppression and prejudice conducted against Myanmar's Islamic faction (Biver, 2014). "To be a Barman is to be a Buddhist" became the spirit of Myanmar's nationalism during its time under the British Empire, which is undoubtedly in line with the desire of hardline monks (Al-Amin, 2021). The Rohingya Muslims subsequently became the main enemy of the Buddhist population as the Bamar sought to unite the country on the basis of a single ethno-religious cultural identity—that is, Buddhism (Ali, n.d.). Further, Buddhist nationalism frequently takes the form of ethnocentrism in which the preservation of the Buddhist identity of Myanmar is emphasized in propaganda and Islam is portrayed as an existential threat to the faith and the nation, justifying its preemptive persecution. For example, in October 2017, senior Buddhist monk Sitagu Sayadaw preached a lecture in front of an audience of military officers in which he argued that violence was permissible against the Rohingya minority because, as Muslims, they are not fully human (Rowand & Artinger, 2021). The government of Myanmar disseminated this propaganda in order to uphold Buddhist supremacy and humiliate the Muslims in Myanmar. The political and religious authorities in Myanmar consistently and knowingly conveyed this false information through a variety of channels, including mainstream media, social media, security forces, political and religious leaders, popular writers, propaganda apps, official documents, school syllabi, and other policies and laws.

5.8 *Mainstream Media*

The mainstream media plays a significant role in othering the Rohingyas in Myanmar. The state authority and government has frequently used news media to disseminate propaganda against the Rohingya with a view to achieve public support for their aims. Since the military takeover in 1962, the media has been subject to censorship and stringent regulations in Myanmar. Apart from concerns over punishment under such laws, the state exerts tight control over media institutions by enforcing harsh defamation laws. For a long time, the state authority and government-controlled media denied the ethnic identity of the Rohingya. The private media and general public have followed the official narrative to portray the Rohingyas as "immigrants," Bengalis, or "illegal Bengali immigrants" (Albert & Chatzky, 2018, as cited in Siddique, 2019). If one looks closely at the headlines and news reports from the Global New Light of Myanmar since August 2017, one finds that they use terms other than "Rohingya" in reference to this group. This media outlet simply reproduces the government narrative while reporting on the crisis in Rakhine, which results in biased reporting that oversimplifies the complexity of the crisis. According to a report by Radio Free Asia (2016), the Myanmar government had ordered the state-run media not to refer to the persecuted Muslim minority group that lives in western Myanmar's Rakhine State by the divisive term "Rohingya" during visits by United Nations human rights officials. The Ministry of Information's letter, dated June 16, 2016, instructed official news outlets to describe the 1.1 million Rohingya who live in Rakhine as the "Muslim community in Rakhine state" during a visit by Yanghee Lee, the UN's special envoy on the situation of human rights in Myanmar, who visited the country from June 20 to July 1 of that year (Radio Free Asia, 2016). Further, Kironska and Peng, (2021) observes that there are five state-run daily newspapers that primarily disseminate propaganda against the Rohingya, including Myanmar Alinn, Kyemon, Yadanabon, Myawady Daily, and The Global New Light of Myanmar (GNLM). Through analyzing newspaper reports, it becomes clear that Rohingyas are depicted as a homogeneous, active group of perpetrators who threaten national stability. For example, the GNLM has likened the Rohingya to "detestable human fleas" (November 26, 2017) and suggested as a solution that "the thorn has to be removed as it pierces." On the other hand, Myanmar Alinn (August 26, 2017) promoted the government's efforts to combat terrorism with reporting that painted the non-Muslim inhabitants of Rakhine State as falling victim to "ARSA extremist Bengali terrorists" (Kironska & Peng, 2021). Kironska and Peng, (2021) also explores how the anti-Rohingya public opinion in the country is a direct result of the military's mass propaganda campaign, aided by state-run media in depicting the Rohingya as "Islamicists and Bengali invaders," which helped to influence people's anti-Rohingya perception and legitimized the military's action in the region.

5.9 Social Media

Human rights groups have claimed that the Tatmadaw, Myanmar's armed forces, uses Facebook to boost propaganda against the Rohingya and to amass public support for their military campaign of rampant killings, rape, and arson targeting the predominantly Muslim minority. In 2018, the New York Times reported that members of the Myanmar military have systematically used Facebook as a tool as part of the government's campaign of ethnic cleansing against the country's mostly Muslim minority group. This report also added that the military's Facebook operation began several years ago and allegedly had as many as 700 people who worked to create troll accounts and news and celebrity pages on Facebook, and then flooded them with inflammatory comments and posts in order to disseminate anti-Rohingya propaganda. In another report by The New York Times in March 2018, it noted that a UN fact-finding mission highlighted the role of social media networks, and Facebook in particular, in fueling hate speech against the Rohingya minority in Myanmar, telling the UN Human Rights Council that "incitement to violence" is rampant and unchecked (Mexsler, 2018).

According to a report by Ebbighausen Rodionat DW, while the military operation was underway, a huge number of posts appeared on Facebook calling for murder and violence against the Rohingya. Comments like the following were shared and "Liked" thousands of times: "We have to fight against the Rohingya the way Hitler did against the Jews, damned Kalar!" A picture showing Rohingya refugees on an overfilled boat was given the caption: "Pour on gas and light it so they got to Allah faster." Many people in Myanmar see the Rohingya as illegal immigrants, even though many Rohingya have been living in the country for decades (Ebbighausen, 2018). In a special investigation, Reuters found more than 1000 examples of posts, comments, images, and videos attacking the Rohingya or other Myanmar Muslims on Facebook. Almost all were in the main local language, Burmese.

The anti-Rohingya and anti-Muslim invectives were collected by Reuters and the Human Rights Center at UC Berkeley School of Law, which collection includes material that has remained public on Facebook for as long as six years. The poisonous posts call the Rohingya or other Muslims dogs, maggots, and rapists, suggest they be fed to pigs and urge they be shot or exterminated (Stecklow, 2018). The material also includes crudely pornographic anti-Muslim images. Here are some Facebook posts (translated into English) against the Rohingya found by Stecklow and Reuters (Table 1):

In his report, Stecklow also said that in Myanmar, Twitter (now X) is far less popular than Facebook. But after the army crackdown in August 2017, hundreds of new Twitter accounts suddenly sprang up in Myanmar. Some tweets on these accounts were in broken English. Two examples of these are as follows (Table 2):

Table 1 Facebook posts about the Rohingya population in Myanmar, 2013–2018

Facebook posts about the Rohingya population in Myanmar, 2013–2018	Date of post
"Cut off those necks of the sons of the dog and kick them into the water"	April 2018
"Pour fuel and set them on fire so that they can meet Allah faster"	April 2018
"Stuff pig's fat inside the damn kalar's mouth"	September 2017
"Just feed them to the pigs"	October 2016
"If it is a kalar, get rid of the whole race"	October 2016
"The non-human kalar dogs, the Bengalis, are killing and destroying our land, our water, and our ethnic people, and we need to destroy their race"	December 2013
"May the Rakhine people…and all Myanmar citizens be free from the dangerous sons of a dog, grandchildren of a kalar, and rapists"	September 2013

Table 2 Twitter posts about the Rohingya population in Myanmar, 2017

Twitter posts about the Rohingya population in Myanmar, 2017	Date of post
"There is no Rohingya in Myanmar, they are only illegal immigrants and terrorist"	August 2017
"They are originally Bengalis, illegally migrants and Land Robbers"	August 2017

In addition, Reuters analyzed more than 1200 of the new Twitter accounts following Matthew Smith, co-founder of Fortify Rights (a Southeast Asia-based human rights group) that were created between August 27 and August 31, at the height of the military crackdown against the Rohingya in western Rakhine State. A review of 564 of those accounts found that 349, or 62 percent, were anti-Rohingya (Stecklow, 2018). Human Rights activists accused Facebook of inciting offline violence through spreading hatred and nationalist propaganda online against the Rohingya community. And Facebook has been under fire for allegedly failing to identify hate speech and anti-Rohingya sentiment on its site (Aziz, 2021). Following intense pressure from rights groups, Facebook removed the Facebook accounts of some military officers and Buddhist monks. In a report on August 28, 2018, on its site the company stated: "today, we removed 425 Facebook Pages, 17 Facebook Groups, 135 Facebook accounts, and 15 Instagram profiles in Myanmar for engaging in 'coordinated inauthentic behavior' on Facebook" (Aziz, 2021).

5.10 Books

Books and booklets have been used as a means of propaganda for othering the Rohingyas. In July 2018, the Myanmar Army published a book titled "True News" on the Rohingya Crisis, which featured three fictitious images, one of which was from the War of Liberation in Bangladesh. A 117-page book published by the army's department of public relations and psychological warfare includes what it calls "documentary photos" and a chilling rewriting of history, in what appears to be an attempt to justify the killing of thousands of Rohingya over the last year in attacks by the army—what the UN has condemned as genocide. A Reuters investigation revealed that the provenance of three of the eight historical photographs contained in the book was faked (Reuters, 2018). The book purports that these photographs were taken in the western state of Rakhine, when in fact one was taken in Bangladesh, one in Tanzania, and the third is falsely labeled as depicting Rohingya entering Myanmar from Bangladesh, when in reality it shows them attempting to leave.

Another image depicts a crowd of men who appear to be on a long march with their backs bent over. "Bengalis intruded into the country after the British Colonialism occupied the lower part of Myanmar," the caption reads. The photo is apparently intended to depict Rohingya arriving in Myanmar during the colonial era, which ended in 1948. Reuters determined that the picture is in fact a distorted version of a color image taken in 1996 of refugees fleeing the genocide in Rwanda. The photograph was taken by Martha Rial for the Pittsburgh Post-Gazette. The newspaper did not immediately respond to a request for comment on the use of its photo. Another picture, also printed in black and white, shows men aboard a rickety boat. "Bengalis entered Myanmar via the watercourse," the caption reads. Actually, the original photo depicts Rohingya and Bangladeshi migrants leaving Myanmar in 2015, when tens of thousands fled to Thailand and Malaysia. The original has been rotated and blurred so the photo looks grainy. It was sourced from Myanmar's own Ministry of Information.

5.11 MRTV App

Through Myanmar Radio and Television (MRTV) propaganda apps, the Myanmar military junta uses MRTV to disseminate propaganda and fake news, including regular content representing democratic actors as "terrorists" and publishing photos of torture victims to spread fear. MRTV was also complicit in the 2017 genocide against the Rohingya, denying Rohingyan identity, portraying Rohingyas as "terrorists," and denying the military's "clearance operations." The MRTV apps were developed by the US Company Apps Web Social LLC, which listed them on the App Store and Google Play store on behalf of the junta in Myanmar. Min Aung Hlaing has launched these apps on Apple's App Store and Alphabet's Google Play Store as well as a third-party website, using Google and Apple logos as the backdrop. The apps are claimed to livestream-broadcast content via international satellites, and to distribute news articles (Justice for Myanmar, 2022). However, according to a report by the Sai (2022), the junta's state propaganda MRTV app was removed from Apple's App Store and the Google Play Store a day after it was launched (Sai, 2022). The report also indicated that MRTV is the junta's propaganda unit run by the Ministry of Information, led by retired major general Maung Maung Ohn—who is sanctioned by the EU—adding that MRTV portrays democracy activists as "terrorists" and publishes photos of torture victims to spread fear.

5.12 Religious Leaders or Monks

The Burmese government could not function without monks or monasteries until recently. Most of the post-independence Burmese governments felt compelled to either co-opt or repress the monks in order to reduce their power over the people (Hlaing, 2007, as cited in Al-Amin, 2021). Because of the sociopolitical context, governments were compelled to form alliances with the monkhood and relationships between the two were either friendly or hostile. The allied government, on the other hand, would not tolerate any monk who supported the opposing parties. The ultra extremist monks like Wirathu, Sitagu and even the chairman of Ma Ba Tha, Ashin Tiloka, propagated relentlessly against Rohingya Muslims in the name of protecting race and religion. Ashin Tiloka gave a speech in a public meeting in Karen State, when he threw questions one after another to the audience until finally the audience answered only with "yes." His propaganda was as follows:

> Outside people don't want our family to be peaceful. They want our properties like our land, that is why they provoke us. Look at the area where we living. It's in the Indochina region. What area? Indochina. What 'sindo? Kalars (Muslim) from the west. What's indo? Kalars from the west. "So our country could be disappeared?" Yes, it could. "So do you want to be careful and not have them separate us?" Yes, we have to! "These people, who don't like you, will try to separate you in different ways. To protect from the wild tiger we have to prepare our fences. Is it important to know why they want us to be divided?" Yes, it's important! "It's not only them. Are there some amongst us who are maggots and want to make things worse in our country?" Yes! They are! "So we also have to be careful with them?" Yes! (Lianes, 2019, as cited in Al-Amin, 2021)

Buddhist monk Ashin Wirathu, who has been described as the "Buddhist Bin Laden" and head of Ma Ba Tha, a Buddhist organization spreading anti-Muslim rhetoric for years, portrays the Rohingya as people from Bangladesh who entered Myanmar illegally and have encroached on native lands. Referring to the Rohingya as "mad dogs" and "snakes" through his numerous posts, Wirathu persistently spreads the propaganda that "We should not mix socially with Muslims" (Bengal, 2015). While Wirathu was jailed in 2003 by the military junta for 25 years for distributing anti-Muslim leaflets and preaching about evicting Muslims from Myanmar's Rakhine State, he was released in 2012 and began touring Myanmar, spreading hatred against Muslims through his sermons (Sumon, 2019).

6 Rohingya Persecution and the Propaganda Model

Based on Herman and Chomsky's propaganda model, it can be observed that the regime in Myanmar has consistently applied propaganda to target the Rohingya minority group there. According to Herman and Chomsky (2010), among other things, the media propagandizes on behalf of the influential socioeconomic interests that finance and control them. In their model, they argued that the information provided to the public will be biased or slanted in favor of these interests since the mainstream media, which is made up of major corporations or conglomerates, considers its financial interests first. The authorities of the Myanmar government used well-known news sources like the GNLM and the Myanmar Alinn as their propaganda tools to represent the Rohingya as "Bengali invaders or Islamicists." This is due to the fact that in Myanmar, the media is not free and is instead tightly controlled by the government's various rules and regulations, and media is also dependent on the government for information and finance in different ways. As a result, national perceptions of the Rohingya and the political rhetoric that predominates in society have an impact on media coverage, which is also expressed by Herman and Chomsky (2010) through their propaganda model. Following the events of August 25, 2017 and through the end of that year, articles in these newspapers in Myanmar propagated the view that Rohingya were a homogeneous, active group of culprits who posed a threat to national stability (Kironshka & Peng, 2021).

Additionally, the idea of Buddhist nationalism is another effective tactic used by radical monks in Myanmar to legitimize the persecution of the Rohingya by spreading the notion that Buddhism could be in danger, because Muslims are a threat to the nation's culture and religion as they attempt to convert the country to Islam through their reproduction and business strategies. For instance, Buddhist monks alleged that Muslim men may contribute to the mass Islamization of Myanmar because they marry both Muslim and non-Muslim women, and convert non-Muslim women to Islam and have many children with them. These rumors about Muslims circulate through both traditional media and social media, especially Facebook, which has contributed to an anti-Muslim moral panic. According to Azeem Ibrahim (2022), famous Buddhist monks, most notably Ashin Wirathum, used Facebook to incite hatred and spread false information about the Rohingya. Wirathu posted incendiary sermons to his millions of followers in which he referred to the Rohingya as "Bengalis" in an effort to persuade his fellow Burmese that they were foreign invaders rather than fellow citizens (Ibrahim, 2016). The Tatmadaw also used Facebook to spread anti-Rohingya propaganda, using hundreds of military personnel to create false accounts and news and entertainment pages and posting defamatory articles depicting Rohingyas as "terrorists" (Mozur, 2018). Without much accountability, Tatmadaw officials continue to propagate misinformation and hate speech on Facebook about the Rohingya community, which has "a detrimental effect on freedom of expression, assembly and association for Myanmar's most vulnerable users" (Stevenson, 2018). In a report, Amnesty International claims that Facebook's algorithms "proactively amplified" anti-Rohingya content and it ignored civilians' and activists' pleas to curb hate-mongering while profiting from increased engagement (Guzman, 2022). Here, it was also possible to see echoes of Herman and Chomsky's argument about funding or financial interest, as Facebook found it profitable as a business to stir hatred and propagate false information about the Rohingya. Additionally, it complies with the propaganda model's final ideological filter, which claims that anti-ideologies prey on people's fears and animosities toward groups that could pose a threat. For instance, Buddhist nationalism raised the voices of the elite, in this case the radical monks in Myanmar, and threatened the press's freedom to tell the truth about the persecution of the Rohingya. As a result, the portrayal of the Rohingyas' persecution in Myanmar's media, both the mainstream and social, is skewed and spreads the opinion of the ruling class or elites.

Moreover, even the largest media outlets cannot afford to send reporters and camera crews wherever there are breaking news stories; therefore, they depend on influential sources that have a tendency to influence media policies, and the media is forced to use these sources to ensure a steady flow of news. In the case of covering the Rohingya crisis, international media and monitoring organizations criticized Myanmar's journalists for their coverage of the war, claiming that the majority of their stories were biased and lacked diverse viewpoints. Studies have shown that limited government and military cooperation, pressure from the Rakhine people, difficulties reaching Muslims in the Rohingya community, and limited access to the conflict zone continue to make it difficult for journalists to fully engage in conflict-sensitive reporting (Lynn, 2020). Since the majority of Myanmar's media had to rely on the Tatmadaw for information about the issue, the Rohingya crisis is an example of how the third filter of Herman and Chomsky's (2010) propaganda model, "source," has an impact on media coverage of the crisis.

7 Conclusion

There is a proverb that states, "If a lie is repeated 100 times, it eventually becomes the truth," which is also a law of propaganda that is widely attributed to the Nazi propagandist Joseph Goebbels. Propaganda has been a very effective technique across the globe for disseminating untruths and lies about a certain group, community, race, or gender. The persecution and othering process of the Rohingyas is no exception. Propaganda is not only used to influence public opinion, but also used to advance a specific social and political stance in order to "other" a particular group or incite hatred and contempt against it. In Myanmar, propaganda targeting the Rohingya as "Bengalis," "outsiders," "economic migrants," and "Muslim terrorists" has been extensively prevalent. The government of Myanmar justified and continued institutionalized prejudice and tyranny through constant propaganda, which also fanned mob violence and abuse against the Rohingya. Additionally, the Myanmar junta government employed social media, mass media, and other platforms extensively for propagandist dissemination in order to shape public opinion and make it resemble the observations predicted by Herman and Chomsky's propaganda model (2010). There are some debates about whether the negative propaganda against the Rohingya in Myanmar resulted in persecution of the Muslim minority or not. But for decades, Rohingyas in Myanmar have been denied their existence by the Buddhist majority, which has falsely portrayed them as illegal immigrants from Bangladesh, while others maintain that though the Rohingyas of Rakhine State have been discriminated and excluded against related to their identity and citizenship issues from the very beginning of the country's independence, the negative propaganda on mainstream and social media intensified the situation after the brutal campaign against the Rohingya people in 2017. The massive military offensive targeting Rohingya civilians in 2017 in Myanmar had clearly been pre-planned; in the weeks beforehand, there had been troop build-ups, ethnic Rakhine civilians had been given training and weapons, and under the pretext of the attacks as an anti-terrorism operation, the military launched a campaign to drive most of the Rohingya out of the country (Khin, 2017).

References

Ahsan Ullah, A. (2016). Rohingya crisis in Myanmar: Seeking justice for the "stateless." *Journal of Contemporary Criminal Justice, 32*(3), 285–301.

Akesson, B., & Basso, A. R. (2022). *From bureaucracy to bullets: Extreme domicide and the right to home*. Rutgers University Press.
Al-Amin, M. (2021). Examining religious extremism and political violence in Myanmar: An experience from Rohingya crisis. *Asian Studies, 40*, 87–110.
Albert, E., & Chatzky, A. (2018). The Rohingya crisis. Available at: https://www.cfr.org/backgrounder/
Albert, E., & Maizland, L. (2017). *The Rohingya crisis. Council on foreign relations.*
Ali, A. B. (n.d.). Buddhist nationalism and making Rohingya Muslim "other." *Burmese nationalism, Rohingya crisis and contemporary politics*, 29.
Allott, A. J. (1994). Burmese ways. *Index on Censorship, 23*(3), 87–91.
Ananna, S. (2022). *We have seen this before: Grounding the Rohingya's genocidal alienation within sociological theories* (SSRN Scholarly Paper 4077938). https://doi.org/10.2139/ssrn.4077938
Anwary, A. (2020). Interethnic conflict and genocide in Myanmar. *Homicide Studies, 24*(1), 85–102.
Aziz, A. (2021). A repertoire of everyday resistance and technological (in) security: Constructing the Rohingya diaspora and transnational identity politics on social media. In *Selected papers in internet research 2021: Research from the annual conference of the association of internet researchers*. Association of Internet Researchers (AoIR).
Aziz, A. (2022). Rohingya diaspora online: Mapping the spaces of visibility, resistance and transnational identity on social media. *New Media & Society*, 14614448221132241.
Bakali, N. (2021). Islamophobia in Myanmar: The Rohingya genocide and the 'war on terror.' *Race & Class, 62*(4), 53–71. https://doi.org/10.1177/0306396820977753
Bari, M. A. (2018). *The Rohingya crisis: A people facing extinction*. Kube Publishing Ltd.
Barkun, M. (2013a). *A culture of conspiracy: Apocalyptic visions in contemporary America* (Vol. 15). University of California Press.
Barkun, M. (2013b). *A culture of conspiracy: Apocalyptic visions in contemporary America*. University of California Press.
BBC News. (2018, March 13). UN: Facebook has turned into a beast in Myanmar. *BBC News*. Retrieved from https://www.bbc.com/news/technology-43385677
Bengal, S. (2015, May 24). *Monk dubbed 'Buddhist Bin Laden' targets Myanmar's persecuted Muslims*. Los Angeles Times. Retrieved from https://www.latimes.com/world/asia/la-fg-ff-myanmar-monk-20150524-story.html
Bilay, Z. (2022). The characteristics of violent religious nationalism: A case study of Mabatha against Rohingya Muslim in Myanmar. *Journal of Human Rights and Peace Studies, 8*(1), 86–106.
Biver, E. (2014). *Religious nationalism: Myanmar and the role of Buddhism in anti-Muslim narratives*.
Bradley. (2022, April 22). *Technology: A problem or a solution in Myanmar's revolution?* Global Voices. Retrieved from https://globalvoices.org/2022/04/21/technology-a-problem-or-a-solution-in-myanmars-revolution/
Brooten, L., Ashraf, S. I., & Akinro, N. A. (2015). Traumatized victims and mutilated bodies: Human rights and the 'politics of immediation' in the Rohingya crisis of Burma/Myanmar. *International Communication Gazette, 77*(8), 717–734.
Brooten, L. (2016). Burmese media in transition. *International Journal of Communication, 10*, 182–199, https://ijoc.org/index.php/ijoc/article/view/3358
Cantril, H. (1938). Propaganda analysis. *The English Journal, 27*(3), 217–221.
Chakraborty, I. (2021). Wizards first: The muggle and mudblood crisis reflecting the Rohingya crisis. *New Literaria, 2*(1), 37–49. https://doi.org/10.48189/nl.2021.v02i1.005
Chowdhory, N., & Mohanty, B. (2020). *Citizenship, nationalism and Refugeehood of Rohingyas in Southern Asia*. Springer.
Cunningham, S. B. (2002). *The idea of propaganda: A reconstruction*. Greenwood Publishing Group.
Datawrapper. (2023). *Datawrapper—Create and share charts and maps online*. Retrieved on December 1, 2023, from https://www.datawrapper.de/_/Kj2XH/

D'Costa, B. (2012). *The Rohingya and the denial of 'the right to have rights'*. The Democratic Voice of Burma.

de Guzman, C. (2022). Meta's facebook algorithms 'proactively' promoted violence against the Rohingya. New amnesty international report asserts. *TIME, 28*(9), 2922.

Ebbighausen, R. (2018, August 25). *Inciting Rohingya hatred on social media.* Deutsche Welle (DW) Asia. Retrieved from https://www.dw.com/en/inciting-hatred-against-rohingya-on-social-media/a-45225962

Eindasekka Bhiwuntha, A. (2014). Bouddha-youn-kyi-khyek-athek-sun-wun-thū-tayā- Daw ["*A Sermon about Those Who Dare to Sacrifice Their Lives for Their Trust in the Buddha* [*Dhamma and Sangha*]"]. Shan State, Lashio, November 12, 2014.

Fink, C. (2001). *Living silence: Burma under military rule.* Zed Books.

Foxeus, N. (2019). The Buddha was a devoted nationalist: Buddhist nationalism, ressentiment, and defending Buddhism in Myanmar. *Religion, 49*(4), 661–690. https://doi.org/10.1080/0048721X.2019.1610810

Foxeus, N. (2022). Buddhist nationalist sermons in Myanmar: Anti-Muslim moral panic, conspiracy theories, and socio-cultural legacies. *Journal of Contemporary Asia*, 1–27.https://doi.org/10.1080/00472336.2022.2032801

Frontières, M. S. (2017). MSF surveys estimate that at least 6700 Rohingya were killed during the attacks in Myanmar. *Relief Web, 14.*

Frydenlund, I. (2021). Protecting Buddhist women from Muslim men: "Love Jihad" and the rise of Islamophobia in Myanmar. *Religions, 12*(12), 1080. https://doi.org/10.3390/rel12121082

Fujita, A. (2017, March 16). *Tackling Asia's final technology frontier.* CNBC. https://www.cnbc.com/2017/03/16/myanmar-technology-tackling-asias-final-tech-frontier.html

Godrej, D. (2008). A short history of Burma. *Journal of New Internationalist, 6*(1), 24–25.

González Villa, L. (2019). *The Rohingya genocide: The internationally neglected people of the Rakhine state.*

Gowan, A. (2014). Cellphone use transforms Burmese life after government opens mobile market. *Washington Post.*

Gupta, C. (2009). Hindu women, Muslim men: Love Jihad and conversions. *Economic and Political Weekly*, 13–15.

Habib, M. R. (2023). Rohingya refugee–host community conflicts in Bangladesh: Issues and insights from the "field." *Development in Practice, 33*(3), 317–327.

Haque, M. M. (2017). Rohingya ethnic Muslim minority and the 1982 citizenship law in Burma. *Journal of Muslim Minority Affairs, 37*(4), 454–469.

Harvey, G. E. (2019). *History of Burma: From the earliest times to 10 March 1824 the beginning of the English conquest.* Routledge.

Herman, E. S., & Chomsky, N. (2010). *Manufacturing consent: The political economy of the mass media.* Random House.

Herman, E. (2018). The propaganda model revisited. *Monthly Review, 69*(8), 42–54

Hlaing, K. Y. (2007). The politics of state—Society relations in Burma. *South East Asia Research, 15*(2), 213–254.

Hossain, M. A., Huda, M. N., Ullah, A. M. A., & Renzaho, A. (2022). Risk factors, contemporary challenges and psychological well-being of the Rohingya refugees in Bangladesh: Policy implications. *The International Journal of Health Planning and Management, 37*(4), 1912–1917.

Hukil, R., & Shaunik, N. (2013). *Rudderless & drowning in tears: The Rohingyas of Myanmar.* Institute of Peace and Conflict Studies. https://www.jstor.org/stable/resrep09219

Human Rights Watch. (2000, May 1). *Burmese refugees in Bangladesh: Still no durable solution.* https://www.hrw.org/report/2000/05/01/burmese-refugees-bangladesh/still-no-durable-solution

Human Rights Watch. (2013, April 22). *All you can do is pray: Crimes against humanity and ethnic cleansing of Rohingya muslims in Burma's Arakan State.* https://www.hrw.org/report/2013/04/22/all-you-can-do-pray/crimes-against-humanity-and-ethnic-cleansing-rohingya-muslims

Ibrahim, A. (2016). *The Rohingyas: Inside Myanmar's hidden genocide*. Oxford University Press.
Ibrahim, A. (2022). *Authoritarian century: Omens of a post-liberal future*. Hurst Publishers.
International Crisis Group. (2014). *Myanmar: The politics of Rakhine state* (Asia Report No. 261). Retrieved from https://www.crisisgroup.org/asia/south-east-asia/myanmar/myanmar-politics-rakhine-state
Justice for Myanmar. (May 5, 2022). *US tech firms enabling Myanmar Junta propaganda*. https://www.justiceformyanmar.org/press-releases/us-tech-firms-enabling-myanmar-junta-propaganda
Karim, D. A. (2016). *The Rohingyas: A short account of their history and culture*. Jatiya Sahitya Prakash.
Kemp S. (2022). Digital Myanmar. Retrieved from https://datareportal.com/reports/digital-2022-myanmar
Khan, N.-U.-Z. (2022). *Rohingya crisis: Security implications on Bangladesh and ways ahead*.
Khin, T. (2017). Rohingya: A preventable genocide allowed to happen. *Insight Turkey, 19*(4), 43–54.
Kingston, L. N. (2018). Protecting the world's most persecuted: The responsibility to protect and Burma's Rohingya minority. In *The responsibility to protect* (pp. 179–191). Routledge.
Kipgen, N. (2021). The 2020 Myanmar election and the 2021 coup: Deepening democracy or widening division? *Asian Affairs, 52*(1), 1–17.
Kironska, K., & Peng, N.-N. (2021). How state-run media shape perceptions: An analysis of the projection of the Rohingya in the global new light of Myanmar. *South East Asia Research, 29*(1), 16–31.
Knight, P. (Ed.). (2003). *Conspiracy theories in American history: An encyclopedia: Conspiracy theories in American history [2 volumes]: An encyclopedia*. ABC-CLIO.
Kyaw, N. N. (2015). Alienation, discrimination, and securitization: Legal personhood and cultural personhood of Muslims in Myanmar. *The Review of Faith & International Affairs, 13*(4), 50–59. https://doi.org/10.1080/15570274.2015.1104971
Kyaw, N. N. (2016). Islamophobia in Buddhist Myanmar: The 969 movement and anti-Muslim violence. *Islam and the state in Myanmar: Muslim-Buddhist relations and the politics of belonging* (pp. 183–210).
Lee, R. (2019). Extreme speech|extreme speech in Myanmar: The role of state media in the Rohingya forced migration crisis. *International Journal of Communication, 13*, 22.
Lewa, C. (2009). North Arakan: An open prison for the Rohingya in Burma. *Forced Migration Review, 32*, 11.
Lwin, N. S. (2012). Making Rohingya statelessness. *New Mandala, 29*.
Lynn, N. (2020). The danger of words: Major challenges facing Myanmar journalists on reporting the Rohingya conflict. *Media Asia, 47*(1–2), 4–22. https://doi.org/10.1080/01296612.2020.1824569
Marcuse, H. (1964). *One dimensional man: The ideology of industrial society*. Sphere Books Limited.
Marshall, A. R. (2013). Myanmar gives official blessing to anti-Muslim monks. *Reuters, June, 27*.
Matsui, M. (2015). Foreign providers, price competition spur growth. *Nikkei Asian Review*.
Mexsler, E. (2018, March 13). *U.N. fact finders say Facebook played a 'Determining' role in violence against the Rohingya*. New York Times. Retrieved from https://time.com/5197039/un-facebook-myanmar-rohingya-violence/
Minahan, B. J. (2016). *Encyclopedia of stateless nations: Ethnic and national groups around the World*, Second Edition (pp. 353–354). Greenwood, ABC-CLIO LLC, Santabarbara, Califorinia.
Moe, M. (2018). Ma Ba Tha changes name, still officially illegal. [Online]. Dalam. https://www.Irrawaddy.Com/News/Ma-Ba-Tha-Changes-Name-Still-Officiallyillegal.html. [Diakses September 2019].
Mozur, P. (2018). *A genocide incited on Facebook, with posts from Myanmar's military*.
Parmar, P. K., Leigh, J., Venters, H., & Nelson, T. (2019). Violence and mortality in the northern Rakhine State of Myanmar, 2017: Results of a quantitative survey of surviving community leaders in Bangladesh. *The Lancet Planetary Health, 3*(3), e144–e153.

Pattison, C. (2012). Barriers to reform in Myanmar: Displacement of civilians in Kachin State. *Oxford Monitor of Forced Migration, 2*(2), 64.
Postman, N. (1993). *Technology: The surrender of culture to technology.* Vintage Books
Radio Free Asia. (2016, June 21). *Myanmar government orders state media not to use 'Rohingya'*. Retrieved from https://www.rfa.org/english/news/myanmar/myanmar-government-orders-state-media-not-to-use-rohingya-06212016155743.html
Rahim, A., & Khan, S. (2021). Representation of the Rohingyas in media and new media: Narrative, analysis, and re-thinking. *International Journal of Research and Innovation in Social Science, 05*. https://doi.org/10.47772/IJRISS.2021.51246
Rao, M. (2011). Love Jihad and demographic fears. *Indian Journal of Gender Studies, 18*(3), 425–430. https://doi.org/10.1177/097152151101800307
Reuters. (August 15, 2018). *Why Facebook is losing the war on hate speech in Myanmar.* https://www.reuters.com/investigates/special-report/myanmar-facebook-hate/
Rowand, M., & Artingr, B. (February 16, 2021). When Buddhists back the army. Foreign Policy. Retrieved December 26, 2022, from https://foreignpolicy.com/2021/02/16/myanmar-rohingya-coup-buddhists-protest/
Sai, K. (2022, May 7). *Myanmar Junta propaganda app ditched by apple and Google.* The Irrawaddy. https://www.irrawaddy.com/news/burma/myanmar-junta-propaganda-app-ditched-by-apple-and-google.html
Shamsuddoha, M. (2019). *Paradox of Rohingya crisis: A legacy of history* (pp. 51–69).
Shani, G., & Saeed, S. (n.d.). *Othering the Rohingya: Religion, human insecurity and the colonial legacy in Maynmar.*
Siddiquee, Md. A. (2019). The portrayal of the Rohingya genocide and refugee crisis in the age of post-truth politics. *Asian Journal of Comparative Politics, 5*, 205789111986445. https://doi.org/10.1177/2057891119864454
Siddiqui, H. (2019). The myth of 'Bengali Migration' to Arakan debunked. *SSRN Electronic Journal.* https://doi.org/10.2139/ssrn.3334098
Siddiquee, M. A. (2020). The portrayal of the Rohingya genocide and refugee crisis in the age of post-truth politics. *Asian Journal of Comparative Politics, 5*(2), 89–103.
Smith, M. (1991). Myanmar: The Burmese way to rack and ruin. *Index on Censorship, 20*(10), 43–45.
Soe, P. P. P. S. (2021). *Media bias and framing analysis of local media and foreign based media coverage on the case of "Rohingya: Gambia files case against Myanmar at international court of justice".*
Sohel, M. (2017). The Rohingya crisis in Myanmar: Origin and emergence. *Saudi Journal of Humanities and Social Sciences, 2.*
Stecklow, S. (2018, August 15). Why Facebook is losing the war on hate speech in Myanmar, Reuters. Retrieved from https://www.reuters.com/investigates/special-report/myanmar-facebook-hate/
Stevenson, A. (2018). Facebook admits it was used to incite violence in Myanmar. *The New York Times, 6.*
Sumon, S. (2019, July 30). *Ashin Wirathu: The Buddhist bin Laden.* ARAB NEWS. https://www.arabnews.pk/node/1532846/world
Tareque, M. (2021). *Is ethnic cleansing of Rohingyas solely for retaining Burmese political power? Unfolding Reality.*
Tay, A. K., Riley, A., Islam, R., Welton-Mitchell, C., Duchesne, B., Waters, V., Varner, A., Moussa, B., Alam, A. M., & Elshazly, M. (2019). The culture, mental health and psychosocial wellbeing of Rohingya refugees: A systematic review. *Epidemiology and Psychiatric Sciences, 28*(5), 489–494.
Thawpaka, A. (2015). Amyou-bhāthā-thāthanā-ne-amyou-saung-upaday ["*Nation, Religion and the Sāsana, and the Law Protecting the Nation*"]. September 12, 2015, Mawlamyaing.
TIME. (2018, May 16). *About 60 Rohingya babies are born every day in refugee camps, the U.N. says.* https://time.com/5280232/myanmar-bangladesh-rohingya-babies-births/

Turner, A. (2017). *Saving Buddhism: The impermanence of religion in colonial Burma*. University of Hawaii Press.
Uddin, N. (2015). Chapter 4. State of stateless people: The plight of Rohingya Refugees in Bangladesh. In *The human right to citizenship: A slippery concept* (pp. 62–77). University of Pennsylvania Press. https://doi.org/10.9783/9780812291421-005
Uddin, N. (2020). *The Rohingya: An ethnography of 'subhuman' life*. Oxford University Press.
Ullah, A. A., & Chattoraj, D. (2023). *The unheard stories of the Rohingyas: Ethnicity, diversity and media*. Policy Press.
Vatti, S. (2017). *The Plight of the Rohingya: sorting through the propaganda*. Liberation School. Retrieved October 5, from https://www.liberationschool.org/the-plight-of-the-rohingya-sorting-through-the-propaganda/
Washaly, N. (2019). Rohingya: The identity crisis. In *Ecos de La Academia*.
Whitecombe, H. (2017). MSF surveys estimate that at least 6700 Rohingya were killed during the attacks in Myanmar. *Medecins Sans Frontiers*. Retrieved August 28, 2023, from https://prezly.msf.org.uk/msf-surveys-estimate-that-at-least-6700-rohingya-were-killed-during-the-attacks-in-myanmar
Wirathu, U. (2013). Amyou-thā-yay-atwek pay-hsap-myi ["*We Will do Selfless Service for Nationalism*"]. May 19, 2013, Muse, Shan State
Yawnghwe, C. T., & Sakhong, L. H. (2002). *Rebuilding the Union of Burma*.
Yegar, M. (1972). *The Muslims of Burma: A study of a minority group*. Harrassowitz.
Yin, K. M. (2005). Salience of ethnicity among Burman Muslims: A study in identity formation. *Intellectual Discourse*, *13*(2), Article 2. https://journals.iium.edu.my/intdiscourse/index.php/id/article/view/108
Zarni, M., & Brinham, N. (2017). *Reworking the colonial-era Indian peril: 1*.
Zarni, M., & Cowley, A. (2014). The slow-burning genocide of Myanmar's Rohingya. *23*(3).

Chapter 12
"Framing" the Rohingya Crisis: Mainstream Media Coverage and Shifting Narratives

Kawser Ahmed and Rukiya Hassan

Abstract This chapter analyzes how mainstream media framed the Rohingya crisis in two periods (2010–2017 and 2017–2022) through Western and non-Western media coverage, exploring dominant narratives, influences, and shifts after global attention in 2017. The analysis reveals diverse portrayals in the first period, with Western media highlighting the plight of refugees and criticizing Myanmar's government, while non-Western media offered alternative perspectives. Post-2017, coverage shifted dramatically, focusing on the military crackdown and humanitarian crisis. The study examines the far-reaching impacts of media framing on international engagement, policy decisions, and public perception, highlighting ethical considerations in reporting genocide and humanitarian crises. The findings offer valuable insights for various stakeholders and contribute to understanding the role of media in shaping discourse and responses to crises.

1 Introduction

The Rohingya crisis, an ongoing humanitarian dilemma since 2010, has garnered widespread attention from global mainstream media. These media outlets have been instrumental in framing the narrative of the crisis, significantly shaping public perception and influencing policy responses at both national and international levels. The evolving nature of media coverage and its potential bias or objectivity in representing the crisis has become a pivotal aspect of understanding the role of journalism in conflict situations. To delve into the media's role in framing the Rohingya crisis, a comprehensive examination of published articles is indispensable. This involves analyzing not just how the crisis is described but also how various aspects of the

K. Ahmed
University of Winnipeg, Winnipeg, Canada
e-mail: k.ahmed@uwinnipeg.ca

R. Hassan (✉)
Bangladesh University of Professionals, Dhaka, Bangladesh
e-mail: rh.phool@gmail.com

K. Ahmed and Md. R. Islam (eds.), *Understanding the Rohingya Displacement*, International Perspectives on Migration, https://doi.org/10.1007/978-981-97-1424-7_12

humanitarian response are portrayed (Lee, 2021). By assessing the textual elements used in media coverage, including linguistic choices and thematic focuses, this study aims to reveal the underlying narratives and biases in reporting on the Rohingya situation (Lee, 2021).

Additionally, the influence of media framing on public opinion and policy-making cannot be overstated. In this context, it is also pertinent to explore the role of digital and social media in amplifying or altering these narratives. The advent of social media has given rise to diverse perspectives and narratives, challenging the traditional media's monopoly over information dissemination. The interaction between traditional news media and social media platforms has created a complex information ecosystem where narratives about the Rohingya crisis are continuously shaped and reshaped. This dynamic raises critical questions about the authenticity, reliability, and impact of the news consumed by the public and policymakers alike. Smith and Doe (2022) highlight the interplay between mainstream media narratives and social media trends, suggesting that this synergy significantly affects the global understanding of the crisis. Thus, this chapter will not only assess mainstream media coverage but also consider the broader context of digital information dissemination and its impact on framing the Rohingya crisis (Smith & Doe, 2022).

2 Context

The Rohingya crisis can be traced back to the early 2010s, when tensions between the Rohingya Muslim minority and the Buddhist majority in Myanmar escalated. These tensions resulted in outbreaks of violence and forced displacement, with thousands of Rohingya fleeing their homes and seeking refuge in neighboring countries.

Factors contributing to the escalation of the crisis in 2010–2017 include discrimination and persecution based on ethnicity and religion, the denial of citizenship rights to the Rohingya community in Myanmar, government-sanctioned violence and military operations against the Rohingya population, and the lack of accountability for human rights abuses.

Key events and developments during this period include the violence in 2012 that led to mass displacement of the Rohingya, attacks by government forces in 2016 and 2017 resulting in a significant influx of Rohingya refugees into neighboring Bangladesh, and the international attention that these events garnered. The Buddhist Ma Ba Tha movement was also instrumental in fueling anti-Rohingya sentiments and supporting policies that further marginalized the Rohingya population. The primary contribution of this movement was the grassroots mobilization of people in Myanmar in general and Rakhine in particular. Another factor is the democratic transition of Myanmar from military to civilian rule, which raised hopes for improved human rights and democratic reforms but also exposed underlying tensions and challenges within the country. Facebook first opened its gates to Myanmar in 2011, allowing for the rapid spread of hate speech and misinformation targeting the Rohingya community.

In Rakhine, the use of Facebook has become synonymous with accessing the internet, and conversely, not having access to Facebook is akin to being completely disconnected from online platforms. This unique relationship between the region's population and this particular social media platform highlights both the influence and limitations of technology in their lives. However, it is important to note that while individuals in Rakhine heavily rely on Facebook as their primary source of online connectivity, there are many other aspects related to digital inclusion that need further exploration.

The rise of Chinese influence needs to be understood during this period as it inaugurated its Belt and Road Initiative (BRI), which earmarked the southern part of Rakhine as an important node connecting its sea route to the Indian Ocean. As a result, Suu Kyi's NLD government witnessed a significant increase in economic ties with China, further complicating the Rohingya crisis by hindering international efforts to hold Myanmar accountable for its human rights abuses and the persecution of the Rohingya population. In this period, regional competition also ensued between Japan, India, and Singapore, which caused billions of dollars to be invested in the Rakhine area.

To gain a more comprehensive understanding of how this dynamic affects the people living in Rakhine and potentially shapes their perspectives on various issues, including current events such as the Rohingya crisis, it would be insightful for future studies to delve into qualitative interviews or surveys conducted within communities directly affected by these circumstances. Incorporating diverse voices can help researchers identify any potential biases or inherent dynamics that may arise due to an over-reliance on Facebook for information dissemination. During this time, media coverage of the Rohingya crisis played a crucial role in shaping public perception and influencing foreign policies. Throughout the period from 2010 to 2022, media coverage of the Rohingya crisis underwent various shifts and changes. These shifts and changes can be observed through several thematic frames that are employed to describe and interpret the crisis. Media coverage of the Rohingya crisis has been a crucial factor in shaping public perception and influencing foreign policies.

3 Literature Review

In the context of the Rohingya crisis, previous studies have highlighted the need to examine media coverage to understand how the crisis is described and framed. Researchers Chyi and McCombs emphasize that the news media engages in reframing events, consciously or unconsciously, in order to keep a particular story in the spotlight (Afzal, 2016). Their study suggests that media frames may change over time, but the aim is to investigate whether these frames favor one side of the crisis over another. Our study builds upon such previous research by examining the content of published articles to understand how the Rohingya crisis is described and framed in order to influence public opinion and shape foreign policies toward humanitarian interventions (Lee, 2021).

To adequately understand the body of literature on the Rohingya crisis, it is important to have a conceptual framework of both refugees and migrants. The concepts of refugee and migrant carry certain differences. In accordance with The Office of the United Nations High Commissioner for Human Rights (OHCHR), migrants are considered those who are not living in their country of birth or country of nationality. Therefore, a neutral group of individuals who do not hold any citizenship in the country where they are currently residing would represent a baseline definition of the term "migrant." The distinction between a migrant and a refugee is that the vulnerability of a migrant is not inherent. A refugee is someone who is escaping persecution or violence in their place of origin and is therefore considered a refugee according to international law.

The representation of migrants and refugees actively contributes to the construction of identities that are ultimately accepted by the broader public. In light of this, it is critical to examine how immigrants and refugees are represented in the media (Lawlor & Tolley, 2017). Scheufele (1999) investigates important frames in newspaper articles and focuses on the process of frame construction. He explains how several factors that influence the frame-building process influence the media frame. Chouliaraki and Zaborowski (2017) claim in their study that refugees were largely classified according to their nationality. Hoewe (2018) uses a content analysis of US media newspapers to investigate the consequences of how refugees are portrayed in international news and how the term "immigrant" is used inappropriately. This latter study examines how the public was informed by news stories about those who were impacted by the wars in Syria, Afghanistan, and Iraq. In press reports, "immigrants" from Syria, Iraq, and Afghanistan are more commonly linked to terrorism. The findings revealed a tendency for American newspapers to mix up the terms "refugee" and "immigrant" more frequently than non-American news organizations. The American participants did not clearly distinguish between their opinions on "refugees" and "immigrants." It is conceivable that American viewers have inferred that those seeking asylum from political unrest are more likely to engage in terrorist activities if the American news media conflates "refugees" and "immigrants," and immigrants are related to terrorism.

On the other hand, a study conducted by Roman et al. (2017) shows a contrast in media coverage. Reports were analyzed from four daily newspapers: Izvestia (Russia), The New York Times (US), Den (Ukraine), and the Guardian (UK). Ukrainian individuals who were forced to leave their country and their portrayal in the media coverage in the United States, United Kingdom, Ukraine, and Russia were the topic of this study. The study found a few unfavorable comments, but the majority of the impressions of Ukrainian migrants were good. Commonly used frames in the coverage of migration, like "Crime" and "Security threat," were absent. Media coverage analysis revealed a difference between the depictions of Ukrainians who were forced to dislocate and other refugees. Compared to the populations into which they migrated, Ukrainians look the same or similar, wear similar clothing, and frequently speak languages that are similar. Using gender, name, and profession, media coverage portrayed the Ukrainians as significant figures in their individual communities. These descriptions of immigrants were highly human, as opposed to the menacing ones from prior studies. According to this study, the political atmosphere of the nation and the characteristics of media organizations have an impact on the frames employed in reporting on Ukrainian refugees. The study also demonstrates that how migrants are portrayed in the news may be influenced by the linguistic and cultural proximity of their countries of origin (Roman et al., 2017).

Other past studies have indicated that news organizations frequently align with the foreign policy of their own nation in their coverage of international news. Reporting on political, ideological, and financial concerns makes this alignment particularly clear (Novais, 2007). There are various works on US media coverage of international crises and the representation of refugees. Herman (1993) looked at how the media portrayed the acts, inactions, and invasions the US government carried out in several nations in the 1980s and 1990s. He proved, using empirical data, that when it comes to covering foreign affairs, the mainstream media frequently follows the government's goal. Herman also discovered that media outlets occasionally served as outposts for official public relations initiatives.

To understand the Western coverage pattern, this study examined several pieces of literature. Patrik (2016) and Gruley and Duvall (2012) observed the reporting of violent conflicts in Africa in Western media. Their observations revealed reasonably traditional war reporting; additionally, wide coverage of The Rwandan genocide (1994) was found in American and British newspapers. However, Patrick (2016) examined those publications and found that there was relatively little coverage of Rwanda, and that scant reportage was based on stereotypes about Africa.

Since the Rohingya crisis has been an ongoing issue in South Asia, scholars have extensively researched the topic. The 2014 Pulitzer Prize-winning Reuter's reports were investigated by Brooten (2015). The conflict between Rohingya Muslims and Rakhine Buddhists in Western Myanmar was the main subject of these reports. Brooten's purpose was to examine how the international media represented Burmese Buddhism in their coverage of the Rohingya issue, highlighting their portrayal as barbaric and supporting the notion that there was a need for an outside savior. Brooten used five in-depth investigative papers and two shorter companion articles from the Reuters news agency to conduct the analysis. Textual analysis, specifically using the SVS framework, also known as the "savages-victims-saviors" paradigm, was the main methodology used. Using this framework, the author was able to determine how important conflict participants were rhetorically portrayed as victims, barbarians, or prospective saviors. The analysis discovered that the news outlet minimized the crucial work being done by regional groups to resist violence against the Rohingya (Brooten, 2015). Kanaker et al. (2020) conducted a study on the Rohingya crisis settlement reports of Al Jazeera and the BBC. The study followed both qualitative and quantitative analysis. The results showed that news frames have the power to influence the way individuals understand situations. The study found the newscasts on Al Jazeera and the BBC used three primary frames: responsibility, human impact, and powerlessness.

Several comparative studies on the Rohingya crisis have been conducted over the years. For example, four newspapers selected from four different countries—the Globe and Mail from Canada, the Daily Star from Bangladesh, the Dawn from

Pakistan, and the New York Times from the United States—were examined in a study conducted by Irom et al. (2022). The study looked at important news frames, refugee descriptions, and sources in the Rohingya crisis coverage of the selected newspapers. The most frequently used frames were the victim and administrative frames. In order to determine the coverage of the management of the Rohingya crisis by the Myanmar government in newspapers, Afzal (2016) did a content analysis of the editorial viewpoints of newspapers from America, the United Kingdom, and Pakistan. His research revealed that emotional sentiments were mostly used in newspaper editorials to actively connect readers with situations. In a textual analysis from the Inter Press Service and the New York Times, Brooten et al. (2015) identified human rights news reports that portrayed Myanmar Buddhists' eruption of violent activities and identified a wide range of victims, villains, and heroes.

Many studies have included countries from South Asia to analyze the crisis. Islam (2018) examined how the media reported on the Rohingya crisis in three distinct nations. The quantitative and qualitative content analyses of six newspapers from three surrounding nations examined Myanmar's portrayal in their media: Bangladesh, India, and China. Significant differences were found in the coverage of the Rohingya situation in both qualitatively studied news reports and quantitatively analyzed news items in all three nations. In the newspapers of Bangladesh and India, frames such as the protest frame and the human interest frame were found frequently. On the other hand, security and conflict frames were mostly employed in the Chinese media. As the majority of these migrants are hosted by the neighboring countries of Bangladesh and India, a study conducted by Awny (2019) analyzed how Rohingya refugees are portrayed in their media. In the researcher's quantitative content analysis of newspaper articles, two Indian newspapers—the Hindustan Times and the Times of India—as well as two Bangladeshi newspapers—the daily Prothom Alo and the New Nation—were all examined. Finding and analyzing the frames used in these newspaper stories were the aim of this investigation. Analysis revealed frames such as the responsibility frame, the victim frame, the return home frame, the intruder frame, and the administrative frame. The investigation found that while discussing Rohingya refugees, Bangladeshi newspapers tended to use the victim frame more frequently, but Indian journalists tended to use the intruder frame more frequently.

The United Nations High Commissioner for Refugees (2021) calculated that Bangladesh was hosting almost 860,000 Rohingya refugees. In light of this increasing number, Bangladesh's media plays a crucial role in the crisis. Uddin (2021) examined how Bangladeshi media portrays the Rohingya population through a total of 40 articles from Bangladesh's top four newspapers: the Daily Star, Prothom Alo, Bangladesh Protidin, and Daily Sun. According to the research's findings, the Rohingyas are portrayed in mainstream Bangladeshi newspapers using four major frames: conflict, securitization, attribution of blame, and human interest. The most commonly used frames were the human interest frame, the securitization frame, the attribution of blame frame, and the conflict frame. When compared to Bengali newspapers, it was found that English newspapers tended to use human interest framing more frequently. However, it was found that Bengali publications employed the securitization frame more often than their English counterparts. The securitization frame, which was first identified in articles appearing in 2018, is notable because it suggests a shift in how the Rohingya issue has been covered in the media since the mass crisis began in 2017. By providing new insights on the securitization of refugees and the shifting Rohingya media narrative in Bangladesh, this study contributed to the body of scholarly knowledge on the subject. Another study, conducted by Wadud (2020), looked at the changing media narratives about the Rohingya crisis. The study analyzed how Bangladeshi media outlets covered the Rohingya refugee crisis between August 2017 and December 2019 by parsing two online news portals and six daily newspapers. The study used qualitative content analysis and examined opinion write-ups and news reports using framing theory. The major objective was to identify the most common narratives used by Bangladeshi media outlets to represent Rohingya refugees, looking at how these frames transformed over the selected time period in addition to whether there were any variations in framing dependent on the characteristics and beliefs of the news outlets. The results of the study showed that the frames used by Bangladeshi news organizations changed over time. Compared to major newspapers, online news sites displayed a more antagonistic attitude toward the Rohingya refugees. Surprisingly, the study found that in contrast to prior research, right-wing media sources took a pro-refugee posture during the Rohingya crisis.

4 Theoretical Framework

Our research follows framing theory to study the dominant frames and narratives used to describe the Rohingya crisis in Western and Eastern media while framing refugee issues.

Goffman raised the idea of framing as an analytical research instrument for the first time in 1974. Giltin (1980) outlined the idea that frames are sets of guidelines that determine what information is chosen, how it is presented, and what aspects are highlighted. These guidelines are based on unspoken assumptions about what is real, what occurs, and what is important. Frames provide a clear understanding of the problem by explaining its essence and suggesting how it should be viewed and comprehended (Nelson & Kinder, 1996).

The effectiveness of textual messages is closely related to the framing theory of mass communication. By strategically presenting and packaging information for the general public's consumption, the media engages in framing. According to Scheufele (1999), in addition to the act of framing itself, a variety of other elements also have an impact on how the media uses frames. The collection, structuring, and organization of material within a news report are all part of this process. The media has the power to shape how an audience views an event by framing it in a specific way. Headlines, audio-visual elements, metaphors, and storytelling strategies are only a few of the textual components used in news stories that have the power to force the audience to understand the news item in a predefined way (Rhee, 1997, pp. 26–48).

It is fundamental for media organizations to frame their news effectively. This is because the language they use to express a text's message, whether it be about a person, a group of people, an event, a process, the state of things, or any other subject or theme found in newspaper writings, frames the story in explicit and unavoidable ways (Richardson, 2007, 49). Because of the potential for misrepresentation of any event, media frames can affect how audiences perceive and understand it (Entman, 2007), especially by their simplification of complicated information and events. There are numerous approaches to aligning and applying the framing analysis. Because of its wide scope of research, it is understandable how framing analysis has become a popular inquiry tool during the past few decades.

Iyengar (1994) studied how political issues were covered in the media and discovered two basic frames: episodic and thematic. Thematic frames place more emphasis on social attributions for political issues than episodic frames do. Thematic framing emphasizes broader trends throughout time and offers a contextual understanding of the issues at hand, whereas episodic framing tends to downplay public dialogue by focusing on isolated case studies. Semetko and Valkenburg (2000), in particular, have identified five common news frames used in conflict coverage: conflict, human interest, economic consequence, moral, and responsibility frames.

As framing theory offers useful insights into the reasons and effects of media coverage on crisis-related issues, the main goal of this study is to examine how the media has framed the Rohingya crisis. Our examination of the literature finds that many studies have looked into media frames to determine how they affect authorities' perception of reality when making foreign policy decisions.

5 Methodology

When we gathered the data in the Spring of 2023, we considered five newspaper agencies: three in the Western countries (UK, the United States, Canada), one from the Middle East, and one from Bangladesh, all of whom have expressed consistent interest in the crisis. The UNHCR and International Organization for Migration's (IOM's) repositories were used to collect data from which the statistics for Rohingya placements were obtained. We selected the newspaper of record from each nation for a total of five news sources. The press is free in these countries. The Daily Star from Bangladesh, the Guardian from the United Kingdom, Al Jazeera from Qatar, the Globe and Mail from Canada, and the New York Times from the United States were the selected publications. The five newspapers all have a substantial readership. We included coverage from January 2010 to December 2022 in two segments: 2010–2017 and 2017–2022. We included all articles that contained the word "Rohingya" in our search parameters. As previous content analyses have used a comparable chronology, the time frame was judged appropriate for the analysis (Brooten et al., 2015). Each article served as the study's analytical unit.

In terms of social media analysis, we considered a few activists' Twitter (now known as X) accounts such as: Wai Wai Nu, Akila Radhakrishnan, Burma campaign, Free Rohingya Coalition (FRC), Poppy McPherson, Razia Sultana, Ro Nay San Lwin, Tun Khin, Women's Peace Network, Tirana Hasan, and Zaw Htay. They come from a wide variety of sectors such as activists (diaspora and local), human rights lawyers, and international NGOs.

6 Coding

We used NVivo 12 qualitative data analysis software for coding purposes. News articles were first coded according to the title of the newspaper, the year, and the date. The majority of the coding categories were established with the aid of earlier studies (such as Chouliaraki & Zaborowski, 2017; Dimitrova et al., 2018). First, Chavez (2011), Dimitrova et al. (2018), and Iyengar (1994) investigated the most prevalent frames utilized in the coverage.

Ten categories made up the variables: *victim, culture, human rights, identity, impact, military, opinion, policy, Rakhine refugees, and Rohingya representation.* The first inquiry is about the main categories of framing. If an article addressed refugees as a threat to the host nation, it was categorized as a *threat framing*. These could represent refugees as a threat to national security (a demographic threat, environmental threat, or threat to culture). Descriptions of the refugees' sufferings mostly made up the *victim frame.* These included accounts of deplorable living situations and deplorable refugee camp circumstances such as regular fire break-outs, flooding of ground, or inter-group atrocities committed by several miscreant groups. Stories involving local or national bureaucracies, refugees at border crossings, the legal status of refugees, or lawyers who help with refugees were all included in the *administrative framing*. The use of the term *genocide* consists of a fourth frame, whereby several news outlets qualified it as a systematic genocide. A few Western nations also recognized it as a genocide. Finally, the *military coup and repatriation potential* frame was explored to find out whether Western and non-Western media were hopeful or otherwise about the potential of the return of a million refugees to Rakhine. These five frames have mostly been employed in earlier studies for comprehensive coverage of refugee or asylum-seeker crises (Chávez, 2011; Dimitrova et al., 2018; Nickels, 2007). We also included thematic and episodic frameworks (Iyengar, 1994), which have been applied in many settings, including child abuse (Hove et al., 2013), terrorism, and climate change (Hart, 2011). To grasp the total breadth of the coverage, episodic and thematic categories were added to the news frames variable. Stories that were classified as episodic featured isolated examples of Rohingya refugees without making a connection to the crisis's overall background. The second research inquiry was looking at notable sources or figures that were cited in the articles. Politicians (mostly those of the host country), refugees, NGOs, security personnel, the press, diaspora activists, community/religious leaders, and international communities were the seven categories represented by this variable. The categories were taken from earlier studies, such as those of Chouliaraki and Zaborowski (2017). The third query was about finding the traits that the Rohingyas featured in the publications have in common (Chouliaraki & Zaborowski, 2017). The country, age or age group, gender, name, and occupation of the refugees were the five elements that made up this variable.

7 Findings

An examination of Western media framing, including portrayals of the Rohingya, the Myanmar government, and the international response to the Rohingya crisis, reveals several key trends.

First, the media predominantly used a thematic frame strategy to depict the Rohingya crisis as a humanitarian emergency and crisis situation perpetrated by the Myanmar military. This strategy involved highlighting the dire conditions faced by Rohingya refugees, emphasizing the urgency of their situation, and framing it as a matter of human rights and international responsibility. Second, there was a shift in framing over time. Initial media coverage of the Rohingya crisis tended to focus on episodic frames, highlighting individual stories and isolated examples of Rohingya refugees without providing a broader context or analysis of the crisis. However, as the crisis persisted and garnered more international attention, media coverage shifted toward a more thematic frame that emphasized the systemic issues and root causes of the crisis (for example, the genocidal intent of the Myanmar government, persecution of Rohingyas, and systemic discrimination). This shift in framing allowed for a deeper understanding of the complexities and underlying factors contributing to the Rohingya crisis. Furthermore, the study found that certain sources were more prominently cited in media coverage of the Rohingya crisis. For example, political figures from the host country, such as government officials and politicians, were frequently mentioned, and their perspectives often shaped the narrative surrounding the crisis. Additionally, international humanitarian organizations and NGOs were frequently cited as sources of information, and their perspectives influenced the framing of the crisis.

However, it is important to note that the media coverage was not entirely uniform in its portrayal of the Rohingya crisis. Certain media outlets and journalists took a more critical stance toward the Myanmar government's handling of the crisis, highlighting allegations of human rights abuses and ethnic cleansing. Meanwhile, other media outlets emphasized the complexities of the situation and sought to provide a balanced perspective by including perspectives from government sources and local communities in Myanmar. Overall, the media coverage of the Rohingya crisis demonstrated a shift in framing and narrative over time, from episodic to thematic frames, allowing for a more comprehensive understanding of the complexities and root causes of the crisis. Identity was mentioned both in terms of ethnic and religious perspectives in this crisis, while the military was mentioned as the main perpetrator of the crisis.

Western media started framing the crisis as "genocide" from 2019/20 onwards. The framing of the Rohingya crisis as a genocide by Western media has been a significant aspect of the changing coverage. This framing gained attention and momentum following the release of several reports documenting widespread human rights abuses, including killings, sexual violence, and forced displacement targeting the Rohingya population. As a result, journalists and news organizations began to use stronger language and labels, such as genocide, to describe the atrocities committed against the Rohingya. This framing of the crisis as a genocide served to highlight the severity and systematic nature of the violence perpetrated against the Rohingya, placing responsibility on the Myanmar government and calling for international intervention to address the crisis. This framing was, in part, influenced by the narratives put forth by human rights organizations and diaspora activists who had been calling for action to address the situation. The framing of the Rohingya crisis, as discussed by various scholars and experts in the field, not only serves to keep the story in focus but also exerts pressure on governments and international organizations to respond effectively. This pressure can often lead to concrete actions being taken against those responsible for the atrocities committed against the Rohingya population. For instance, as a direct consequence of this framing, both Canadian government officials and numerous international human rights organizations have publicly condemned Myanmar's role in the crisis. Such condemnation has resulted in Suu Kyi being stripped of her citizenship due to her apparent involvement in these horrific events. In addition to framing the Rohingya crisis as a genocide, mainstream media coverage has also shifted over time to highlight the broader humanitarian and security implications of the crisis.

For each newspaper, a word cloud was employed to visually demonstrate the prevalence of various themes in its reporting. These graphics portray the frequency of each given theme by its relative size. Word clouds, graphical representations of text data, have been employed in the analysis of media framing of the Rohingya crisis for their multifaceted utility. By visualizing the frequency of words, they reveal key themes such as "refugee," "persecution," and "human rights," and uncover underlying biases and perspectives in media reporting. They enable comparative analysis across different sources, highlighting variations in understanding and representation, and enhance accessibility by translating complex textual data into engaging visuals. Chosen for this research, word clouds offer efficiency in handling large data sets, appeal to various disciplines by bridging qualitative and quantitative analysis, and facilitate further in-depth exploration of specific themes and narratives. Their use in this context underscores their value in understanding and communicating complex issues in an accessible and insightful manner. The word cloud visualization for the Guardian prominently displays terms such as "Rohingya," "military," "Muslims," Rakhine," and "violence." Here, the authors identified five major themes: ethnic identity (Rohingya), persecutors (military), religious identity (Muslims), geographical location (Rakhine), and human rights (violence).

Subsequently, cluster analysis through a word tree (or dendrogram) was generated to show the pattern of similarities within the articles that reported on the crisis. By the word similarity under the classification of various nodes of parent themes, articles were analyzed cluster-wise that are closer (measured the similarity of the themes used in framing in the selected news articles using Pearson correlation coefficient). Word trees, as graphical representations illustrating the connections of specific words or phrases within a text, hold significant value in the analysis of media framing, such as in the Rohingya crisis. They provide a contextual understanding of how terms are used, revealing nuanced meanings and connotations. By exploring the relationships and patterns between words, word trees identify recurring themes and framing techniques, uncovering hidden insights that might be missed in traditional analysis. This ability to delve into the subtleties of text complements other tools like word clouds; while word clouds emphasize frequency, word trees focus on contextual relationships, offering a more comprehensive view. The visual nature of word trees enhances interpretation and communication, making complex textual data accessible to a diverse audience, including scholars, policymakers, and the general public. Furthermore, word trees facilitate targeted analysis, allowing researchers to concentrate on specific words or phrases of interest, such as "refugee" or "human rights," and explore how they are framed within the media discourse. In essence, the use of word trees in analyzing the Rohingya crisis adds depth, complexity, and precision to the understanding of media framing, serving as both an analytical instrument and a communicative device that bridges quantitative and qualitative insights. Their application enriches the research by providing a multifaceted perspective on the language, representation, and underlying messages in the media portrayal of this significant humanitarian issue. The results for the Guardian are shown below in Fig. 1.

The Guardian's dendrogram shows a connection between culture, media ("account" and "Facebook" representing factors that triggered sectarian violence),

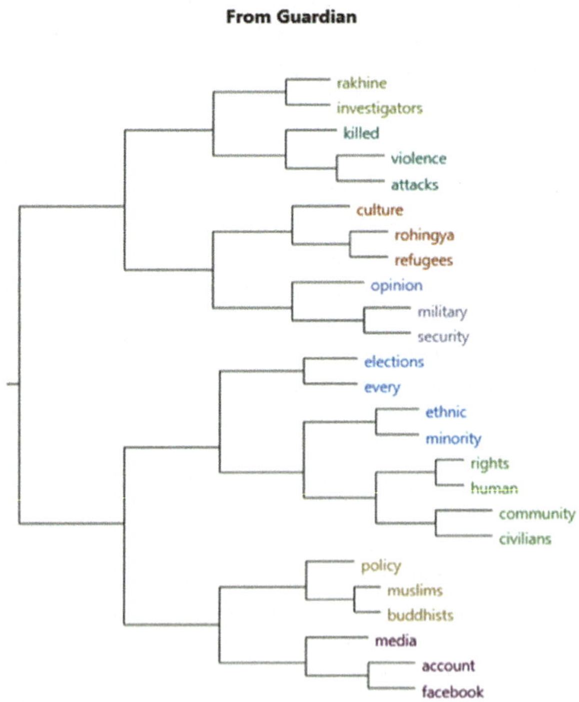

Fig. 1 Dendrogram result from the Guardian

and contested ethnicity and human rights. The cluster suggests that "violence" and "attacks" are related closely with the term "Rakhine" and "investigators." That the terms "military" and "security" are connected with the term "opinion" shows that the articles gathered from The Guardian frequently mentioned the involvement of military in the crisis. Terms such as "minority," "ethnic," "elections," and "rights" being mentioned in a cluster provide insight about the underlying relationship with the theme.

In the New York Times word cloud, common keywords dominate the framing themes such as identity, the persecutor (military and Buddhists), and genocide. Terms such as "Muslims" and "Rakhine" are included in the identity theme. The word cloud suggests that terms like "military," "violence," "Muslims," and "rights" are frequently used in the reports of the New York Times (Fig. 2).

In the corresponding dendrogram, human rights are closely associated with the term "genocide" and "court" (pointing to the ICJ process). A cluster containing the term "Facebook" and its association with other terms like "general," "leader," "military," "images," and "campaign" suggests the role of Facebook in the crisis and the action of military personnel.

Analysis of the Globe and Mail's frequently used terms generated persecutor, identity, and genocide themes. One particularly significant point can be noticed in

Fig. 2 Dendrogram result from the New York Times

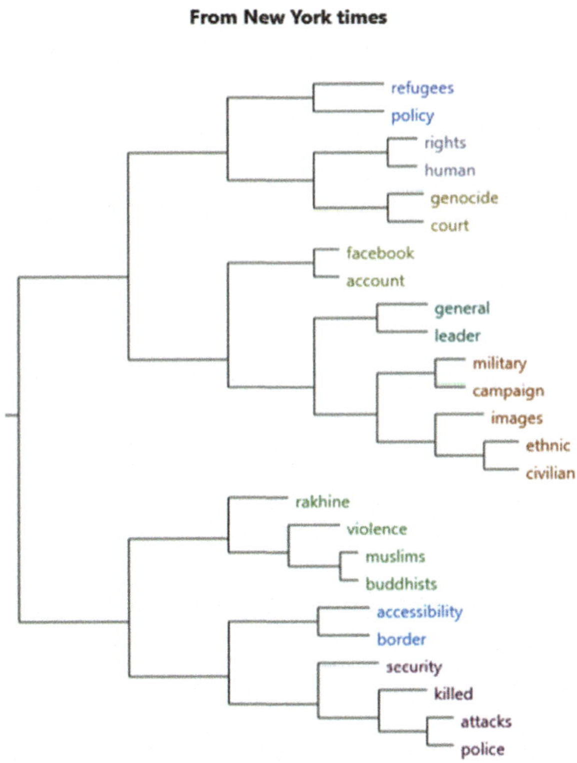

this word cloud: the terms "boat" and "Indonesia" are shown here, indicating that the Globe and Mail focused on the unsafe migration of Rohingya refugees (Fig. 3).

Examining the dendrogram, relational aspects of democracy in Myanmar can be observed. Genocide is also closely associated with the court system (ICJ), as Canada is one of the countries which has supported Gambia in pursuing an ICJ court case against Myanmar, along with Netherlands. The term "refugee" drew close associations with the terms "camps" and "work," and this association indicates the working (livelihood) matters of Rohingya refugees.

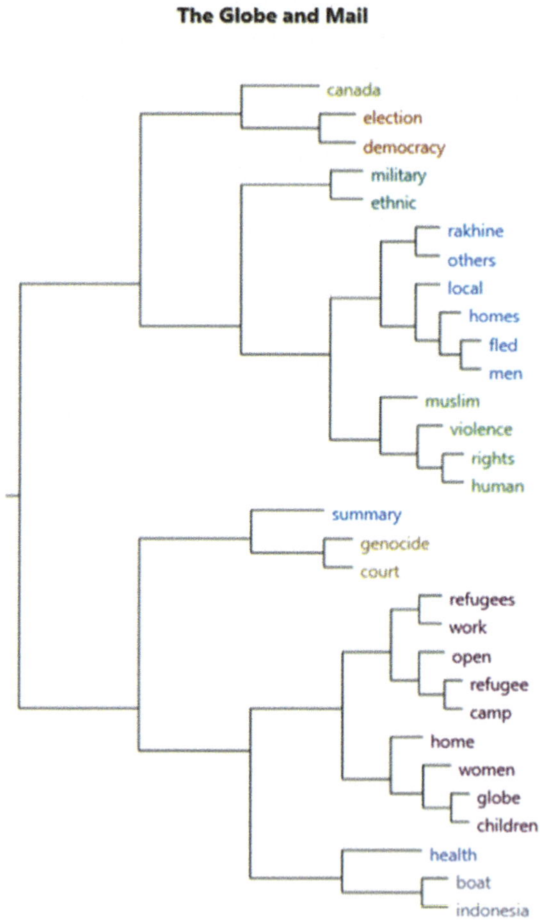

Fig. 3 Dendrogram result from the Globe and Mail

8 Analysis of Non-western Media Framing

Turning to the non-Western media sources, we first examine perspectives from Al Jazeera—one of the media outlets that covered the crisis most extensively. Our analysis drew from news coverage as early as October 28, 2015, and as late as April 11, 2023.

The Al Jazeera word cloud visualization underscores the now-common themes of genocide, military, rights, humans, and policy. The presence of terms like "military," 'genocide," "investigative," "refugees," "policy," and "Muslim" indicates that the reports have focused mostly on policy discussion, racial identities, human rights, military involvement, and investigative reporting (Fig. 4).

The Al Jazeera dendrogram shows that the term "genocide" is closely related to the terms "investigation," "Muslim," and "violence." This linkage suggests that investigative reports have focused on understanding the causes and factors of the genocide on the Muslim community. Furthermore, the terms "media" and "trust" being connected to the terms "election," "politics," and "party" indicate the media's role in electoral issues and the involvement of political parties in the crisis.

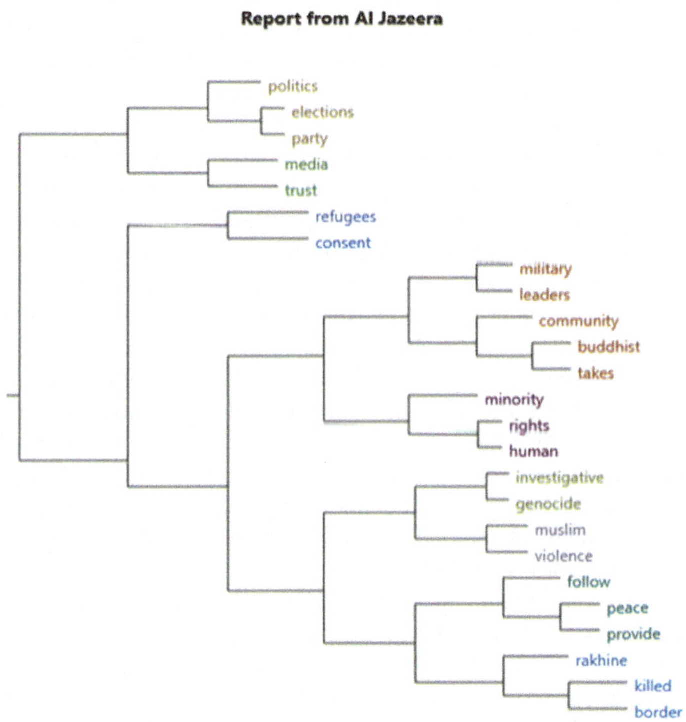

Fig. 4 Dendrogram result from Al Jazeera

We have compiled news headlines published by Al Jazeera between 2017–18 and 2022–23 to examine and illustrate how the framing shift occurred in coverage. Table 1 shows the summary of this analysis.

Being the largest host nation, examining the Bangladesh media reveals a more nuanced and complex portrayal of the Rohingya crisis. The media sources often emphasize the challenges faced by Bangladesh as a host country for Rohingya refugees and highlight the potential threats to internal stability. Furthermore, the framing of the Rohingya crisis in non-Western media often focuses on geopolitical factors and historical tensions within the region, highlighting the complexity of the Rohingya crisis and the challenges in finding a comprehensive solution. None of these media mentioned the term "genocide" in explaining the crisis. Despite Bangladesh providing material evidence to the International Court of Justice and potentially at the International Criminal Court, as discussed in a webinar by the Conflict and Resilience Research Institute Canada's (CRRIC's) Payam Akhaban, it did not take on the role of complainant in the ICJ case brought against Myanmar. Instead, Gambia filed the case and continues to pursue it. This raises questions about why Bangladesh, despite being a member of the Organization of Islamic Cooperation, chose not to initiate legal action itself. One possible explanation for Bangladesh's decision not to initiate legal action itself may be the delicate diplomatic and political considerations involved in maintaining its relationships with other countries, particularly Myanmar.

The media framing of the Rohingya crisis has undergone significant shifts from 2017 to 2022. Initially, the media focused on the atrocities committed by Myanmar's army against the Rohingya Muslims and framed it as a textbook example of ethnic cleansing. However, as time has passed and the crisis has continued to unfold, mainstream media coverage has expanded to include a range of other factors and implications. For example, in Bangladesh, media coverage has shifted to emphasize the challenges faced by the country in hosting a large number of Rohingya refugees. This shift in media framing highlights the complex nature of the Rohingya crisis and the multiple perspectives that need to be considered. Importantly, from the policy level, the framing started to shift from a purely humanitarian issue to a potential threat to Bangladesh's internal stability. This shift in media framing can be attributed to several factors. First and foremost, the influx of hundreds of thousands of Rohingya refugees into Bangladesh has put immense strain on the country's resources and infrastructure. As a result, the media has started to highlight the challenges faced by Bangladesh in providing for and accommodating such a large number of refugees. Additionally, the media has started to explore the potential security implications of the Rohingya crisis for Bangladesh.

This shift in media attention includes examining the potential for conflict, socioeconomic dilemmas, and insecurity arising from the presence of Rohingya refugees in the country. Since 2017, Bangladesh government has consistently denied the presence of the miscreant group ARSA in the camps; yet, from 2022 onwards, most of the news outlets in Bangladesh began reporting on the alleged involvement of ARSA in criminal activities within the refugee camps, further reinforcing the narrative of a potential threat to Bangladesh's internal stability posed by the Rohingya crisis. The question of narcoterrorism came into play through the media coverage, as there have

Table 1 The United States went from imposing sanctions on Myanmar to recognizing the crisis as a genocide, which is significant[1]

Headlines	Date	Broad thematic shifts
Rape used as a weapon in Myanmar to ignite fear	Oct, 2015	Human rights violation (rape), terrorism, UN, and roles of international actors
The case of French aid worker Moussa Tchantchuing (**terrorism**)	July, 2016	
The Rohingya crisis and the role of the **OIC**	Feb, 2017	
ARSA fighters declare truce amid Rohingya crisis	Sept, 2017	
UN Security Council to discuss Rohingya situation	Sept, 2017	
'We will kill you all': Rohingya beg for safe passage	Sept,2017	
Rohingya refugees share stories of **sexual violence**	Sept, 2017	
Cox's Bazar: **Chaos** all around at Rohingya camps	Sept, 2017	
US mulls **sanctions** on Myanmar over Rohingya crisis	Oct, 2017	
The **mental health toll** of the Rohingya crisis	Oct, 2017	
India is complicit in the Rohingya suffering	Oct, 2017	
Rohingya survivor: The army threw my baby into a fire	Oct, 2017	
'Everywhere they go, the Rohingya are **exploited**'	Feb, 2023	Frustration, human trafficking, hopefulness about ICJ (?), genocide
Rohingya are **drowning at sea**. Asia's leaders are to blame	Feb, 2023	
At least three women die after Rohingya **boat sinks** off Bangladesh	Jan, 2023	
'Feeling like prisoners': The plight of Rohingya refugees today	Aug, 2022	
ICJ to rule on Myanmar objections to Rohingya genocide case	Jul, 2022	

(continued)

[1] https://www.aljazeera.com/tag/rohingya/

Table 1 (continued)

Headlines	Date	Broad thematic shifts
UN refugee agency **'shocked'** at Rohingya deaths in Malaysia escape	Apr, 2022	
US declares Myanmar army committed **genocide** against Rohingya	Mar, 2022	
Myanmar military **accused of war crimes, genocide** in German suit	Jan, 2023	
Myanmar's military **honors anti-Muslim monk, frees prisoners**	Jan, 2023	
Rohingya in Bangladesh **protest** to be **sent home** after UN aid cut	Jun, 2023	

been reports of drug trafficking and other criminal activities within the Rohingya refugee camps.[2]

The inter-group violence and targeted killings of Rohingya leaders in the camps have received extensive media coverage, which has framed the Rohingyas as "violent," "criminals," and "dangerous." However, it is essential to examine this framing with more depth. The portrayal of an entire community based on the actions of a few individuals perpetuates stereotypes and fails to capture the complexities and nuances of the situation.

It is important to recognize that during times of crisis such as this one, media often resort to certain frames or narratives that may align with preconceived notions or dominant discourses. This can lead to biased representations which uphold existing power structures or reinforce negative perceptions about marginalized communities like the Rohingyas.

Therefore, it becomes crucial for journalists and news organizations not only to provide timely updates but also to investigate deeper into these events before attributing blame solely to a particular group. By delving beyond surface-level explanations, journalists can offer more nuanced understandings that shed light on underlying causes behind inter-group violence while avoiding perpetuating harmful stereotypes. Furthermore, the role of media in framing and shaping public opinion cannot be underestimated. The study found identity, prosecutor, administrative, human rights, and violence themes among the frequently used words in the Daily Star's reports. The presence of terms like "refugees," "Rakhine," and "Muslims" suggests that news reports have emphasized constructing a coherent identity for the Rohingya people (Fig. 5).

In the Daily Star's dendrogram, one notable cluster bearing the terms "rights" and "killed" is connected with the terms "police," "leader," and "Mohibullah." This connection suggests that Daily Star focused on the killing of Rohingya leader

[2] Myanmar, Narco-terrorism, Rohingya and the world, by Dr. Imtiaz Ahmed, https://diplomats.news/archives/952

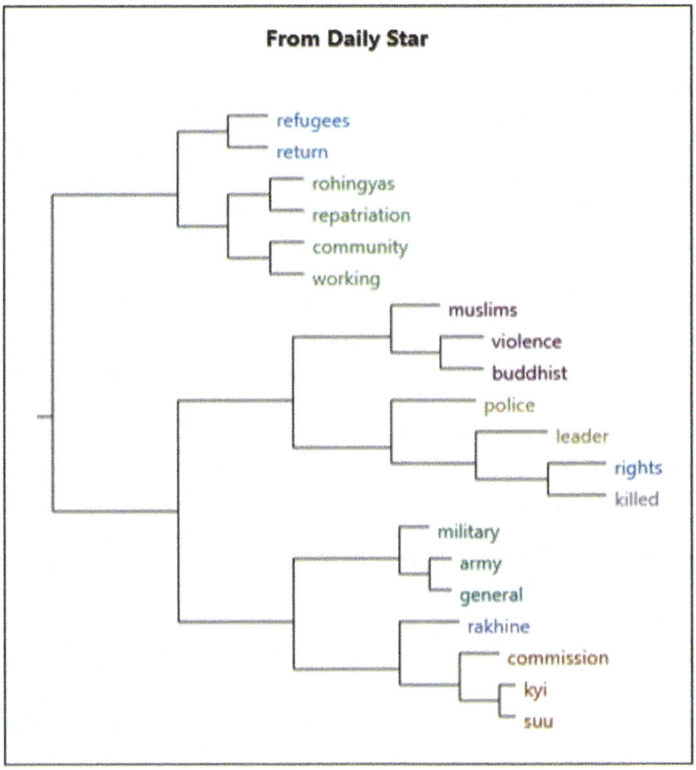

Fig. 5 Dendrogram result from the Daily Star

Mohibullah. That the term "general" is associated with the terms "military" and "army" shows the discussion of military involvement, the role and impact of army personnel, and their connection to the crisis. Furthermore, the term "commission" connected with the terms like "Rakhine," "Suu" and "Kyi," implies a reference to addressing the crisis before an investigative body, and how the leadership of Aung San Suu Kyi is related to this crisis.

9 Factors Shaping Media Framing of the Rohingya Crisis

Several factors contribute to the framing of the Rohingya crisis in mainstream media both in the West and East. These include geopolitical interests, media ownership, political and cultural contexts, and humanitarian considerations.

Geopolitical interests play a significant role in shaping the media framing of the Rohingya crisis. Countries with vested interests in Myanmar, such as neighboring states or major global powers, may have specific political agendas that influence the way they frame the crisis. For example, Japan does not acknowledge the Rohingya issue as a crisis, as is the case with most ASEAN members (although a subtle change became apparent recently when Myanmar's General Min Aung Hlang was denied attendance at the ASEAN summit in 2021).

Media ownership is another crucial factor that affects the framing of the Rohingya crisis. Media organizations may be influenced by their ownership structures, which can have ties to political parties or business interests. These affiliations can shape the narrative and agenda-setting of media coverage, influencing how the Rohingya crisis is framed.

In addition to the factors mentioned earlier, it is worth noting that political and cultural contexts also have a significant impact on how the Rohingya crisis is framed. Particularly in countries where there are longstanding ethnic or religious tensions, media coverage of this crisis may exhibit biases toward favoring the dominant group or perpetuating existing prejudices. These biases can manifest themselves through selective reporting, omissions of certain perspectives, or even the use of loaded language to manipulate public opinion. The influence of such framing becomes especially pronounced when media outlets align themselves with specific political agendas or cater to audiences with preconceived notions about certain groups.

Furthermore, humanitarian considerations also necessarily play a role in the framing of the Rohingya crisis by mainstream media. Humanitarian organizations and activists often play a crucial role in bringing attention to the plight of the Rohingya people. They may use various strategies to frame the crisis as a humanitarian issue, highlighting the suffering and human rights abuses faced by the Rohingya. These narratives can evoke empathy and support for intervention or assistance, shaping public opinion and influencing foreign policies toward the crisis. For example, although the Government of Bangladesh officially labels the newly arrived Rohingyas as forcibly displaced Myanmar nationals (FDMN), UNHCR in their reports consistently refers to them as "Rohingya refugees," emphasizing their status as victims of persecution and displacement. This framing choice by UNHCR serves to emphasize the urgency and severity of the crisis, appealing to the international community for assistance and protection for the Rohingya people.

10 Impacts of Media Framing in the Crisis

Examination of the effects of media framing on public perception, policy-making, and humanitarian response reveals that it can shape public perception and understanding of the crisis.

Media can influence public opinion and mobilize support for or against certain actions or interventions. Media framing can also influence policy-making decisions, as politicians and policymakers often rely on media coverage to inform their understanding of a crisis. In the case of the Rohingya crisis, media framing has played a role in shaping foreign policies toward humanitarian interventions (Afzal, 2016). Media coverage that portrays the Rohingya crisis as a humanitarian issue with clear victims and perpetrators may lead to increased support for intervention and pressure on governments to take action. The Canadian Prime Minister, for example, assigned a special envoy to the crisis—Bob Rae—between 2017 and 2020, and Canada remains committed to providing financial aid to support the Rohingya cause. However, the Government of Bangladesh expresses its concerns and reservations about this approach, as it believes such aid impedes its intended aim of repatriating the Rohingyas to Rakhine. One example is found in the comments of the foreign minister of Bangladesh Mr. Momen, who expressed concerns about the potential long-term consequences of providing assistance and support to the Rohingya refugees, stating that it could hinder efforts for their repatriation and create a dependency on external aid. He also opined that having easy access to aid makes Rohingyas comfortable in Bangladesh and could discourage them from returning to their homeland. The Twitter feed of the Bangladesh High Commission in Ottawa takes the position that the "sympathetic" approach is not working; rather, it claims Canada and other international actors should act in concert to "put pressure" on Myanmar to take back the Rohingyas. Similarly, a few Bangladesh media outlets have also been critical of the international community's response to the crisis, particularly their emphasis on humanitarian aid instead of addressing the root causes and holding accountable those responsible for the persecution of the Rohingya population.

This highlights the complex relationship between media framing, public perception, and policy-making. Although Myanmar is now ruled by a military junta, hopes are still high that a repatriation plan will materialize sooner than later. Some mainstream news outlets actually expressed optimism for the military leadership to start the much-touted repatriation process, which was followed by Chinese mediation and a token of repatriation in April 2023 to Rakhine. However, others portrayed it as a white lie and highlighted the lack of credibility in Myanmar's promises regarding repatriation.

11 Conclusion

The Rohingya crisis has presented a significant challenge for both Bangladesh and Myanmar. The process of repatriation has been marred by accusations that it is not voluntary and that the government of Myanmar denies the national identity of the Rohingya. As a result, many refugees do not feel safe returning to their homes. Despite these challenges, Bangladesh has shown remarkable efforts in providing support to the Rohingya refugees and their displaced children. However, there is still more to be learned in order to effectively respond to their humanitarian needs, particularly in terms of education for Rohingya children who are missing out on basic educational opportunities. It is clear that addressing this crisis requires a coordinated and comprehensive approach from the international community.

Similarly, the role of mainstream media in framing the Rohingya crisis and shaping public perception cannot be ignored. Throughout the course of the crisis, mainstream media outlets have played a crucial role in shaping the narrative and framing the events surrounding the Rohingya crisis.

References

4imn. (n.d.). *Top 100 newspapers in Europe*. 4imn. https://www.4imn.com/topEurope/

Afzal, N. (2016). Elements of pathos and media framing as scientific discourse: A newspaper perspective on Rohingya crisis. *International Journal of Advanced and Applied Sciences, 3*(10), 89–99. https://doi.org/10.21833/ijaas.2016.10.014

Awny, M. (2019). *The Rohingya refugee issue: Differences in media framing in Bangladesh and India* [Doctoral dissertation, Iowa State University]. https://dr.lib.iastate.edu/handle/20.500.12876/31822

Brooten, L. (2015). Blind spots in human rights coverage: Framing violence against the Rohingya in Myanmar/Burma. *Popular Communication, 13*(2), 132–144. https://doi.org/10.1080/15405702.2015.1021466

Brooten, L., Ashraf, S. I., & Akinro, N. A. (2015). Traumatized victims and mutilated bodies: Human rights and the 'politics of immediation' in the Rohingya crisis of Burma/Myanmar. *International Communication Gazette, 77*(8), 717–734. https://doi.org/10.1177/1748048515611022

Chávez, K. R. (2011). Identifying the needs of LGBTQ immigrants and refugees in Southern Arizona. *Journal of Homosexuality, 58*(2), 189–218. https://doi.org/10.1080/00918369.2011.540175

Chouliaraki, L., & Zaborowski, R. (2017). Voice and community in the 2015 refugee crisis: A content analysis of news coverage in eight European countries. *International Communication Gazette, 79*(6–7), 613–635. https://doi.org/10.1177/1748048517727173

Dimitrova, D. V., Ozdora-Aksak, E., & Connolly-Ahern, C. (2018). On the border of the Syrian refugee crisis: Views from two different cultural perspectives. *American Behavioral Scientist, 62*(4), 532–546. https://doi.org/10.1177/0002764218756920Entman, R. M. (2007). Framing bias: Media in the distribution of power. Journal of communication, 57(1), 163-173.

Gruley, J., & Duvall, C. S. (2012). The evolving narrative of the Darfur conflict as represented in The New York Times and The Washington Post, 2003–2009. *GeoJournal, 77*, 29–46. https://doi.org/10.1007/s10708-010-9384-4

Hart, P. S. (2011). One or many? The influence of episodic and thematic climate change frames on policy preferences and individual behavior change. Science Communication, 33(1), 28-51.Herman, E. (1993). The media's role in US foreign policy. *Journal of International Affairs, 47*(1), 23–45. https://www.jstor.org/stable/24357083

Hoewe, J. (2018). Coverage of a crisis: The effects of international news portrayals of refugees and misuse of the term "immigrant." *American Behavioral Scientist, 62*(4), 478–492. https://doi.org/10.1177/0002764218759579Hove, T., Paek, H. J., Isaacson, T., & Cole, R. T. (2013). Newspaper portrayals of child abuse: Frequency of coverage and frames of the issue. Mass Communication and Society, 16(1), 89-108.

Irom, B., Borah, P., Vishnevskaya, A., & Gibbons, S. (2022). News framing of the Rohingya crisis: Content analysis of newspaper coverage from four countries. *Journal of Immigrant & Refugee Studies, 20*(1), 109–124. https://doi.org/10.1080/15562948.2021.1906472

Islam, M. K. (2018). *How newspapers in China, India and Bangladesh framed the Rohingya crisis of 2017* [Master's Dissertation, University of Mississippi]. Electronic Theses and Dissertations. https://egrove.olemiss.edu/etd/648/Iyengar, S. (1994). Is anyone responsible?: How television frames political issues. University of Chicago Press.

Kanaker, O., Abughazlih, M. O., Battour, M., Awais, I. A., & Tahat, K. M. (2020). News framing of the Rohingya crisis settlement: A study on Aljazeera and BBC.

International Online Journal of Language, Communication, and Humanities, 3(1), 41–58. https://www.researchgate.net/publication/337623183_News_Framing_of_the_Rohingya_Crisis_Settlement_Efforts_a_Study_on_Aljazeera_and_BBC

Lawlor, A., & Tolley, E. (2017). Deciding who's legitimate: News media framing of immigrants and refugees. *International Journal of Communication, 11*, 967–991. https://ijoc.org/index.php/ijoc/article/view/6273/1946Lee, M.. (2021, October 16). Media influence on humanitarian interventions: analysis of the Rohingya refugee crisis and international media coverage. https://scite.ai/reports/10.1186/s41018-021-00108-5

Lee, M. J. (2021). Media influence on humanitarian interventions: analysis of the Rohingya refugee crisis and international media coverage. *Journal of International Humanitarian Action, 6*(1), 20.

Nelson, T. E., & Kinder, D. R. (1996). Issue frames and group-centrism in American public opinion. The Journal of Politics, 58(4), 1055-1078.Nickels, H. C. (2007). Framing asylum discourse in Luxembourg. *Journal of Refugee Studies, 20*(1), 37–59. https://doi.org/10.1093/jrs/fel029

Novais, R. A. (2007). National influences in foreign news: British and Portuguese press coverage of the Dili massacre in East Timor. *International Communication Gazette, 69*(6), 553–573. https://doi.org/10.1177/1748048507082842

Patrick, D. (2016). A concern for humanity? Anglo-American press coverage of Bosnia and Rwanda, 1992–1995. *International Politics, 53*(1), 138–153. https://doi.org/10.1057/ip.2015.41

Rhee, J. W. (1997). Strategy and issue frames in election campaign coverage: A social cognitive account of framing effects. Journal of communication, 47(3), 26-48.Richardson, J. E. (2017). Analysing newspapers: An approach from critical discourse analysis. Bloomsbury Publishing.Roman, N., Wanta, W., & Buniak, I. (2017). Information wars: Eastern Ukraine military conflict coverage in the Russian, Ukrainian and U.S. newscasts. *International Communication Gazette, 79*(4), 357–378. https://doi.org/10.1177/1748048516682138

Scheufele, D. A. (1999). Framing as a theory of media effects. *Journal of Communication, 49*(1), 103–122. https://doi.org/10.1111/j.1460-2466.1999.tb02784.xSemetko, H. A., & Valkenburg, P. M. (2000). Framing European politics: A content analysis of press and television news. Journal of communication, 50(2), 93-109.

Uddin, M. R. (2021). *Representation of the Rohingya people in Bangladeshi media: A framing analysis of mainstream newspapers* [Master's thesis, Tampere University], Trepo. https://trepo.tuni.fi/bitstream/handle/10024/130699/UddinMdRiaz.pdf?sequence=2

United Nations High Commissioner for Refugees. (2021). *The displaced and stateless of Myanmar in the Asia-Pacific region*. Retrieved from https://reporting.unhcr.org/sites/default/files/The%20Displaced%20and%20Stateless%20of%20Myanmar%20in%20the%20Asia-Pacific%20Region%20-%20January%202021.pdf

Wadud, M. (2020). *Good Rohingyas, bad Rohingyas: How narratives of Rohingya refugees shifted in Bangladesh media, 2017–2019* [Doctoral dissertation, University of Nevada], Scholar Works. http://hdl.handle.net/11714/7549

Part IV
Right to Return, Rehabilitation, Peacebuilding, and Camp Management

Chapter 13
Displaced Rohingya Management in Bangladesh and Law Enforcement Agencies' Role

Md. Zillur Rahman

Abstract This paper explores the security issues which are handled by the Bangladesh Police as a Law Enforcing Agency due to the Rohingya presence in Cox's Bazar and assesses the capability of Armed Police Battalions (APBn) to maintain a law-and-order situation in the Rohingya camps. Since 2017, more than 1.3 million Rohingyas have been living in Cox's Bazar while their human rights have remained suspended. The large number of migrated stateless people are generating security issues in Cox's Bazar and are thus threatening the daily lives of the refugees and local people of the host community. Using a mixed-method approach via content analysis, questionnaire surveys, KIIs, and FGDs, this study has explored the security issues, difficulties, weaknesses, and limitations of the APBn and assessed the capability of the APBn. The available sparse literature on the topic focuses on mostly social security dimensions of the Rohingya issue in Bangladesh. This study seeks to shift the focus from social changes to the more physical dimensions of safety and security for the Rohingya population as well as the host communities and assess the capability of Armed Police Battalions in handling the security issues of the Rohingya camps. The recommendations generated from this study will seek to provide reliable policy directives to better equip the Armed Police Battalions in handling the changing dynamics due to the emergent security threats generated by the Rohingya presence in Cox's Bazar, Bangladesh.

1 Introduction

The Rohingyas are considered one of the world's largest stateless populations (Human Rights Watch, 2023). The Buddhist nationalist 969 Movement and the actions of race and religious organization Ma Ba Tha's leaders, Buddhist monks Ashin Wirathu and Ashin Wimala, led to claims against Muslims that they planned to take over Rakhine State, and accused them of marrying and converting Buddhist

Md. Z. Rahman (✉)
Bangladesh University of Professionals, Dhaka, Bangladesh
e-mail: zillur2010@gmail.com

K. Ahmed and Md. R. Islam (eds.), *Understanding the Rohingya Displacement*, International Perspectives on Migration, https://doi.org/10.1007/978-981-97-1424-7_13

women. They spread anti-Muslimism propaganda within the Buddhist and ruling-class community. General Ne Win declared Rohingyas illegal during his rule in 1962, and he denied them citizenship according to Myanmar's 1982 Citizenship Law; thereby the Rohingya became one of the largest stateless ethnic populations in the world. The state-sponsored persecution, religious conflicts with Buddhism, and the atrocities of Myanmar's military compelled them to cross the border and take shelter in the Cox's Bazar district of Bangladesh. "The number of registered and unregistered Rohingyas residing in thirty-three congested camps at Cox's Bazar in the southern part of Bangladesh varies from 900,000 to 1.3 million" (UNHCR, 2022). This is therefore one of the biggest man-made catastrophes in the entire world.

Bangladesh is a non-signatory state of the UN Refugee Convention of 1951 and its Protocol of 1967. No instruction from the UN is followed in how refugees will be treated in Bangladesh. Bangladesh had welcomed the displaced Rohingyas on humanitarian grounds and by international communities' demand. In the crisis's early days, national organizations, international communities, and aid agencies provided then-adequate facilities to the Rohingyas, but those supports are fading away. "Instead, they are getting involved in criminal and militant activities making the existing problems diversified and exacerbated" (Zafar, 2020). The security situation is deteriorating day by day, threatening to create anarchy in Cox's Bazar as well as create tensions around the national security of Bangladesh. "Moreover, the involvement of the Rohingya people in unlawful activities concerning the narcotic trade and the importation of small arms and light weapons and human trafficking have put the host populations into a state of dire insecurity" (Banerjee, 2019). According to the district police administration, the law-and-order situation is deteriorating inside and outside the camps. The Rohingya refugees have become involved in serious crimes including human trafficking, drug trafficking, arms smuggling, kidnapping, passport and NID card forgery, rape, murder, and more. Beside this, potential for militancy among refugees is echoed by Rahman (2010): "The Rohingya camps in Cox's Bazar District are fertile grounds for recruitment by Islamic militants." The Bangladesh government has deployed three Armed Police Battalions (APBn) to maintain the security of the Rohingya camps. "The capacity of these Armed Police Battalions (APBn) brigades APBn-16, APBn-8 and APBn-14 have been tested due to a high number of deaths involving armed confrontations with organized narcotic dealer groups in Cox's Bazar" (Rahman, 2022).

This research is crucial for assessing the capabilities of the APBn to handle the security of the Rohingya camps, which has not yet been explored in detail in the literature. This study is based on surveys, KIIs, FGDs, and secondary data from local police stations, and other reliable and reputable sources. This study will provide a set of recommendations for strengthening the capacity of APBn as well as the Bangladesh Police. Moreover, this study can greatly contribute to the overarching literature concerning the Rohingya crisis as well as provide a solid foundation regarding the available countermeasures on security issues for both the short and long term.

2 Background

The story of how the Rohingya came to Myanmar has many, many versions. "The Rohingya people are a stateless Indo-Aryan ethnic group who believe in Islam and reside in Rakhine State, Myanmar. The term 'Rohingya' is derived from the Arabic word 'Rahm' which means mercy" (Ullah, 2011). "The myth tells of a ship of Arab traders that arrived on shores of Ramree Island in the eighteenth century and wrecked off the Burmese coast, and the survivors asked for Rahm of the local king. The king allotted a piece of land for them, and they were allowed to settle there. Over time Rahm changed to Rhohang and eventually to Rohingya" (Chowdhury, 2006). "Another version of the 'Rohigya' is that the 'Roh' in Rohingya means 'mountain' in Sanskrit and that the region of mountains in northwest India was known as 'Roh'" (Ahmad, 2012). All these are interesting explanations, but there are no historical or linguistic proofs. The Rohingya population first arrived in the old coastal country in Southeast Asia, which is a historical region named Arakan. They came to Arakan for business purposes as well as to spread the religious views of Islam. There is confusion as to who the original settlers of Arakan were. According to the Burmese traditional history, the Rakhine have inhabited Arakan since 3000 BCE, but there is no archaeological evidence in favor of that claim. The earliest Indianized kingdom in South Asia was Arakan. The Chandra dynasty ruled Arakan in the early eighth century. The British historian Daniel George Edward Hall (1955) stated that "The Burmese do not seem to have settled in Arakan until possibly as late as the tenth century CE." Hence earlier dynasties are thought to have been Indian, ruling over a population similar to that of Bengal. All the capitals known to history have been in the north near modern Akyab. The Mrauk-U dynasty ruled Rakhine State and some parts of Bangladesh and India until Burmese occupation in 1785.

Before the advent of Buddhist rule, the Rohingya and Buddhist Magh lived together with communal harmony; but when Burmese rule began, the Buddhist Magh's leader Ga Than De with his other associates destroyed Muslim mosques, temples, shrines, and libraries. During that time, a huge number of Rohingya Muslims fled from Arakan to Chittagong due to persecution. "More than 100,000 Muslims Rohingya were killed by them and about 80,000 fled from Rakhine state to the Chittagong division of British India" (Ullah & Faisal, 2022). In the year 1826 Arakan was annexed under British India and in 1885 British took full control over Burma. Due to dividend rule, the Muslim Rohingya again faced discrimination from the British authorities. But during the Second World War, Rohingya Muslims worked in support of the British Army; on the other hand, Burma's independent army worked with the Japanese Army. Due to heavy airstrikes by the Japanese Army, the British authorities withdrew their forces in March and April 1942. During that time, Burma's independent army, along with the Japanese Army and local Buddhist Maghs, attacked Muslim villages.

In 1947–48, all Burmese community leaders worked jointly for the independence of Burma, but Arakan Muslims showed interest in joining with Pakistan. During that time, the leader of Pakistan, Mohammad Ali Jinnah, ensured that Arakan Muslims' identities and fundamental rights would be protected like any other ethnic community. However, communal unrest began just after independence, and a Muslim militant organization formed to fight for a separate Muslim country. The Prime Minister of Burma, U Nu, declared the Rohingya an indigenous ethnic community with all fundamental rights like the other ethnic groups and even took some initiatives to protect the Rohingya community from Buddhist Maghs during his rule. During this period, Rohingya Muslim leader Mr. Sultan Mahmud also participated in the elections of 1956 and 1960 and was appointed health minister. But after military chief General Ne Win took power in 1962, all of these processes failed.

The military ruler Ne Win declared the Rohingya illegal and adopted the unlawful Citizenship Act of 1982. General Ne Win destroyed the economic backbone of the Rohingya, expelled them from any government opportunities, and imposed restrictions on the Rohingya population in many different ways. This precipitated the rise of the Ma Ba Tha Buddhist Association for the Protection of Race and Religion, alongside the government's continued plotting against the Rohingya Muslims of Arakan. "With their unlawful citizenship act of 1982, they defined 135 ethnic groups, among which the Rohingyas were not one of them" (Aye & Sercombe, 2014). "Myanmar Army carried out its operation against 'so called insurgents' at Rakhine state after several police posts and military outposts were attacked by Arakan Salvation Army (ARSA), a separatist outfit, on 25 August 2017" (Fair, 2018). The Myanmar military has committed genocide several times over, raped children and women, taken valuable assets, set fire to Rohingya villages, and burnt almost all their houses—which definitely constitutes a crime against humanity. ZeidRa'ad al-Hussein, former UN High Commissioner for Human Rights (2014–2018), described the atrocities perpetrated against the Rohingyas of Rakhine as the "textbook example of ethnic cleansing" (UN Nation, 2017). The brutality of Myanmar's military compelled Rohingyas to cross the border into Bangladesh (Fig. 1).

"Before the largest influx of Rohingya in August, 2017 Bangladesh has experienced some influx of Rohingyas in the year of 1978, 1991, 1992, and 2012" (Parnini et al., 2013). Aid provided to the Rohingya population in the camps in the initial days has faded away with the passing of time. The Bangladeshi government imposed restrictions on the Rohingya population not to venture beyond the camps, but very

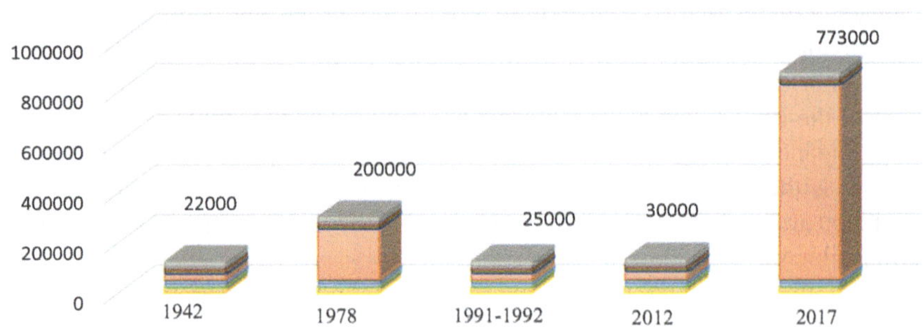

Fig. 1 Rohingya influx to Bangladesh (OCHA and UNHCR). *Source* Developed by the author

often they are found doing so. Crime is a regular phenomenon of the Rohingya camps, and the most desperate faction of the Rohingya population is becoming involved in different organized crimes, including transnational crimes. Religious extremist groups are also taking advantage of the vulnerable Rohingya for their recruitment, and they consider the Rohingya camps as fertile land for advancing their causes. "Al-Qaeda has urged Muslims in Southeast Asia (including Bangladesh) to support the Rohingya in Myanmar 'financially, militarily and politically' and has warned that: The savage treatment meted out to our Muslim brothers… shall not pass without punishment. The government of Myanmar shall be made to taste what our Muslim brothers have tasted" (Moore, 2017). The government of Bangladesh has deployed three Armed Police Battalions (APBn) to the Cox's Bazar area in recent years to better handle the security threats of the Rohingya presence.

It is still unclear whether the security force is having a desirable effect on improving the security situation. The security situation becomes more complicated day by day, and this creates a tense situation for Cox's Bazar as well as a threat to the national security of Bangladesh. Such security implications seriously jeopardize the safety and security of the local host community as well as the vulnerable part of the Rohingya population, and both groups have come under immense threats of harm due to the aforementioned activities of many organized groups among the Rohingya refugees. Thus, in addition to assessing the security implications of the Rohingya crisis in terms of physical safety and security, the capabilities of the Bangladesh Police to handle such issues need to be assessed. This study can provide crucial data on refugee management as well as security measures and improvements for handling crisis situations concerning displaced populations and refugees.

3 Methodology

The study has been conducted through mixed-method analysis, i.e., quantitative and qualitative. The methodology of the proposed study has also followed a participatory and multi-disciplinary approach. The key methods and steps are as follows: Review of literature and secondary data, Contextual analysis, and Focus Group Discussions (FGDs). Relevant literature and secondary data have been critically examined to summarize, evaluate, and compare the main development and current debates in the field, which are especially relevant to the subject of research. Relevant criminal activities recorded as the responsibility of the Rohingya have been collected from the relevant security agencies, i.e., local Thana, Union Parishad, BGB camps, etc., to critically analyze and ascertain the existing security threat scenario. This context analysis has helped to quantify the number and types of crimes performed by the Rohingya. To discern the overall views, opinions, and perceptions of the problem and potentials for safety and security issues, FGDs have also been conducted within host community and Rohingya camps. Each of the FGDs has involved six to eight participants from the host community, security experts, local government representatives including adult males and females, and Rohingya people. FGD participants were pre-selected by the researcher as those willing to participate in this study, in consultation with the appropriate authorities.

4 Refugee Management

The Cox's Bazar area of Bangladesh has become home to the largest concentration of Rohingya refugees in the world. As a result, the sociopolitical dynamics of the area have become more complex, and the physical safety and security of the region have become a significant concern. Despite the availability of some literature on the subject, a comprehensive understanding of the situation has not been achieved, and significant research gaps remain. One such research gap involves the effectiveness of the Bangladesh Armed Police Battalions (APBn) in handling security issues that arise due to the presence of Rohingya refugees in the Cox's Bazar area. It is difficult to adequately evaluate their limitations, weaknesses, and capabilities. Addressing these difficulties is critical in developing effective policies and strategies to maintain law and order in the area and ensure the security of both the local and refugee populations. Therefore, let us briefly review the UN's sometimes complicated relation to refugees, with a particular eye toward the situation in Bangladesh.

The United Nations (UN) has established protocols for the management of refugees through the Office of the United Nations High Commissioner for Refugees (UNHCR). The 1951 Refugee Convention, which defines the rights of refugees and the obligations of states toward them, is fundamental to these protocols. The Convention outlines that a refugee is a person who has been forced to flee their country due to a well-founded fear of persecution based on race, religion, nationality, political opinion, or membership in a particular social group. The Convention also outlines the rights of refugees, which include the right to work, education, and basic human needs such as shelter, food, and medical care. In addition to the 1951 Refugee Convention, the UN also established the 1967 Protocol Relating to the Status of Refugees, which expands the definition of a refugee to include those who flee due to generalized violence, foreign aggression, or events seriously disturbing public order. The UNHCR is responsible for ensuring that refugees are protected and their rights are respected, regardless of their location. The agency provides assistance to refugees, including protection, shelter, and basic necessities such as food, water, and healthcare. The UNHCR also works to find durable solutions for refugees, such as voluntary repatriation, resettlement, or local integration (Government of Bangladesh, 2022).

Despite not being a signatory to the UN Refugee Convention of 1951 and its protocol of 1967, Bangladesh is still bound by certain principles and protocols of the Convention with regard to managing its Rohingya refugee population. These principles and protocols are recognized as customary international law and are thus applicable to all states, regardless of whether or not they have ratified the Convention. One of the key principles that Bangladesh follows is the principle of non-refoulement, which prohibits the expulsion or return of refugees to a country where they face a risk of persecution or serious harm (Ashikuzzaman et al., 2022).

This principle has been widely accepted as a norm of customary international law (Meer et al., 2021). Bangladesh has reiterated its commitment to this principle and has repeatedly stated that it will not forcibly repatriate the Rohingya refugees to Myanmar, where they face a risk of persecution and violence. Another protocol of the Convention that Bangladesh follows is the principle of providing basic humanitarian assistance to refugees. This includes providing access to food, water, shelter, and healthcare services. The UNHCR and various international organizations have been working with the Bangladesh government to provide essential services to the Rohingya refugees in Cox's Bazar. The Bangladesh government has allowed these organizations to establish camps and facilities to provide humanitarian assistance to the refugees. Bangladesh has also allowed the UNHCR to register Rohingya refugees and issue identification cards to them (Government of Bangladesh, 2022). This has helped the government and aid agencies to provide targeted assistance to the refugees and ensure that their basic needs are met. Bangladesh has been working with the international community to find a sustainable solution to the Rohingya crisis, including the safe and voluntary repatriation of the refugees to Myanmar.

5 Security Forces of Bangladesh

The main responsibility of the Armed Police Battalions is to ensure the law and order of the Rohingya camps, but they are not performing any investigation of criminal cases in the camps. Armed Police Battalions have also performed administrative and secondary services. Generally, Bangladesh Armed police Battalions perform the following categories of responsibilities in the Rohingya camps, illustrated in Table 1.

Bangladesh Armed Police Battalions have taken the following measures for prevention and controlling of crime in the refugee camps, illustrated in Fig. 2.

Table 1 Responsibilities of APBns in Rohingya camps

Primary line or operational police tasks	Secondary and auxiliary service tasks	Administrative or managerial police tasks
• Patrol • Conduct information-based operations • Intelligence collection from the Rohingya community • Access control • Bit policing • Prepare databases • Apprehensions • Arbitration	• Records • Property • Transportation • Communication	• Personnel • Planning • Budgeting • Training • Public/community relations

Source Developed by the author

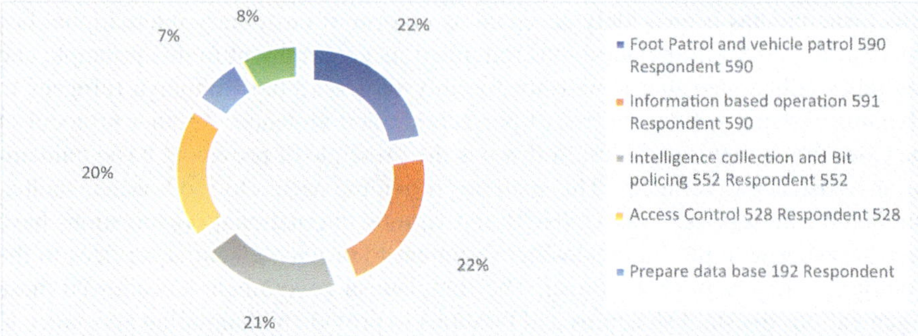

Fig. 2 APBn activities (Reproduced from survey on 795 APBn forces). Developed by author based on field data

5.1 Foot and Vehicle Patrol in the Rohingya Camps

Every Armed Police Battalion camp covers 3/4 of a Rohingya camp. The area of each Rohingya camp is near about 2/3 square kilometer. One mobile team consisting of 8–10 police members conducts foot patrols for each Rohingya camp during the night. But in daytime, only one mobile patrol covers all the Rohingya camps, dispatched from the one APBn camp. The supervising officer along with his team consisting of 4–5 members supervises all the mobile patrols by pickup truck. Vehicle patrols cannot cover all the camp areas due to a lack of roads, and inside the camps, there are many narrow passages just for walking. Even three or four persons cannot go through those passages together. A survey carried out on 795 members of the APBn revealed that among them, 22% think that effective patrolling can control the security situation in the Rohingya camps.

5.2 Information-Based Operations in the Rohingya Camps

Armed Police Battalions have their own intelligence wing that collects real-world information, and the APBn also receives intelligence from other agencies. APBn therefore conducts operations to collect intelligence and information. This type of operational team consists of 25–30 members of the APBn. Sometimes, the APBn conducts block raids with the help of district police, RAB-15 (the Rapid Action Battalion), and the executive magistrate. The APBn also makes requisitions for manpower from regional headquarters for any major operations being undertaken. In the aforementioned APBn survey, 22% of battalion members think that information-based operations can control the security situation in the Rohingya camps.

5.3 Intelligence Collection from the Rohingya Community

The Armed Police Battalion has enlisted sources inside the camps, and they collect information secretly from the Rohingya people and the Majhis of the camps. Only those police members who understand the language of the Rohingya very well are engaged for intelligence collection. A few police members have been injured during intelligence collection by the Rohingya people. Usually, Rohingya people do not cooperate with police, and they do not want to be witness to any incident. They just say "N JANI N DEKHI," which means, "I don't know and I don't see." Among the 795 members of APBn surveyed, 21% think that intelligence is highly required to improve the security situation in Rohingya camps.

5.4 Access Control

The Rohingya camps were initially surrounded by fencing, but Rohingya people created more than a thousand passages to enable them to leave the camps. There are now many entry points into the Rohingya camps. APBn sets up their checkpoints mostly on those roads which are made of bricks, since many Rohingya people and vehicles use those roads. All the checkpoints work 24 h a day, and sometimes they seize illegal items, confiscate arms, and stop illegal goods from entering and leaving the camps. In the APBn survey, 20% think that proper access control can help to control the security situation in the Rohingya camps.

5.5 Bit Policing

The Armed Police Battalion camp commander has assigned one officer as a "bit officer" for bit policing in the Rohingya camps. Bit policing can engage the community with involvement, and on the other hand, it helps to get proper information from the community. The community will help to prevent crime to enhance their engagement. Each camp has one bit officer. They have not yet established a formal bit office in the Rohingya camps, but currently use learning centers, volunteers' rooms, or NGO offices as bit office. The bit officers listen to complaints from the Rohingya people and try to solve their problems.

5.6 Preparing a Database of All Rohingyas

The Armed Police Battalion do not have a comprehensive database of Rohingya people and do not even have access to an updated database of criminals. UN agencies have made a database of all Rohingyas for purposes of providing aid, and they have issued FCN cards to all Rohingya families. But the Armed Police Battalions don't have any access to that database. Only the Office of the Refugee Relief and Repatriation Commissioner (RRRC) has access, and even then only to read. For verification purposes and to better identify criminals, Armed Police Battalions should prepare a database of the entire Rohingya community.

Besides this, Armed Police Battalions also perform administrative tasks, secondary tasks, coordination meetings, protocols, and other crime-related tasks.

6 Discussion and Conclusion

The Rohingya crisis is an ongoing humanitarian catastrophe that has resulted in the displacement of hundreds of thousands of Rohingya people from Myanmar. The crisis has also significantly impacted Bangladesh, where many of the displaced people have fled to. While Bangladesh has been providing shelter and support to the Rohingya refugees, the situation remains far from ideal due to a range of issues related to policing, security, and logistical challenges, particularly in the area of Cox's Bazar.

One of the key issues facing the Bangladesh Police is the lack of a cohesive policy to address the Rohingya issue in light of Myanmar's continued upheaval. Additionally, the Bangladesh Armed Police Battalions have not developed appropriate procedures or identification databases for all Rohingya refugees, nor have they updated the criminal database with recent pictures. This has led to a lack of effective measures to prevent and combat crime in the refugee camps, including drug trafficking and smuggling of arms and gold. Another challenge faced by the Bangladesh Armed Police Battalions is the absence of a strong and effective intelligence and research wing, which has hampered efforts to gather crucial information about criminal activities and terrorist groups operating in the camps. Additionally, there is a severe shortage of manpower and logistical support, including inadequate patrol vehicles and limited road infrastructure, which has made it difficult to provide effective security in the camps. The service records of the police officers working in the Rohingya camps indicate that many are not satisfied with their work, and they face numerous challenges and threats while on duty. They do not receive hardship allowances like other government organizations, and cooperation from other required agencies is also not forthcoming. The situation is further exacerbated by the lack of lighting, effective fencing, and digital surveillance equipment, which has allowed criminals to exploit the numerous entry points to the camps.

One of the most significant challenges facing the Bangladesh Police is the reluctance of the Rohingya community to cooperate with law enforcement. The language barrier has made it difficult to engage the Rohingya community effectively, and the community is unable to choose Majhi (representatives of the Rohingya camps) without seeking any opinion from the police/camp authority (i.e., those in charge of the camps). Moreover, the transportation of illegal drugs such as "Yaba" continues unabated inside the camps, which poses a significant security risk.

To address the Rohingya crisis, it is crucial to find a permanent solution, and strong diplomacy is required to create pressure on Myanmar to take the Rohingya back. China, India, and other powerful countries can play a vital role in this regard. However, the Bangladesh Police must also take proactive measures to address the challenges facing them, including developing appropriate policy frameworks, investing in logistical support and intelligence gathering, and ensuring adequate training and incentives for police personnel.

There are several areas where the Bangladesh Armed Police Battalions can make a significant impact on the safety and security of the Rohingya camps. First, it is essential to have a policy framework that takes into account Myanmar's ambivalence regarding the Rohingya issue. Armed Police Battalions should prepare appropriate procedures founded on research-based guidelines, and ensure that all officers in the camps are aware of them. Providing additional skilled police personnel to the Armed Police Battalions in the Rohingya camps might greatly aid in keeping the region secure and safe for both innocent Rohingyas and host Bengali people. The additional police personnel can aid in keeping the spread of crime in check, since a lack of personnel has been a significant deficit for the police force working in the Rohingya camps, and a sizeable police force can both keep the area safer and also aid the Border Guard Bangladesh (BGB) in keeping the border safe.

Second, up-to-date digital communications and surveillance equipment are essential for the modern age when activities are harder to track than ever before. The digital age has brought several innovations for security forces, which involve cutting-edge communications and surveillance equipment that can facilitate tracking potential suspects of unlawful activity, as well as communicating crucial information during important operations. Getting such equipment in adequate supply in the hands of the Bangladesh Armed Police Battalions of the Rohingya camps is only part of the solution in bringing their communications and surveillance equipment into the modern era. In connection with this, strict access control, separately fencing every camp, adequate light, and a reliable power supply are highly required in all the Rohingya camps. Appropriate training to utilize such equipment is paramount to fully integrating such technology into the Bangladesh Armed Police Battalions as well as Bangladesh as a whole.

Third, the study findings have revealed that the enforcement equipment and transportation vehicles of the APBn of the Rohingya camps are not sufficient to combat the rising criminal activities in that area. Their gear and vehicle insufficiency needs to be addressed. This is a key priority alongside the addition of an increased road infrastructure within the Rohingya camps, including peripheral roads with watchtowers and effective fencing of the camp.

Fourth, Bangladesh APBns should establish a strong and effective intelligence and research wing with adequate support of logistics, modern digital surveillance equipment, and skilled manpower. They should prepare a required database of all Rohingya for effectively handling the security situation in the camps. All members of APBns should be provided need-based training for capacity building and adequate logistics for smooth handling operations in the Rohingya camps. Like other government organizations, Armed Police Forces should provide hardship allowance for motivation. After serving a certain period in the Rohingya camp, a member will be transferred and rewarded by the appropriate authority.

Fifth, Bangladesh APBns are not getting the expected level of cooperation from other required agencies. The level of coordination among all the required organizations is not satisfactory. Though APBns work 24/7, other organizations are not available 24/7 in the camp, and APBns are not getting assistance during the night from any other organizations. Camp In Charge (CIC) should stay within the Rohingya camps 24/7 and cooperate with the law enforcement agencies.

Lastly, it is important to address the issue of community policing in the Rohingya camps. Community policing involves creating a partnership between the police and the community to prevent crime and promote public safety. The community is encouraged to actively participate in identifying problems and coming up with solutions, which can help to foster a sense of ownership and responsibility toward the security of the area. The police, in turn, are encouraged to work closely with the community, to understand their concerns and needs, and to collaborate with them to address issues in a timely and effective manner. Community policing has been successfully implemented in many parts of the world and has been proven to be an effective tool in crime prevention and detection. In the context of the Rohingya camps, community policing can be used to build trust between the police force and the refugee population. It can help to bridge the gap between the two parties and promote cooperation and collaboration in maintaining law and order within the camps.

In conclusion, the Rohingya crisis is a complex issue that requires a multi-faceted approach to address. The Bangladesh Police has a crucial role to play in ensuring the security and safety of the Rohingya camps. To effectively address the issue, the police force should have a dynamic policy framework, adequate equipment, and skilled personnel. It is important to establish clear communication channels and protocols that involve the refugee population in cooperation with the police force to handle crime and criminal activities in the region. Moreover, community policing can be used as an effective tool to build trust and promote cooperation between the police force and the refugee population. By adopting these measures, the Bangladesh Police can play a pivotal role in addressing the Rohingya crisis and promoting peace and security in the region. The Rohingya crisis presents significant challenges to the Bangladesh Police and requires a multi-faceted approach that addresses both the immediate security concerns and the root causes of the crisis. It is thus essential to develop a comprehensive policy framework that considers the unique challenges of the Rohingya issue, invest in logistical support and intelligence gathering, and build effective partnerships with the Rohingya community and other relevant agencies. Only by taking a holistic approach can the Bangladesh Police contribute effectively to resolving the Rohingya crisis and ensuring the safety and security of all affected communities.

References

Ahmad, A. (2012, January 30). The Rohingya: Myanmar's outcasts. *Al Jazeera English*. https://www.aljazeera.com/opinions/2012/1/30/the-rohingya-myanmars-outcasts

Ashikuzzaman, Gazi, A. K., & Abir, T. M. (2022). The key scenarios of Rohingya refugees in Bangladesh: A narrative study. In *Worldwide Inter-Disciplinary Research* (pp. 252–269). New Delhi: Notion Press India.

Aye, K. K., & Sercombe, P. (2014). Language, education and nation-building in Myanmar. In P. Sercombe & R. Tupas (Eds.), *Language, education and nation-building: Assimilation and shift in Southeast Asia* (pp. 148–164). Palgrave Macmillan. https://doi.org/10.1057/9781137455536_8.

Banerjee, S. (2019, March 15). *Drug trafficking and Rohingya refugees in Bangladesh*. Observer Research Foundation. https://www.orfonline.org/expert-speak/drug-trafficking-and-rohingya-refugees-in-bangladesh-49005/

Chowdhury, M. A. (2006, October 22). *The advent of Islam in Arakan and Rohingyas*. Arkan Rohingya National Organisation. https://www.rohingya.org/the-advent-of-islam-in-arakan-and-the-rohingyas/

Fair, C. C. (2018, December 9). *Arakan Rohingya Salvation Army: Not the Jihadis you might expect*. Lawfare Institute. https://www.lawfaremedia.org/article/arakan-rohingya-salvation-army-not-jihadis-you-might-expect

Gazi, A. K., & Abir, T. M., Ashikuzzaman. (2022). The key scenarios of Rohingya refugees in Bangladesh: A narrative study. In B. Bhattacharya, N. Karunakar, V. Shukla, S. Dey & W. K. Yadav (Eds.), *Worldwide inter-disciplinary research* (pp. 252–269). Notion Press India.

Government of Bangladesh. (2022). *Rohingya refugee response/Bangladesh: Rohingya population by location (as of 31 Jan 2022)*. UNHCR. https://data2.unhcr.org/en/documents/details/90958

Hall, D. G. E. (1955). *A history of South-East Asia*. Macmillan.

Human Rights Watch. (2023). *Rohingya*. Retrieved August 28, 2023, from https://www.hrw.org/tag/rohingya#:~:text=The%20Rohingya%20have%20faced%20decades,stateless%20populations%20in%20the%20world

Moore, J. (2017, September 13). Al-Qaeda promises jihad against Myanmar over Rohingya crackdown. *Newsweek*. https://www.newsweek.com/al-qaeda-promises-punishment-myanmar-pledges-jihad-over-crimes-against-663956

Parnini, S. N., Othman, M. R., & Ghazali, A. S. (2013). The Rohingya refugee crisis and Bangladesh-Myanmar relations. *Asian and Pacific Migration Journal, 22*(1), 133–146. https://doi.org/10.1177/011719681302200107

Rahman, M. M. (2022). Challenges and strategies to conduct research at restricted Rohingya refugee camps of Bangladesh. *Indiana Journal of Humanities and Social Sciences, 3*(9), 22–31. https://doi.org/10.5281/zenodo.7123481

Rahman, U. (2010). The Rohingya refugee: A security dilemma for Bangladesh. *Journal of Immigrant & Refugee Studies, 8*(2), 233–239. https://doi.org/10.1080/15562941003792135

Ullah, A. A. (2011). Rohingya refugees to Bangladesh: Historical exclusions and contemporary marginalization. *Journal of Immigrant & Refugee Studies, 9*(2), 139–161. https://doi.org/10.1080/15562948.2011.567149

Ullah, R., & Faisal, Md. M. (2022). Challenges in a host country: A study on Rohingya refugees in Bangladesh. *Middle East Journal of Refugee Studies, 6*(2), 5–19. https://dergipark.org.tr/en/download/article-file/2181252

United Nations. (2017). *UN rights expert 'disappointed' by Myanmar's decision to refuse visit*. Retrieved from: https://news.un.org/en/story/2017/12/639982-un-rights-expert-disappointed-myanmars-decision-refuse-visit

United Nations High Commissioner for Refugees. (2007). *Statistical yearbook, 2005: Trends in displacement, protection and solutions*. UNHCR. https://www.unhcr.org/statistics/country/464478a72/unhcr-statistical-yearbook-2005.html

Zafar, A. (2020). The Rohingya refugees: A review of security threats for Bangladesh. *Global Scientific Journals, 8*(9), 2104–2109. https://www.researchgate.net/publication/355734262_THE_ROHINGYA_REFUGEES_A_REVIEW_OF_SECURITY_THREATS_FOR_BANGLADESH

Chapter 14
Social Cohesion and Integration of Rohingyas in the Host Community in Bangladesh

Mahabuba Islam Meem

Abstract Given the influx of nearly a million Rohingya refugees into the Cox's Bazar region of Bangladesh in 2017, it was inevitable that the demographics and social makeup of the area should change. The refugee population is now more than double that of the host community. Though efforts for repatriation are ongoing, the continued lack of success in that regard leads to the conclusion that long-term initiatives for improving social cohesion between the Rohingya and the Bangladeshi host community are required. We begin by constructing a definition of social cohesion in the context of the Rohingya crisis, first sketching out several frameworks from the literature before homing in on the specific region at hand. Next, a careful examination is performed of the many factors which adversely affect social cohesion in Cox's Bazar today, as it is only through an understanding of these factors that a path forward can be discovered. It is doubly important to emphasize social cohesion in the area where they live, since the current repatriation initiative is in limbo and nobody knows when such a large population of Rohingyas would be able to return to Rakhine. Finally, we draw upon global examples as well as expectations from international bodies like the UN in suggesting ways that the integration of the Rohingyas can be achieved using long-term strategic planning.

1 Introduction

Bangladesh has a long history of hosting Rohingyas from the northern Rakhine State of Myanmar, with the earliest arrivals recorded in 1948 (Ullah, 2011). The Rohingya people of Myanmar have faced decades of systematic discrimination and targeted violence (Alam, 2019). The latest of these episodes, in late August 2017, caused almost one million people to flee to Bangladesh, creating a large-scale humanitarian crisis. The response to this crisis, which saw the involvement of a wide range of formal and informal aid actors, prevented the loss of many lives and helped to stabilize the

M. I. Meem (✉)
North Carolina State University, Raleigh, USA
e-mail: meem.mahabuba@gmail.com

K. Ahmed and Md. R. Islam (eds.), *Understanding the Rohingya Displacement*, International Perspectives on Migration, https://doi.org/10.1007/978-981-97-1424-7_14

situation. This is a significant achievement given the formidable challenges that confronted the humanitarian community.

The large influx of Rohingyas to Cox's Bazar has changed its sociopolitical, demographic, and economic dimensions (Kudrat-E-Khuda, 2020; Ullah et al., 2021; UNDP, 2018). Furthermore, the pre-existing stressors in terms of high poverty rates, low employment and education rates, high rates of crime, and fragile topography have progressively worsened the relationship between the host community and refugee community (Islam, 2023; Islam, & Wara, 2022). This problematic context has led to social tensions, competition over resources, negative perception of refugees, strain on public services, and other situations that further degrade the social cohesion between the host community and refugees residing in Cox's Bazar (Islam & Wara, 2022; Yasmin & Akther, 2019). However, aspects of the crisis may also have created jobs, provided international recognition, attracted aid, boosted local economies, and increased the size of the market, all phenomena which have improved social cohesion. Therefore, this study aims to understand the social cohesion and integration between Rohingya refugees and host communities in Bangladesh. The chapter specifically attempts to answer two questions: What does social cohesion mean in the context of Rohingya refugees residing in Cox's Bazar? And what are the factors that affect the social cohesion between Rohingya refugees and host communities? Based on the secondary literature, this chapter first provides literature on social cohesion and its diverse meaning in a refugee receiving society. Secondly, this chapter presents the issues of social cohesion in the context of Bangladesh. Then, this chapter outlines the factors which are affecting the social cohesion issues in Cox's Bazar. Finally, this chapter highlights how social cohesion can be achieved between the local people and Rohingyas with a conclusion.

2 Literature Review

2.1 Social Cohesion

Social cohesion was first formally described by Emile Durkheim in the context of division of labor and its impacts through mechanical and organic solidarity (Kuhnt et al., 2017). Mechanical solidarity is based on shared collective values, beliefs, traditions, and lifestyles—which is more linked with a traditional society—whereas organic solidarity deals with aspects of industrialization and division of labor (Lyytinen & Kullenberg, 2013). The concept of social cohesion evolves from different academic disciplines and policies developed by different countries (Acket et al., 2011). Freud defined social cohesion from the perspective of identity, wherein individuals are identified with each other who share the same characteristics, and cohesion provides intense emotional ties (Fonseca et al., 2018). Similarly, Organization for Economic Cooperation and Development (OECD) defined social cohesion through the lens of overall well-being, in which "a cohesive society works toward the well-being of all its members, fights exclusion and marginalization, creates a sense of belonging, promotes trust, and offers its members the opportunity of upward mobility" (OECD, 2012). The Social Cohesion Research Network defined social cohesion most comprehensively from three perspectives: (1) willingness to cooperate, where people are willing to cooperate, participate, and trust each other or institutions despite their backgrounds; (2) respect for diversity, meaning respect for different values and opinions and the ability to leverage this diversity in the absence of social sameness, shared values, or social orderliness; and (3) implementation of social liberal values such as freedom of expression, equality, tolerance, respect for human rights, etc. (Stanley, 2003).

Additionally, the vagueness of social cohesion makes it adaptable to various situations, but leaves it difficult to conceptualize social cohesion as a whole (Bernard, 1999, cited in Kuhnt et al., 2017). Its wide framework is adaptable to every aspect of social life, but because of its vagueness it is difficult to pin down and to develop its definition and concept (De Berry & Roberts, 2018). The concept of social cohesion is often formally developed from policy framework, and such policies are often politicized and driven by the agenda of invested agencies.

2.2 *Social Cohesion in the Context of Forced Displacement*

People are forcefully displaced in the event of war, conflict, generalized violence, disaster, and persecution. Forced displacement has both positive and negative impacts on the receiving society (De Berry & Roberts, 2018; Kuhnt et al., 2017). Within this context of forced displacement, the people who are forced to flee their own country are called refugees. Of the refugees who are registered with UNHCR, 84% are hosted by low- and middle-income countries (UNHCR, 2019). This situation puts an immense burden on such countries, who are already struggling to provide basic needs to their own people (De Berry & Roberts, 2018; Kuhnt et al., 2017).

The structural barriers, combined with lack of government leadership, lack of appropriate government institutions, and high levels of poverty and unemployment, do not allow countries to adequately respond to the needs of refugees and host communities, which ultimately affects social cohesion (UNHCR, 2019). The link between high poverty and unemployment rates with low levels of social cohesion can be further illustrated with the example of South Africa. Despite the enactment of various acts and policies, and the establishment of institutions at township levels, South Africa continues to experience a vast range of xenophobic attacks toward migrants and refugees (Anderson, 2012). The most pertinent reasons for this are South Africans feeling neglected by their own government, widespread poverty, high levels of unemployment, and drug abuse (Anderson, 2012).

Similarly, the literature shows that appropriate government leadership and the installation of government institutions at the central and local levels have positive impacts on social cohesion. Putnam (1995) conceptualizes social cohesion from the perspective of bonding and bridging, which is applicable in the refugee context.

Bonding is an intra-group concept that is inward-looking and refers to exclusive social ties that are built around the same kind of people, like family members and community (Lyytinen & Kullenberg, 2013). In the case of refugees, they can be considered a group, and the support systems or relationships which are developed within them are examples of bonding. Connections between individuals of the same community, i.e., bonding, is considered helpful in the refugee context to allow people to get along and assist each other during times of crisis (Lyytinen & Kullenberg, 2013). However, overreliance on bonding is not considered positive, as it will make people more dependent on the group and isolate them from the larger frame of society (Cheong et al., 2007; Lyytinen & Kullenberg, 2013). Bridging, on the other hand, is an inter-group concept that is outward-looking and involves forming voluntary associations that intersect horizontal setups, which are based on the common interest of a heterogeneous group of people (Cheong et al., 2007). It is well established that refugees use social networks to leverage their other assets and capital. In the refugee context, the interconnectedness between the refugee and host community is one classic example of bridging relating to social cohesion (Acharya, 2020). The relationship between refugees and government institutions or government authorities of the host country is another example of bridging.

In the context of forced displacement, UNHCR (1996) environmental guidelines mention six different categories that affect the host community's overall environment. The categories are the following:

1. natural resource degradation
2. irreversible impact on natural resources
3. impact on health
4. impact on social condition
5. social impact on local population
6. social impact on economic condition.

Similarly, a study conducted by World Vision measured social cohesion from the perspective of its structural cause, socioeconomic cause, and proximate cause (Guay, 2015). The structural cause deals with issues such as poverty, lack of resources, and absence or lack of effective government institutions (Guay, 2015). The socioeconomic cause deals with issues related to differences in religious, cultural, and social values and norms between the refugee and host community; and the proximate cause deals with the shrinking labor market, rise in the cost of living in terms of food prices, transport and housing costs, competition over natural resources, and feelings of being neglected due to distribution of international aid targeting refugees only (Guay, 2015).

A further study conducted on social cohesion in times of forced displacement defines the Relational Capacity Index (RCI) and Social Cohesion Index (SCI) as tools developed to measure and conceptualize social cohesion (Kuhnt et al., 2017). RCI, developed by Giruad et al. (2013), includes three dimensions which are as follows:

1. integration into networks (socioeconomic integration)

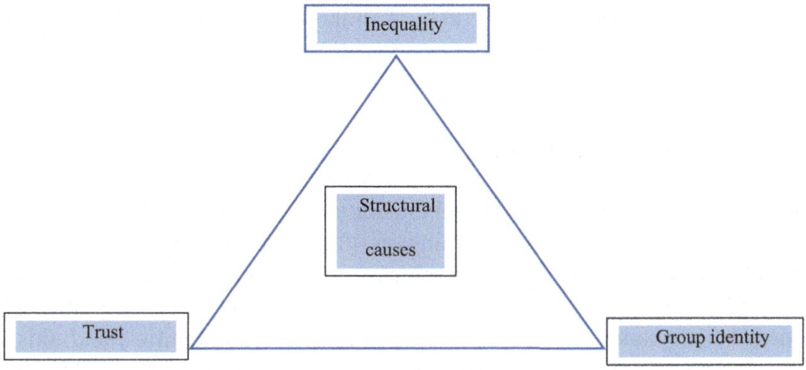

Fig. 1 Social cohesion in the context of forced displacement (Acharya, 2020)

2. private relations (sociocultural integration)
3. civic commitments (civic and political integration).

SCI was developed by Langer et al. (2016) and focuses on three relationship which are as follows:

1. relationship among individuals of same groups (bonding)
2. relationship among individual across groups (bridging)
3. relationship between individual, group and state (linking).

These relationships are further analyzed by considering three components which are inequality, trust, and group identity; while linked to each other, these factors are independent components (Fig. 1).

3 Data Analysis

3.1 Social Cohesion in the Context of the Rohingya Crisis

Social cohesion is an important construct that is required for the overall prosperity of all involved in the Rohingya crisis in Cox's Bazar, especially for Ukhiya and Teknaf, as these two sub-districts are heavily affected by the habitation of refugees. It is imperative to define social cohesion as per the local context because the concept of social cohesion has plasticity and as there is no widely held, theoretically derived, clearly articulated, and reasonably operationalized definition for social cohesion (Acharya, 2020).

Social cohesion in the context of the Rohingya crisis in Cox's Bazar is defined through three different categories: willingness to cooperate, respect for diversity, and conformity toward social liberal values such as freedom, equality, tolerance, and respect for human rights (Stanley, 2003). If all these issues are insured between the local people and Rohingyas, social cohesion can be possible to attain.

3.1.1 Willingness to Cooperate

The host and refugee community must be willing to cooperate to survive and prosper (Stanley, 2003). In the case of the Rohingyas, this could range from simple interactions between refugees and host communities to complex decision-making processes. It could be buying, selling, or lending of goods. This willingness telegraphs collaboration and understanding between host and refugee communities, and aids both in living together in harmony. Experience shows that local people welcomed the Rohingyas and provided logistics and opportunities so that they could sustain in the new place (Yasmin et al., 2020; Ansar & Md. Khaled, 2021). Bangladesh government, security forces, and local people worked together to shelter the Rohingya people in 2017 when more around 8 hundred thousand people arrived and sought humanitarian help and support.

3.1.2 Respect for Diversity

A socially cohesive society must respect diversity, in opposition to mono-culturalism, social sameness, and homogeneity. In the case of the Rohingya context, it means respecting the existence of Rohingya refugees despite their different backgrounds in terms of culture, education, religion, and identity. This is important for the emergence of a new community within the host society, and interventions that are made to tackle mistrust and lack of tolerance are linked with respect for diversity. The local people, administration, and security forces not only welcomed the Rohingyas but also ensured favorable environment so that the displaced people could live without compromising their culture and religious traits (Siddique, 2019). Since the settlement of Rohingyas in 34 camps in Cox's Bazar, mosques, Madrasha, schools, and institutions connected to the Rohingya culture have been established so that these displaced people live without discrimination.

3.1.3 Conformity Toward Social Liberal Values

Both the host and refugee communities in Cox's Bazar are supported toward developing social liberal values. Rohingya refugees are provided lifesaving support in terms of food, health, shelter, education, and fuel, which is a sign of respect for human rights. Similarly, tailor-made interventions are made for the host community as per their needs and priorities (Olney et al., 2019). Many interventions are being undertaken to tackle the problem of Rohingya refugees and host communities.

Therefore, social cohesion in the Rohingya context is a process that enables development of an environment where both host and refugee communities are willing to cooperate, to respect the diversity of both communities, and to show compliance toward social liberal values. In fact, social cohesion has been possible when Rohingya people came during 1980s and 1990s. The local people supported, cooperated, and lived together. However, the influx of large number of Rohingyas in 2017 has changed the scenario in Cox's Bazar which is generating conflict and mistrust between the local people and Rohingyas (Islam, 2023). This mistrust and frustration are challenging the notion of social cohesion in Cox's Bazar.

3.2 Factors Affecting Social Cohesion Between Rohingyas and the Host Community

3.2.1 Structural Problems

Ukhiya and Teknaf are sub-districts of Cox's Bazar situated in the southern part of Bangladesh, with a Bangladeshi population of around 471,000 (Bangladesh Bureau of Statistics, 2013a). Both sub-districts are characterized by a high level of poverty, high unemployment rate, and low level of education combined with poor food habits resulting in severe malnutrition (JRP, 2018; UNDP, 2018). Furthermore, difficult terrain, bad roads, insufficient infrastructure, and a lack of drinking water and sanitation contribute to the poor living conditions (ADB, 2019). The average and extreme poverty rates in Cox's Bazar, including Ukhiya and Teknaf, are 33% and 16%, respectively (Strategic Executive Group, 2020).

To exacerbate the situation, 59 and 41% of land in Ukhiya and Teknaf is reserved for forest land (Bangladesh Bureau of Statistics, 2013a). In Ukhiya, 63% of the total households are involved in agricultural activities, whereas in Teknaf, 81% of total households are involved in agricultural activities (Bhatia et al., 2018; UNDP, 2018). This shows the livelihood options are not diversified and most people are doing agricultural work, which leads to the vicious circle of poverty and unemployment. Since 2017 Rohingyas have been putting enormous pressure on agricultural land and forest resources, now this is a major obstacle to establishing social cohesion between local people and Rohingyas.

In the meantime, both sub-districts are prone to natural disasters such as cyclones, flooding, landslides, and heavy rainfall that disrupts the overall well-being of people residing in these sub-districts. The huge pressure of the Rohingyas on the overall environment has had significant negative impacts on land use, rainfall patterns, and management of disasters. The settlement of the Rohingyas and rapid urbanization have also caused impacts on sub-districts in Cox's Bazar (Hossain et al., 2023). These structural causes that predate the Rohingya crisis are some of the factors that negatively affect social cohesion.

3.2.2 Demographic Change

The sudden arrival of many Rohingyas in a new location obviously induced a demographic change. The arrival of refugees altered the previous composition and distribution of ethnicity and race, ultimately impacting the overall balance of tolerance, social acceptance, and cohesion (UNHCR, 2019). Therefore, the sudden arrival of Rohingya refugees from Myanmar brought extreme new demographic changes, which further worsened the situation in Ukhiya and Teknaf—where the margin of tolerance was already thin because of its many structural problem mentioned above. The total population of the host community in Ukhiya and Teknaf is around 471,000 (Bangladesh Bureau of Statistics, 2013b), and the total population of refugees residing in these sub-districts is 855,00 (Strategic Executive Group, 2020). Clearly the refugee population outnumbers the host community by a large margin. Around 64% of the total population in Ukhiya and Teknaf are refugees, while 36% are the host community. Local populations argue that they are outnumbered in their own regions, leading to demographic insecurities. The newborn children in Rohingya families are also generating a question of their identity and how these children would get their basic human rights including education.

Two out of five interviewees mentioned that a demographic change in Ukhiya and Teknaf has taken place with the arrival of huge number of refugees.

3.2.3 Environmental Degradation

Environmental resource scarcity is considered one of the factors for violent conflict, which is often intrastate, small scale and within the context of poverty (Martin, 2005). The presence of refugees in an area can place considerable stress on natural resources, leading to adverse environmental and social impacts. (Martin, 2005). Deforestation is widely cited as the most prominent cause of environmental degradation.

The arrival of the Rohingyas exerted extra pressure on the environment of Ukhiya and Teknaf, as Cox's Bazar and especially these two sub-districts are prone to environmental degradation and climate change (UNDP, 2018). Six thousand acres of government land, which is primarily forest reserve land, was allocated to them for their settlement. Apart from the settlement itself, refugees are heavily dependent on the forest for fuel, medicinal plants, and raw materials for construction, and such dependency has already damaged an additional 5125 acres of land (Bashar, 2021; Hossain, 2023; UNDP, 2018). Many host community families are dependent on the forest for timber, fuel, fodder, and medicinal plants, and the presence of refugees in the same area engenders competition over these resources affecting both populations (UNDP, 2018). According to Needs and Population Monitoring (NPM) round 7 which happened in December 2017, 65% of refugee households were dependent on the forest for firewood (NPM, 2017). Deforestation activities, depletion of water level, and loss of flora and fauna have caused significant damage to the environment and it has adversely affected social cohesion.

3.2.4 Rise in Cost of Living

With a huge number of refugees living in the vicinity of the host community, the demand for daily essentials has risen, leading toward price hikes and ultimately increasing the cost of living (Yasmin & Akther, 2019). Further, there has been a rise in transport costs and the cost of accommodations. Apart from this, the labor market has become saturated with refugees, as they work for lower rates compared to the local people or host community (Ahmad & Naeem, 2020; UNDP, 2018). There is no official data for reduced labor rates; however, many studies conducted in the area suggest the pay rate of daily labor has been reduced by as much as 50% (Krehm & Shahan, 2019; Huang et al., 2019). The daily wage has declined from 500 to 200 Taka per day (Yasmin & Akther, 2019). Two participants mentioned that a fall in the rate of daily labor and the lack of livelihood opportunities were major factors that affected social cohesion. Further, another participant mentioned that changes in market dimensions relating to the rise in food prices and unavailability of resources affect social cohesion. Refugees sell relief items at cheap prices to fulfill their other needs, which disrupts the market equilibrium (Yasmin & Akther, 2019). Some sell their goods as individuals, while others have created small-scale businesses in the camps. Additionally, the presence of refugees has affected some economic activities, such as the cross-border trade between Bangladesh and Myanmar, and fishing at the Naf River—which is now prohibited. The tourism industry is also affected, as there is a restriction on the movement of watercraft. Such a situation has facilitated the environment of unemployment or lack of economic opportunities for the host community. Therefore, tension is observed in the host communities because of economic frustration, business competition, and lowering of wages. According to Multi Sector Need Assessments (MSNA) conducted in December 2018, nearly eight out of ten members of the host community reported a significant or moderate increase in the cost of living (Strategic Executive Group, 2018). To further exacerbate the situation, most of the humanitarian organizations working in Ukhiya and Teknaf tend to hire workers, employees, and volunteers from the refugee community. This has further fueled discontent in the host community and led to several demonstrations being held in Ukhiya and Cox's Bazar.

According to an International Federation of Red Cross and Red Crescent Societies (IFRC) report on social cohesion, the Bangladeshi host community identified their most important challenges are unemployment and rise in the cost of living, which is further linked to reduced labor opportunities and agricultural land and increase in competition for markets and jobs (IFRC, 2020).

3.2.5 Perception

One factor that undermines social cohesion is perception (Guay, 2015). Perception in most cases is negative, and negative perceptions are built against different groups such as government vs refugee community, host community vs refugee community, host community vs humanitarian community, and other binary oppositions. The most common variables that determine perception in the context of the Rohingya crisis are as follows:

(a) **Perception of being neglected**: As per a report from World Vision, social cohesion in Jordan is affected because of negative perceptions that are being built regarding humanitarian aid which is delivered to refugees (Guay, 2015). In the case of Cox's Bazar, too much attention and assistance were given to the refugee community (Sohel & Siddiqui, 2019). The host community reported that they felt the government and non-government organizations had placed too much of their priority on refugees (Jerin & Mozumder, 2019). Further similar expressions were mentioned by the UNDP (2018), in which the host community believed assistance was exclusively provided to refugees and their own problems were not given priority, which made them feel ignored.
(b) **Perception created by media**: The media plays a huge role in developing perception. A report by UNHCR (2019) further confirmed how social media at times creates a negative perception for refugees, as it connects or suggests them as terrorists. For example, 17.6 million tweets were made related to the Berlin terror attack suggesting refugees were terrorists. In the context of Cox's Bazar, according to an IFRC report that quoted a statement of the assistant RRRC (Refugee Relief and Repatriation Commission), 99% of media reports categorically failed to address the crisis properly, and the spreading of false information can only increase the chances of conflicts flaring up between the host community and the refugee people (IFRC, 2020). Perceptions created by both social media and print media that refugees are snatching jobs or increasing crime levels are extremely detrimental to social cohesion.
(c) **Perception of being unsafe**: The host community in Bangladesh also feels unsafe, as they must pass through multiple checkpoints in their daily life; notably, there are no female officers in the checkpoints, which makes women more vulnerable to sexual harassment (UNDP, 2018). There is a widespread perception that the number of crimes like kidnapping, robberies, drug trafficking, human trafficking, and many more have increased with the arrival of the refugees, which makes the host community fearful of the refugee community; this has a huge impact on social cohesion (UNDP, 2018).
(d) **Perception of being different from refugee community**: According to Jerin and Mozumder (2019), the host community feels that the refugees' moral values are not aligned with their own. A similar opinion is mentioned in an IFRC report, whereby the host community perceives refugees differently because of cultural differences and the way they follow their religion (IFRC, 2020). Such othering of refugees is the basis of discrimination and affects social cohesion as well.

4 Increasing Social Cohesion and Integration Between Rohingyas and the Host Community

The issue of Rohingya repatriation to Myanmar has caused frustration, because refugees want to ensure their civil rights in Myanmar before any repatriation begins. This has created a complex situation for both the host community and the Rohingyas. Social cohesion and peaceful coexistence must therefore be achieved within the existing situation. Peaceful coexistence is a complex issue that is blended not only within the nearest local host community but also with the broader consensus of the district's and country's sentiments. UNHCR and other UN agencies are supporting the solidarity approach, which needs broader (district- and national-level) dissemination. In many cases, social cohesion and integration programs are designed based on loose conceptualization and implicit assumptions that do not reflect the real scenario (De Berry & Roberts, 2018).

To begin with, the government and all involved parties, including refugees, need to define the concept of social cohesion and its measurable indicators as per the local context. Such conceptual frameworks are imperative, as all the stakeholders need to identify and understand social cohesion unilaterally. Similarly, the government and the involved parties should develop policies for social cohesion along with the establishment of a specific government institution that deals with the matter. For example, Uganda and Turkey have created appropriate institutions to deal with matters of refugees, including social cohesion. Any developed policies should enable mutual growth, trust, and opportunities for both communities.

Second, the government should accept the presence of the Rohingya refugee population in their territory and accordingly make proper analyses regarding their stay in Bangladesh. Their stay is likely going to be protracted, as the prospects of durable repatriation solutions are not yet finalized. The moment the government starts to send positive messages about Rohingya refugees, most of the negative perception will subsided and the host communities will also accept them. Further, the government should start implementing a long-term approach for this response, which means a proper plan spanning five or ten years plan should be developed for Rohingya refugees that envisions their growth and overall development in terms of education, training, and self-reliance (Acharya, 2020).

Third, the Rohingya operation lacks an effective and efficient coordination mechanism for social cohesion matters, and therefore a coordinating mechanism needs to be established within government departments and between government counterparts, humanitarian communities, development communities, and relevant partners. The coordination mechanism should not limit itself to organizing meetings and reporting activities on social cohesion; rather, this mechanism should be able to produce plans and strategies for social cohesion.

Fourth, the government should increase the framework of its engagement with multiple partners. The government should engage not only with humanitarian partners, developing partners, and banks, but also with a diverse range of partners such as private organizations, multinational organizations, small- and medium-scale businesses, education institutions, and community-led banks and foundations.

Fifth, effective communication is essential to erase doubts for both refugees and host communities, and therefore clear and appropriate communication channels need to be established. Such clear and timely communication will help to reduce anxiety, stress levels, and prejudiced attitudes during both normal and crisis times. For example, a clear communication strategy on available, durable solutions would have cleared up many doubts for the refugees and the host community. The government should communicate its stance, strategies, and plans for the overall operation.

Sixth, projects that strengthen the relationship between refugees and the host community need to be implemented, such as community-led projects that allow both communities to share and learn from each other. Projects that allow the establishment of dialogue to curtail small-scale conflicts need to be established.

Lastly, a whole-of-society approach is essential to obtain a maximum output of social cohesion, which means both host and refugee communities should be viewed in an equal manner and a balanced approach should be practiced. Such an approach will allow both communities to lead a meaningful life with all available opportunities.

5 Conclusion

The arrival of the Rohingyas has completely changed the demography of the Ukhiya and Teknaf regions, and this has caused fear among host communities, as they are now a minority community. They feel the refugee community is much more powerful than them. Apart from this, a direct impact on the overall environment, a rise in the cost of living, and a disturbance in market equilibrium has been observed, which has significantly degraded social cohesion. Perception of refugees has changed drastically from their initial time of arrival, and now refugees are seen as job snatchers, criminals, ethically suspect, and more, which has also affected social cohesion negatively. Another important factor that affects social cohesion is finding and communicating durable solutions for refugees. Neither the refugee community nor the host community has a clear idea of the prospects of any available durable solutions. This situation has agitated both refugee and host communities. There is no clear timeline regarding the stay of the refugees, which bring anxiety and fear for both communities.

Further, with regard to this crisis, the government policies are focused on repatriation, and therefore short-term policy and restrictive measures are implemented which are predominately used to only save the lives of refugees. Such an approach will directly affect social cohesion between both refugee and host communities. In addition to this, the lack of livelihood opportunities, insufficient education opportunities, and scarce recreational activities lead refugees to exist in a difficult environment without growth and development. This phenomenon has cumulatively affected social cohesion between refugee and host communities. In summary, both refugees and host communities are living in a hostile environment owing to their own vulnerabilities, and this may considerably damage the social cohesion between both communities. Their mutual existence has been treated as a threat and problem.

Under this scenario, it is necessary to properly evaluate the consequences of the adverse impact on the hosts and to ensure proper distribution of humanitarian relief and the implementation of refugee and host community support projects, mainly in the protracted phase of the crisis. The local constraints must also be recognized for the comprehensive management of the refugee situation. A refugee-centric humanitarian response will only lead to the further deterioration of social cohesion and host–refugee relationship dynamics. The Rohingya crisis has slowly transformed into a protracted crisis, and therefore, an all-inclusive and comprehensive humanitarian engagement by focusing on capacity development of the state and by ensuring integrated refugee–host humanitarian support programs are needed.

References

Acharya, S. (2020). *Social cohesion between Rohingya refugees and host communities in Cox's Bazar*. University of London.

Acket, S., Borsenberger, M., Dickes, P., & Sarracino, F. (2011, January 20–21). Measuring and validating social cohesion: A bottom-up approach. In *International Conference on Social Cohesion and Development*, Luxembourg. http://www.oecd.org/dev/pgd/46839973.pdf

Ahmad, S. M., & Naeem, N. (2020). Adverse economic impact by Rohingya refugees on Bangladesh: Some way forwards. *International Journal of Social, Political and Economic Research, 7*(1), 1–14.

Alam, J. (2019). The current Rohingya crisis in Myanmar in historical perspective. *Journal of Muslim Minority Affairs, 39*(1), 1–25.

Anderson, J. L. (2012). *Urban displacement and peacebuilding: An analysis of South African social cohesion interventions*. United Nations High Commissioner for Refugees. https://www.unhcr.org/sites/default/files/legacy-pdf/5040ae509.pdf

Bangladesh Bureau of Statistics. (2013a). *District Statistics 2011 Cox's Bazar*. Ministry of Planning, Government of the People's Republic of Bangladesh. http://203.112.218.65:8008/WebTestApplication/userfiles/Image/District%20Statistics/Cox%60s%20Bazar.pdf

Bangladesh Bureau of Statistics. (2013b). *District Statistics 2011 Cox's Bazar*. Bangladesh: Bangladesh Bureau of Statistics.

Bangladesh Resident Mission. (2019). *Summary poverty reduction and social strategy*. South Asia Department. https://www.adb.org/sites/default/files/linked-documents/52174-001-sprss.pdf

Bashar, S. (2021). *The Rohingya refugee crisis in Bangladesh: Environmental impacts, policies, and practices*. Master's Thesis. Oregon State University, USA. Available online: https://ir.library.oregonstate.edu/concern/graduate_projects/m326m865f

Bhatia, A., Mahmud, A., Fuller, A., Shin, R., Rahman, A., Shatil, T., Sultana, M., Morshed, K.M., Leaning, J., & Balsari, S. (2018). The Rohingya in Cox's Bazar: when the stateless seek refuge. *Health and Human Rights, 20*(2), 105.

De Berry, J. P., & Roberts, A. J. (2018). *Social cohesion and forced displacement: A desk review to inform programming and project design*. The World Bank. http://documents.worldbank.org/curated/en/125521531981681035/Social-cohesion-and-forced-displacement-a-desk-review-to-inform-programming-and-project-design

Cheong, P., Edwards, R., Goulbourne, H., & Solomos, J. (2007). Immigration, social cohesion and social capital: A critical review. *Critical Social Policy, 27*(1), 24–49. https://doi.org/10.1177/0261018307072206

Fonseca, X., Lukosch, S., & Brazier, F., (2018). Social cohesion revisited: A new definition and how to characterize it. *Innovation: The European Journal of Social Science Research, 32*(2), 231–253. https://doi.org/10.1080/13511610.2018.1497480

Guay, J. (2015). *Social cohesion between Syrian refugees and urban host communities in Lebanon and Jordan.* World Vision. https://www.wvi.org/disaster-management/publication/social-cohesion-between-syrian-refugees-and-urban-host-communities

Hossain, F., Kamal, A. M., Sadeak, S., & Gazi, M. Y. (2023). Quantitative soil erosion risk assessment due to rapid urbanization in the Cox's Bazar district and Rohingya refugee camps in Bangladesh. *Stochastic Environmental Research and Risk Assessment, 37*(3), 989–1006.

Hossain, M. P. (2023). The Rohingya refugee crisis: Analysing the international law implications of its environmental impacts on Bangladesh. *The International Journal of Human Rights, 27*(2), 238–257.

International Federation of Red Cross and Red Crescent Societies. (2020). *Community feedback: Social cohesion - population movement operation (PMO), Cox's Bazar, Bangladesh—January.* ReliefWeb. https://reliefweb.int/attachments/d18c62cc-8a18-3c68-8236-f5bb09574605/02-Social-Cohesion-Draft-2-FINAL_compressed.pdf

Islam, M. R., & Wara, U. (2022). Conflict potential of the Rohingya people in Bangladesh and beyond. *JAS (Journal of ASEAN Studies), 10*(1).

Islam, R. (2023). The state of social cohesion in the post-settlement of Rohingyas in Cox's Bazar, Bangladesh. *International Journal on Minority and Group Rights*, 1(aop), 1–32.

Jerin, M., & Mozumder, M. K. (2019). Exploring host community attitudes towards Rohingya refugees in Bangladesh. *Mental Health and Psychological Support in Conflict Affected Areas, 17*(2).

Krehm, E., & Shahan, D. A. (2019). *Access to justice for Rohingya and host community in Cox's Bazar.* International Rescue Committee. https://www.rescue.org/sites/default/files/document/3929/accessingjusticeassessmentexternalfinalsmall.pdf

Kudrat-E-Khuda (Babu). (2020). The impacts and challenges to host country Bangladesh due to sheltering the Rohingya refugees. *Cogent Social Sciences, 6*(1), 1770943.

Kuhnt, J., Rischke, R., David, A., & Lechtenfeld, T. (2017). *Social cohesion in times of forced displacement: The case of young people in Jordan.* Georg-August-Universität Göttingen. https://www.researchgate.net/publication/322006817_Social_cohesion_in_times_of_forced_displacement_-_the_case_of_young_people_in_Jordan

Lyytinen, E., & Kullenberg, J. (2013). *Urban refugee research and social capital: A roundtable report and literature review.* International Rescue Committee, Women's Refugee Commission. https://www.researchgate.net/publication/313161471_Urban_Refugee_Research_and_Social_Capital_A_Roundtable_Report_and_Literature_Review

Martin, A. (2005). Environmental conflict between refugee and host communities. *Journal of Peace Research, 42*(3), 329–346. https://doi.org/10.1177/0022343305052015

Needs and Population Monitoring. (2017). *NPM R7 report.* International Organization for Migration. https://displacement.iom.int/system/tdf/reports/NPM%20Round%207%20Report.pdf?file=1&type=node&id=2587

Olney, J., Badiuzzaman, M., & Hoque, M. A. (2019). Social cohesion, resilience and peace building between host population and Rohingya refugee community in Cox's Bazar, Bangladesh. BRAC, Dhaka. Available online: https://dspace.bracu.ac.bd/xmlui/handle/10361/16294

Organisation for Economic Co-operation and Development. (2012). *Social cohesion.* https://www.oecd.org/dev/inclusive-societies-development/social-cohesion.htm

Putnam, R. D. (1995). Bowling alone: America's declining social capital. *Journal of Democracy, 6*(1), 65–78. https://doi.org/10.1353/jod.1995.0002

Siddique, W. (2019). *The impact of Rohingya refugees on the local host community: The case of Cox's Bazar in Bangladesh* (Master's thesis). Tampere University, Finland. Available online: https://trepo.tuni.fi/handle/10024/116089

Sohel, I. M., & Siddiqui, P. (2019). *Tensions and potential conflict between host communities and Rohingya refugees*. The Independent. http://www.theindependentbd.com/printversion/details/194317

Stanley, D. (2003). What do we know about social cohesion: The research perspective of the Federal Government's social cohesion research network. *The Canadian Journal of Sociology, 28*(1), 5–17. https://doi.org/10.2307/3341872

Stategic Executive Group. (2020). *2020 Joint response plan: Rohingya humanitarian crisis (January–December 2020)—Bangladesh*. ReliefWeb. https://reliefweb.int/attachments/c3584bb5-6582-374b-86f3-cd8d703e4a30/jrp_2020_final_in-design_280220.2mb_0.pdf

Strategic Executive Group. (2018). *2018 Joint response plan for Rohingya humanitarian crisis*. United Nations High Commissioner for Refugees. https://www.unhcr.org/sites/default/files/legacy-pdf/5ab8e23a7.pdf

Ullah, A. A. (2011). Rohingya refugees to Bangladesh: Historical exclusions and contemporary marginalization. *Journal of Immigrant & Refugee Studies, 9*(2), 139–161.

Ullah, S. A., Asahiro, K., Moriyama, M., & Tani, M. (2021). Socioeconomic status changes of the host communities after the Rohingya refugee influx in the Southern coastal area of Bangladesh. *Sustainability, 13*(8), 4240.

United Nations High Commissioner for Refugees. (1996). *UNHCR environmental guidelines*. https://www.refworld.org/pdfid/42a01c9d4.pdf

United Nations Development Programme. (2018). *Impacts of the Rohingya refugee influx on host communities*. UNDP, Policy Research Institute of Bangladesh. https://reliefweb.int/attachments/a3fa1614-8cfc-3790-aeb3-93aeef40afb2/Impacts%20of%20the%20Rohingya%20Refugee%20Influx%20on%20Host%20Communities.pdf

United Nations High Commissioner for Refugees. (2019). *UNHCR global trends 2018*. UNHCR. https://www.unhcr.org/sites/default/files/legacy-pdf/5d08d7ee7.pdf

Yasmin, L., & Akther, S. (2019). The locals and the Rohingyas: Trapped with an uncertain future. *Asian Journal of Comparative Politics, 5*(2). https://doi.org/10.1177/2057891119865021

Yasmin, L., & Akther, S. (2020). The locals and the Rohingyas: Trapped with an uncertain future. *Asian Journal of Comparative Politics, 5*(2), 104–120.

Chapter 15
Repatriation of Rohingya Refugees: Prospects and Challenges

Md. Rafiqul Islam and Muhammad Mazedul Haque

Abstract This chapter critically examines the potential for Rohingya refugee repatriation from Bangladesh to Myanmar, adopting an interdisciplinary approach. It combines political, legal, and humanitarian perspectives to highlight the complexities and challenges. The research includes stakeholder interviews, official statements, and literature reviews to present a nuanced understanding of prospects, obstacles, and pathways for safe and voluntary returns. Beginning with an overview of the Rohingya crisis, it contextualises within the historical backdrop of the Rohingya-Muslim minority in Myanmar, emphasising the need for a sustainable, rights-based solution. The chapter explores Bangladesh's perspective on repatriation, analysing its humanitarian approach, challenges in hosting refugees, and diplomatic efforts. Expert opinions on feasibility and challenges, Bangladesh–Myanmar relations, geopolitical factors, and international roles are incorporated. Rohingya voices are amplified to reveal fears and aspirations, while Myanmar's position and crisis-addressing efforts are examined. Key success factors, such as citizenship frameworks and trust-building mechanisms, are meticulously evaluated, along with the roles of regional and international stakeholders and ongoing legal proceedings. Concluding with synthesised insights, it underscores sustained dialogue and cooperation for a just and sustainable solution, ensuring the safe and voluntary return of Rohingya refugees within a comprehensive approach.

Md. R. Islam (✉)
University of Dhaka, Dhaka, Bangladesh
e-mail: rislampacs@du.ac.bd

M. M. Haque
Bangladesh Institute of International and Strategic Studies, Dhaka, Bangladesh

K. Ahmed and Md. R. Islam (eds.), *Understanding the Rohingya Displacement*, International Perspectives on Migration, https://doi.org/10.1007/978-981-97-1424-7_15

1 Introduction

The Rohingya refugee crisis has emerged as one of the most pressing humanitarian challenges of our time. The Rohingya-Muslim minority has faced longstanding discrimination and marginalisation in Myanmar. References to their historical presence in Rakhine State can be traced back centuries, with Rohingya communities residing in the region for generations (Alam, 2019). However, their status has been a subject of contention, and successive Myanmar governments have denied them citizenship rights, rendering them stateless (Alam, 2019; Kajla & Chowdhory, 2020). This exclusionary policy, coupled with discriminatory practices and violence against the Rohingya population, has perpetuated their vulnerability and eventual displacement (Ullah, 2011).

The scale of the Rohingya refugee crisis is staggering. Following a major influx of Rohingya refugees into Bangladesh in 2017, the number of displaced individuals reached unprecedented levels (Idris, 2017). Reports of human rights abuses, including violence, extrajudicial killings, sexual assault, and mass displacement, have drawn international attention and condemnation (Ashikuzzaman et al., 2022). The United Nations has described the situation as ethnic cleansing and genocide (Beyrer & Kamarulzaman, 2017; Khin, 2017). Given the gravity of the crisis, there is an urgent need for a sustainable solution that addresses the root causes of the Rohingya refugee problem and paves the way for their safe and dignified return to their homeland. Such a solution must uphold the principles of human rights, justice (Ullah, 2016), and non-discrimination, ensuring that the Rohingya population is accorded full citizenship rights and protections (Alam, 2019). The repatriation of Rohingya refugees is a complex process that requires the collaboration and commitment of multiple stakeholders, including the governments of Bangladesh and Myanmar, international organisations, and the Rohingya community itself. However, any repatriation effort must be conducted in a manner that prioritises the safety, security, and well-being of the Rohingya refugees, guaranteeing their protection from further persecution and ensuring a sustainable reintegration process (Gorlick, 2020; Inter Sector Coordination Group, 2019).

In the light of these considerations, the proceeding discussion involves a critical examination of the prospects and challenges surrounding the repatriation of Rohingya refugees. By analysing the perspectives of the Government of Bangladesh, experts, Rohingya refugees, and Myanmar, as well as drawing on scholarly research and official statements, the chapter aims to contribute to a comprehensive understanding of the complexities involved and to provide insights into potential pathways for the resolution of this humanitarian crisis. The multidimensional nature of the Rohingya refugee crisis must be acknowledged in recognising that the resolution of the issue extends beyond repatriation alone. While repatriation is a crucial component, it must be accompanied by broader efforts to address the underlying causes of the crisis, such as systemic discrimination, lack of citizenship rights, and the need for sustainable development in Myanmar's Rakhine State (Ullah & Chattoraj, 2018).

The international community has a significant role to play in supporting the repatriation process and advocating for the rights and well-being of Rohingya refugees. Efforts to secure justice and accountability for the atrocities committed against the Rohingya population are underway, including legal proceedings at the International Court of Justice and the pursuit of accountability mechanisms at both the national and international levels (Alam, 2019; Takemura, 2023). These actions underscore the importance of ensuring that the repatriation process is not only voluntary but also takes into account the need for justice and redress for the victims. Moreover, the success of any repatriation effort hinges on the cooperation and commitment of the Myanmar government. Myanmar's willingness to address the concerns raised by the international community, implement sustainable solutions, and uphold the rights of the Rohingya population is essential (Beyrer & Kamarulzaman, 2017; Haider, 2018). A key consideration involves the establishment of a comprehensive citizenship framework that recognises the rights of the Rohingya community and ensures their equal and non-discriminatory treatment under the law (Alam, 2019; Takemura, 2023). Additionally, efforts to promote reconciliation, intercommunal dialogue, and sustainable development in Rakhine State are paramount to creating an environment conducive to the safe and dignified return of Rohingya refugees (Islam et al., 2022a, 2022b).

By critically analysing the perspectives and experiences of various stakeholders, this discussion seeks to contribute to the ongoing discourse on the repatriation of Rohingya refugees. It aims to provide insights into the complexities, challenges, and potential pathways for addressing this humanitarian crisis in a just and sustainable manner. Through an interdisciplinary approach that incorporates political, legal, and humanitarian perspectives, this discourse endeavours to contribute to the understanding of the Rohingya refugee crisis and the pursuit of effective and lasting solutions. The significance of understanding the perspectives and voices of the Rohingya refugees themselves must also be recognised. Their experiences, aspirations, and concerns must be at the forefront of any discussion on repatriation. Engaging with the Rohingya community, listening to their narratives, and respecting their agency are vital components of formulating inclusive and sustainable solutions (Lewis, 2019). Testimonies and first-hand accounts from Rohingya refugees are used to substantiate a nuanced understanding of their desires, fears, and expectations regarding repatriation.

It requires special emphasis that the regional dynamics and geopolitical considerations surrounding the Rohingya refugee crisis warrant attention. The involvement of neighbouring countries, international organisations, and influential stakeholders in facilitating the repatriation process is essential for its success (Ahsan, 2018). Cooperation among regional actors, including Bangladesh, Myanmar, and the Association of Southeast Asian Nations (ASEAN), can play a pivotal role in creating an enabling environment for the repatriation and addressing the underlying causes of the crisis. The proceeding discussion underscores the urgency and complexity of the Rohingya refugee crisis, emphasising the need for a comprehensive and sustainable approach to repatriation. It recognises the historical context, the magnitude of the crisis, and the voices of various stakeholders involved. By critically analysing the perspectives, challenges, and potential pathways for repatriation, this discussion aims to contribute to the academic discourse, policy formulation, and advocacy efforts towards resolving the Rohingya refugee crisis and ensuring a just and dignified future for the Rohingya population.

2 Background: The Repatriation Team's Visit to Rakhine

In early May 2023, a significant development took place regarding the repatriation of Rohingya refugees when a delegation consisting of 20 Rohingya Muslims and government officials from Bangladesh visited Myanmar's Rakhine State. This visit aimed to encourage voluntary homecoming and marked a major step forward in the long-stalled Rohingya repatriation process (Nath, 2023). The Rohingya delegation travelled across the Naf River, which serves as the transboundary boundary between Bangladesh and Myanmar, to visit a community in Rakhine State (Nath, 2023). The Rohingya refugees, who have been residing in camps in Bangladesh's Cox's Bazar since fleeing the military-led crackdown in Myanmar in 2017, expressed their desire to return home with all their rights and security (Nath, 2023). However, their concerns about violence and the lack of guarantees for their safety and citizenship in Myanmar have hindered previous repatriation efforts (Nath, 2023; Mostafiz, 2023). The May visit by the Rohingya delegation was seen as a confidence-building measure to assess the situation in Rakhine State and explore the feasibility of repatriation (Nath, 2023). It was the first time that a Rohingya refugee team had visited Rakhine to investigate the conditions there (Nath, 2023). Bangladesh has been host to over 1.2 million Rohingya refugees, and the socioeconomic and security situation in the country has been deteriorating due to the large refugee population (Babu, 2020). Repatriation has become the primary pathway for Bangladesh to address this issue, which has remained unresolved for six years (Nath, 2023).

The recent shift in Myanmar's stance and its willingness to collaborate on repatriation efforts can be attributed to several factors. Myanmar's military junta, which seized power in a coup in February 2021, has faced increasing international pressure and criticism for human rights abuses (OHCHR, 2023). The military's control is under stress due to resistance from the deposed National League for Democracy (NLD) and ethnic organisations, as well as pressure from Europe, the United States, and ASEAN. The exclusion of the junta from ASEAN summits, a UN Security Council resolution, and various sanctions have pushed Myanmar to take action on the Rohingya repatriation issue (Nath, 2023). Furthermore, Myanmar's military regime has an interest in demonstrating progress on repatriation before the International Court of Justice (ICJ) hearings on the Rohingya genocide case. The ICJ has issued temporary measures to protect the Rohingya, and Myanmar is expected to provide updates on its actions to the court (Palma, 2022).

While repatriation efforts seem promising, concerns have been raised about Myanmar's sincerity and the lack of a conducive atmosphere for safe returns. The Rohingya lack confidence in Myanmar's government, which has been accused of genocide by the United Nations (OHCHR, 2023). The limited number of refugees to be repatriated and the timing of the initiative raise suspicions that Myanmar's military regime is attempting to relieve international pressure and gain an advantage in the ICJ case (Aljazeera, 2022). The repatriation process, which was planned to begin with the return of 1076 Rohingya in May, might face delays due to the impact of Cyclone Mocha on Rakhine State (Mostafiz, 2023). China facilitated tripartite talks between Bangladesh, Myanmar, and China in April to initiate the repatriation before the monsoon season. However, the visit of Myanmar officials to the Cox's Bazar Rohingya camps has been deferred due to the cyclone's devastation in Rakhine State (Mostafiz, 2023). The Rohingya delegation's visit to Rakhine State earlier in May aimed to assess the resettlement camps and gather first-hand information to determine the conditions for a safe return (Mostafiz, 2023). However, the delegation raised concerns about the detention-like conditions in the camps, the lack of full citizenship rights, and the absence of a conducive environment for a secure and sustainable return. Human Rights Watch (HRW) has also voiced its opposition to the small-scale repatriation initiative, urging Bangladesh to halt the process. HRW argues that the repatriation is being pursued without consulting the Rohingya community and without addressing the significant risks they face in terms of their lives and freedom (Hossain et al., 2022a, 2022b). The organisation emphasises that the reasons for the Rohingya's displacement remain unchanged, and repatriating them to Myanmar under the control of the current military junta would only set the stage for another devastating exodus (Mostafiz, 2023).

The Rohingya refugees who participated in the go-and-see visit expressed dissatisfaction with the situation in Rakhine State. They emphasised that the camp conditions and the denial of full citizenship rights do not create a conducive environment for a safe return. The Rohingya refugees have consistently stated their desire to return home, but only when their security, access to land and livelihoods, freedom of movement, and citizenship rights are guaranteed (Islam et al., 2021, 2022a, 2022b). During the visit, the Rohingya delegation observed the Hla Poe Kaung transit camp and the Kyein Chaung resettlement camp in Maungdaw Township, Rakhine State. These camps were built by Myanmar authorities on land that had previously belonged to the Rohingya, which was burned and bulldozed by Myanmar security forces in 2017 and 2018 (Ruser et al., 2019). The transit camp is surrounded by barbed-wire fencing and security outposts, resembling the confinement experienced by Rohingya in other detention camps across central Rakhine State.

These current developments highlight the complexity and challenges involved in the repatriation process. The concerns raised by the Rohingya refugees, as well as the opposition from human rights organisations like HRW, underscore the need for a comprehensive approach that addresses the underlying issues and ensures the protection and rights of the Rohingya population. The delays caused by the cyclone further underscore the need for thorough assessments of the conditions in Rakhine State and the establishment of a conducive environment for a safe and voluntary return. The pilot repatriation initiative, although facing setbacks, represents a potential starting point for future repatriation efforts. However, it is crucial that the concerns of the Rohingya refugees, as well as international human rights standards, are addressed before any large-scale repatriation takes place. Continued engagement and cooperation among Bangladesh, Myanmar, and the international community are necessary to overcome the challenges, establish trust, and create the conditions required for a just and sustainable solution that upholds the rights and dignity of the Rohingya refugees.

3 Prospects for Rohingya Repatriation: Views of Government of Bangladesh

In the context of the Rohingya refugee crisis, the prospects for repatriation have been subject to extensive analysis and scrutiny. This section delves into the perspectives of the Government of Bangladesh regarding the potential for repatriation. By examining official statements, policy positions, and diplomatic engagements, this analysis aims to provide a nuanced understanding of Bangladesh's views on the matter. Central to the Government of Bangladesh's stance on repatriation is its commitment to ensuring the protection and well-being of Rohingya refugees. Bangladesh recognises the vulnerability of the stateless Rohingya population and the need for their rights to be safeguarded throughout the repatriation process. In this regard, the government insists on guarantees from Myanmar authorities that the principle of non-refoulement will be respected, ensuring that no Rohingya refugee will be forcibly returned to a situation of persecution or danger. Additionally, Bangladesh emphasises the importance of granting Rohingya individuals access to citizenship, eliminating discriminatory practices, and addressing the root causes of their displacement (Siddique, 2019). These considerations reflect Bangladesh's adherence to international human rights standards and its responsibility to protect the rights of Rohingya refugees. The Government of Bangladesh recognises that repatriation efforts must extend beyond the physical return of Rohingya refugees. A comprehensive approach to repatriation is deemed crucial, encompassing not only the safe and voluntary return of individuals but also their successful reintegration into society. Bangladesh emphasises the importance of addressing the underlying causes of the Rohingya crisis, including issues related to citizenship, discrimination, and access to basic services in Myanmar's Rakhine State (Sejan, 2020). To ensure the sustainability of the repatriation process, the government advocates for measures that foster reconciliation, promote intercommunal dialogue, and facilitate socioeconomic development in Rakhine State. By addressing these multifaceted challenges, Bangladesh aims to create an environment conducive to the long-term viability and well-being of Rohingya returnees.

Recognising the complexity of the repatriation process, the Government of Bangladesh places significant emphasis on international cooperation and engagement. The successful repatriation of Rohingya refugees requires the collective efforts of various stakeholders, including neighbouring countries, regional organisations, and international humanitarian agencies. Bangladesh actively seeks the involvement of the international community in addressing the intricate challenges associated with repatriation (Mallick, 2020). This collaboration spans logistical coordination, financial support for rehabilitation and reintegration programmes, and the monitoring of the progress and welfare of returnees. By fostering robust international cooperation, Bangladesh aims to establish an enabling environment that facilitates a safe, voluntary, and dignified repatriation process for the Rohingya population. The perspectives of the Government of Bangladesh on the prospects of Rohingya repatriation reveal its unwavering commitment to protecting the rights and welfare of Rohingya refugees. The government's emphasis on comprehensive repatriation, sustainable reintegration, and international cooperation underscores its dedication to finding a just and durable solution to the Rohingya crisis. Nonetheless, the multifaceted nature of the repatriation process necessitates continued engagement and collaboration between Bangladesh, Myanmar, and the international community to address underlying challenges and ensure the long-term success of repatriation efforts.

4 Prospects for Rohingya Repatriation: Views of Experts

The prospects for Rohingya repatriation have drawn the attention of experts who offer valuable insights into the complexities surrounding the issue. Analysing perspectives of experts who have closely observed the socioeconomic and security implications of the Rohingya crisis can enable a deeper understanding of the challenges and potential solutions concerning repatriation. The Rohingya crisis has not only had a significant impact on Myanmar but has also permeated into the internal situation within Bangladesh, resulting in various dimensions of crisis. In an interview with a security analyst, the complex nature of the crisis and its potential consequences were discussed.[1] He emphasised that Myanmar bears the responsibility for creating this crisis through its oppressive treatment and forcible expulsion of the Rohingya population. The crisis has negatively affected the bilateral relations between Bangladesh and Myanmar and has resulted in a crisis for peace, security, and the sociopolitical fabric of both countries. The humanitarian problems faced by the Rohingya people have also strained the limited resources in Bangladesh, leading to social, environmental, and governance challenges.

From a social perspective, the influx of Rohingya refugees has put a strain on the local host community in Cox's Bazar. The increasing population has resulted in the scarcity of resources and strained intercommunal relations. At the national level, Bangladesh's economy, environment, governance, and security have been significantly affected. Efforts have been made to improve the quality of life for the Rohingyas, such as the Bhasan Char project, which aims to provide better living conditions. However, the rise in crime rates, including human trafficking facilitated by organised Rohingya groups, has raised concerns about social stability in the region. The environmental dimension of the crisis is closely tied to resource scarcity, which

[1] Expert interview conducted in Dhaka in November 2022.

has not only caused an environmental conflict but has also resulted in a comprehensive crisis encompassing humanitarian, security, and economic risks. The presence of a large Rohingya population in Cox's Bazar, near the strategically important Chittagong Hill Tracts region, has created a conflict with multiple dimensions that require careful examination.

Furthermore, the prolonged stay of Rohingyas and their proximity to the Chittagong Hill Tracts region raise concerns about destabilisation and potential conflicts. The mingling of Rohingya, Bengali, and indigenous communities in certain areas, such as Bandarban district, has already complicated the local situation. Such developments pose vulnerabilities that could be exploited by third parties, jeopardising Bangladesh's development and national plans.

In assessing the gravity of the Rohingya predicament in Arakan, it becomes evident that their national identity holds significant bearing. The interviewee stressed that,

> If they were prepared to change or abandon their national identity, then their current predicament in Arakan would not have been so grave. (Expert interview conducted in Dhaka in December 2022)

In terms of bilateral relations between Bangladesh and Myanmar, there is a possibility of progress in other areas despite the contentious issues surrounding the Rohingya crisis. Economic relationships have often shown resilience even in the face of territorial disputes, as observed in the case of India and China. However, the sensitive nature of the Rohingya issue has led to mutual distrust and a deterioration of military relations between the two countries. While efforts have been made to improve military relations, the lack of progress on the repatriation of Rohingya refugees hampers the overall relationship. Resolution of the repatriation issue could positively influence economic and other relationships between the two countries. The outlook for repatriation depends on the foresight and willingness of Myanmar's government (Alam, 2019). Although there have been instances of positive decisions by military governments in practical matters, Myanmar's current government, including Aung San Suu Kyi, has shown a narrow and oppressive standpoint towards the Rohingya issue. The current geopolitical situation, particularly the pressure exerted by the Ukraine crisis on countries like China and Myanmar, may create an opportunity for resolving the crisis and benefiting all parties involved. The expert emphasises that the conflict within the Rohingya community has its roots in Myanmar. The history of oppression and suppression faced by the Rohingya people since the military came into power in 1962 has shaped their struggle for survival. Various organisations such as the Rohingya Solidarity Organisation (RSO) and the Arakan Rohingya Salvation Army (ARSA) have attempted to address the issue, but with limited success (Alam, 2019; Lee, 2021). The lack of a clear and sustainable defence against oppression has contributed to the ongoing conflict within the Rohingya community.

To address the refugee problem, including the Rohingya crisis, three standard models are typically employed globally: social integration, voluntary repatriation, and systematic resettlement to third countries (Hansen, 2018). While Bangladesh has implemented all three models, the expert emphasises that social integration has already occurred to some extent, as many Rohingyas have integrated into the local community through marriage and other means. Despite the efforts made, achieving social cohesion between the Rohingya refugees and the host community in Bangladesh poses significant challenges. Firstly, the burden on the host community has increased, both economically and socially. The local labour market has been affected, as Rohingyas are willing to work for lower wages, disrupting the local labour dynamics (Interviewee #1). Additionally, the fishing industry, among others, has witnessed a shift in ownership, with a significant number of fishing boats now owned by Rohingyas.[2]

The presence of Rohingyas in the host community has also resulted in environmental and human costs. The overpopulation of the camps has led to the degradation of grazing lands and the destruction of natural habitats, affecting the lives of both humans and animals (Babu, 2020). The lack of policies to address these issues further exacerbates the social imbalance faced by the host community. The Rohingya crisis has the potential to create regional and interstate concerns. The expert highlights the possibility of an interstate conflict, with militant activities targeting vulnerable groups like the Rohingyas for recruitment (Islam et al., 2022a, 2022b). The South Asian region, including Bangladesh and India, faces significant challenges due to the presence of militant groups and arms trafficking in the border areas (Interviewee #2). India, in particular, is concerned about the regional imbalance that could arise from the Rohingya crisis, especially in relation to the Tripura region. The expert also discussed the perspectives of Southeast Asian countries, such as Indonesia and Malaysia, which have sizable Rohingya populations. The Association of Southeast Asian Nations (ASEAN) has a non-interference policy regarding internal matters of member states. Consequently, the Rohingya crisis has been considered Myanmar's internal problem by ASEAN.

5 Prospects for Rohingya Repatriation: Views of Rohingya Refugees

The repatriation of Rohingya refugees stands as a critical and complex issue, deeply intertwined with the aspirations, concerns, and hopes of the Rohingya population itself. The discussion moves on to elaborating upon the perspectives of the Rohingya refugees in Bangladesh regarding their repatriation and its future. The interviews conducted with Rohingya refugees residing in Bangladesh unveiled a consistent and unequivocal desire among them to return to their homeland in Myanmar. One Rohingya refugee aptly captured the sentiments of many by stating,

> We long to go back to our ancestral land, to reclaim our homes and rebuild our lives there. (FGD conducted in Kutupalong Camp in Cox's Bazar in February 2022)

[2] Expert interview conducted in Dhaka in December 2022.

This quote underscores the deep-rooted longing and attachment that Rohingya refugees have for their homeland and their eagerness to restore their lives in Myanmar. However, their willingness to repatriate hinges on several crucial conditions. The interviews revealed that Rohingya refugees demand a safe and secure environment upon their return, free from persecution, discrimination, and violence (Ullah & Chattoraj, 2023). They emphasise the imperative need for the protection of their human rights, including the right to citizenship, freedom of movement, access to education, healthcare, and livelihood opportunities. Ensuring the preservation of their dignity and guaranteeing non-recurrence of the atrocities that led to their displacement are fundamental to their willingness to return. The foremost concern among Rohingya refugees contemplating repatriation is the assurance of safety and security upon their return. The experiences of violence, persecution, and displacement have deeply scarred their lives and engendered a profound sense of fear and mistrust. Consequently, any repatriation plan must address these anxieties by establishing robust security measures, fostering an environment free from intimidation, and ensuring the protection of their physical and psychological well-being.

The perspectives of Rohingya refugees living in Bangladesh emphasise their strong desire to return to Myanmar, their ancestral homeland. However, their willingness to repatriate hinges on the assurance of safety, security, and protection of human rights, preservation of dignity, and the prevention of future atrocities. The repatriation process must be underpinned by comprehensive legal and policy reforms (Hossain et al., 2022a, 2022b), robust security measures, and international support to ensure the successful return and reintegration of the Rohingya population. By addressing these concerns and upholding the principles of justice, reconciliation, and non-recurrence, a just and sustainable resolution to the Rohingya crisis can be achieved.

6 Prospects for Rohingya Repatriation: Views of Myanmar's Government

The repatriation of Rohingya refugees to Myanmar has remained a pressing concern in the international community. This section examines the perspectives of Myanmar's government regarding the prospects for Rohingya repatriation, drawing insights from expert interviews. By exploring the viewpoints of government officials, this section aims to shed light on the key factors and considerations influencing Myanmar's stance on the repatriation process.

To understand the government's perspective on Rohingya repatriation, it is crucial to examine the historical context of the Rohingya crisis in Myanmar. The Rohingya, an ethnic minority group primarily residing in Rakhine State, have long faced systemic discrimination and marginalisation within the country. The outbreak of violence in 2017 resulted in a mass exodus of Rohingya refugees to neighbouring Bangladesh, leading to an international outcry. The complex historical background and the ongoing conflict have significantly shaped the government's approach to repatriation. Through confidential interviews with experts closely connected to Myanmar's government, valuable insights into the country's perspective on Rohingya repatriation were obtained. One interviewee, who has deep knowledge of the government's policy formulation, shared an important perspective:

> ...even a highly educated civilian leader such as Aung Sun Suki has been shown to have a very narrow and oppressive standpoint toward the Rohingya issue...Therefore, it is a concern whether we will be seeing an enlightened perspective from Myanmar's military government, even though military governments have from time to time made some positive decisions when considering their practical implications.

This statement highlights the government's viewpoint and provides a foundation for understanding their position. One major aspect that emerged from the interviews was the government's emphasis on security concerns as a significant factor influencing their approach to repatriation. Myanmar's government has repeatedly expressed apprehensions about potential security threats posed by Rohingya returnees. The government fears that some individuals may have links to armed insurgent groups, leading to the possible re-emergence of violence and destabilisation in the region. These concerns, while subject to debate, have played a pivotal role in shaping the government's cautious stance on repatriation.

Another key aspect highlighted during the interviews was the issue of citizenship and documentation. The government maintains that the repatriation process must adhere to Myanmar's existing legal framework, which requires individuals to possess valid citizenship and proper documentation. This requirement poses challenges for many Rohingya refugees, as they have historically been denied citizenship and face difficulties in obtaining necessary documents. The government's insistence on these legal requirements has been viewed as a significant hurdle to achieving meaningful progress in repatriation efforts.

Experts also noted that socioeconomic factors play a role in the government's perspective on repatriation. The interviewees highlighted the strain that hosting a large number of refugees' places on local resources and infrastructure. Myanmar's government, already grappling with development challenges, raises concerns about the long-term socioeconomic implications of absorbing a substantial population of Rohingya returnees. These concerns, while indicating the government's commitment to stability and sustainable development, have been viewed as contributing to a cautious and gradual approach to repatriation.

7 The Future of Rohingya Repatriation: A Critical Analysis

The future of Rohingya repatriation remains a topic of immense significance and complexity. One expert emphasised the role of political will and international pressure in determining the future of Rohingya repatriation. The expert stated,

> The successful repatriation of Rohingya refugees hinges upon the sincere commitment and political will of the Myanmar government, as well as the sustained pressure exerted by the international community.

This statement highlights the importance of political commitment from the Myanmar government and the influence exerted by international stakeholders, such as neighbouring countries, regional organisations, and the United Nations. The interplay between political will and international pressure is a crucial factor that will shape the success or failure of future repatriation efforts.

The international community has a vital role in exerting diplomatic pressure on the Myanmar government to ensure compliance with international human rights standards and to create an enabling environment for repatriation. Sanctions, targeted measures, and diplomatic negotiations can be employed to encourage the Myanmar government to take concrete steps towards addressing the underlying causes of the Rohingya crisis and facilitating the safe and voluntary return of displaced individuals. Furthermore, regional organisations like ASEAN and the Organisation of Islamic Cooperation (OIC) can play a significant role in fostering dialogue, mediation, and cooperation among relevant stakeholders.

Addressing the root causes of the Rohingya crisis is fundamental to ensuring the sustainable repatriation of Rohingya refugees. Experts stress the necessity of addressing issues related to citizenship rights, discriminatory policies, and social integration within Myanmar. The expert interviewees highlighted that the discriminatory policies against the Rohingya, including the denial of citizenship and restricted access to education, healthcare, and livelihood opportunities, have fuelled the ongoing displacement crisis.

To lay the groundwork for repatriation, comprehensive political, legal, and social reforms are required to promote inclusivity, non-discrimination, and the protection of minority rights in Myanmar. This entails amending or repealing discriminatory laws, such as the 1982 Citizenship Law, which has rendered the Rohingya stateless. The provision of legal recognition and pathways to citizenship for the Rohingya population is crucial for their successful reintegration into Myanmar society. Additionally, efforts should be made to ensure their access to essential services, including education, healthcare, and employment opportunities, to foster their long-term well-being and self-sufficiency. International actors, including governments, NGOs, and human rights institutions, can support these reforms by providing technical assistance, capacity building, and funding for initiatives aimed at promoting equality, human rights, and inclusive governance. Collaboration with civil society organisations and Rohingya representatives is vital to ensure that the perspectives and needs of the affected population are adequately represented in the repatriation process. Ensuring the safety and security of Rohingya returnees is paramount for successful repatriation. Experts highlighted the need for robust security measures and mechanisms to protect the returnees from potential violence, discrimination, and human rights abuses. The expert interviews revealed concerns regarding the prevailing climate of fear, mistrust, and impunity in Myanmar, which could hinder the willingness of Rohingya individuals to return voluntarily.

To instil confidence among the Rohingya community, it is crucial to establish an independent monitoring mechanism, preferably with international involvement, to oversee the repatriation process and ensure the safety and well-being of the returnees. This mechanism should have the mandate to investigate and address any allegations of human rights violations or discriminatory practices, fostering an environment conducive to safe and dignified returns. Additionally, efforts should be made to rebuild trust and foster reconciliation between the Rohingya and other communities in Myanmar, promoting social cohesion and harmony. International actors, including peacekeeping missions, human rights organisations, and humanitarian agencies, can provide technical expertise and financial support to strengthen the capacity of the Myanmar government to ensure the security and protection of the returnees. Cooperation between the Myanmar security forces and international actors can help build trust and facilitate a coordinated approach to safeguarding the rights and well-being of the Rohingya community.

Collaboration among stakeholders and sustained international support are vital elements in shaping the future of Rohingya repatriation. Experts emphasised the need for regional and international cooperation to facilitate repatriation efforts. This includes active engagement with Bangladesh, the host country for a significant number of Rohingya refugees, as well as involvement from regional organisations, international humanitarian agencies, and donor countries. The complex nature of the crisis necessitates a comprehensive and coordinated response from multiple actors.

Bangladesh, as a key stakeholder, plays a crucial role in facilitating the repatriation process. Bilateral negotiations between Myanmar and Bangladesh should continue to address issues related to the verification of returnees, the restoration of property rights, and the provision of humanitarian support during the repatriation and reintegration phases. International actors, including the UNHCR, the IOM, and other relevant agencies, should provide technical assistance and financial resources to support the implementation of repatriation initiatives. Moreover, donor countries and international financial institutions should allocate adequate funding to address the immediate humanitarian needs of the returnees and support long-term development programmes in Rakhine State. Such investments should prioritise the improvement of infrastructure, education, healthcare, and livelihood opportunities for both the returnees and the host communities, fostering social cohesion and sustainable reintegration.

A critical evaluation of existing approaches to Rohingya repatriation is essential for informing future strategies. By examining the strengths and limitations of previous initiatives, policymakers and stakeholders can identify lessons learned and implement more effective and sustainable repatriation measures. Repatriation efforts undertaken in the past have faced significant challenges, including incomplete implementation, insufficient safeguards, and a lack of genuine commitment from the Myanmar government. The international community should critically evaluate past repatriation attempts and draw lessons from them. It is crucial to ensure that any future initiatives are based on the principles of voluntariness, safety, dignity, and sustainability. Monitoring and evaluation mechanisms should be established to assess the progress and impact of repatriation efforts, allowing for the identification of shortcomings and the adaptation of strategies accordingly. Regular reporting and transparency in the repatriation process can foster accountability and enhance the credibility of the overall endeavour.

8 Conclusion

The repatriation of Rohingya refugees stands as a formidable challenge, intricately entangled with the complex web of political, social, and historical dynamics between Myanmar and Bangladesh. This chapter has critically examined the prospects and challenges of repatriation in the context of the bilateral relations between the two countries, shedding light on the multifaceted dimensions that shape the repatriation process. By drawing upon expert interviews, existing literature, and comprehensive analysis, this chapter has sought to provide a nuanced understanding of the complexities involved and offer insights for policymakers, stakeholders, and scholars invested in finding a just and sustainable resolution to the Rohingya crisis.

Throughout this chapter, expert insights have played a crucial role in informing the analysis. One expert highlighted the delicate nature of the repatriation process, stating, "The repatriation of Rohingya refugees requires a delicate balancing act between addressing the concerns of the Rohingya population and navigating the political landscape between Myanmar and Bangladesh." This statement underscores the need for a nuanced and sensitive approach that takes into account the interests and rights of both the Rohingya refugees and the governments involved.

Experts emphasised the pivotal role of political will, international pressure, and collaboration in shaping the prospects for successful repatriation. The Myanmar government's commitment to creating an enabling environment, ensuring the safety and security of the returnees, addressing root causes of the crisis, and fostering social integration are critical components for a sustainable repatriation process. International stakeholders, including neighbouring countries, regional organisations, and the international community at large, can exert significant influence through diplomatic pressure, mediation, and financial support. Collaboration between Myanmar and Bangladesh, particularly in the areas of verification, restoration of property rights, and provision of humanitarian assistance, is essential for establishing a viable framework for repatriation. The resolution of the Rohingya crisis necessitates a comprehensive approach that addresses the root causes, particularly issues related to citizenship rights, discriminatory policies, and social integration. The discriminatory policies against the Rohingya, exemplified by the denial of citizenship and limited access to education, healthcare, and livelihood opportunities, have perpetuated the displacement crisis. To ensure the sustainable return and reintegration of Rohingya individuals, comprehensive political, legal, and social reforms are indispensable. Efforts should be directed towards amending or repealing discriminatory laws, such as the 1982 Citizenship Law, which has rendered the Rohingya stateless. The provision of legal recognition and pathways to citizenship for the Rohingya population is fundamental for their successful reintegration into Myanmar society. Concurrently, investments in infrastructure, education, healthcare, and livelihood opportunities must be made to facilitate their long-term well-being and self-sufficiency. International actors, including governments, NGOs, and human rights institutions, can support these efforts through technical assistance, capacity building, and financial support, ensuring the inclusion of the perspectives and needs of the Rohingya population.

The safety and security of Rohingya returnees must be guaranteed to engender confidence and facilitate successful repatriation. Experts underscored the necessity of robust security measures and mechanisms to protect returnees from potential violence, discrimination, and human rights abuses. Given the prevailing climate of fear, mistrust, and impunity in Myanmar, an independent monitoring mechanism, preferably with international involvement, should be established to oversee the repatriation process and ensure the safety and well-being of the returnees. The collaboration between the Myanmar security forces and international actors can help build trust and facilitate a coordinated approach to safeguarding the rights and well-being of the Rohingya community. Moreover, efforts to foster reconciliation and social cohesion between the Rohingya and other communities in Myanmar are crucial for sustainable repatriation. It is imperative to address historical grievances, promote intercommunal dialogue, and implement reconciliation programmes that pave the way for peaceful coexistence and a shared future. Collaboration among stakeholders and sustained international support are essential for the success of repatriation efforts. The involvement of regional organisations, neighbouring countries, and the international community at large can provide the necessary political leverage, technical expertise, and financial resources to facilitate repatriation initiatives. Bangladesh, as a key stakeholder, plays a significant role in ensuring the smooth implementation of repatriation processes, including the verification of returnees and the provision of humanitarian support. International actors such as the UNHCR, the IOM, and other relevant agencies should actively engage in supporting repatriation efforts through technical assistance, financial resources, and capacity building. Donor countries and international financial institutions should allocate adequate funding to address the immediate humanitarian needs of the returnees and support long-term development programmes in Rakhine State, focussing on infrastructure, education, healthcare, and livelihood opportunities for both the returnees and the host communities.

In conclusion, the repatriation of Rohingya refugees is an immensely complex and multifaceted process that requires a comprehensive and multidimensional approach. By addressing root causes, ensuring safety and security, and fostering collaboration and international support, the prospects for successful repatriation can be enhanced. The involvement and commitment of the Myanmar government, the active engagement of the international community, and the rights-based approach that upholds the dignity and well-being of the Rohingya population are indispensable for achieving a just and sustainable resolution to the crisis.

References

Ahsan, S. B. (2018). The Rohingya crisis: Why the world must act decisively. *Asian Affairs, 49*(4), 571–581. https://doi.org/10.1080/03068374.2018.1528791

Alam, J. (2019). The current Rohingya crisis in Myanmar in historical perspective. *Journal of Muslim Minority Affairs, 39*(1), 1–25. https://doi.org/10.1080/13602004.2019.1575560

Al Jazeera. (2022, July 22). ICJ to rule on Myanmar objections to Rohingya genocide case. *Al Jazeera*. https://www.aljazeera.com/news/2022/7/22/icj-to-rule-on-myanmar-objections-to-rohingya-genocide-case

Ashikuzzaman, Gazi, A. K., & Abir, T. M. (2022). The key scenarios of Rohingya refugees in Bangladesh: A narrative study. In *Worldwide inter-disciplinary research* (pp. 252–269). Notion Press India.

Babu, K. E. K. (2020). The impacts and challenges to host country Bangladesh due to sheltering the Rohingya refugees. *Cogent Social Sciences, 6*(1), 1770943. https://doi.org/10.1080/23311886.2020.1770943

Beyrer, C., & Kamarulzaman, A. (2017). Ethnic cleansing in Myanmar: The Rohingya crisis and human rights. *The Lancet, 390*(10102), 1570–1573. https://doi.org/10.1016/s0140-6736(17)32519-9

Gorlick, B. (2020). The Rohingya refugee crisis: Rethinking solutions and accountability. *Refugee Studies Centre, Working Paper Series No. 131*, 1–28. https://doi.org/10.2139/ssrn.3506638

Haider, S. A. (2018). *Capitalizing on the Rohingya crisis by transnational militants—Assessing the security threat*. Retrieved July 2, 2022, from https://www.academia.edu/48846180/Capitalizing_on_the_Rohingya_Crisis_by_Transnational_Militants_Assessing_the_Security_Threat

Hansen, R. (2018). The comprehensive refugee response framework: A commentary. *Journal of Refugee Studies, 31*(2), 131–151. https://doi.org/10.1093/jrs/fey020

Hossain, M. A., Huda, M. N., Ullah, A. K. M. A., & Renzaho, A. (2022a). Risk factors, challenges, and psychological well-being of the Rohingya refugees in Bangladesh: Policy implications. *International Journal of Health Planning and Management, 37*(4), 1912–1917.

Hossain, M. A., Ullah, A. K. M. A., & Mohiuddin, M. (2022b). Rohingya Refugee in the pandemic: Crisis and policy responses. *Global Policy, 14*(1), 183–191. https://doi.org/10.1111/1758-5899.13156

Idris, I. (2017). *Rohingya refugee crisis: Impact on Bangladeshi politics*. Retrieved from NYU Faculty Digital Archive. https://archive.nyu.edu/handle/2451/43693

Inter Sector Coordination Group. (2019). *Gender reflections: Two years of the Rohingya refugee response. Achievements, challenges and recommendations*. Retrieved June 30, 2022, from https://www.humanitarianresponse.info/en/operations/bangladesh/gender-hub

Islam, M. R., Islam, M. T., Alam, M. S., Hussain, M., & Haque, M. M. (2021). Is Bhasan Char Island, Noakhali district in Bangladesh a sustainable place for the relocated Rohingya displaced people? An empirical study. *SN Social Sciences, 1*, 1–24. https://doi.org/10.1007/s43545-021-00281-9

Islam, M. R., Islam, M. T., Alam, M. S., Hussain, M., & Haque, M. M. (2022a). An assessment of the sustainability of living for Rohingya displaced people in Cox's Bazar camps in Bangladesh. *Journal of Human Rights and Social Work, 7*, 331–345. https://doi.org/10.1007/s41134-022-00212-5

Islam, R., Haque, M. M., & Wara, U. (2022b). Intra-group conflict among Rohingya displaced people in Bangladesh. In K. Ahmed & H. Mohiuddin (Eds.), *The Rohingya crisis and the two-faced god of Janus: What lies ahead* (pp. 31–52). Lexington Books.

Kajla, M., & Chowdhory, N. (2020). The unmaking of citizenship of Rohingyas in Myanmar. In N. Chowdhory & B. Mohanty (Eds.), *Citizenship, nationalism and refugeehood of Rohingyas in Southern Asia* (pp. 51–70). Springer.

Khin, T. (2017). Rohingya: A preventable genocide allowed to happen. *Insight Turkey, 19*(4), 43–54. https://www.jstor.org/stable/26300556

Lee, R. (2021). Myanmar's Arakan Rohingya salvation army (ARSA): An analysis of a new Muslim militant group and its strategic communications. *Perspectives on Terrorism, 15*(6), 61–75. https://www.jstor.org/stable/27090916

Lewis, D. (2019). Humanitarianism, civil society and the Rohingya refugee crisis in Bangladesh. *Third World Quarterly, 40*(10), 1884–1902. https://doi.org/10.1080/01436597.2019.1652897

Mallick, A. H. (2020). Rohingya refugee repatriation from Bangladesh: A far cry from reality. *Journal of Asian Security and International Affairs, 7*(2), 202–226. https://doi.org/10.1177/2347797020938983

Mostafiz, M. (2023, May 19). *Pilot scheme of Rohingya repatriation faces hurdle*. Retrieved June 02, 2023, from The Financial Express: https://thefinancialexpress.com.bd/national/pilot-scheme-of-rohingya-repatriation-faces-hurdle

Nath, S. S. (2023, May 18). Is Rohingya repatriation finally moving forward? *The Diplomat*. https://thediplomat.com/2023/05/is-rohingya-repatriation-finally-moving-forward/.

OHCHR. (2023, September 19). *A/HRC/54/59: Situation of human rights in Myanmar - Report of the United Nations High Commissioner for Human Rights (Advance unedited version).* https://www.ohchr.org/en/documents/country-reports/ahrc5459-situation-human-rights-myanmar-report-united-nations-high

Palma, P. (2022, July 24). ICJ ruling on genocide case: Time to mount pressure on Myanmar. *The Daily Star*. https://www.thedailystar.net/rohingya-influx/news/icj-ruling-genocide-case-time-mount-pressure-myanmar-3077621

Ruser, N., Thomas, E., & Walker, M. (2019). *Mapping conditions in Rakhine State*. International Cyber Policy Centre. http://www.jstor.com/stable/resrep23035

Sejan, S. (2020). Analyzing the legal issues in the Rohingya crisis: A Bangladesh perspective. *International Journal on World Peace, 37*(1), 23–42.

Siddique, F. B. (2019). Non-refoulement & other durable solutions in refugee law: Rohingyas in perspective. *SCLS Law Review, 2*(1), 2523–9228. https://ssrn.com/abstract=3413948

Takemura, H. (2023). The relationship between the Rohingya case before the International Court of Justice and the Bangladesh-Myanmar situation before the International Criminal Court. In H. Takemura (Eds.), *The Rohingya crisis and the International Criminal Court* (pp. 63–111). Springer. https://doi.org/10.1007/978-981-99-2734-0_4

Ullah, A. K. M. A. (2016). Rohingya crisis in Myanmar: Seeking justice for the 'stateless.' *Journal of Contemporary Criminal Justice, 32*(3), 285–301.

Ullah, A. K. M. A. (2011). Rohingya refugee to Bangladesh: Historical exclusions and contemporary marginalization. *Journal of Immigrant and Refugee Studies, 9*(2), 139–168.

Ullah, A. K. M. A., & Chattoraj, D. (2018). Roots of discrimination against Rohingya minorities: Society, ethnicity and international relations. *Intellectual Discourse, 26*(2), 541–565.

Ullah, A. K. M. A., & Chattoraj, D. (2023). *The untold stories of The Rohingyas: Ethnicity, diversity, and media*. Bristol University Press.

Chapter 16
Updates on Rohingya Repatriation to Myanmar: The Tale of a Never-Ending Process

Md. Rafiqul Islam and Etu Ahmed

Abstract The Rohingyas of Myanmar have suffered from persecution and discrimination virtually from the moment Myanmar gained independence in 1948. Over several distinct waves of migration, displaced Rohingyas fled into neighboring countries, most significantly Bangladesh. Though there have been numerous attempts to repatriate these Rohingya refugees, who now number above one million, to date very little success has been achieved. We provide an overview of the four largest and most distinct waves of Rohingya migration to Bangladesh, before moving to a discussion and analysis of the various repatriation initiatives attempted. These initiatives broadly fall under two categories: first, attempts under the Suu Kyi Government; and second, attempts under the current military junta, which are continuing today. Based on the recent repatriation initiative taken by China, we conclude with cautious optimism and exhortations for responsible conduct on the part of Myanmar, Bangladesh, and the global community in continuing to negotiate the complex issue of Rohingya repatriation.

1 Introduction

The Rohingyas, a Muslim minority ethnic group previously living in the Rakhine State of Myanmar, were denied their citizenship under Myanmar's 1982 Citizenship Act and are now referred to as the largest group of stateless people in the world; they have suffered years of persecution in Myanmar. The Rohingya Muslims, being the victims of extensive physical torture as well as killings by the Myanmar military junta over several years, fled to many of the neighboring countries of Myanmar, including Bangladesh. After the mass migrations of the Rohingya population into Bangladesh in 1977–1978, 1991–1992, 1996, 2012, and 2016, the largest influx of Rohingyas into Bangladesh occurred in the year of 2017 after "Operation Scorched Earth" by the Myanmar military junta. Around 700,000 Rohingyas were expelled from Rakhine

Md. R. Islam (✉) · E. Ahmed
Bangladesh University for Professionals (BUP), Dhaka, Bangladesh
e-mail: rislampacs@du.ac.bd

K. Ahmed and Md. R. Islam (eds.), *Understanding the Rohingya Displacement*,
International Perspectives on Migration, https://doi.org/10.1007/978-981-97-1424-7_16

State and took refuge in Bangladesh. Since then, Myanmar has faced pressure from the international community to resolve the Rohingya crisis, and within three months of the mass Rohingya influx to Bangladesh, in November 2017, Myanmar signed an agreement with Bangladesh to repatriate the Rohingyas who had fled the country. This very first initiative after the largest Rohingya exodus failed due to the mistrust and fear of the Rohingya people toward Myanmar due to their horrific prior experiences. In the following years, 2018 and 2019, there were two more initiatives between the two governments under Suu Kyi's regime regarding Rohingya repatriation; however, these initiatives also did not see any success due to the opaqueness in their underlying policies. After the military coup in 2021 led to the withdrawal of Myanmar's first democratic leader, Suu Kyi, the repatriation talks remained almost halted until the recent sudden initiative taken by the Myanmar military junta to repatriate the Rohingya group.

This chapter gives an overview of the Rohingya influx into Bangladesh, highlighting the four major waves of Rohingya migration. This is followed by two consecutive and distinct sections of discussions regarding the repatriation initiatives undertaken during Suu Kyi's regime and the initiatives undertaken during the recent military regime. Then comes a brief discussion about the loopholes in the recent Pilot Project for Rohingya Repatriation, followed by our conclusion.

2 Overview of the Rohingya Influx into Bangladesh

The Rohingya crisis in the Rakhine State of Myanmar has a long history, as its roots can be found shortly after Myanmar's independence in 1948. The "Constitution of the Union of Burma" and the "Union Citizenship Act" set Rohingya citizenship rules after Burma's independence from the British in 1948 (Ullah & Chattoraj, 2018). A harmonious understanding of these two works reinforced the constitution's objective of simultaneous Buddhist and Muslim citizenship. U Nu, Burma's longest-serving civilian prime minister, recognized Rohingya, Kachin, Kayah, Karen, Mon, Rakhine, and Shan as ethnic groups. Independent Burma's first president, Sao Shwe Thaik, and second prime minister, U Ba Swe, advocated for Rohingya nationalism (Abdul, 2020). However, following the coup d'état in 1962, the citizenship rights of the Rohingya population were indefinitely suspended, and their access to citizenship papers was systematically denied, resulting in their statelessness (Alam, 2019). Regrettably, successive administrations in Myanmar have failed to address the issue of Rohingya citizenship since the malicious seizure of power by General Ne Win in 1962, which marked the overthrow of the civilian government (Alam, 2019; Rahman, 2021). The region of Arakan, also known as Rakhine State, has historically been the homeland of the Rohingya community for generations (Alam, 1999). However, due to recurring cycles of violence, persecution, and severe limitations on their freedom of movement, they have been compelled to flee their ancestral homes and seek sanctuary in Cox's Bazar, Bangladesh. Over the years, four waves of

Rohingya refugees have sought refuge in Bangladesh, occurring during the periods of 1977–1978, 1991–1992, 2012–2016, and 2017–2018.

2.1 The First Wave of Rohingya Migration to Bangladesh, 1977 to 1978

In 1978, the military junta in Myanmar initiated operation "Naga Min," or "King Dragon," against the Rohingya Muslims living in the Rakhine State of Myanmar. According to reports, over 10,000 Rohingya were killed during this operation, and approximately 250,000 refugees fled to Bangladesh following a wave of torture, rape, and forced eviction by the Myanmar military junta; approximately 40,000 Rohingya women, children, and elderly people died during their journey to Bangladesh (Mathieson, 2009; Ahsan Ullah, 2016; Uddin, 2022). In the host country of Bangladesh, the refugees were accommodated in 13 refugee camps in Cox's Bazar and Bandarban, in addition to a few remote areas which were all established with assistance from the UN. Human Rights Watch (HRW) said that these evictions occurred during national census efforts to register citizens and exclude immigrants or foreigners from influencing Myanmar's national policies. The International Committee of the Red Cross (ICRC) and the government of Bangladesh provided emergency assistance to the Rohingya people coming into Bangladesh, but were soon swamped by the level of need. However, the Burmese regime took back these refugees under the "Operation Golden Eagle" program in 1979, following an agreement with the Bangladeshi government signed under the pressure from the UNHCR and some Muslim countries (Habib, 2022). The first wave of Rohingya refugees happened in the 1980s, and it was solved through an agreement between two countries, and displaced people returned to their place of origin afterward.

2.2 The Second Wave of Rohingya Migration to Bangladesh, 1991 to 1992

In 1991, another operation by the Myanmar military junta was perpetrated upon the Rohingyas living in the Rakhine State of Myanmar with the goal of assigning them the status of "illegal immigrants" (Zawacki, 2013). This operation was named "Operation Pyi Thaya," or "Operation Clean and Beautiful Nation," and it resulted in further violence and an influx of almost 200,000 Rohingya into Bangladesh (Ahmed, 2023;). During the operation, again, the Myanmar military junta was accused of rape, forced labor, and religious persecution. Following that, in the two districts of Bangladesh, the country's government established temporary camps for the Rohingyas fleeing from Myanmar.

Even though the governments of Bangladesh and Myanmar reached a bilateral agreement on April 28, 1992, the repatriation of the refugees proceeded only at a snail's pace (Abrar, 1995; Gorlick, 2019). However, in the verification procedure handled by the UNHCR, which established a sub-office to handle the work, refugee registration cards issued by the Bangladeshi government were taken into consideration as documentation. Around 200,000 Rohingya refugees were able to return as a result of this procedure, yet approximately 30,000 Rohingya people were forced to remain in Bangladesh because they lacked proper documents. In the late 1990s, specifically in 1996 and 1997, there were some additional Rohingya influxes, and the repatriation process of these Rohingyas nearly ceased from 2005 onward (Habib, 2022). In this phase, many of the Rohingyas remained in Bangladesh as stateless, and these people are still living in the camps in Bangladesh.

2.3 *The Third Wave of Rohingya Migration to Bangladesh, 2012 and 2016*

This wave of the mass exodus took place as a consequence of widespread riots and clashes between the Buddhists and Rohingya Muslims in June 2012 that broke out in the Rakhine State of Myanmar, sparked by the rape and murder on May 28, 2012, of a Buddhist Arakanese woman (Van Klinken et al., 2017; Ware, 2015). The violence forced thousands of refugees to sneak into Bangladesh. Following the sectarian violence, government authorities destroyed mosques, conducted violent mass arrests, and blocked aid to displaced Muslims, according to an HRW report published in 2013, which accused the Myanmar government of engaging in a "campaign of ethnic cleansing." At least 125,000 Rohingya and other Muslims, and a smaller number of Arakanese, were displaced to internally displaced persons camps (Burma: End 'Ethnic Cleansing' of Rohingya Muslims, 2013).

Three large-scale coordinated attacks were operated in Myanmar along the Bangladesh border in October 2016 (Alam, 2019) and the military actions that followed led to yet another exodus of Rohingya people into Bangladesh. The majority of the immigrants started residing in the temporary settlement in Cox's Bazar. Over the next several months, more than 74,000 Rohingya refugees fled to Bangladesh, as the UNHCR reported. The majority of refugees interviewed by UNHCR asserted that their dwellings in Myanmar had been looted, scorched, or destroyed (Habib, 2022). In this stage, the Myanmar army systematically launched an attack on the Rohingya Muslims. The ultra-Buddhist people coordinated with the military and persecuted the innocent people. Many of them fled to Bangladesh and took shelter in adjacent areas in Bangladesh. However, no initiative has been undertaken from the Myanmar side to receive these displaced people despite Bangladesh raising the issue of repatriation of the Rohingya people to their land in Arakan.

2.4 The Fourth and Largest Wave of Rohingya Migration to Bangladesh, After 2017s August Incident

When violence erupted in Rakhine State on August 25, 2017, Bangladesh witnessed its largest and most rapid influx of Rohingya refugees. Between August 25 and August 31, according to the UNHCR, more than 940,000 refugees escaped to Bangladesh, the majority of whom started to reside in 34 overloaded settlements—the largest of which is the Kutupalong–Balukhali Expansion Site, which is home to over 635,000 Rohingya refugees (Alam, 2019; Uddin, 2023). Bangladesh is presently host to more than 1.2 million Myanmar nationals who have been forcibly displaced. These Rohingya people had to flee as the Myanmar military destroyed entire villages in Rakhine, murdered many Rohingyas, separated a lot of Rohingya families, and abused and raped Rohingya women and girls in gangs (Islam et al., 2022). It has been almost six years since that massive 2017 Rohingya inflow into Bangladesh, yet not a single Rohingya refugee has managed to be repatriated to their homes in Myanmar despite formal repatriation efforts in November 2018 and August 2019 (Habib, 2022).

Therefore, there were four major waves of Rohingya inflow into Bangladesh, of which the fourth was both the largest one and the only one after which not a single person from the Rohingya community in the Bangladeshi camps has been repatriated to date. However, recently, initiatives are being undertaken to begin the repatriation of the Rohingya refugees. In different times, both countries signed repatriation agreements; however, Myanmar shows very little positive interest in receiving the displaced people. Moreover, the military authority of Myanmar often blames other side not for holding appropriate initiatives for Rohingya repatriation.

3 Repatriation of the Rohingya: Myanmar's Initiative

The Rohingyas, a Muslim ethnic minority group that has lived for generations in the primarily Buddhist nation of Myanmar, were denied citizenship under Myanmar's 1982 Citizenship Act and have become the largest community of stateless people across the globe. Rohingya families are denied basic rights and protection in Myanmar due to their statelessness, making them particularly susceptible to exploitation, sexual and gender-based violence, and other forms of abuse. The persecution of the Rohingya people, who originally resided in the Rakhine State of Myanmar, dates back to the military coup that took place there in 1962. In Myanmar, the Rohingya have endured decades of violence, prejudice, and persecution (Alam, 2019; Ahsan Ullah, 2016). Their greatest migration started in August 2017 when Rakhine State in Myanmar saw a tremendous wave of violence by the Myanmar military that drove more than 700,000 people, half of whom were children, to seek refuge in Bangladesh. Thousands of families were slain or torn apart, entire towns were set ablaze, and grave human rights crimes were documented (Rohingya Refugee Crisis Explained, 2022).

Since the massive Rohingya exodus in 2017, the Myanmar Government has received harsh criticism from the world community and has been accused of perpetrating ethnic cleansing in the country. Under massive condemnation and pressure from the international community and human rights organizations, the Myanmar government has taken some initiatives to resolve the Rohingya issue in the last few years. Here, the initiatives taken by Myanmar are discussed under two sections: first, the initiatives taken by the Suu Kyi Government during its regime; and second, the initiatives taken by the military junta of Myanmar in recent years.

4 The Initiatives Under the Suu Kyi Government

Myanmar has mostly existed under complete military control since its independence in 1948, but finally, in 2015, Suu Kyi's political party won its victory in the first-ever democratic election held in Myanmar. The perpetrators of the Rohingya massacre in Rakhine State was explicitly the Tatmadaw, which is Myanmar's Military; therefore, after Suu Kyi's win, the world community as well as the Rohingyas had high hopes for the former human rights activist regarding a forthcoming solution to the years of sufferings of the Rohingyas. The citizens of Myanmar, the Rohingya people living in the Arakan state of Myanmar, and those who had taken refuge in different camps in Bangladesh were eagerly waiting for the first speech of Aung San Suu Kyi about the ongoing Rohingya crisis.

Suu Kyi delivered the speech in English, widely taken to mean that it was directed more at an international audience than her own people, and she canceled a planned appearance at the United Nations General Assembly in New York. This took place in September 2017, amid calls for Myanmar's security forces to be held responsible for atrocities against the Rohingya Muslims. After 2016s violence against the Rohingya Muslims in Myanmar, Suu Kyi limited her travels abroad and also skipped 2016s UN General Assembly, at which she was expected to discuss the increasingly complex Rohingya Crisis (Aung et al., 2021). Aung San Suu Kyi, the state counselor of Myanmar, spoke out about the Rohingya issue for the first time since the Myanmar military's crackdown in Rakhine State in 2017—which Zeid Ra'ad al-Hussein, the UN's human rights chief, called a "textbook case of ethnic cleansing"—in the nation's capital, Naypyidaw. She stated that her nation was not "afraid of international scrutiny" (McPherson, 2017).

Suu Kyi's 30-min speech addressing the Rohingya crisis for the first time in 2017 drew widespread criticism for her failure to denounce alleged atrocities against the Rohingya community and her statement that the Myanmar government needed more time to determine "what the real problems are" in Rakhine State, despite the fact that the United Nations, numerous rights groups, and the Myanmar government itself had issued reports detailing the causes of the interethnic violence. In her speech, Suu Kyi attempted to portray the Rohingya crisis in Myanmar as a complicated internal problem and compared the violence, which she claimed to be an isolated event, with the government's continuous development program, particularly its attempts to bring "peace, stability, harmony, and progress" to the country as a whole. Amnesty International characterized the address as a "mix of untruths and victim blaming," since Suu Kyi only once addressed the Rohingya by name, explicitly mentioning the Arakan Rohingya Salvation Army (ARSA), who she claimed was engaged in terrorist operations.

However, Suu Kyi added in her speech that they would welcome others to join them in their efforts regarding the Rohingya issue by visiting their homes (Wright et al., 2017). But before and after the event on August 25, 2017, access to Rakhine State has been severely limited for the media, human rights organizations, and diplomats. (Myanmar: End Harassment of Rakhine Media Outlets, 2020). Early in September 2017, the government organized a tightly supervised media journey to the state of Rakhine. However, it was nearly impossible for journalists to visit the area independently and conduct interviews without official interference (Head, 2017). Even almost a year before, in December 2016, Ghanaian diplomat Kofi Annan appeared to criticize the Myanmar government's refusal to allow humanitarian organizations and other NGO' access to Rakhine State (Westcott & Maung, 2016).

Many people outside of Myanmar, who see Suu Kyi as a champion of human rights due to her struggle against military rule, have been disappointed by her ambiguous stance on the Rohingya issue. But the big crowds in Yangon City in Myanmar, who had gathered in a festive mood to watch her speech live on huge outdoor screens, cheered and celebrated. Suu Kyi, according to analysts, calculated politically that taking a stronger stance on the Rohingya would have lost her popularity domestically (Wright et al., 2017).

Penny Green, a professor of law at Queen Mary University of London who studies the Rohingya conflict, said in 2016 that Suu Kyi's position regarding the Rohingya crisis was "disingenuous" and "filled with underlying denials," a position she considered "a familiar and integral strategy deployed by criminal states to deflect blame" (Aung San Suu Kyi is legitimizing genocide in Myanmar and has entrenched the persecution of Rohingya Muslims, warn state crime academics, 2016).

The repatriation of Rohingyas has been a topic of extensive discussion, not only in Bangladesh but also in various other countries. In response to the influx of Rohingyas who sought refuge in Bangladesh following the Myanmar Military's "Operation Scorched Earth" campaign in August 2017, Suu Kyi's government undertook three official repatriation initiatives in 2017, 2018, and 2019. Regrettably, all of these efforts proved to be unsuccessful. The subsequent sections provide a concise overview of the repatriation endeavors during the aforementioned years.

4.1 Agreement Between Bangladesh and Myanmar in 2017

More than 620,000 Muslim Rohingyas have crossed the border into Bangladesh since August 2017s military crackdown in Rakhine State of Myanmar, which has been referred to as a planned ethnic-cleansing operation. Myanmar and Bangladesh signed an initial deal for the possible repatriation of hundreds of thousands of Rohingya

Muslims who fled violence in Rakhine State in November, 2017 (Bin Siddique, 2019). Aung San Suu Kyi, the de facto leader of Myanmar, and Abul Hassan Mahmood Ali, the foreign minister of Bangladesh, met in Naypyidaw, Myanmar's capital, to sign the agreement (Homes, 2017). The agreement stated that Myanmar would take all feasible steps to ensure that returnees are not settled in temporary locations for an extended period of time and that their freedom of movement in Rakhine State is guaranteed in accordance with existing laws and regulations. The memorandum also stated that Myanmar would authenticate their return and identity certificates would be issued based on "evidence of past residence in Myanmar." However, many activists expressed their concern about effective Rohingya repatriation under this agreement, as a large number of Rohingya documents had been seized prior to August 25 or lost when their villages burned during the ongoing assaults in the preceding months (Westcott et al., 2017). Even if the Rohingyas were repatriated, where the persecuted minority would live—as hundreds of their villages had been demolished—and how they would be safeguarded in a nation where harsh anti-Muslim sentiment prevails were the concerns of various rights groups and NGOs (Siddique, 2022). Aung San Suu Kyi's administration in response stated that they were trying to amicably resolve the issue with their neighbor, Bangladesh, through a friendly bilateral negotiation to attain a win–win situation for both countries (Homes, 2017).

4.2 The Repatriation Initiative in 2018

In November 2017, a plan to repatriate the Rohingya from Bangladesh, where refugee camps were overflowing and well beyond capacity, to Myanmar was announced. However, the repatriation, scheduled for January 22, 2018, was postponed as the Rohingya people did not feel safe going back to their homeland; they continued to bear extensive fears of persecution from the Myanmar government, and its military, back in Rakhine State (Smith, 2018a, 2018b). On January 10, the Myanmar Army acknowledged that some of its soldiers had captured, summarily executed, and buried 10 Rohingya civilians but to date, no soldier or commander has been held accountable for the assaults, murders, and arson attacks (Smith, 2018a, 2018b). State Counselor Suu Kyi continued to rigidly deny full access to United Nations fact finders, journalists, and human rights monitors in the Rakhine State to avoid questions regarding the massacre perpetrated by the Myanmar military forces (Watson & Griffiths, 2017).

Later on, on November 15 of the same year, another plan was formed to begin repatriating hundreds of thousands of Rohingya Muslim refugees to Myanmar. Repatriation of an initial batch of 2200 Rohingyas again stalled amid protests by refugees at camps in Bangladesh and accusations between the officials in both the countries. The Myanmar government's lack of transparency and openness with the international community gave rise to much confusion as well as fears among both the Rohingya people and the world community. The UN human rights office continued to receive reports of ongoing rights violations against Rohingya in Myanmar including allegations of killings, disappearances, and arbitrary arrests. Moreover, there was no assurance in the agreement of repatriation that the Rohingya would receive their fundamental rights, like the ability to work, the right to be free from violence and persecution, and most importantly, the right to citizenship as Rohingyas. Without these safeguards, there was a significant concern that the Rohingya would return home only to face conditions identical to those they previously fled from (Prabandari & Tobing, 2018).

Bangladesh had pledged not to coerce anyone into returning, and therefore, on November 15, 2018, hundreds of Rohingya Muslim refugees protested in Bangladesh to demonstrate against any attempt to send them back; by late afternoon, no refugees had returned to Myanmar. Officials on both sides placed the responsibility for the absence of progress on the bilateral plan, which had been agreed upon in late October 2018, on the other side (Paul & Naing, 2018).

4.3 The Repatriation Initiative in 2019

The authorities again failed to convince the thousands of Muslims from the Rohingya minority who fled to Bangladesh from Myanmar to participate in repatriation in 2019. No Rohingya volunteered to board the buses heading for Myanmar, despite the Myanmar government having authorized the return of more than 3000 Rohingya starting on August 22, 2019. Four families, or roughly 18 persons, from Shalbagan Camp 26 in Cox's Bazar initially showed a desire to return, a Bangladeshi government official revealed. They were on the verge of boarding a vehicle to cross the border when other migrants warned them that they would not be able to go back to their home communities or have a path to citizenship (Ellis-Petersen & Rahman, 2019).

The refugees again protested after the repatriation plan was disclosed, demanding accountability for those responsible for the past atrocities. In addition, they demanded that the Myanmar government assure full citizenship rights and return of land and properties to the refugees, including compensation for the homes and businesses burnt down by the Myanmar military forces (Myanmar/Bangladesh Halt Rohingya Returns: Ensure Refugees' Security, Basic Rights, Equal Access to Citizenship, 2019). The Tatmadaw, that is, the Myanmar military, had used sexual violence as "part of a deliberate, well-planned strategy to intimidate, terrorize, and punish a civilian population" during the "clearance operations" in 2016 and 2017, according to a UN fact-finding mission, and as a result, the Rohingyas could not have confidence that they would be safe upon returning to Myanmar (Ellis-Petersen & Rahman, 2019).

Although Suu Kyi stated several times that she would work for the facilitation of the Rohingya people residing in Bangladesh, and even signed agreements with Bangladesh in 2017, 2018, and 2019, she was never successful in this aspect. Moreover, Suu Kyi never managed to deal with the actual crisis during her regime: reaching toward a sustainable resolution of the underlying tensions regarding the minority Rohingya Muslims. With the Military coup in February 2021, Suu Kyi's regime was overthrown and the military junta, the Tatmadaw, took control of Myanmar. As Suu Kyi had failed to meet the Rohingya Muslims' expectations several times, the

Rohingya minority group did not feel sorry for Suu Kyi, though the initiation of the military regime in Myanmar seemed to quash their hopes for repatriation to their homeland (Mahmud, 2021).

5 The Initiatives Under the Military Junta

After the repeated failure of the repatriation of the Rohingyas in 2018 and 2019 under Suu Kyi's government, the repatriation initiatives were losing credibility. The COVID pandemic and the coup in Myanmar in 2021 made the repatriation initiatives more complex, and discussions regarding the issue have since largely fallen flat. As the Rohingya people had terrible experiences with the Myanmar military, they saw little hope for returning home after the Myanmar military took power in the country and detained Suu Kyi in February 2021. Since then, Bangladesh has continued attempting to draw the attention of the world community regarding the repatriation of the Rohingya refugees. The United Nations has made its own position very clear, that a repatriation process must be "voluntary, safe, and dignified" (Sheikh, 2022).

Myanmar has suddenly shown an interest in Rohingya repatriation primarily due to pressure from China (Nath, 2023a, 2023b). The Myanmar government was given until April 24, 2023, to submit a counterargument in the Rohingya genocide case before the International Court of Justice (ICJ). The question of whether this is perhaps a reason for Myanmar's recent upsurge in interest in Rohingya repatriation is also being raised. Myanmar might be attempting to demonstrate to the ICJ and the world community that they are making efforts toward improving the situation (Ejaj, 2023).

5.1 Diplomats Visit Rakhine State

In the first week of March 2023, Yangon-based diplomats from eight nations were transported to Rakhine as part of Myanmar's Rohingya repatriation initiative. They included diplomats from Bangladesh, India, and China. The Pilot Project is planned to bring back over a thousand Rohingyas to Myanmar from Bangladesh. Diplomats visiting Rakhine noted that the situation improved from 2018 to 2020, as the internally displaced Rohingyas in Myanmar could now travel to Sittwe, which was nearly impossible even two years prior. Moreover, in 2022, Sittwe University accepted 230 Rohingya students, which reflects the highest number of Rohingya students to be admitted to that institution since 2012 (Begum, 2023). Scrutinizing the list of 862,000 Rohingyas that the Bangladeshi government sent to Myanmar, the country announced it would choose about 70,000 from among them to repatriate initially. According to recent reports, about 1000 Rohingyas would be sent home to start, through family-based repatriation. Myanmar initially said that once the Pilot Project got underway, at least 1500 Rohingyas from each community will be relocated to nine villages in Myanmar. However, before the next national election, Bangladesh wants the repatriation process to get underway, even if on a small scale (Ejaj, 2023).

5.2 *Myanmar Delegation's Five-Day Visit to Bangladesh*

According to the Bangladesh–Myanmar Repatriation Agreement, the repatriation of Rohingyas must be voluntary, safe, and dignified, and no Rohingya can be forcibly sent back to Myanmar (Ibrahim, 2023). A 17-member delegation led by Ministry of Foreign Affairs Maungdu Regional Director Aung Myew visited Bangladesh on March 15 to verify some Rohingya families as a part of the initiation for their repatriation in Myanmar. The Myanmar delegation gathered the details of 499 Rohingyas from 149 families, interviewing Rohingyas at Teknaf Shal Port in Bangladesh, according to the Office of the Refugee Relief and Repatriation Commissioner (RRRC). Bangladesh provided a list of 830,000 Rohingyas residing in 33 camps in Cox's Bazar's Ukhya and Teknaf areas and Noakhali's Bhasan Char area for repatriation, and Myanmar chose only 60,000 Rohingyas for repatriation, stating that it needed to verify the identity of the others (Rohingya repatriation: Myanmar delegation's 5-day visit to Cox's Bazar ends, 2023).

5.3 *Rohingya Delegation's One-Day Visit to Myanmar*

As a preliminary stage of Myanmar's Pilot Project, Myanmar invited a Rohingya delegation to Myanmar to observe the camps that had been constructed for them. On May 5, 2023, a 20-member Rohingya delegation led by Bangladesh Refugee, Relief, and Repatriation Commissioner Mohammad Mizanur Rahman and accompanied by seven other members from various organizations, including the Ministry of Foreign Affairs of Bangladesh, visited Rakhine State to evaluate the local environment and situation.

They visited at least 15 villages surrounding the township of Maungdaw. This is undeniably the most significant move toward initiating the repatriation of Rohingyas through trust-building. During the visit, the Maungdaw Deputy Commissioner stated that the Rohingyas returning from Bangladesh would be kept at the Maungdaw Transit Center for three days and would then be moved directly to the Model Village (Sadi, 2023). A Model Village had been constructed for the would-be repatriation of Rohingyas, where each of the Rohingya families would be given one house and one acre of farmland, along with fertilizer and seeds. Each community would have access to a hospital, a mosque for worship, and a sports field, and the opportunity for children to attend education, access to commerce, and other income-generating opportunities (Model Villages built in Myanmar, Rohingyas to get houses and agricultural land, 2023). After shifting the repatriated Rohingyas to the Model Village,

National Verification Certificates (NVCs) would be issued to the Rohingyas as citizens of Myanmar and National Identity Cards would be issued to them later on in phases (Sadi, 2023).

But the Rohingya delegates objected to this idea and asked that prior to repatriation, they be given citizenship, security, and they insisted to return to their villages in Rakhine sooner. Under the Pilot Project, Myanmar will first repatriate 1176 individuals. The high demand for repatriation from the Rohingyas is clearly seen in the "Bari Cholo" movement in the Cox's Bazar camps. On the July 19, 2022, a day before World Refugee Day, thousands of Rohingyas conducted a peaceful rally in Ukhia, Cox's Bazar, to announce to the world that they wish to return to Myanmar and asserting their citizenship of Myanmar, as Myanmar is their birthplace. On the first day of the Bari Cholo ("Let's Go Home") campaign, the Rohingya community organized a rally at 23 camps—21 in Ukhia and 2 in Teknaf Upazila—demanding justice for the genocide in Myanmar. In addition, they distributed leaflets with their seven-point demand, which included the prompt repatriation of Rohingyas to Myanmar, the repeal of Myanmar's Citizenship Act of 1982, the protection of Rohingya dignity and security in Myanmar, and an end to the persecution of Myanmar's innocent Rohingya population. Additionally, they called on Myanmar and the international community to create a safe environment in Rakhine State to ensure the dignified repatriation of the Rohingyas, and this campaign created public opinion within the camps in favor of repatriation ("Let's go home; let's go to Myanmar": Rohingya rally tells world, 2022).

Bangladeshi officials expressed satisfaction after visiting Rakhine, declaring that Myanmar was now suitable for Rohingya repatriation. Conversely, the Rohingya leaders, after the visit to Myanmar, said that the conditions for repatriation had not yet been met. They believed that they would not be able to revisit the residences they fled from in 2017, as their towns had been demolished and replaced with military and law enforcement barracks and installations. According to them, the Rohingyas are unwilling to return as merely visitors with National Verification Cards; repatriation should begin with citizenship. A sub-group of Rohingyas, on the other hand, believes that some Rohingyas should accept repatriation in order to fully understand the situation in Rakhine. These trailblazers could then disclose the true state of affairs in Rakhine and cast light on the true stance and goals of the Myanmar government. Otherwise, it will remain an uncertain predicament and the crisis will continue for a longer period of time (Sadi, 2023).

5.4 *Myanmar Government Officials' Visit to Bangladesh*

As part of the proposed repatriation plan, a team from the Myanmar government visited Rohingya refugee camps in Bangladesh on May 25, 2023. When the group of 14 Myanmar officials arrived in Teknaf, Bangladesh, they proceeded to the camps and spoke with over 200 individuals while dressed in civilian attire.

However, according to the Myanmar government officials who visited the camps, the Rohingyas they came across were not convinced of the need for repatriation. The Rohingyas stated they did not want to return to their motherland as non-citizens and requested citizenship from Myanmar, something the visiting authorities would not guarantee. In response to these demands from the Rohingya community in Bangladesh, the Myanmar team "assured that the confusions that are being created will be resolved gradually," according to Mainul Kabir, the head of the Rohingya wing in Bangladesh's foreign ministry (Joshi, 2023).

5.5 Proposed Facilities for the Rohingyas by the Myanmar Military

During their visit to Myanmar, the Rohingya delegation was given a booklet that detailed the government's plans for the resettlement of Rohingya refugees once they had returned home. The leaflet said that the Rohingya will be provided with eight distinct facilities upon their return to their homeland. These include:

1. **Humanitarian Assistance**: Those Rohingya people who will be repatriated to Myanmar as a part of the recent Pilot Project will be kept in special repatriation centers. They will be given clothes and lodging that is appropriate for their age and gender as well as their needs. In accordance with established standards, they will be provided with soap, food, and blankets.
2. **House for Resettlement**: The Rohingyas returning to Myanmar will be temporarily accommodated in camps immediately after their re-entrance in Myanmar, for not more than 60 days. After their stay in the camps in the beginning, they will be provided with houses for their resettlement.
3. **Employment Opportunities**: The Rohingya people, on returning to Myanmar, will be given the rights and facilities to work on agricultural land in the villages where they will be resettled. Additionally, rice, crop seedlings, fertilizer, agricultural apparatus, and agricultural instruction will be distributed to them.
4. **Health Services**: COVID-19 antigen test (RDT) screening facilities have been established for the Rohingya returnees. If there is a long distance between the health center and the village of the Rohingyas, new health centers will be built nearby for fulfilling their requirements.
5. **Education Facility**: The education of Rohingya children who return to their villages will be prioritized in the schools located closest to them.
6. **Security Arrangements:** To maintain peace and security and to ensure law and order during the return of the displaced Rohingyas, border police battalions and township police stations have already been prepared. The townships will gradually adopt security measures. The entire procedure will be supervised by the appropriate UNDP and UNHCR officials. Depending on what the Myanmar government wants, they will help with the procedure.

7. **National Verification Card (NVC)**: The NVC is a procedure for verifying citizenship of the Rohingya people in Myanmar. It is required for freedom of movement, professional activities, and access to education and health services. In accordance with the 2017 agreement between Myanmar and Bangladesh regarding Rohingyas, displaced Rohingyas will be issued identity cards at re-entry centers following screening and registration. Religion and ethnicity are not specified on this NVC certificate, which is issued during the citizenship verification procedure. The NVC certificate essentially demonstrates that the recipient is a resident of Myanmar. This document will enable Rohingyas to file for citizenship verification, and it must be carried until the verification process is complete.
8. **Citizenship**: According to the 1982 Myanmar Citizenship Act, there are three types of citizenship. These are citizens, associate citizens, and naturalized citizens. The right to apply for citizenship (or extra-citizenship) with pertinent information is granted to those who fulfill the requirements of the Citizenship Act of 1982. The Citizenship Act states that after reviewing the applicants' information, a central committee will determine whether or not a person has the right to become a citizen.

These are the eight specific facilities which are to be provided by the Myanmar authority toward the Rohingya returnees under the recent Pilot Project of Rohingya Repatriation (Karim & Alam, 2023).

5.6 The Loopholes in the Pilot Project for Rohingya Repatriation

Despite the agreement signed between the Bangladesh and Myanmar governments in 2017 and the two consecutive efforts in 2018 and 2019, repatriation of the Rohingyas never began after the largest influx of Rohingyas into Bangladesh in 2017, due to Myanmar's lack of sincerity and the Rohingya's objections to returning to an unfavorable environment in Rakhine (Sajjad, 2020). To address these issues, Bangladesh is seeking to incorporate the UNHCR into the repatriation process. However, the military administration of Myanmar is reluctant to do so. Consequently, the Rohingya's lack of trust has never been resolved (Nath, 2023a, 2023b).

Myanmar's military regime appears to have used the agreement to repatriate slightly more than one thousand Rohingya as a ploy to avoid pressure and accountability from the international community. The decision to repatriate only one thousand refugees seems, specifically, to be an effort to alleviate pressure from China and other nations. The military administration of the country announced in April that it will begin repatriating Rohingya from Bangladesh. In addition, they assert that Myanmar is conducting a trial operation to repatriate 1500 Rohingya and that, as part of this, a Myanmar representative team traveled to Bangladesh and carried out its inspection responsibilities. However, Myanmar's government may have initiated this campaign to gain an advantage before the International Criminal Court begins hearings in Gambia's case accusing Myanmar of genocide against the Rohingya.

In February 2022, a noteworthy shift occurred when Myanmar demonstrated a sudden and notable interest in the joint working group meeting with Bangladesh. This development ignited discussions on repatriation and was presented as evidence in favor of Myanmar's efforts. Subsequently, the International Court of Justice (ICJ) granted an extension until August 24, 2023, to Myanmar's military government to present their arguments, despite concerns raised by Gambia. Myanmar is likely to view this extension as an opportunity to achieve a favorable disposition from the court, and may seek to commence the repatriation of Rohingya before the specified deadline (Nath, 2023a, 2023b).

However, rights group leaders and diplomats are skeptical about the state of the citizenship verification process as most Rohingyas, while fleeing Myanmar to Bangladesh's territory to save their lives, did not have any valid documents to prove their citizenship, or had lost or damaged them during their various travels. This is despite the fact that officials and Rohingya members of the delegation found the initiatives and arrangements conducive to starting repatriation during their spot visit on May 5, 2023.

Shahidul Haque, a former foreign secretary, expressed worry about how Myanmar would provide citizenship to Rohingyas and how many would be granted it. He claimed that there was a lot of deceit going on and that, in his experience, Myanmar does not follow through on its promises.

The Myanmar government's demands should in any case be viewed with some skepticism, according to Md. Nur Khan, executive director of Ain o Salish Kendra (ASK), who reminded the Business Standard that the country had questioned the citizenship of the Rohingyas long before the 2017 persecution. He said that the ethnic animosity the Myanmar junta government has for the Rohingyas will make getting citizenship much more difficult. "In the pretext of repatriation, Myanmar could have plans to imprison these people [Rohingyas] in the barracks." Therefore, given this situation, Md. Nur Khan continued, it is important to prioritize the Rohingya residents of Bangladesh. According to migration expert Asif Munier, a thorough examination is required to ascertain whether Myanmar's acceptance of their requirements extends beyond mere rhetoric. Munier emphasizes the need to verify Myanmar's long-term commitment to upholding these obligations (All hands-on deck: The world cannot dally on this issue any longer, 2023).

The international community is going to see seventh year of Rohingya displacement and living in cramped conditions in refugee camps in Bangladesh. A huge cry has already been raised from different sources to repatriate the Rohingyas. The Rohingyas have become crazy for returning to their homes. They do not like to live in the camps in Bangladesh. They very much care for their children's education and good future. However, no light for hope is yet to be seen from the international context to reinitiate the repatriation process. China has a big power, and the mediator of this crisis is not taking positive initiative to start the process of repatriation. This is delaying the process and deepening the crisis in Bangladesh.

6 Conclusion

The recent Pilot Project of Rohingya Repatriation has provided some positive motion amid the prevailing confusion and ambiguity. For the first time since the significant influx of Rohingya in 2017, a delegation representing the Rohingya community visited Myanmar to gather first-hand information on the preparations made for their return. Notably, China, a prominent regional power, has adopted the role of mediator in the process, which has shown some promise. This offers a slight hope that repatriation, albeit on a limited scale, could commence, marking the first tangible success since the massive influx of Rohingya into Bangladesh. The international community can play a constructive role by closely monitoring ongoing repatriation efforts and advocating for the protection of the Rohingyas' rights throughout. Myanmar's military junta currently faces legitimacy challenges both domestically and internationally, alongside grappling with multiple conflicts involving insurgent factions within the country. This presents a crucial opportunity to exert pressure on the military rulers, with the assistance of China, to take genuine measures to facilitate a lasting solution for the Rohingya.

The Rohingya Crisis stands as one of today's most pressing global concerns, and demands the attention of the international community. Multiple international bodies and human rights organizations are eagerly awaiting a resolution to this protracted crisis. The substantial presence of Rohingya populations in a densely populated country like Bangladesh poses significant economic and security challenges. Despite Myanmar's independence, the Rohingya crisis has persistently evaded a lasting solution over the years. Notably, since the mass exodus of Rohingyas in 2017, the repatriation of a single Rohingya refugee from Bangladesh to Myanmar has not materialized, despite the signing of agreements and the implementation of initiatives by both governments. The historical backdrop of Rohingya suffering, intertwined with Myanmar's military power, has further dimmed the prospects of repatriation following the military coup in 2021. However, recent actions taken by Myanmar's military junta have instilled a glimmer of hope among the Rohingya people and the international community for the initiation of Rohingya repatriation, which has remained stagnant for six years. Although the military's intentions regarding repatriation and granting citizenship to Rohingyas remain unclear, skepticism persists among many human rights organizations, casting doubt on the repatriation process's potential benefits for the vulnerable Rohingya population. Nonetheless, the visit of Rohingya delegations, accompanied by Bangladeshi officials, to Model Villages in Myanmar with necessary facilities after six years of wishful thinking offers hope for an effective and timely commencement of the repatriation process. To ensure the successful and sustainable repatriation of Rohingyas, the collective efforts of different human rights organizations, the United Nations, and as well as the international community must be mobilized.

References

Abdul, H. (2020). The Rohingyas of Rakhine State: Social evolution and history in the light of ethnic nationalism. *Social Evolution & History, 19*(2), 115–144.

Abrar, C. R. (1995). Repatriation of Rohingya refugees. *UNHCR's Regional consultation on refugee and migratory movements, Colombo.*

Ahmed, K. (2023). *I feel no peace: Rohingya fleeing over seas & rivers.* Hurst Publishers.

Ahsan Ullah, A. K. M. (2016). Rohingya crisis in Myanmar: Seeking justice for the "stateless". *Journal of Contemporary Criminal Justice, 32*(3), 285–301.

Alam, M. A. (1999). *A short historical background of Arakan.* Arakan Historical Society, Chittagong (Bangladesh), 27–28. Available online: https://kaladanpress.org/images/document/2018/A%20Short%20Historical%20Background%20%20of%20Arakan.pdf

Alam, J. (2019). The current Rohingya crisis in Myanmar in historical perspective. *Journal of Muslim Minority Affairs, 39*(1), 1–25.

All hands-on deck: The world cannot dally on this issue any longer. (2023, May 22). *The Dhaka Tribune.* Retrieved May 29, 2023, from https://www.dhakatribune.com/editorial/2023/05/22/all-hands-on-deck.

Aung San Suu Kyi is legitimizing genocide in Myanmar and has entrenched the persecution of Rohingya Muslims, warn state crime academics. (2016, November 23). *International State Crime Initiative.* Retrieved March 23, 2023, from http://statecrime.org/isci-press-release-nov2016/

Aung, T. S., Unruh, J., & Ali, F. (2021). Modelling the determinants of voluntary repatriation: The role of ecosystem services in postconflict reconstruction in Rakhine. *Journal of Environmental Management, 290,* 112540.

Begum, S. (2023, April 20). China mediated BD-Myanmar meet: Small-scale Rohingya repatriation talks end in Kunming, Momen sees glimmer of hope. *The Daily Observer.* Retrieved May 28, 2023, from https://www.observerbd.com/news.php?id=416390

Bin Siddique, F. (2019). Non-refoulement & other durable solutions in refugee law: Rohingyas in perspective. *SCLS Law Review, 2*(1).

Burma: End 'Ethnic Cleansing' of Rohingya Muslims. (2013, April 22). Human Rights Watch. Retrieved May 24, 2023, from https://www.hrw.org/news/2013/04/22/burma-end-ethnic-cleansing-rohingya-muslims

Ejaj, R. (2023, March 12). Myanmar takes sudden initiative for Rohingya repatriation, pressure from China. *The Prothom Alo.* Retrieved May 27, 2023, from https://en.prothomalo.com/bangladesh/6intv2y3oi

Ellis-Petersen, H., & Rahman, S. A. (2019, August 22). Rohingya refugees turn down second Myanmar repatriation effort. *The Guardian.* Retrieved March 28, 2023, from https://www.theguardian.com/world/2019/aug/22/rohingya-refugees-turn-down-second-myanmar-repatriation-effort

Gorlick, B. (2019). The Rohingya refugee crisis: Rethinking solutions and accountability. *Refugee Studies Centre, Working Paper Series,* (131). University of Oxford, UK.

Habib, W. B. (2022, December 10). The Rohingya refugee crisis throughout the years. *The Daily Star.* Retrieved April 5, 2023, from https://www.thedailystar.net/supplements/oxfam-human-rights-day-special-magazine-2022/news/three-generations-stateless-3193491

Head, J. (2017, September 11). Rohingya crisis: Seeing through the official story in Myanmar. *The BBC News.* Retrieved May 2, 2023, from https://www.bbc.com/news/world-asia-41222210

Homes, O. (2017, November 22). Myanmar signs pact with Bangladesh over Rohingya repatriation. *The Guardian.* Retrieved May 1, 2023, from https://www.theguardian.com/world/2017/nov/23/myanmar-signs-pact-with-bangladesh-over-rohingya-repatriation

Ibrahim, D. A. (2023, May 22). Rohingya repatriation must address safety, citizenship and dignity. *The Arab News.* Retrieved May 26, 2023, from https://www.arabnews.com/node/2308236#:~:text=Attempts%20to%20initiate%20repatriation%20in,to%20return%20under%20unfavorable%20conditions

Islam, M. R., Islam, M. T., Alam, M. S., Hussain, M., & Haque, M. M. (2022). An assessment of the sustainability of living for Rohingya displaced people in Cox's Bazar Camps in Bangladesh. *Journal of Human Rights and Social Work, 7*(3), 331–345.

Joshi, M. (2023, May 26). Myanmar officials visit Rohingya camps in Bangladesh over repatriation plan. *WION*. Retrieved May 27, 2023, from https://www.wionews.com/south-asia/myanmar-officials-visit-rohingya-camps-in-bangladesh-over-repatriation-plan-596754

Karim, R., & Alam, N. (2023, May 8). Rohingya repatriation: Myanmar pledges 8 facilities, will it work this time? *The Business Standard*. Retrieved May 25, 2023, from https://www.tbsnews.net/bangladesh/rohingya-repatriation-myanmar-pledges-8-facilities-will-it-work-time-628526

"Let's go home; let's go to Myanmar": Rohingya rally tells world. (2022, June 8). *The Daily Star.* Retrieved April 11, 2023, from https://www.thedailystar.net/news/bangladesh/rights/news/nid-correction-be-made-easy-3341226

Mahmud, F. (2021, February 2). *'Don't feel sorry for Suu Kyi': Rohingya refugees on Myanmar coup.* Al Jazeera. Retrieved April 16, 2023, from https://www.aljazeera.com/news/2021/2/2/dont-feel-sorry-for-suu-kyi-rohingya-refugees-on-myanmar-coup

Mathieson, D. S. (2009). Plight of the damned: Burma's Rohingya. *Global Asia, 4*(1), 84–89.

McPherson, P. (2017, September 19). Aung San Suu Kyi says Myanmar does not fear scrutiny over Rohingya crisis. *The Guardian.* Retrieved April 21, 2023, from https://www.theguardian.com/world/2017/sep/19/aung-san-suu-kyi-myanmar-rohingya-crisis-concerned

Model villages built in Myanmar, Rohingyas to get houses and agricultural land. (2023, May 6). *The Daily Bangladesh.* Retrieved May 28, 2023, from https://www.daily-bangladesh.com/english/national/83089

Myanmar: End Harassment of Rakhine Media Outlets. (2020, September 1). Human Rights Watch. Retrieved April 25, 2023, from https://www.hrw.org/news/2020/09/01/myanmar-end-harassment-rakhine-media-outlets

Myanmar/Bangladesh Halt Rohingya Returns: Ensure Refugees' Security, Basic Rights, Equal Access to Citizenship. (2019, August 20). Human Rights Watch. Retrieved April 9, 2023, from https://www.hrw.org/news/2019/08/20/myanmar/bangladesh-halt-rohingya-returns

Nath, S. S. (2023, May 13). China hosting Bangladesh-Myanmar Rohingya talks: Is there a hope? *The Financial Express.* Retrieved May 29, 2023, from https://thefinancialexpress.com.bd/views/china-hosting-bangladesh-myanmar-rohingya-talks-is-there-a-hope

Nath, S. S. (2023, May 18). Is Rohingya Repatriation Finally Moving Forward? *The Diplomat.* Retrieved May 27, 2023, from https://thediplomat.com/2023/05/is-rohingya-repatriation-finally-moving-forward/

Paul, R., & Naing, S. (2018, November 14). *Rohingya repatriation process stalls amid refugee protests, recriminations.* Reuters. Retrieved May 2, 2023, from https://www.reuters.com/article/us-myanmar-rohingya-bangladesh-idUSKCN1NJ2K1

Prabandari, A., & Tobing, D. H. (2018, February 13). The Rohingya repatriation deal: What is at stake and what needs to be done. *The Conversation.* Retrieved May 12, 2023, from https://theconversation.com/the-rohingya-repatriation-deal-what-is-at-stake-and-what-needs-to-be-done-91082

Rahman, M. K. (2021, August 24). Citizenship of the Rohingya in Myanmar: A historical account. *The Daily Star.* Retrieved May 21, 2023, from https://www.thedailystar.net/law-our-rights/news/citizenship-the-rohingya-myanmar-historical-account-2159176

Rohingya Refugee Crisis Explained. (2022). UNHCR. https://www.unrefugees.org/news/rohingya-refugee-crisis-explained/

Rohingya repatriation: Myanmar delegation's 5-day visit to Cox's Bazar ends. (2023, March 22). *The Daily Star.* Retrieved May 26, 2023, from https://www.thedailystar.net/rohingya-influx/news/rohingya-repatriation-myanmar-delegations-5-day-visit-coxs-bazar-ends-3277781?amp

Sadi, A. (2023, May 21). Rohingya repatriation pilot project: A call for comprehensive and sustainable solutions. *The Geopolitics.* Retrieved May 25, 2023, from https://thegeopolitics.com/rohingya-repatriation-pilot-project-a-call-for-comprehensive-and-sustainable-solutions/

Sajjad, T. (2020). Refugees welcome?: The politics of repatriation and return in a global era of security. In *Displacement* (pp. 79–96). Manchester University Press.

Sheikh, S. (2022, October 31). The perils of repatriation for Rohingya refugees. *The Asia Times*. Retrieved May 19, 2023, from https://asiatimes.com/2022/10/the-perils-of-repatriation-for-rohingya-refugees/

Siddique, S. (2022). *Sustainable displacement and the Rohingya refugee camps*. University of California.

Smith, M. (2018, January 28). Rohingya repatriation is premature and dangerous. *CNN*. Retrieved May 6, 2023, from https://edition.cnn.com/2018/01/28/opinions/rohingya-repatriation-matthew-smith-intl/index.html

Smith, N. (2018, January 22). Rohingya refugees made to wait as repatriation delayed. *The Telegraph*. Retrieved May 18, 2023, from https://www.telegraph.co.uk/news/2018/01/22/rohingyarefugees-made-wait-repatriation-delayed/

Uddin, N. (2022). The voices of Rohingyas: Contexts and settings. *Voices of the Rohingya people: A case of genocide, ethnocide and 'Subhuman' life* (pp. 1–25). Springer International Publishing.

Ullah, A. A., & Chattoraj, D. (2018). Roots of discrimination against Rohingya minorities: Society, ethnicity and international relations. *Intellectual Discourse, 26*(2), 541–565.

Van Klinken, G., & Aung, S. M. T. (2017). The contentious politics of anti-Muslim scapegoating in Myanmar. *Journal of Contemporary Asia, 47*(3), 353–375.

Ware, A. (2015). Secessionist aspects to the Buddhist–Muslim conflict in Rakhine State, Myanmar. In *Territorial Separatism in Global Politics* (pp. 153–168). Routledge.

Watson, A., & Griffiths, J. (2017, December 20). Myanmar bans UN official as military finds mass grave in Rakhine. *CNN*. Retrieved March 28, 2023, from https://edition.cnn.com/2017/12/20/asia/myanmar-grave-journalists-intl/index.html

Westcott, B., & Maung, M. (2016, December 6). Kofi Annan calls on Myanmar to allow aid and media access to Rakhine. *CNN*. Retrieved April 2, 2023, from https://edition.cnn.com/2016/12/06/asia/myanmar-rakhine-kofi-annan/index.html

Westcott, B., et al. (2017, November 27). Bangladesh-Myanmar agreement on Rohingya refugees revealed. *CNN*. Retrieved May 13, 2023, from https://edition.cnn.com/2017/11/27/asia/rohingya-myanmar-bangladesh-agreement/index.html

Wright, R., et al. (2017, September 19). Aung San Suu Kyi breaks silence on Rohingya, sparks storm of criticism. *CNN*. Retrieved April 19, 2023, from https://edition.cnn.com/2017/09/18/asia/aung-san-suu-kyi-speech-rohingya/index.html

Zawacki, B. (2013). Defining Myanmar's "Rohingya Problem". *Human Rights Brief, 20*(3), 2. Available online: https://digitalcommons.wcl.american.edu/cgi/viewcontent.cgi?article=1873&context=hrbrief

Chapter 17
Rohingya Relocation to Bhasan Char Island: A Sustainability Assessment

Rehnuma Mahjabin and Kawser Ahmed

Abstract With the repeated difficulties encountered in the repatriation of Rohingya refugees from Bangladesh to Myanmar, the Bangladeshi Government has become increasingly aware that the Rohingya crisis represents a long-term logistical challenge. Conditions in the overflowing refugee camps in Cox's Bazar have become critical. The government's most highly touted solution is the relocation of a large number of Rohingya to the island of Basan Char, where living facilities have already been constructed, and indeed, a small number of refugees have already been sent. Initially, although the international communities were skeptical due to the geographic location of the island, eventually they came onboard with the ongoing relocation process. Proceeding from an analysis of two global case studies of population resettlement, this chapter discusses the myriad reasons cited in claiming the necessity for Rohingya relocation. We continue with an in-depth description of the Bangladeshi relocation program and raise the question of the program's sustainability, along with responses from the various parties involved. We conclude by finding both merit in the relocation, as well as cause for caution and meticulous oversight.

1 Introduction

The Rohingyas, a Muslim community that has its roots in Bengali culture, has lived in Myanmar for centuries as an ethnic minority (Ahmed et al., 2021). After 1962, Burma came under military power, and since then Rohingyas have been targeted for their religion and culture (Ahmed & Mohiuddin, 2019). To escape the unjust persecution, Rohingyas began migrating to Bangladesh for the first time in 1978. At that time, Bangladesh accepted the Rohingyas and opened refugee camps for them. In 1982, the government of Myanmar refused to give citizenship to the Rohingya

R. Mahjabin (✉)
University of Manitoba, Winnipeg, Canada
e-mail: mahjabir@myumanitoba.ca

K. Ahmed
University of Winnipeg, Winnipeg, Canada
e-mail: k.ahmed@uwinnipeg.ca

K. Ahmed and Md. R. Islam (eds.), *Understanding the Rohingya Displacement*, International Perspectives on Migration, https://doi.org/10.1007/978-981-97-1424-7_17

population, and they were denied any kind of citizen rights and facilities. In 1992, more than 200,000 Rohingya people migrated to Bangladesh because of horrific violence (Yesmin, 2016). In August 2017, the third and largest Rohingya migration happened, and almost 947,000 Rohingya people fled to Bangladesh from Rakhine State, Myanmar, to save their lives from the brutal attacks of the Myanmar military and police (Labib et al., 2018). On humanitarian grounds, Bangladesh accepted the Rohingyas and arranged temporary camps for them. The situation was unexpected for Bangladesh, and the country was not prepared for it. Although national as well as international organizations came forward to help, they could not provide all the necessary resources that the displaced population needed (Ahmed & Khan, 2022). The government of Bangladesh provided 6500 acres of land in Teknaf and Ukhiya Upazila of the Cox's Bazar district to build refugee camps for the Rohingyas (Habib, 2023). At that time the government of Bangladesh had no other option to give the helpless community a shelter.

However, the Cox's Bazar district, where the refugee camps have been established, is ecologically crucial for Bangladesh. The district consists of reserve forests, national parks, and wildlife sanctuaries, and the land allocated for the Rohingyas was mostly forestry and agricultural land (Imtiaz, 2018). With the help of local and international NGOs, the government of Bangladesh cleared the area by cutting down about 3000 ha of forest; this action of the authorities was contrary to the protected-area policy of the country (Habib, 2023). The situation quickly got out of control because of the extreme population pressure on the area and on the resources. The forest protection policies of the government lost their effectiveness (Sadat al Sajib et al., 2022). The host community as well as the government treated this situation as a temporary condition. However, it has been six years and there are no signs of successful repartition to date. When the impact of the Rohingya influx became tangible, the host population—who were cordial before—became hostile toward the migrated community (Macdonald et al., 2023). Therefore, to protect the peace and reduce the immense population pressure and harmful environmental impacts, the government of Bangladesh is planning to relocate 100,000 Rohingyas to a 13,000-acre island named Bhasan Char (Islam et al., 2021). The island is located in Hatiya Upazila, and it is 60 km away from the mainland (Fig. 1). However, this decision of the government of Bangladesh has been questioned by many human rights organizations. The organizations expressed their doubts about the sustainability of the island, but at this time Bangladesh has moved ahead with the relocation plan (Islam et al., 2021).

2 Global Relocation Programs and Impacts

In the contemporary world, displaced populations are a growing challenge. A UNHCR 2020 report noted that 82.4 million people in the world are displaced, having left their homes to ensure their safety. The complexity of these population movements is a problem, and the world has no overarching solution for it (Judith &

Fig. 1 Location of Bhasan Char Island. Reproduced from The Rohingya Post (2021)

Chidiebere, 2022). Relocating these populations in a planned and sustainable way is stressful and difficult. Despite this fact, every year millions of people are uprooted from their original homes and relocated to facilitate development projects, or they are migrated populations who had no other option (Xi & Hwang, 2011). In 1992, China approved a massive development project named the Three Gorges Dam (TGD). This dam is one of China's largest-ever engineering projects, and the Chinese government made full preparations to ensure a successful project. Building a 185-m-high dam in a populous country like China across the Yangtze River was not easy (Jackson & Sleigh, 2000). The government had to relocate 1.3 million people from 1711 villages, 356 communes, 116 towns, and 20 cites to create space for the dam. The resettled population faced several struggles like financial uncertainty and social conflict. They become impoverished and vulnerable people in their internal host communities (Carney, 2021). Although the government tried to devise a foolproof plan for relocation, they overlooked some important factors. The first thing is that this plan did not give priority to environment and resource carrying capacity (Heggelund, 2006). The number of relocated people increased from 1.3 million to 1.6 million and continued to grow, but there was no official communication about the growing population (Jackson & Sleigh, 2000). Among the resettled population, 40% were farmers. The Government of China allocated 45,000 ha of unused land for farming to the displaced peoples. Despite this allocation, the farmers could not generate their previous levels of income, as they were used to farming on the fertile land beside the river. The farmers were not familiar with the new land, which reduced their productivity. Among the other 60%, it was difficult to find jobs, because unlike farming other jobs do not pass through generations. Most of them migrated to other cities to seek jobs and eventually became unemployed (Heggelund, 2006). The relocated population received material wealth, but they lost their healthy social life. They faced conflict from the host population because of preferred treatment from the government. Despite the best efforts by China's government agencies to transfer them in their groups, the family and community cohesion broke down as it was difficult to distinguish the number of people who stayed together (Heggelund, 2006). From these experiences, the government of China brought changes to their future resettlement regulations. Among the modifications, the most important changes were adding environmental protection and resource capacity in the resettlement document, removing the clause where agriculture was the only economic basis for the resettled area, and manage the funding of resettlement in defined sections. The revised resettlement regulation was more concrete, and it solved the problem to some extent (Heggelund, 2006).

In 2002, the Victorian Horn of African Community Network (HACN) made a deal with the government of Australia to resettle some refugees from the Horn of Africa in the Victoria region of Australia. It was a beneficial situation for both locations, as Victoria was suffering from a lack of labor. However, after the resettlement of 55 people to the Swan Hill area of Victoria, 37 of these people left the area because of various challenges. One of the major challenges for the relocated population was working in that area. They lacked training and language proficiency. The employers tried to test them before giving them permanent jobs, and the relocated refugees did not have that luxury to be tested (Broadbent et al., 2007). In most cases of displaced population relocation, the major issue that arises is the lack of economic opportunity, lack of housing opportunity, and the missing sense of belonging. Observing the situation in Australia leads one to suggest putting more focus on a holistic approach. The mere availability of opportunities and facilities is not enough. The authorities must establish links between the relocated community and available opportunities (McDonald-Wilmsen et al., 2009). In the Swan Hill case, the Australian government had a six-month planning period, and in most global relocation cases, the authorities have planned over a few months. But the population resettlement process requires continuous observation for several years until the desired integration is achieved (Broadbent et al., 2007).

3 Why is Relocation Necessary?

The Rohingyas are currently living in 34 camps in the Cox's Bazar district. The lack of space, fresh water, and sanitation facilities makes life miserable for Rohingyas. Naturally, when an area experiences a sudden population influx, the competition for resources increases (Imtiaz, 2018). The extra population pressure has become a threat for the natural resources of Cox's Bazar. Within two years of the influx, 744 ha of forest has been destroyed just to collect firewood. Now the displaced populations are moving toward deeper forest two to three kilometers from their settlement to fetch the needed firewood (Hasan, 2019). The Rohingyas burn almost 50,000 kg of fuel wood each day for cooking alone, as reported by Dhaka Tribune. They even remove the roots of the trees, which can cause (or is already causing) major landslides (United News of Bangladesh, 2017). Moreover, different organizations have constructed permanent structures near Rohingya camps by clearing hills and forests, even though it is illegal to construct permanent structures in that area (Hasan, 2019). Massive deforestation has increased the vulnerability of the area to natural disasters. Cox's Bazar receives 3770 mm of rainfall every year during monsoon season. Due to landslides and topsoil erosion, the Rohingyas as well as the host community suffer every year during these monsoons (Ahmed et al., 2021). When these environmental impacts became visible, the host community started blaming the Rohingya people (Macdonald et al., 2023). Destruction of vegetation, top soil degradation, landslides, and massive land-cover changes in the area are altering the dynamics of the relationship between the migrated population and host population (Ahmed & Khan, 2022). Therefore, the resettlement of at least some of the Rohingyas from those temporary refugee camps appears necessary to give the Rohingya people better living conditions and to protect the ecological resources of the Cox's Bazar district.

4 Overview of the Relocation Program in Bangladesh

Bangladesh started to relocate Rohingyas to Bhasan Char Island on December 4, 2020 (Rahman, 2022). Bhasan Char Island is located 28 nautical miles away from the Chittagong district and 4 nautical miles away from the nearest island, Sandwip (Islam et al., 2021). It takes two hours by boat to travel to the island from the mainland (Islam & Siddika, 2022). The island was newly formed nearly two decades ago. The area of the island is 36 km^2 (Islam et al., 2021). The local population coined the term "Bhasan Char," which means "floating island." The island was previously underwater; however, over time the accumulation of silt made the central part of the island quite stable. In 2015, the government of Bangladesh began an island development plan on Bhasan Char. The goal of this plan was a thorough development of the island by the Bangladesh Navy. Before 2017s large influx, Bangladesh was already host to nearly 30,000 Rohingyas from prior migrations. Therefore, the plans for the Rohingya relocation were already being developed (Islam & Siddika, 2022).

In 2018 after the Rohingya influx, the relocation initiative was accelerated and the government of Bangladesh now planned to relocate 100,000 Rohingyas to Bhasan Char Island (Islam & Siddika, 2022). The average altitude of the island is 2.84 m above sea level. The Bangladesh Navy has filled many low-lying areas to protect the island from erosion and floods, and to prevent natural disasters and tidal waves, a three-meter flood-protection embankment has been built. Sinohydro, a Chinese construction firm, and HR Wallingford, a British engineering company, helped the Bangladeshi government set up the relocation (Banerjee, 2020).

According to the government of Bangladesh, the relocation of the Rohingyas is an attempt to provide them enough space, necessary facilities, and better options for livelihood that are not possible to provide in Cox's Bazar (Afrin, 2022). Under the Ashrayan-3 project, to accommodate the 100,000 Rohingyas, semi-permanent shelters have been built which are expandable enough to accommodate 400,000 Rohingyas in the future (Banerjee, 2020). The budget of the Ashrayan-3 project is more than 350 million USD (Islam & Siddika, 2022). This funding has mainly come from donor organizations; to date, the USA has been the largest donor country for the Rohingyas (Loy, 2022). On 6.7 km^2 of land, steel and concrete barrack rows have been built (Banerjee, 2020). Each barrack consists of 16 rooms, and each room can accommodate four people. At the middle of the barrack rows, there is a courtyard with a pond in it. Every barrack has two kitchens and a total of 12 toilets and 8 bathrooms for men and women separately (Hossain, 2020). There are 12 barracks in a cluster, and a total of 120 clusters on the island, in which a total of 92,160 people can live comfortably. To protect from high tidal waves, the houses are built at 4 feet in height. One storm shelter has been built in every cluster. Each shelter is strong enough to withstand 260 km-per-hour winds and has room for almost 1000 people and 200 head of cattle (Banerjee, 2020). The shelters are multipurpose and can be used as administrative offices, educational institutions, or hospitals. Among the shelters, three are marked for mosques, one is marked for a superstore, and four will be used as community clinics. The plan also includes an orphanage, daycare center, and guest house. Apart from these facilities, the island also includes two helipads, a police camp, and eight high-speed boats for transportation (Islam et al., 2022) (Table 1).

4.1 Livelihood

A sustainable livelihood option is a must for any community to be resilient. The livelihood options for Rohingyas in Bhasan Char are not outstanding. They are dependent on several natural and anthropological disturbances and seasonal issues. On the other hand, a lack of knowledge and skills in the Rohingya community limits the scope of alternative livelihood activities (Islam et al., 2021). However, the Government of Bangladesh has taken some initiatives to create stable livelihood options for the Rohingya people on Bhasan Char Island. The plan has allocated much natural capital for the Rohingyas. Providing agricultural land for farming, fishing facilities, seeds,

Table 1 Summary of the facilities available on Bhasan Char Island (Banerjee, 2020)

Facilities	Amount/measurement
Solar-power streetlights	1000
Solar-power lights	52,000 in 1440 buildings
Wide roads	22 feet, 16 feet, and 12 feet, running approximately 42 km
Ponds	120 ponds of 5461 square feet
Mobile towers	2
Per person living area	3.6 m^2
Lights in each building	36
Steel-construction beds	4 in each room
Ceiling fan and light	1 in each room

and wood are some initiatives taken by the government toward this sustainable livelihood (Afrin, 2022). To meet the nutritional needs of the families, the government will provide fast-growing vegetable seeds of beans, spinach, bottle gourds, and sweet potatoes. Bangladesh Rural Advancement Committee (BRAC), a renowned NGO in Bangladesh, provided materials for rooftop, vertical, tower, and sack-bag gardening. A total of 10,000 juvenile fish have also been released in the 38 ponds of the area (Islam et al., 2022) (Table 2).

Crab fattening and Biofloc aquaculture are some highly productive businesses on the island which can be initiated with proper training and educational procedures. For women, livestock rearing, making fishing nets, pottery, cane basketry, jute products, and artificial flower cultivation are among the best options for sustainable livelihoods. Although all these activities look promising, the Rohingyas will still need intensive training and skill development programs to earn profit from these livelihood activities. Moreover, the restriction of communication with the mainland may create a barrier to their livelihood activities flourishing (Islam et al., 2022).

Table 2 Livelihood capital provided by the government for Bhasan Char Island (Islam et al., 2022)

Livelihood capital	Amount
Juvenile fish	Distributed among 200 Rohingyas
Grocery items	Distributed among 100 Rohingyas
Ducks & chickens	5000 of each
Carpenter's tools	50 sets
Haircutting kits	45 sets
Van repair kits	25 sets
Electricians equipment	7 sets
Sewing machines	100
Vans	50

4.2 Education Facilities

The UN human rights commission's 2019 joint response plan expressed that among children aged 3–14 years, 39% of Rohingyas did not receive any education, and for the youth aged 15–24, the rate of illiteracy was 97%. From this information, it is clear that Rohingyas need attention in the education sector (Banerjee, 2020). To escape enduring misfortune, they need quality education. The government of Bangladesh has collaborated with different NGOs toward educational purposes. Recently, the government set up 10 model classrooms for 500 Rohingya children. These classrooms are directed by trained teachers who offer primary education along with other extra-curricular activities (Children on the Edge, n.d.). Although the Government of Bangladesh has allocated concrete structures for schooling purposes, which are in much better condition than those in the congested refugee camps, education still did not receive enough priority in the plan (Banerjee, 2020). Education has been the top requested facility from the camp residents (Children on the Edge, n.d.).

4.3 Security

Security was one of the major reasons for which the Bangladesh government planned to relocate the Rohingyas (Hossain & Janmyr, 2022). The congested camps of Cox's Bazar are becoming the birthplace of crimes like drug dealing, illegal weapons, prostitution, gender-based violence, and human trafficking (The Business Standard Sunday, 2023). The Bangladesh government claimed that Bangladesh wants to give the Rohingyas a secure living environment. Therefore, the government has taken many security measures on Bhasan Char Island to protect Rohingyas from all kinds of threats. The government has established a watchtower, a perimeter fence, and several police posts to prevent theft, murder, drug dealing, and human trafficking. The government has installed security cameras and monitors to observe the people closely, so that any kind of violence can be prevented (Banerjee, 2020). In a recent survey, the residents of Bhasan Char Island asserted that no criminal acts or political violence occur on Bhasan Char. In the same survey, a security officer in charge revealed that there are 30 officers, 31 members of Armed Police Battalion Units (APBNs), and 10 female police officers assigned to protect the area from crime. Moreover, Navy ships and two Navy boats are stationed there constantly (Islam et al., 2021). However, the security measures of the government have been criticized by different human rights organizations. They have complained that Bhasan Char Island is a kind of jail for the Rohingya people. The government's plans will invade their privacy, and the place is like a detention center in the name of security (Hossain & Janmyr, 2022).

4.4 Healthcare

All the medical facilities have been arranged on Bhasan Char keeping in mind that the area is isolated from the mainland. Four community clinics and two hospitals have been established which can treat serious illnesses. Accommodation facilities with high standards have been arranged for the doctors. The hospitals and clinics have adequate medicine storage capacity. Moreover, in case of emergency, speedboats, helipads, and helicopter facilities are in place to transport patients to the city center for better treatment (Islam et al., 2021). Although the government has claimed all kinds of medical facilities are available on the island, this fact is arguable, as some human rights agencies have expressed doubts about the capacity of the hospitals. During the recent diarrhea outbreak on the island, hospitals were unable to accommodate all the patients and there is news that a number of children died as a result. Moreover, according to experts, going to the mainland in an emergency—a two-hour journey by boat from the island—is not a feasible option (Ganguly, 2021).

4.5 Freedom of Movement

Residents of the Bhasan Char Island have claimed that they can move anywhere inside the project area. They can even go to the sea to catch fish. As it seems in different documents, the island is not that small, and it is not possible for a person to cross the whole island by walking. For religious purposes they have mosques and community halls where they can perform any religious activities and can celebrate festivals (Islam et al., 2021). The isolation of the island has been a triggering point for many human rights organizations. They think isolated areas and the permission system to leave the area is a violation of freedom of movement rights. Many international authorities complained that the relocation act is forceful, not voluntary, which is a breach of human rights regulations (Hossain & Janmyr, 2022). There is a news that several Rohingyas has been detained by the Bangladesh Navy because they wanted to escape the island. After the relocation began in December 2020, within the first three months of 2021, almost 84 Rohingyas were rescued on the way to Chittagong and detained by the Bangladesh Navy. Though no exact official number has been published by the authorities, according to Rohingya residents in Bhasan Char, almost two to three hundred Rohingyas have tried to escape the island. Among the escapees, teenagers and young males are predominant. According to the director of the project, Commodore Rashed Sattar, the ambitious young generation are using their connections in Thailand, Malaysia, and the Middle East and are trying to move there for better opportunities (Soma, 2021). The government of Bangladesh has claimed that the shifting of Rohingyas to Bhasan Char Island will be voluntary. However, there are several reports that government officials tried to use threats and cash incentives to convince the Rohingyas to move to the island. Human Rights Watch interviewed 12 families whose names suddenly appeared on the list for relocation, and found they did not give any consent to relocate to Bhasan Char. Different humanitarian organizations complained that Rohingyas are offered incentives like priority during repartition to Myanmar, medicine for specialized illnesses, and even opportunities to settle in another country (McPherson & Paul, 2020).

5 The Question of Sustainability on Bhasan Char Island

The term "sustainability" has different meanings in different contexts. Sustainability can be connected to environmental, economic, and social dimensions. In the case of Rohingya relocation to Bhasan Char Island, environmental sustainability refers to the island's stability and safety during natural calamities, economic sustainability refers to sustainable livelihood and economic activities for Rohingyas, and social sustainability refers to the human development elements such as education, poverty alleviation, skill, and experience (Islam et al., 2021). The Government of Bangladesh considers Bhasan Char as a much better and more sustainable location for the Rohingyas. However, global organizations like Human Rights Watch and Amnesty International have consistently expressed concerns in declaring Rohingya relocation to Bhasan Char Island as sustainable (Islam & Siddika, 2022). The major reason behind these concerns is that Bangladesh is a country vulnerable to global warming and climate change. The results of climate change, like rising sea levels, changing precipitation patterns, and constant storm surges will affect the island areas of the country before the mainland. In fact, in the last 120 years, the rate of extreme storms in Bangladesh has increased by 20%. Bhasan Char is located at the focal point of Ganges–Brahmaputra–Meghna River system. Therefore, the area is more vulnerable to disasters like landslides, flash floods, and cyclones compared to other parts of the country (Banerjee, 2020). Bhasan Char Island is a newly formed island, and because of these sustainability issues, the United Nations and other humanitarian groups have declared the island as unfit for habitation. However, the Government of Bangladesh arranged all the facilities in the island and finally convinced the United Nations of its suitability. In 2021, the United Nations and Bangladeshi government signed an agreement to work together to provide the relocated population a good living standard (Aljazeera, 2021).

5.1 The Bangladeshi Government Response

In the question of sustainability, the government of Bangladesh has presented several justifications to support their relocation decision. The government assured the safety of the island and claimed that the strong infrastructure on the island will protect it from any kind of disasters. According to the government, the Rohingya camps in the Cox's Bazar district are becoming unlivable. The overpopulation problem of those congested camps is preventing the authorities from helping the Rohingyas with healthcare and educational facilities. Bhasan Char Island is a spacious place with all-new facilities, and the Rohingya community can enjoy a good standard of life on the island. Another justification is the environmental degradation in Cox's Bazar. This ecologically crucial area is degrading because of population pressure. Therefore, the Rohingya relocation to Bhasan Char Island will save the country from environmental degradation (Islam & Siddika, 2022). And finally, increasing criminal acts and the growing tension between the host community and displaced community is increasingly alarming for the authorities (Afrin, 2022).

5.2 *Rohingya Community Response*

As of May 2022, almost 28,000 Rohingyas have already relocated to Bhasan Char Island (Hasan, 2022). At first, the Rohingya population did not like the idea of relocation because they were afraid of physical and social isolation (Shahpur & Wardani, 2022). The relocated Rohingyas have now expressed mixed feelings. A leading German News Agency named Deutsche Welle has interviewed some Rohingyas from Bhasan Char, and reported that some of the Rohingya said unnamed Bangladeshi authorities had promised them a monthly stipend if they agreed to live on Bhasan Char. Government officials denied the news entirely. Some of the Rohingyas complained about the lack of emergency medical facilities (Islam & Siddika, 2022). On the other hand, a research team from the University of Dhaka interviewed several Rohingya and found that relocated Rohingyas were satisfied, as they had received good accommodations, less-crowded spaces, and much needed security (The Business Standard Sunday, 2023). Foreign diplomats from the USA, UK, France, Germany, and European Union have visited the island and reported that Rohingyas are happy on the island due to the secure environment. In 2021, the UNHCR also gave a positive report of living conditions on Bhasan Char Island (Islam & Siddika, 2022).

5.3 *International Organizations' Response*

The International Humanitarian Organization (IHO) was not so happy about the decision to relocate Rohingyas to Bhasan Char Island. One of the major reasons for this dissatisfaction is the isolation of the island from the mainland. The communication between the mainland and the island was only via waterways. Secondly, the newly risen island has a high risk of sinking again (Hossain & Jannyr, 2022). Many donor organizations became reluctant to donate toward this relocation process (Loy, 2022). However, the United Nations ultimately agreed to the relocation process and emphasized that the relocation process should be voluntary. Though some positive points of views emerged, the project still bears some controversy among the stakeholders (Afrin, 2022). Another major concern that the international organizations showed regarding this relocation is freedom of movement. Some organizations stated that Bhasan Char Island is a big prison for the displaced Rohingya population, and they have no right to move according to their will (Hossain & Janmyr, 2022).

6 What Lies Ahead?

The Government of Bangladesh has made several attempts for Rohingya repatriation through negotiation. In 2019, UNHCR and China tried to mediate and start the repatriation process. Bangladesh worked according to the agreement and provided IDs of the Rohingyas. All the effort Bangladesh put into Rohingya repatriation went in vain, as no Rohingya were able to return to Myanmar. Since February 2021, Myanmar has been ruled by the military, which makes the repatriation process more difficult. Therefore, Bangladesh should accept the fact that Rohingyas are not a temporary problem anymore (Ahmed & Khan, 2022). The safety and sustainability of Bhasan Char Island may represent the future of Rohingyas in Bangladesh. Geologically, Bhasan Char Island is located at Meghna Estuary. Per year the river carries almost 1.7 billion tons of sediment. With this huge amount of sediment, the area of the island is gradually getting larger. Since 2018 there is no sign of erosion on the island, which proves that the island is stable. The island is completely safe during tidal surges up to 6.8 m in height (Gazi et al., 2022). In 2007, cyclone Amphan was the strongest cyclone after cyclone Sidr, and during Amphan Bhasan Char Island was completely safe. All the evidence proves that geologically the island is sustainable. Now, Bangladesh must think about economic and social sustainability of the Rohingyas on Bhasan Char Island. The Bangladeshi government tried to provide all kinds of economic options to the Rohingyas. Yet the isolation of the island from the mainland will obstruct the flourishing of their livelihood (Islam et al., 2021). The relocation of the Rohingyas is not a good permanent option (Rahman, 2022). In future, it will be best for the Rohingyas to return to their home country safely, with respect and recognition (Islam et al., 2021).

7 Conclusion

The newly relocated Rohingyas may be getting better facilities than their previous refugee camps in Cox's Bazar, yet the international community is not fully doubt-free about the relocation process. To make the Rohingyas more comfortable and confident about living in Bhasan Char, Bangladesh should maintain the life standard in the island that the government has promised. A growing population can provide a challenge in maintaining all the facilities on the island. In that case, long-term planning is needed. Bangladesh can follow the impoverishment risks and reconstruction model (IRR), a conceptual tool which helps to prevent impoverishment during resettlement. The model focuses on eight major problem sectors which a community faces during the resettlement. The major sectors of this model are landlessness, joblessness, homelessness, marginalization, food insecurity, increased mortality, loss of access to common property, and social disarticulation. The model provides a framework for resettlement and a guideline to fight the problems based on equity, human rights, and social justice (Vivoda et al., 2017). To build a sustainable community on Bhasan Char, it is necessary to increase financial resilience and reduce aid dependency (Hossain, 2020).

References

Afrin, I. (2022). Rohingya refugee future: Narratives from history, memory, & relocation. In I. A. Hussain (Ed.), *Rohingya camp narratives: Tales from the 'lesser roads' traveled* (pp. 273–297). Springer Nature.

Ahmed, K., & Khan, N. I. (2022). *The Rohingya crisis and the two-faced god of Janus: What lies ahead*. Lexington Books.

Ahmed, K., & Mohiuddin, H. (2019). *The Rohingya crisis: Analyses, responses, and peacebuilding avenues*. Lexington Books.

Ahmed, S., Simmons, W. P., Chowdhury, R., & Huq, S. (2021). The sustainability–peace nexus in crisis contexts: How the Rohingya escaped the ethnic violence in Myanmar, but are trapped into environmental challenges in Bangladesh. *Sustainability Science, 16*(4), 1201–1213. https://doi.org/10.1007/s11625-021-00955-6

Associated Press. (2021, October 11). UN, Bangladesh sign deal to aid Rohingya relocated to island. *Aljazeera*. https://www.aljazeera.com/news/2021/10/11/un-bangladesh-deal-rohingya-refugees-bhasan-char-island-aid

Banerjee, S. (2020). From Cox's Bazar to Bhasan Char: An assessment of Bangladesh's relocation plan for displaced Rohingyas. *Observer Research Foundation Brief, 357*, 1–16.

Broadbent, R., Cacciattolo, M., & Carpenter, C. (2007). A tale of two communities: Refugee relocation in Australia. *Australian Journal of Social Issues, 42*(4), 581–601.

Carney, T. M. (2021). China's three Gorges Dam: Development, displacement, and degradation. *Nebraska Anthropologist, 29*, 20–27. https://digitalcommons.unl.edu/cgi/viewcontent.cgi?article=1193&context=nebanthro

Children on the Edge. (n.d.). *Education for Rohingya refugee children on Bhasan Char Island*. Children on the Edge. Retrieved August 28, 2023, from https://www.childrenontheedge.org/bhasanchar.html

Ganguly, M. (2021, June 30). Rohingya refugees facing medical crisis on Bhasan Char. *Asian Times*. https://www.hrw.org/news/2021/06/30/rohingya-refugees-facing-medical-crisis-bhasan-char

Gazi, M., Kamal, A., Uddin, M., Bhuiyan, M., & Rahman, M. (2022). The stability and suitability of the Bhasan Char Island as an accommodation for the forcibly displaced Myanmar nationals (FDMN). *Sustainability, 14*(2), 747. https://doi.org/10.3390/su14020747

Habib, M. R. (2023). Rohingya refugee–host community conflicts in Bangladesh: Issues and insights from the "field." *Development in Practice, 33*(3), 317–327. https://doi.org/10.1080/09614524.2022.2090516

Hasan, K. (2022, May 25). UNHCR's Grandi urges redoubled support for Rohingya refugees, host communities in Bangladesh. *UNHCR*. https://www.unhcr.org/news/news-releases/unhcrs-grandi-urges-redoubled-support-rohingya-refugees-host-communities

Hasan, R. (2019, October 18). Rohingya settlements: 8,000 acres of forests razed. *The Daily Star*. https://www.thedailystar.net/frontpage/news/rohingya-settlements-8000-acres-forests-razed-1815400

Heggelund, G. (2006). Resettlement programmes and environmental capacity in the Three Gorges Dam project. *Development and Change, 37*(1), 179–199. https://doi.org/10.1111/j.0012-155X.2006.00474.x

Hossain, I. (2020). After humanitarianism: Bangladesh's evolving Rohingya policy. *German Institute of Global and Area Studies (GIGA)*, 1–12.

Hossain, M. S., & Janmyr, M. (2022, May 12). Bhasan Char: Prison Island or paradise? Are Rohingya refugees being denied their right to freedom of movement? *Lacuna Magazine: Migration.* https://lacuna.org.uk/migration/bhasan-char-rohingya-refugees-right-to-freedom-of-movement/

Imtiaz, S. (2018). Ecological impact of Rohingya refugees on forest resources: Remote sensing analysis of vegetation cover change in Teknaf Peninsula in Bangladesh. *Ecocycles, 4*(1), 16–19. https://doi.org/10.19040/ecocycles.v4i1.89

Islam, M. R., Islam, M. T., Alam, M. S., Hussain, M., & Haque, M. M. (2021). Is Bhasan Char Island, Noakhali district in Bangladesh a sustainable place for the relocated Rohingya displaced people? An empirical study. *SN Social Sciences, 1*, 277. https://doi.org/10.1007/s43545-021-00281-9

Islam, M. D., & Siddika, A. (2022). Implications of the Rohingya relocation from Cox's Bazar to Bhasan Char, Bangladesh. *International Migration Review, 56*(4), 1195–1205. https://doi.org/10.1177/01979183211064829

Islam, Md. M., Barman, A., Khan, M. I., Goswami, G. G., Siddiqi, B., & Mukul, S. A. (2022). Sustainable livelihood for displaced Rohingyas and their resilience at Bhasan Char in Bangladesh. *Sustainability, 14*(10), 6374. https://doi.org/10.3390/su14106374

Jackson, S., & Sleigh, A. (2000). Resettlement for China's Three Gorges Dam: Socio-economic impact and institutional tensions. *Communist and Post-Communist Studies, 33*(2), 223–241. https://doi.org/10.1016/S0967-067X(00)00005-2

Judith, A., & Chidiebere, O. (2022). Land allocation and conflicts among refugees and host communities, a case of Nakivale and Oruchinga refugee settlements in western Uganda. *International Journal of Research and Innovation in Social Science, 6*(8), 132–138. https://www.rsisinternational.org/journals/ijriss/Digital-Library/volume-6-issue-12/132-138.pdf

Labib, S. M., Hossain, N., & Patwary, S. H. (2018). Environmental cost of refugee crisis: Case study of Kutupalong Balukhali Rohingya camp site: A remote sensing approach. In *26th Annual GIS Research UK Conference.* https://doi.org/10.13140/RG.2.2.14086.22085

Loy, I. (2022, April 5). Q&A: The aid policy 'limbo' on Bangladesh's refugee island. *The New Humanitarian.* https://www.thenewhumanitarian.org/interview/2022/04/05/aid-policy-limbo-bangladesh-refugee-island-bhasan-char#:~:text=Donor%20reluctance%20to%20fund%20aid,of%20a%20leading%20Bangladeshi%20NGO

Macdonald, G., Mekker, I., & Mooney, L. (2023, April 12). Conflict dynamics between Bangladeshi host communities and Rohingya refugees. *United States Institute of Peace Special Report*, 1–19.

McDonald-Wilmsen, B., Gifford, S. M., Webster, K., Wiseman, J., & Casey, S. (2009). Resettling refugees in rural and regional Australia: Learning from recent policy and program initiatives. *Australian Journal of Public Administration, 68*(1), 97–111. https://doi.org/10.1111/j.1467-8500.2008.00611.x

McPherson, P., & Paul, R. (2020, December 3). Rohingya coerced into going to remote island, refugees and aid workers say. *Reuters.* https://www.reuters.com/article/us-bangladesh-rohingya-idUSKBN28D0RQ

Rahman, S. A. (2022, January 14). Relocated Rohingyas finding a better life in Bhasan Char. *Independent Australia.* https://independentaustralia.net/life/life-display/relocated-rohingyas-finding-a-better-life-in-bhashan-char,15934

Sadat al Sajib, S. M., Islam, S. A. M. Z., & Sohad, M. K. N. (2022). Rohingya influx and socio-environmental crisis in southeastern Bangladesh. *The International Journal of Community and Social Development, 4*(1), 89–103.https://doi.org/10.1177/25166026211067604

Shahpur, T., & Wardani, A. A. (2022). Relocation, climate change and finding a place of belonging for Rohingya refugees. *Journal of Peacebuilding & Development, 17*(3), 274–288. https://doi.org/10.1177/15423166221129487

The Business Standard Sunday. (2023, June 25). Study finds Bhasan Char perfectly livable. *The Business Standard Sunday.* https://www.tbsnews.net/rohingya-crisis/study-finds-bhasan-char-perfectly-liveable-211897

The Rohingya Post. (2021, July 6). *Bhasan Char Map.* Retrieved from https://www.rohingyapost.com/report-an-island-jail-in-the-middle-of-the-sea-bangladeshs-relocation-of-rohingya-refugees-to-bhasan-char/bhasan-char-map/

United News of Bangladesh. (2017, October 29). Rohingya camps: Deforestation takes back seat to humanitarian concerns. *Dhaka Tribune.* https://archive.dhakatribune.com/bangladesh/nation/2017/10/29/rohingya-camps-deforestation-takes-back-seat-humanitarian-concerns

Vivoda, V., Owen, J., & Kemp, D. (2017). *Applying the impoverishment risks and reconstruction (IRR) model to involuntary resettlement in the global mining sector.* Centre for Social Responsibility in Mining. http://www.miningresettlement.org/media/downloads/IRR_Workbook_UQ_Consortium.pdf

Soma, L. J. (2021, July 19). *Why are Rohingya refugees attempting an escape from Bhasan Char?* [Video]. WION, YouTube. https://www.youtube.com/watch?v=W8looPSlfF4

Xi, J., & Hwang, S. S. (2011). Relocation stress, coping, and sense of control among resettlers resulting from China's Three Gorges Dam Project. *Social Indicators Research, 104*(3), 507–522. https://doi.org/10.1007/s11205-010-9758-5

Yesmin, S. (2016). Policy toward Rohingya refugees: A comparative analysis of Bangladesh, Malaysia, and Thailand. *Journal of the Asiatic Society of Bangladesh, 61*(1), 71–100. http://cgsdu.org/wp-content/uploads/2019/03/4-H_883.pdf

Chapter 18
Civic Education as Peacebuilding in the Rohingya Refugee Camps

Rafa Nailah Sattar

Abstract This chapter seeks to investigate the ways education can catalyze social cohesion or further conflict in the Rohingya refugee camps of Bangladesh. While research has identified the value of peacebuilding education to mediate tensions between the host Bangladeshi and Rohingya refugee communities, it has yet to explore the delivery of such interventions. We analyze how teachers can impede or foster peacebuilding processes in the Rohingya refugee camps, through a review of the existing literature. This chapter will alternatively apply the conceptual framework of critical design theory to model how peacebuilding education can be feasibly delivered in the Rohingya refugee camps.

1 Introduction

In Cox's Bazar, Bangladesh, the Rohingya refugee and host communities have begun to cross the borderlines of conflict. Before relations reach a violent point of no return, this chapter sets out to interrogate how education may contribute to conflict and peacebuilding in the region. The Bangladesh government advocates for the eventual repatriation of all Rohingya refugees to Myanmar. In the host country itself, Rohingya refugees are stigmatized as a national security concern. Accordingly, the government does not aim to cultivate a sense of belonging or civic duty in Rohingya refugees. This position has guided the government's approach to delivering education in the camps. Nonetheless, according to a UNHCR survey, less than 30% of Rohingya refugees are willing to repatriate (Ullah, 2011, p. 155). Young Rohingya refugees, especially those who were born and raised in the camps, are a testament to the formation of a new group identity. Efforts to impede their integration have frequently put the Rohingya refugee community in tension with the host community. According to UNICEF (2019, p. 17), educational interventions in the Rohingya refugee camps aim to "build their identity and make them part of the solution," encapsulating the purpose of citizenship and civic education. Levinson (2011, p. 280) defines citizenship as

R. N. Sattar (✉)
Columbia University, New York, USA
e-mail: rafa.sattar@columbia.edu

K. Ahmed and Md. R. Islam (eds.), *Understanding the Rohingya Displacement*,
International Perspectives on Migration, https://doi.org/10.1007/978-981-97-1424-7_18

"the meanings, rights, and obligations of membership in publics, as well as the forms of agency and modalities of participation implicated by such membership." This frames the approach we take to applying civic and citizenship education in the Rohingya refugee context. Levinson (2011, p. 284) further describes how citizenship education defines legitimate expressions of "participation as (democratic) citizens." Citizenship education can thus drive students to collectively work toward a better world or passively accept the status quo.

The study will particularly apply the concept of critical design to examine how civic education in Kutupalong Refugee Camp can empower Rohingya refugee students to re-envision possibilities for their futures. The literature has yet to explore the delivery of civic education through the medium of interactions in a dual-teacher system as used in the Rohingya refugee camps. The dual-teacher system is an unprecedented, unique means for Rohingya refugees and Bangladesh host communities to come into contact despite policies seeking to segregate the Rohingya from the host community. Led by a Bangladesh teacher and a Rohingya facilitator in a single informal classroom, this approach can make tensions hyper-visible or provide students with a model for peaceful coexistence. This research chapter poses the question: How can small openings for civic education emerge through critical design praxis between Bangladesh host community teachers and Rohingya facilitators in temporary learning centers (TLCs) across Rohingya refugee camps in Bangladesh?

To interrogate this question, the chapter will begin with an overview of the methods used to consolidate the literature. Secondly, the chapter provides a contextual overview of the Rohingya refugee crisis and relations between the Bangladesh host and Rohingya refugee communities. Third, the chapter will examine the scale of existing educational interventions. The chapter will analyze macro-level and internal classroom challenges to the delivery of educational interventions in Rohingya refugee camps, and will apply a critical lens to determine how host community teachers can reproduce and exaggerate external conflict. Fourth, the chapter will consider the value and feasibility of peacebuilding education and global civic education in the refugee camps through an analysis of the existing Learning Competency Framework Approach (LCFA) used across the Rohingya refugee camps. Fifth, the chapter considers the alternative incorporation of critical design practices to deliver meaningful civic education in the camps. The chapter concludes with implications for further research on how the relationship between host community teachers and Rohingya facilitators can be leveraged to effectively deliver civic education through teachers' training and best practices in the classroom.

2 Methodology

The methods used to consolidate the literature involved a Boolean search on academic databases (i.e., Columbia Universities Online Catalog and Google Scholar) using the search terms "Rohingya," "education," and "Bangladesh." This initial search produced more than 12,700 results. This presented a holistic but unwieldy overview of the state of education in Kutupalong. The search terms were then narrowed to specify "civic education" and "peace education" to delve into the educational subfields. This respectively returned 136 and 173 results. We used the following criteria to determine which articles addressed the delivery, or lack thereof, of civic education in the Rohingya refugee camps:

- Focus on mediation of conflict between the host and refugee communities
- Focus on themes of belonging and global citizenship education
- Direct mention of civic education, citizenship education, human rights education, or history education
- Analysis of curriculum delivered in the camps.

This selection process consolidated 16 articles and books for review.

3 Contextual Overview and Relations Between the Host and Refugee Communities

The Rohingya have been named "the most persecuted minority in the world" by the United Nations, condemned to statelessness and forced to flee genocide in Myanmar to neighboring Bangladesh (Malik, 2020). The Bangladesh government's policies are guided under the premise of the repatriation of the Rohingya to Myanmar (Ahmed & Mohiuddin, 2019, p. xxviii). Meanwhile, the Myanmar government claims that the Rohingya are not Myanmar's citizens. Restrictions on education rights of the Rohingya in Myanmar have resulted in a literacy rate of only 1% among Rohingya children (Ahmed & Mohiuddin, 2019, p. 52). Ongoing political upheaval in Myanmar makes prospects for the repatriation of the Rohingya unlikely, where the genocide is ongoing (Human Rights Watch, 2022).

Although much of the literature has examined relations between the Rohingya and Myanmar communities, amid a refugee crisis with no end in sight, greater attention must be paid to the immediate context of Rohingya refugee and host community relations. While a pattern of Rohingya migration to Bangladesh goes as far back as 1977, most of the refugees had been repatriated before 2017. In August 2017, an exodus of nearly a million Rohingya refugees took place to Cox's Bazar as the Myanmar military launched a genocidal campaign against the Rohingya, and no repatriation has taken place since (Ahmed & Mohiuddin, 2019, p. 95). Interviewees from the host community have described feeling a sense of compassion and Muslim solidarity during the onset of the crisis in 2017 (Ahmed & Mohiuddin, 2019, p. xxviii). Religious leaders from the host community played a critical role in empowering the host community to welcome and support the Rohingya refugees (Olney et al., 2019, p. 13). The Bangladesh host community received Rohingya refugees based on an ethos of charity and compassion, but social cohesion and trust have sharply broken down due to a resource crisis, a rise of criminality and extremism, and clashes in social values. Researchers have notably observed a concomitant decrease in interactions between the host and refugee communities over the years due to government restrictions on the mobility of Rohingya refugees (Olney et al., 2019, p. 6).

The center of conflict between Rohingya refugees and the host community is perceived inequity in the distribution of resources. Many in the host community expressed concerns regarding competition for wages with the refugee community. Locals have even expressed grievances regarding fair democratic representation for the host community due to the "intense involvement" of their elected representatives in the Rohingya refugee camps (Ahmed & Mohiuddin, 2019, p. 259).

Rohingya refugees have also been stereotyped as vulnerable to criminality and extremism. Local host communities have attributed a rise in drug trafficking to the Rohingya refugees. Human and sex trafficking are also increasing day by day (Ahmed & Mohiuddin, 2019, p. 104). An interviewee even described how the Rohingya are "always searching for a way to get a chance," in doing so reinforcing the rationale for the genocide in Myanmar (Ahmed & Mohiuddin, 2019, p. 258). Locals interviewed from the host community cited the "rude" behavior and lack of "awareness about family planning" of Rohingya refugees (Ahmed & Mohiuddin, 2019, p. 258). This may present a potential opening to frame the need for civic education to instill community-building moral values among Rohingya refugees in Bangladesh.

Such tensions have led to an increase in xenophobia among the local host community. Some have expressed fears of the mobilization of extremist groups and the Arakan Rohingya Salvation Army in Bangladesh. There is a sense of irreconcilability with the Rohingya's conservative interpretation of Islam and a fear of being outnumbered (Ahmed & Mohiuddin, 2019, p. 130). Nonetheless, the historic coexistence of Rohingya refugees with the host community in Cox's Bazar since 1977 may provide hope for harmony despite escalating tensions.

The paucity of long-term conflict may facilitate receptivity to civic education programs between the two communities. Olney et al. (2019, p. 8) has specifically advocated for the introduction of separate civic education programs for host and refugee children to ensure that the values of civic education are taught, while children cultivate separate civic identities. This would be in line with the underlying government stance for the repatriation of the Rohingya to Myanmar. Civic education can provide an opportunity to deconstruct the seeds of conflict that are emerging in real-time between the refugee and host communities.

4 Overview of Education Interventions in the Rohingya Refugee Camps of Bangladesh

Amid stagnant prospects for repatriation, the education of Rohingya refugee children has languished. In fact, 80% of Rohingya refugees are illiterate (Ullah & Chattoraj, 2018). Approximately, 60% of Rohingya refugees in Bangladesh since

2017 are children (Gjerløw et al., 2022). The Rohingya were heavily restricted from accessing education in Myanmar, which does not recognize them as citizens (Gjerløw et al., 2022). This has contributed to a lack of higher education even among older generations who may serve as teachers and mentors.

In Bangladesh, Rohingya refugees are prohibited from accessing formal schools both in the host community and refugee camps (Gjerløw et al., 2022). Since 2017, nongovernmental organizations have delivered nonformal educational interventions to Rohingya refugees through 700 temporary learning centers (TLCs). Rather than a formal or Bangladeshi curriculum, the TLCs use the Learning Competency Framework Approach (LCFA), a framework developed with NGO actors and technical experts. The largest funder of nonformal education programs is UNICEF, while the largest implementing partner is BRAC (Gjerløw et al., 2022).

In 2019, the Bangladesh government planned to deliver the Myanmar Curriculum Pilot (MCP) to provide formal education to Rohingya refugees (Rahman, 2020, p. 117). While the delivery of a formal curriculum is a step in the right direction, the MCP is framed under the premise that Rohingya refugees will return to Myanmar. Nonetheless, as Mansur (2020, p. 48) stresses, young Rohingya refugees are renegotiating their identities in relation to the host community. By predetermining their futures, the MCP does not provide space for the cultivation of civic identities in Bangladesh.

The delivery of the MCP has otherwise been stalled amid the COVID-19 pandemic. The Bangladesh government shut down the education sector in the refugee camps from 2020. TLCs adopting the LCFA have only begun to reopen as of March 2022 (Gjerløw et al., 2022).

5 External Challenges to Delivering Education in Rohingya Refugee Camps in Bangladesh

The government's plan to repatriate the Rohingya to Myanmar is reflected in their draconian educational policies. According to Foucault's theory of governmentality, the state conditions people to make decisions that ultimately align with a state's aims (Rodríguez-Gómez, 2022, p. 315). Through structural violence in education, the Bangladesh government seeks to obstruct the Rohingya from envisioning a long-term future for themselves in Bangladesh. The government regulates the claim to a right to education in the refugee camps through calculated terminology, lack of access to accreditation, and restrictions on language of instruction.

The Bangladesh government uses strategic labels to deprive the Rohingya of their rights in Bangladesh and in doing so frame the only possibility for their future in Myanmar. For instance, the informal schools Rohingya children attend are identified as "temporary learning centers" to reflect the government's position that the crisis is temporary (Bakali & Wasty, 2020, p. 7). Moreover, Rahman (2020, p. 65) describes how the Bangladesh government deliberately identifies the Rohingya as "forcibly displaced people" rather than refugees to legally shield the Bangladesh government from delivering formal education in the camps. The children Rahman (2020, p. 42) interviewed were also self-aware that the Bangladesh government was restricting their access to education due to their identity as Rohingya. This awareness can result in the children internalizing a sense of being less deserving due to their ethnic identity. Rahman (2020, p. 115) particularly cites how TLCs have had to be relabeled as "Child Play Areas" to receive government approval. In a literal sense, governmentality guides people toward a particular decision through "its aspirational, exploratory, and even playful quality" (Rodríguez-Gómez, 2022, p. 318). The playful focus of TLCs has in fact drawn parents and children to question the value of education and to ultimately stop attending and "wasting time" (Rahman & Husain, 2022, p. 6). By drawing the Rohingya to choose the limited future carved out for them, the Bangladesh government ultimately seeks to legitimize its stance for the repatriation of the Rohingya to Myanmar.

Moreover, the Bangladesh government prevents the Rohingya from seeing a future for themselves in Bangladesh through lack of educational accreditation. As Karim and Hussain (2019, p. 677) underscore, "the biggest obstacle" for any "long-term education program for refugees" is accreditation. The TLCs run with short-term goals of providing a learning-friendly space, while Rohingya students are banned from enrolling in government-accredited schools or sitting for board exams in Bangladesh (Karim & Hussain, 2019, p. 117). Rahman and Husain (2022, p. 7) also found that the TLCs do not provide certificates to Rohingya children. Barring the Rohingya from receiving any form of certification is a bid to ultimately prevent the Rohingya from integrating and competing for jobs with the host community. Lack of certification would further prevent Rohingya children from reintegrating into the Myanmar education system. As Williams (2004, p. 477) observes, this political maneuver prevents the Rohingya from "caring for themselves." The Bangladesh government did not consult with Rohingya parents during the development of the curriculum, which has further cultivated a culture of "mistrust" in the education system (Rahman & Husain, 2022, p. 6). While a Bangladesh government official acknowledges that the futures of the Rohingya are "breaking day by day," the government may condemn itself to a self-fulfilling prophecy (Rahman & Husain, 2022, p. 8). The Bangladesh government's efforts to block equitable access to education for Rohingya children will close off their futures in the Myanmar education system, as well.

The Bangladesh government's ban on the teaching of Bengali to Rohingya children has systematically legitimized their ostracization from the host community. As Karim and Hussain (2019, p. 618) highlight, thousands of Rohingya children have been born in Bangladesh due to the protracted nature of the crisis. Accordingly, Rohingya facilitators in TLCs have conveyed the demand for Rohingya children to learn Bengali in class (Rahman & Husain, 2022, p. 4). The government stance, however, is that the Rohingya do not need to learn Bengali because their national language is Burmese (Rahman & Husain, 2022, p. 4). Restricting the languages of instruction to English and Burmese has resulted in barriers around communication in the classroom due to lack of fluency in Burmese among most Rohingya and host community teachers. According to Rahman (2020, p. 115), such communication barriers are the primary reason why children drop out of TLCs.

Such structural restrictions on educational opportunities in the camps ultimately lead Rohingya children to lose hope for their academic futures in Bangladesh. By circumscribing the futures of the Rohingya, the Bangladesh government gives Rohingya children no choice but to envision a future for themselves indistinguishable from the state's aim to repatriate the Rohingya.

6 Internal Challenges to Delivering Education in Rohingya Refugee Camps in Bangladesh

Classroom practices in TLCs are a microcosm of the systemic exclusion of Rohingyas from educational opportunities in refugee camps across Bangladesh. Internal challenges such as lack of qualified teachers, scarcity of teachers' training, and oversized classrooms have resulted in mistrust between teachers and the Rohingya community.

A low threshold for recruitment of teachers has compromised the quality of instruction in the Rohingya refugee camps of Bangladesh. Due to low pay, it is especially difficult to attract qualified candidates for teaching positions (Khan & Kontinen, 2022, p. 7). Instead, Rahman and Husain (2022, p. 5) describes how recruited teachers reflect low competency in the subjects they teach and their skill in managing students' behavior. While Rohingya parents are satisfied with the quality of the curriculum, parents have expressed their lack of interest in sending their children to school due to deficient teaching quality. Rahman and Husain (2022, p. 8), describes how even Grade 4 students have procured teaching positions at the TLCs. During interviews, Rahman and Husain (2022, p. 8) recounted how teachers who taught English required a translator due to lack of proficiency in English.

Moreover, the dearth of pedagogical training and resources in the camps has hindered improvement in teaching quality. Training is not regularly offered in the camps due to lack of funding and time (Karim & Hussain, 2019, p. 681). Rahman (2020, p. 10) delineates how the implementation of separate trainings for Rohingya facilitators and Bengali teachers results in lack of coordination and conflict when the two are put in the same TLC classroom. When the Rohingya teacher is absent, the class on Burmese is also canceled due to the Bengali teachers' lack of language proficiency (Rahman & Husain, 2022, p. 6). Rahman cites how although the trainings are held once a month, the sessions are overcrowded and deliver too much information in a single session. Rohingya teachers themselves have stressed the need for more comprehensive teachers' training due to their own limited formal education. Significantly, an NGO worker attributed dropout rates to the lack of quality training (Rahman & Husain, 2022, p. 5).

High student–teacher ratios and limited teaching time have also prevented teachers from effectively addressing individual learning needs. In fact, Rahman and Husain (2022, p. 6) describes how four subjects are taught in under 90 min in the camps.

Due to scarcity of teachers, teachers are also assigned large classes with students of varying backgrounds and educational levels (Shohel, 2022, p. 115). This can ultimately be to the detriment of student confidence and interest in the subject matter and ultimately in the nonformal education space as a whole.

While Rohingya facilitators were the most outspoken in voicing concerns about teaching practices to researchers such as Rahman, the breakdown of trust between Rohingya refugee parents and teachers is reflective of the marginal role Rohingya facilitators play in the classroom. According to Rahman and Husain (2022, p. 5), transparency should be at the heart of every intervention for refugee communities to cultivate trust. Instead, language barriers and unwillingness on the part of host community teachers has prevented open communication in the Rohingya refugee camps. This is illustrated in the low attendance of TLCs compared to Madrassahs (Islamic Education Centers), which have traditionally been the only pathway for education in the Rohingya community (Karim & Hussain, 2019, p. 678). The sidelined concerns of both Rohingya TLC facilitators and parents are but an aftershock of the macro-level marginalization of the Rohingya.

7 How Teachers Reinforce External Challenges in the Classroom

The systemic discrimination against the Rohingya in refugee camps across Bangladesh percolates into the classroom. As Williams (2004, p. 474) underscores, teachers imbue a classroom with values and norms through their instruction, reinforcing a child's sense of identity. In managing classroom conflict, teachers implicitly instruct students on peace and civic education (Williams, 2004, p. 475). Teachers in TLCs reenact emerging hostility between the host and Rohingya communities through physical and verbal assaults on Rohingya students and subversion of Rohingya teachers.

Bullying of Rohingya students by TLC teachers reproduces emerging tensions between the Rohingya and host communities. Rahman (2020, p. 41) recounts numerous instances where teachers have beaten students "with sticks and other objects" for giving an incorrect answer or being absent. Such negative behavior would provide a license to others in class who would taunt the student (Rahman, 2020, p. 41). Rahman attributed the reason for the bullying, according to those he interviewed, to their refugee status. According to Rubin (2016, p. 659), local students in Guatemala otherize the indigenous population as underperforming, impoverished, and purposeless to imply that they do not share a common civic identity. This alienation aligns with the host teachers' racialization of Rohingya students as "illiterate, unfriendly, and rural" (Rahman, 2020, p. 42). Such violence would manifest in ruthless and irrational ways such as a child who described being beaten "when I smile a little." A child Rahman interviewed also described Bangladeshi teachers taunting and cursing at the Rohingya children. Many of these children described leaving the TLCs because of the beatings. As Rahman (2020, p. 42) writes, the negative perceptions of teachers cause children to lose their academic motivation. This comes as no surprise, as Williams (2004, p. 478) also highlights how conflict diminishes "willingness to learn." Violent pedagogical tactics thus emerge as politicized tools to sharpen the marginalization of the Rohingya in relation to the host community.

Such bullying in the classroom is even reflected in interactions between host community teachers and Rohingya facilitators. As Huhtala (2022, p. 9) describes, each TLC is assigned a host community teacher and a Rohingya facilitator. This dynamic intrinsically demands that the Rohingya facilitator answer to the Bangladeshi teacher. Rahman and Husain (2022, p. 5) further notes how the facilitator is paid less than the teacher. Such systemic inequities manifest in a "cold conflict" between Bengali teachers and Rohingya facilitators. In fact, Rohingya facilitators have described how Bengali teachers attempt to "dominate" and "show supremacy" over facilitators in the classroom (Prodip & Garnett, 2019, p. 213). Prodip and Garnett (2019, p. 213) describes a language facilitator who recounted how Bangladeshi teachers curse at and mistreat Rohingya facilitators. Teachers have demanded unquestioned obedience from facilitators, reasoning that they are "asylum seekers receiving the best support they can get from Bangladesh." Although students may feel most comfortable in addressing their concerns to Rohingya facilitators, such facilitators hold no leverage in the classroom. As Williams (2004, p. 477) describes, this is a form of "alienating violence," which robs a person of their right to psychological and intellectual integrity. By not treating Rohingya facilitators as intellectual equals, Bangladeshi teachers contribute to a culture of "competition and fear" in the classroom (Davies, 2005, p. 359). This climate ultimately rationalizes complacency toward aggression and hatred in mainstream society.

As Williams (2004, p. 478) indicates, substantial time will be needed to restore trust due to the internal projection of conflict through classroom practices in the Rohingya refugee camps. Until then, Rohingya refugees will continue being driven toward the violent, extreme margins of society in search of a "new or better order" (Davies, 2005, p. 358).

8 Value and Feasibility of Civic Education in the Rohingya Refugee Camps

According to Coster and Sigalas (2017, p. 3), citizenship education aims to promote coexistence by instilling in students the knowledge, skills, and values to give back to the society in which they live. While existing educational interventions in the Rohingya refugee camps have been rudimentary and curriculum-based, citizenship education has the potential to not only mitigate conflict between the Rohingya and host communities but empower Rohingya children to expand possibilities for their futures. Most significantly, civic education makes real the radical possibility of Rohingya refugees contributing as active members of Bangladeshi society.

Through civic education, Rohingya students, Rohingya facilitators, and host community teachers have the chance to co-construct an alternative civic identity for the Rohingya in the classroom. As Rubin (2016, p. 644) underscores, civic identity construction is a process taking place within a fixed setting such as a classroom. While the Rohingya and general Bangladeshi society do not share "historical memories," there is space for the host communities surrounding refugee camps and Rohingya refugees to reflect on "shifting social and political landscapes" due to the protracted nature of the crisis (Rubin, 2016, p. 645). According to Hossain (2021, p. 106), citizenship education is critical for Rohingya refugees to understand their roles as refugees both in and outside of Bangladesh. Through active participation, civic education cultivates skills in cross-cultural communication and conflict management by increasing consciousness of political, social, and economic structures (Hossain, 2021, p. 115). In doing so, civic education cultivates students who are "responsible, participatory, and justice-oriented" (Hossain, 2021, p. 115). Although Hossain (2021, p. 116) advocates for the development of a curriculum on civic education, this would prove difficult due to the need for government approval of curriculum. As Hossain (2021, p. 123) acknowledges, there is no sign that the Bangladesh government would promote citizenship education in the refugee camps anytime soon.

Instead, civic education practices can be integrated within the structure of the school itself by providing a forum for democratic practices such as deliberation without resorting to violence. According to Rubin (2016, p. 667), providing space for student and teacher voices can uncover insights needed to engage with the complex civic identities of students and create a new, hybrid civic identity. This is especially relevant for Rohingya refugee children, many of whom were born in and only know of Bangladesh as home. As Coster and Sigalas (2017, p. 24) highlights, school culture is critical to citizenship education. As Hossain (2021, p. 117) indicates, transforming school culture can introduce students to democratic participation and new ways to address local and global problems. Hossain (2021, p. 119) also cites how students problematically identify TLCs as places for "playing" rather than learning. A learning-focused curriculum both Rohingya children and parents value should be delivered by centering the agency and participation of Rohingya students in the classroom.

9 A Critique of Global Citizenship Education in the Rohingya Refugee Camps

Global citizenship education, as described by the United Nations, would provide children the skills to negotiate, solve problems, think critically, and ultimately resolve conflict without violence (Rubin, 2016, p. 640). The problematic root of global democratic citizenship education lies in its purported universality divorced from the local context of conflict zones. As Rubin (2016, p. 640) underscores, global democratic citizenship is inadequate in a setting where a person's sense of belonging is embedded in the positioning of their communities in an unjust power structure. According to Bajaj and Bartlett (2017, p. 27), global citizenship fails to account for forced migration experiences.

Nonetheless, as Mansur (2020, p. 35) stresses, a sense of belonging to a community is essential for the well-being of a refugee child. Social belonging is mediated through the relationship of an individual to the state, peers, and family (Meloni, 2019, pp. 453–454). While such dialogic encounters leave an impression on the self-image of Rohingya refugee children, Mansur (2020, p. 36) finds that children can originate their own sense of belonging even in the most unfavorable conditions.

Global citizenship emerges from a Western normative frame, which can preclude such alternative imaginings of civic belonging. As Pinson (2007, p. 345) makes clear, Palestinian students may connect more strongly with a local or even Muslim civic identity. In the same vein, Rohingya refugees and the neighboring host community may especially find common grounding in a Muslim civic identity. As Karim and Hussain (2019, p. 16) underscore, religious education has historically been the only means for Rohingya people to receive an education in Myanmar and is perhaps the only constant in their lives. According to Kamruzzaman et al., (2022, p. 1862), Rohingyas identify Islam as central to their individual and collective identity. The shared religious identity of the Bangladeshi neighboring host community and the Rohingya has the potential to serve as a common bridge. In fact, Bangladeshi religious leaders have advocated for civic education in the Rohingya refugee community to prevent extremism (Olney, 2019, p. 7).

The normative definitions of global citizenship, however, do not provide space for the local and the religious. Rohingya refugee children must instead be given the space to examine their relationship with the state and cultivate a meaningful civic identity that will catalyze their drive to enrich and resolve conflict in society.

10 Analysis and Application of LCFA

In October 2017, a working group composed of representatives from international nongovernmental organizations, the government of Bangladesh, and curriculum experts from Bangladesh and Myanmar produced the Learning Competency Framework Approach as an alternative, nonformal curriculum for Rohingya refugees settled in Bangladesh (Shohel, 2022, p. 117). The LCFA was drafted over two workshops in 2017 and further revised based on recommendations from teachers, frontline workers, Rohingya children's parents, and Rohingya children. Many Rohingya parents in other studies have contradicted this, stressing that they were not consulted during curriculum development. With fluctuating attendance rates in the TLCs and a constantly developing legal landscape for the delivery of education in the camps, the Rohingya parents consulted with in 2017 may not be representative. The Bangladesh Ministry of Education with technical assistance from UNICEF launched the LCFA through TLCs to deliver education to children up to age 14 (Shohel, 2022, p. 117).

Five learning levels are incorporated into the LCFA including: Pre-primary, Grades 1–2, Grades 3–5, Grades 6–8, and Grades 9–10.

Citizenship education is incorporated into the LCFA in the following ways: life skills from pre-primary–Grade 8 and global citizenship education from Grades 9–10. At the pre-primary level, the goals of citizenship education are captured under a learning competency seeking to foster the self-esteem and confidence of children through individual and group participation. At the Grades 1–2 level, citizenship education is conveyed under a competency seeking to cultivate a child's problem-solving and decision-making skills. At the Grades 3–5 level, social science is introduced toward unpacking "institutions of the social environment" and promoting values such as community, diversity, and tolerance (LCFA, 2019, p. 31). At the Grades 6–8 Level, "civic competencies" and "democratic processes" are particularly identified toward analyzing "interdependent relationships among people and institutions" (LCFA, 2019, p. 38). Finally, the Grades 9–10 level references "global citizenship" as a goal toward fostering debate on macro-level issues such as "peace and human diversity" and "critical local issues" (LCFA, 2019, p. 51). According to an interview conducted with Dr. Kawser Ahmed, these learning competencies are at a pilot phase and are otherwise not being implemented on a wide scale across TLCs due to government restrictions (Dr. Kawser Ahmed, personal communication, April 28, 2023). Notably, there is no reference to religious education in the LCFA despite the central role of religion in Rohingya culture. This again reflects how removed the LCFA is from the realities of life for the Rohingya and elucidates why parents lack trust in the LCFA.

According to Bayezid (2023, p. 56), strengths of the LCFA are the "top priority" given to teachers' professional development and social cohesion. Teachers' professional development is centered on developing competency in content, child protection, pedagogy, and curriculum development (LCFA, 2019, p. 51). The proposed adoption of reflective teacher groups could provide a vital opportunity to cultivate "small openings" (Bekerman & Zembylas, 2012, p. 19) between Rohingya facilitators and host teachers. Moreover, Bayezid (2023, p. 57) describes how the LCFA will "provide certificates and facilitate the transition of graduates into the formal system." None of these aims have been realized in practice.

In principle, Devonald et al., (2021, p. 37) describe how the LCFA sought to promote social cohesion through "transformative action." In reality, depriving the Rohingya of their human rights in the refugee camps prevents the delivery of "meaningful" human rights and civic education (Devonald et al., 2021, p. 28). The launch of the Myanmar Curriculum Pilot was indefinitely paused, and all TLCs were shuttered during the COVID-19 pandemic (Devonald et al., 2021, p. 34). TLCs only reopened in 2022. Advanced levels in the LCFA have also yet to receive government approval (Devonald et al., 2021, p. 37). Far removed from the goals of the LCFA on civic education, the education delivered ultimately reinforces a "confined," nonexistent future in the camps for Rohingya refugee children (Devonald et al., 2021, p. 38).

11 All Play and No Rigor in TLCs

To get around government policies, many NGOs have delivered the LCFA through TLCs. While TLCs have been described as cost-effective and efficient in theory, the centers in practice have not been scalable for demographics such as adolescents and young girls. For adolescents, the TLCs do not provide life skills training. For girls, the TLCs are not adapted to the highly conservative nature of the community (Ahmed & Mohiuddin, 2019, p. 260). The Humanitarian Play Lab (HPL) model is a particular iteration of TLCs in the camps.

The Humanitarian Play Lab is an education intervention to foster play-based learning for Rohingya children aged 0–6 years. Early-child development scholars have described play-based learning as an ideal way to promote learning, native language literacy, social-emotional learning, and creativity for students. The model laudably centers localization and gives Rohingya children a platform to make meaning of their own experiences. Nonetheless, by solely framing the curriculum based on Rohingya culture, the HPL model cultivates a classroom environment trapped in the past, presupposing their repatriation to Myanmar.

By teaching Rohingya values and culture, HPLs seek to cultivate the psychosocial well-being of Rohingya children and prevent radicalization. HPLs are led by a local young Rohingya woman identified as a "playleader," who conducts sessions in Rohingya and draws upon traditional Rohingya oral folk rhymes, folk tales, and traditional games and sports (Iqbal et al., 2022, p. 2). The physical layout of an HPL is designed to be child-friendly, with as the incorporation of wall decorations and bamboo platforms, toward helping Rohingya refugee children manage their trauma through a creative outlet (Baidya, 2020, p. 103). While host community children are welcome to join the sessions, BRAC has given leverage to the Rohingya to design the layout of the HPL centers based on their culture.

Despite a focus on localization, the HPL model adopts a problem-solving approach by seeking to address the immediate problems of radicalization and emotional trauma among Rohingya refugee youth rather than structural factors in the camps contributing to these issues. Positive peace would require the absence of structural and cultural violence (Bajaj, 2019, p. 66). This is not reflected in the HPL model, which fails to empower Rohingya students to interrogate and resist systemic violence in the camps. A truly critical approach to education in the camps would instead question the systemic stigmatization of the Rohingya refugee identity and center the experiences of both the Rohingya refugee and host communities.

The HPL model does not challenge traditional hierarchies of power in the camps. Most fathers of Rohingya refugee children in a study described how "play is not necessary," instead stressing the importance of acquiring life skills, formal education, and religious studies (Baidya et al., 2020, p. 2). The HPL model is thus not accepted as an essential form of instruction by Rohingya refugee parents. The "local turn" in peacebuilding would rethink "authority, rights, and redistribution" by empowering community stakeholders to lead the development of curriculum (Ginty, 2013, p. 769). Notably, the HPL model does not address any of the skills that Rohingya refugee fathers value. This is likely due to the government's stranglehold on the delivery of education in the camps. To uphold local agency, the HPL model must give Rohingya refugees the chance to confront forms of structural violence that aim to circumscribe their livelihoods (Ginty, 2013, p. 770). The integration of forms of education valued by Rohingya parents into the HPL model would go further than centering a romanticized vision of Rohingya culture. Even colonial interventions have strategically used the local focus to co-opt communities as in need of saving "from themselves" (Ginty, 2013, p. 771). The absence of religious references in the HPL model may reflect the stigmatization of the Rohingya as being inclined to radicalization, a form of cultural violence. By embodying a truly "local turn," the HBL model would reclaim the autonomy of Rohingya refugees in centering their nuanced values and motivations.

To catalyze conflict transformation, the HPL model must integrate the needs and culture of the neighboring host community near Kutupalong Refugee Camp to reflect the social realities of the Rohingya refugee community. Conflict transformation demands the need to "address conflict at the local and community levels" (Ginty, 2013, p. 771). The HPL model should instead reflect a culture of integration that reimagines Rohingya refugees as productive neighbors rather than burdens in Bangladesh. By tapping into the structural roots of social problems in Kutupalong Refugee Camp, classroom practices have the potential to model an alternative reality where the Rohingya refugee and host communities can coexist peacefully.

12 Critical Design Praxis to Deliver Civic Education in the Rohingya Refugee Camps

Despite restrictions on the delivery of civic education curricula, practices between host community teachers and Rohingya refugee facilitators can provide the bedrock for reflecting or breaking the radical possibility of peaceful coexistence in Cox's Bazar. Before this can be done, the existing "cold conflict" between teachers and facilitators must be interrogated.

While the literature has underscored the need for more comprehensive teachers' trainings toward fostering trust between teachers and students, not as much attention has been paid to the need to foster trust between host teachers and community facilitators. As Zembylas and Bekerman highlight, peace or civic education is a construct whose meaning is "negotiated by active participants and put to work in complex social relations" (2013, p. 204). While the delivery of curricula is heavily policed in the Rohingya refugee camps, the content of teachers' trainings is not as heavily regulated or standardized. As critical experts of design, Bangladeshi teachers and Rohingya facilitators can deconstruct how their own behaviors are extensions of macro-level policies and can ultimately be reformed (Zembylas & Bekerman, 2013, p. 203). Critical cultural analysis in civic or peace education requires the following steps for teachers: framing community programs to explore the practice of identity and culture, interrogating the use of identity to classify and make sense of the world, engaging in collaborative activities to deconstruct existing classifications, and collaborating to work toward a better world (Zembylas & Bekerman, 2013, p. 209). Fostering dialog can promote conflict negotiation during trainings between teachers and facilitators (Davies, 2005, p. 366). Teachers' trainings can help Bangladeshi teachers and Rohingya facilitators find common ground and develop civic identities in relation to one another. Trainings should give teachers the mobility to find solidarity from a non-normative lens. In particular, NGOs must be more open to the possibility of a civic identity grounded in religion, especially due to the centrality of religion to the identities of the Rohingya and the role of Bangladesh's religious leaders themselves in advocating for civic engagement.

Ideally, such insights will be translated to the classroom in critically engaging with and balancing power dynamics between the Bangladeshi teachers and Rohingya facilitators. As Davies (2005, p. 367) stresses, teachers must model citizenship education in the classroom, such as through the development and enforcement of a code of conduct. More than a focus on curricula, effective citizenship education must be delivered through positive practices that teachers model. Zembylas and Bekerman (2013) urge educators to temper their expectations but underscore the need to still change our immediate contexts and liberate our classrooms. Despite the sequestered lives of Rohingya refugee children, the healthy dynamics Bangladeshi teachers and Rohingya facilitator's model in the classroom can catalyze Rohingya refugee youth to examine the potential for a long-term, harmonious future shared with the host community.

The focal point that is classroom practice for the delivery of citizenship education demands greater mediation between teachers and facilitators in the trainings. Providing a safe space for constructive, democratic dialog between Bangladeshi teachers and Rohingya facilitators is a logical first step toward ensuring better coordination in TLCs across Cox's Bazar.

13 Conclusion

In conclusion, critical design praxis between Bangladesh host community teachers and Rohingya facilitators in TLCs across Rohingya refugee camps in Bangladesh can provide an opening for the delivery of civic education. Further ethnographic research should also be conducted to particularly explore trends in dynamics between Rohingya facilitators and Bangladeshi teachers and to what extent those power dynamics also affect students. These trends should be explored in the context of Rohingya students' learning and sense of belonging in the classroom. It is not yet clear whether the Bangladeshi government would allow the implementation of critical design praxis in teachers' training workshops. Moreover, it is unclear how critical design praxis would manifest in communities that are in the process of experiencing emerging conflict but otherwise do not share a history of animosity and violence. This literature review advocates for the testing of critical design practices within teachers' professional development programs in Bangladesh's Rohingya refugee camps. This will ultimately provide greater clarity on the transformative potential, or not, of critical design praxis as a medium to deliver civic education to Rohingya refugee children across Bangladesh.

References

Ahmed, K., & Mohiuddin, H. (2019). *The Rohingya crisis: Analyses, responses, and peacebuilding avenues*. Lexington Books.

Baidya, E. U. (2020, May). The role of collaborative storytelling in participatory planning: Cases from Bangladesh. In *International Conference of Contemporary Affairs in Architecture and Urbanism* (ICCAUA-2020) (Vol. 6, p. 8). https://doi.org/10.38027/2020ICCAUA316295

Baidya, E. U., Mahboob, F., Polin, F., & Chowdhooree, I. (2020). Designing spaces with victims of humanitarian crisis: action research on spaces for children at Rohingya camps in Bangladesh. *External Interventions for Disaster Risk Reduction: Impacts on Local Communities*, 103–119.

Bajaj, M., & Bartlett, L. (2017). Critical transnational curriculum for immigrant and refugee students. *Curriculum Inquiry, 47*(1), 25–35. https://doi.org/10.1080/03626784.2016.1254499

Bajaj, M. (2019). Conceptualizing critical peace education for conflict settings. *Education and Conflict Review, 2*, 65–69. https://discovery.ucl.ac.uk/id/eprint/10081588

Bakali, N., & Wasty, S. (2020). Identity, social mobility, and trauma: Post-conflict educational realities for survivors of the Rohingya genocide. *Religions, 11*(5), 241. https://doi.org/10.3390/rel11050241

Bayezid, A. (2023). Learning competency framework and approach for the displaced Rohingya children living in Bangladesh: A critical review. *Continuity in Education, 4*(1), 50–66. https://doi.org/10.5334/cie.57

Bekerman, Z., & Zembylas, M. (2012). *Teaching contested narratives: Identity, memory and reconciliation in peace education and beyond*. Cambridge University Press.

Coster, I., & Sigalas, E. (2017). *Citizenship education at school in Europe, 2017*.

Davies, L. (2005). Schools and war: Urgent agendas for comparative and international education. *Compare, 35*(4), 357–371. https://doi.org/10.1080/03057920500331561

Devonald, M., Jones, N., Guglielmi, S., Seager, J., & Baird, S. (2021). Human rights education in humanitarian settings: Opportunities and challenges. *Human Rights Education Review, 4*(1), 27–48. https://doi.org/10.7577/hrer.3986

Ginty, R., & Richmond, O. P. (2013). The local turn in peace building: A critical agenda for peace. *Third World Quarterly, 34*(5), 763–783. https://www.jstor.org/stable/42002156

Gjerløw et al. (2022). *Access to educational services in Cox's Bazar during the COVID-19 Pandemic, 2022*. PRIO Policy Brief. Peace Research Institute Oslo. Retrieved from https://www.prio.org/download/publicationfile/3635/Gjerl%C3%B8w%20et%20al.%20-%20Access%20to%20Educational%20Services%20in%20Cox%E2%80%99s%20Bazar%20during%20the%20COVID-19%20Pandemic,%20PRIO%20Policy%20Brief%2020-2022.pdf

Hossain, A. Z. (2021). Preparedness for education to Rohingya refugee children in Bangladesh: potentials and challenges to citizenship education. *Journal of Social Science Education, 20*(2). https://doi.org/10.11576/jsse-3980

Human Rights Watch. (2022, August 24). *Myanmar: No justice, no freedom for Rohingya 5 years on*. Retrieved May 08, 2023, from https://www.hrw.org/news/2022/08/24/myanmar-no-justice-no-freedom-rohingya-5-years

Huhtala, T. (2022). *A year of isolation, uncertainty, and changes: Experiences and well-being of teachers from the time of COVID-19 pandemic in Cox's Bazar, Bangladesh*. (Master's thesis).

Iqbal, Y., Sunny, S., Alif, A., Yoshikawa, H., & Shorna, M. A. (2022). Family socialization and experiences of early childhood programs in the Rohingya camps: Study protocol. *International Journal of Qualitative Methods, 21*.https://doi.org/10.1177/16094069211062419

Kamruzzaman, P., Williams, K., Wardak, A., Kabir, M. E., & Ayobi, Y. (2022). Exploring dignity in the context of displacement–evidence from Rohingyas in Bangladesh and IDPs in Afghanistan. *Third World Quarterly, 43*(8), 1854–1874. https://doi.org/10.1080/01436597.2022.2074387

Karim, A., & Hussain, F. (2019). 'When will you start teaching the real curriculum?' Challenges and innovations in education for Rohingya refugees. In *Information and Communication Technologies for Development. Strengthening Southern-Driven Cooperation as a Catalyst for ICT4D: 15th IFIP WG 9.4 International Conference on Social Implications of Computers in Developing Countries, ICT4D 2019, Dar es Salaam, Tanzania, May 1–3, 2019, Proceedings, Part I 15* (pp. 675–686). Springer International Publishing.

Khan, A. K., & Kontinen, T. (2022). Impediments to localization agenda: humanitarian space in the Rohingya response in Bangladesh. *Journal of International Humanitarian Action, 7*(1), 14.

LCFA: Revised Draft. (2019). *Learning competency framework and approach for children of displaced people from Rakhine State, Myanmar in Bangladesh.* Revised Draft with level I to V. https://educationcluster.app.box.com/v/BangladeshLCFA2019

Levinson, B. A. U. (2011). Toward an anthropology of (democratic) citizenship education. In B. A. U. Levinson & M. Pollock (Eds.), *A companion to the anthropology of education* (pp. 279–298). Wiley-Blackwell.

Malik, H. F. (2020). Rohingya Muslims: The most persecuted group in the world. *The Boar*. Retrieved April 24, 2023, from https://theboar.org/2020/10/rohingya-muslims-the-most-persecuted-group-in-the-world/

Mansur, N. N. (2020). Notions of belonging for working Rohingya boys in Cox's Bazar, Bangladesh. *Journal of Education in Muslim Societies, 2*(1), 30–57. https://doi.org/10.2979/jems.2.1.03

Meloni, F. (2019). The ambivalence of belonging: The impact of illegality on the social belonging of undocumented youth. *Anthropological Quarterly, 92*(2), 451–479. https://doi.org/10.1353/anq.2019.0022

Olney, J., Haque, N., & Mubarak, R. (2019). *We must prevent a lost generation: community-led education in Rohingya camps*. PRIO Paper. Oslo: PRIO.

Pinson, H. (2007). At the boundaries of citizenship: Palestinian Israeli citizens and the civic education curriculum. *Oxford Review of Education, 33*(3), 331–348. https://doi.org/10.1080/03054980701366256

Prodip, M. A., & Garnett, J. (2019). Emergency education for Rohingya refugee children in Bangladesh: An analysis of the policies, practices, and limitations. In *Comparative perspectives on refugee youth education* (pp. 191–219). Routledge.

Rahman, M. M. (2020). *Barriers to providing basic education among the Rohingyas refugee children: Insights from the Kutupalong unregistered camp, Cox's Bazar, Bangladesh.* [Unpublished Master's thesis, LUP Student Papers, Lund University, Sweden]. Retrieved from https://lup.lub.lu.se/student-papers/search/publication/9026975

Rahman, M. M., & Husain, T. (2022). Structural barriers to providing basic education to Rohingya children in the Kutupalong refugee camp, Cox's Bazar, Bangladesh. *International Journal of Educational Research Open, 3*, 100159. https://doi.org/10.1016/j.ijedro.2022.100159

Rodríguez-Gómez, D. (2022). Disputed futures: Rural entrepreneurship and migration in post-secondary trajectories on the Ecuador-Colombia Border. *Ethnography and Education, 17*(3), 314–330. https://doi.org/10.1080/17457823.2022.2049333

Rubin, B. C. (2016). We come to form ourselves bit by bit: Educating for citizenship in post-conflict Guatemala. *American Educational Research Journal, 53*(3), 639–672. https://doi.org/10.3102/0002831216646871

Shohel, M. M. C. (2022). Education in emergencies: Challenges of providing education for Rohingya children living in refugee camps in Bangladesh. *Education Inquiry, 13*(1), 104–126. https://doi.org/10.1080/20004508.2020.1823121

Ullah AKM Ahsan. (2011). Rohingya refugee to Bangladesh: Historical exclusions and contemporary marginalization. *Journal of Immigrant and Refugee Studies, 9*(2), 139–168.

Ullah AKM Ahsan, & Chattoraj, D. (2018). Roots of discrimination against Rohingya minorities: Society, ethnicity and international relations. *Intellectual Discourse, 26*(2), 541–465.

UNICEF. (2019). Beyond survival, Rohingya refugee children in Bangladesh want to learn.
Williams, J. H. (2004). Civil conflict, education, and the work of schools: Twelve propositions. *Conflict Resolution Quarterly, 21*(4), 471–481. https://doi.org/10.1002/crq.75
Zembylas, M., & Bekerman, Z. (2013). Peace education in the present: Dismantling and reconstructing some fundamental theoretical premises. *Journal of Peace Education, 10*(2), 197–214. https://doi.org/10.1080/17400201.2013.790253

Chapter 19
Conclusion

Md. Rafiqul Islam and Kawser Ahmed

1 Question of Identity and Existence

The Rohingyas are now regarded as one of the unfortunate nations in the world. State-sponsored policies of Myanmar are responsible for excluding the Rohingyas from all forms of rights including citizenship rights. Now, most of the Rohingyas are ousted from their place of origin and living in many parts of the world containing as stateless identity. More than one million Rohingyas are living in Bangladesh of whom around 8 hundred thousand took shelter when they faced serious persecution, killing, rape, and human rights violations in 2017 by the Myanmar army. Thus, the issues of Rohingya identity, citizenship, framing, representation, and repatriation have been a great concern for policymakers and researchers. Much has been written about the issues of Rohingyas as chapters, articles, books, and policy papers. This book is an endeavor to present some important topics—ethnic identity formation of Rohingyas, conflict dynamics and security ramifications of the Rohingyas in Bangladesh and beyond, media narratives and propaganda against the Rohingyas, and humanitarian perspectives and management approaches to this intractable problem. From this perspective, this book carries strong significance in presenting this timely topic.

After the introduction chapter, the next section presents the history of Rohingyas, the meaning of Rohingyas, and how the contested identity has been formed. The Rohingyas are native Arakanian people who have been living in Myanmar from generation to generation. They represented all state machinery including the parliament. Before the independence of Burma, Rohingyas enjoyed due rights in the state

Md. R. Islam (✉)
University of Dhaka, Dhaka, Bangladesh
e-mail: rislampacs@du.ac.bd

K. Ahmed
University of Winnipeg, Winnipeg, Canada
e-mail: k.ahmed@uwinnipeg.ca

K. Ahmed and Md. R. Islam (eds.), *Understanding the Rohingya Displacement*,
International Perspectives on Migration, https://doi.org/10.1007/978-981-97-1424-7_19

system. The first part concludes that the ruling class in Myanmar systematically discriminated against and excluded the Rohingyas. Chapter 11 highlights the history of Rohingya displacement and settlement in Bangladesh. The persecution of the Rohingyas in Myanmar has necessitated the process of displacement of this group of people, and then took shelter in the neighboring countries. Rohingyas settled in Cox's Bazar district as this place is very proximate, the Rakhine state of Myanmar. The settlement process started after 1980s and still continuing. This chapter conclude that Rohingyas settle in Bangladesh in order to escaping from torture and human rights violation.

In part two, this book narrates the conflict potentials of the Rohingya people in Bangladesh after the exodus in 2017. It is a fact that Rohingya displacement and settlement in Bangladesh was handled smoothly by the authority of Bangladesh. Prime Minister Sheikh Hasina welcomed this large number of people and provided possible assistances to them, so that they could live and survive. The authority of Bangladesh perceived that sheltering of Rohingyas is a short-term issue and they must be repatriated shortly. However, the repatriation process is uncertain. On the other hand, Rohingyas are putting enormous pressure on the existing resources, environment, economy, society, and local political issues. Due to pressure on economy, jobs, and services, the local people are being deprived of getting access to the jobs and services which is generating a source of conflict and violence. The environment has been destroyed by the sudden pressure from the Rohingyas. The Rohingyas have destroyed the forest, polluted the environment, and complicated the living spaces of Cox's Bazar. The local people no longer welcome this devastation and damage. Thus, conflict between the local people and Rohingyas is a new reality in the region. Chapter Three has highlighted this conflict potentials of Rohingya people. Some of the Rohingyas are involved in transnational crimes and drug business. They are also involved in human trafficking and terrorist activities which have security implications in regional and international context. The sociopolitical context of the region is also complicated because of the presence of Rohingyas in a longer period of time. Chapter Five shows that some of the Rohingyas are generating social problems and political conflict by using the local people. In this way, they are complicating the social and political environment in the region. Crimes and violence have also become the common scenarios in the camps which has been explored by Chapter Eight. Scholars argued that Rohingyas are involved in crimes and violence because they are frustrated living in such as inhuman conditions. Their statelessness and no hope for their children have made them frustrated and forced them to do any work for their survival.

Part Three highlights the role of media in framing the Rohingyas in Myanmar and in the host society Bangladesh. Media as an important medium of forming public perception played a role in framing the Rohingyas as a trouble maker in Myanmar. The mainstream and social media portrayed the Rohingyas as outsider, terrorist, and anti-state element. This propaganda and framing formed the public perception in Myanmar against the Rohingyas. Chapter Nine and Ten narrated the role of the media in generating the Rohingya crisis in Myanmar and Bangladesh. In host society, media is also playing role in forming public perception against the Rohingyas in the host place. Now, they are branded as the trouble makers, baby boomer, and violent. Sometimes, media represent as the unfortunate nation in the world.

The last part of this book presents humanitarian perspectives and management approaches of this Rohingya crisis. In the course of the time, Rohingyas has become an issue of security concern not only for Bangladesh but also for the region and international perspective. This all stakeholders must consider the humanitarian concern of the Rohingyas as well as the management approaches to manage this conflict potentials.

2 Addressing the Crisis: Two Possibilities

In conclusion, the Rohingya crisis is a complex issue that requires urgent attention from the international community. It has evolved beyond being just a humanitarian crisis and now poses regional security threats as well as places economic burdens on countries receiving refugees. The responsibility for resolving this crisis should not solely rest on the shoulders of the Myanmar government, but also on ASEAN as a regional body that has an obligation to protect minority groups and guarantee human rights.

Furthermore, addressing the Rohingya crisis requires comprehensive solutions that take into account various perspectives including security, media, and humanitarian angles. The ineffectiveness of the UN Security Council in reaching a consensus among its permanent members has contributed to prolonging this crisis. Additionally, the domestic political culture in Myanmar has played a role in the lack of progress and resistance to change. Still further, the displacement of the Rohingya has been mischaracterized and downplayed by both ASEAN and the Myanmar government. The crisis has also been incorporated into the Bali process on people smuggling, trafficking of persons and related transnational crime by ASEAN.[1] This incorporation further emphasizes the need for a multidimensional approach to resolving the Rohingya crisis.

With a cohort of scholars from Bangladesh and Canada, in this book, we have tried to provide a comprehensive analysis of the Rohingya crisis, taking into account the security implications, media coverage, and humanitarian aspects. Particularly, in this section, we also discuss the sustainable management of the Rohingya conflict, with a focus on the theoretical lens of the United Nations High Commissioner for Refugees (UNHCR). The UNHCR approach provides a theoretical framework for managing refugee crises worldwide.

We examine two potential solutions in this section: repatriation of the Rohingyas to their home country of Myanmar, and third-country resettlement. Both approaches must emphasize the importance of protecting the rights of refugees and ensuring their

---

[1] Bali Process on People Smuggling, Trafficking in Persons and Related Transnational Crime: https://www.iom.int/bali-process-people-smuggling-trafficking-persons-and-related-transnational-crime

physical safety, as well as providing them with access to basic needs such as shelter, food, water, and healthcare. The approaches also must recognize the importance of providing refugees with education and employment opportunities to facilitate their eventual integration into the host society.

The first potential solution to the Rohingya crisis is repatriation of the Rohingyas to their home country of Myanmar. This solution would involve ensuring that the refugees can return safely to their homes and have their rights protected. However, the success of repatriation would depend on the willingness and ability of the Myanmar government to provide a safe and sustainable environment for the refugees to return to. The Myanmar government has been accused of human rights violations against the Rohingya people, making this a challenging solution to implement.

The second potential solution is third-country resettlement. This solution would involve resettling the Rohingya refugees in a third country, where they would have the opportunity to start a new life. This solution has gained traction in recent years, with several countries expressing their willingness to accept Rohingya refugees. However, this solution also has its challenges, such as ensuring that the refugees are resettled in a safe and sustainable environment and that they are able to integrate into the host society. Overall, this chapter will explore the UNHCR approach to managing the Rohingya crisis and examine the potential solutions of repatriation and third-country resettlement. It is hoped that the insights and analysis presented in this chapter will contribute to a better understanding of the sustainable management of the Rohingya conflict and facilitate the development of practical solutions to help the Rohingya people.

3 UNHCR's Approach

The UNHCR's approach to sustainable management of the Rohingya conflict is based on the principles of protection, assistance, and solutions. This approach aims to protect the rights of refugees, provide them with necessary assistance, and find sustainable solutions to their displacement. While the UNHCR approach provides a useful theoretical framework for managing refugee crises worldwide, its implementation in the case of the Rohingya crisis has been limited by several challenges.

One of the key challenges to implementing the UNHCR approach to the Rohingya crisis is the lack of political will among the governments involved. The Myanmar government has been accused of human rights violations against the Rohingya people, and its willingness to provide a safe and sustainable environment for the refugees to return to is in question. Similarly, Bangladesh, the primary host country for Rohingya refugees, has been unable to provide a sustainable environment for the refugees due to resource constraints and political pressure.

Another challenge to the UNHCR approach is the lack of coordination and collaboration among international actors involved in managing the Rohingya crisis. The international community must work together to provide sustained support to the refugees and their host communities and find practical solutions to their displacement. This requires a multi-stakeholder approach that includes collaboration among international organizations, governments, civil society organizations, and the private sector. Furthermore, the UNHCR approach needs to be adapted to the specific context of the Rohingya crisis (Ahmed, 2018). The Rohingya refugees are in a particularly vulnerable situation, having fled violence and persecution in Myanmar. They require specialized support, including access to healthcare, education, and legal protection. The UNHCR approach must take into account the unique needs and vulnerabilities of the Rohingya refugees to effectively manage the crisis.

A further challenge to implementing the UNHCR approach is the lack of funding and resources. The UNHCR relies heavily on donor funding to provide assistance to refugees, and the Rohingya crisis has been severely underfunded. The lack of funding has limited the UNHCR's ability to provide essential services such as food, water, shelter, and healthcare to the Rohingya refugees. Third-country resettlement is also challenging due to the limited number of countries willing to accept refugees and the difficulty of integrating refugees into the host society (Parveen & Sahana, 2022). Additionally, the UNHCR approach emphasizes the importance of finding sustainable solutions to displacement, such as repatriation or third-country resettlement. However, these solutions are not always feasible or desirable for refugees. In the case of the Rohingya crisis, repatriation to Myanmar is a challenging solution due to the political situation and human rights violations against the Rohingya people.

While the UNHCR approach provides a theoretical lens for managing the Rohingya conflict, its implementation has been limited by challenges such as political will, funding, and the feasibility of sustainable solutions. To effectively manage the Rohingya crisis, a more comprehensive approach is needed that addresses the root causes of the conflict, including discrimination and human rights violations against the Rohingya people. The international community must work together to provide sustained support to the refugees and their host communities and find practical solutions to their displacement.

4 Refugee Management by the Host Country

The Cox's Bazar area in Bangladesh has become a significant hub for Rohingya refugees, resulting in complex sociopolitical dynamics and concerns about regional safety and security. Although some literature exists on the subject, there are substantial research gaps that need further exploration (Ashikuzzaman et al., 2022). One crucial area lacking adequate investigation is the effectiveness of the Bangladesh Armed Police Battalions (APBn) in addressing security challenges arising from the presence of Rohingya refugees in Cox's Bazar. Existing literature fails to provide sufficient insights into the limitations, weaknesses, and capabilities of the APBn. Additionally, there is a dearth of research on the intricate sociopolitical dynamic between the host community and the Rohingya population. Addressing these research gaps is vital to formulate effective policies and strategies for maintaining law and order in the area and ensuring the safety and security of both the local and refugee populations.

The management of refugees is guided by protocols established by the UN through the UNHCR. The cornerstone of these protocols is the 1951 Refugee Convention, which defines the rights of refugees and the obligations of states toward them. According to the Convention, a refugee is someone who has fled their country due to a well-founded fear of persecution based on various grounds. The Convention guarantees the rights of refugees, including the right to work, education, and basic human needs such as shelter, food, and medical care. Alongside the 1951 Refugee Convention, the UN has also introduced the 1967 Protocol Relating to the Status of Refugees, expanding the definition of a refugee to include those fleeing generalized violence, foreign aggression, or disturbances to public order (Meer et al., 2021). The UNHCR assumes responsibility for protecting refugees, irrespective of their location, by providing essential assistance, including protection, shelter, and basic necessities. The agency also collaborates with governments to develop policies, establish legal frameworks, and offer training and support to officials engaged in refugee-related work.

Although Bangladesh is not a signatory to the 1951 Refugee Convention and its 1967 Protocol, it is bound by certain principles and protocols recognized as customary international law. One crucial principle followed by Bangladesh is non-refoulement, which prohibits the expulsion or forced return of refugees to a country where they face persecution or harm. Bangladesh, in line with this principle, has consistently affirmed that it will not forcibly repatriate Rohingya refugees to Myanmar, where they face risks of persecution and violence (Ashikuzzaman et al., 2022). Another protocol adhered to by Bangladesh is the provision of basic humanitarian assistance to refugees, encompassing access to food, water, shelter, and healthcare services. Collaboration between the Bangladesh government, the UNHCR, and international organizations has facilitated the establishment of camps and facilities to deliver essential aid to Rohingya refugees in Cox's Bazar. The government has also allowed registration and issuance of identification cards to the Rohingya population, enabling targeted assistance in meeting their fundamental needs. Bangladesh has actively engaged with the international community to seek a sustainable solution to the Rohingya crisis, including the safe and voluntary repatriation of refugees to Myanmar.

5 Repatriation of the Rohingyas to Myanmar

This study suggests a speedy and sustainable solution for ensuring the human rights of the Rohingya people and managing the current and future conflicts in the region. The reasonable and sustainable solution to the problem is repatriation to their country, and respectful treatment upon their arrival. Refugee settlements and the issue of their eventual repatriation have theoretical underpinnings in how refugee populations influence the host state in a myriad of ways. The influence can either be as an opportunity, a burden, or as even as a new form of offensive strategic weapon for carrying out armed conflicts (Greenhill, 2004; Stedman & Tanner, 2003). The key to resolving the conflict involving the refugee issues that countries face lies in their eventual repatriation to their state of origin.

The costs of the sudden influx of refugee populations, often in the wake of a violent civil conflict in their country of origin, impose some heavy costs upon the host state. The costs involve economic and social constraints and environmental issues with repurposing land to accommodate the new arrivals. For Bangladesh, the costs have been on many fronts, with added problems of criminal involvement of these refugees over the years of their refuge (Uddin, 2012). In several recent cases of refugee situations, refugees have overwhelmed a host state's capacity to provide even the most basic of services—fresh water, sanitation, basic medical aid, food, and shelter, as well as safety and security. In Congo, as an example, Hutu refugees fleeing from Rwanda during the 1994 Rwandan genocide have disrupted economic activities, accelerated deforestation, and have triggered a civil and interstate war. In other case examples, refugee crises stimulate external intervention and support by international organizations that bring their own personnel with them for humanitarian aid, relief, and development purposes. In some Islamic countries, the presence of foreigners is considered as an anathema, and a government's decision to allow foreigners in, even at a temporary capacity, can destabilize that government or provoke a civil war within its borders. In authoritarian states, the presence of foreigners is unwelcome for other reasons—such as the critical need of certain states to control the local population's access to information about the outside world (Toft, 2007).

Refugee settlement is another concern for UNCHR in which the commission refers to finding a durable solution for the refugee problem. According to UNHCR, "resettlement is the transfer of refugees from an asylum country to another third country that has agreed to admit them and ultimately grant them permanent residence." UNHCR undertakes resettlement as one of three durable solutions, though less than one percent of refugees are resettled each year (UNHCR, 2021). In 1992, the UNHCR declared that the 1990s were to be the "decade of repatriation," and that the UNHCR would strive toward realizing every opportunity in order to make sure voluntary repatriation takes place all over the globe wherever such issues are present (Toft, 2007). The question of refugee settlement comes when some section of refugees live under extreme poverty and perilous health conditions. In such a case, the vulnerable section of the population is transferred to a third country under an international agreement. For example, some countries in Europe (UK and Germany) receive vulnerable refugees and provide shelter and services.

Australia is one of the signatory parties of the 1951 Convention, and therefore, it administers an onshore program and an offshore program. The onshore protection program is for people seeking asylum who arrived in Australia on a valid visa. On the other hand, the offshore program consists of the refugee, special humanitarian, and community support program (CSP). The refugees are the people who have been identified as refugees by UNHCR and referred to Australia for resettlement (UNSW, 2020). Since August 13, 2012, any person arriving in Australia without holding a valid visa has been shifted to Manus Island in Papua New Guinea (UNSW, 2020).

There, they live in a holding camp and Australia pays to take them to Manus Island (BBC News, 2015).

Based on the study findings, the following recommendations can be provided for smoothening the repatriation negotiations and actual repatriation process:

1. To continue rigorous and engaged bilateral diplomacy to expedite and ensure a smooth repatriation process so that both Bangladesh and Myanmar sustain the negotiation process that began immediately after the 2017 influx.
2. Bangladesh should develop a coordinated, proper displaced (refugee) people management strategy with a focus on their dignified return to their home.
3. To engage the regional and international communities as much as possible for continuing the negotiation process for a safe, secure, and dignified repatriation of Rohingyas to their country, Myanmar. One needs to bear in mind that the refugee repatriation negotiation process is a continuous endeavor.

If these steps are followed properly, it can be reasonably safe to predict that the Rohingya crisis would be resolved peacefully between the two countries and that the Rohingyas would be free from their long history of oppression and destitution. However, the nuances of these steps need to be carefully considered for their eventual realization, and the existing barriers to realizing these very steps need to be removed for them to be taken into the implementation phase.

6 Third-Country Resettlement: Rhetorical or a Practical Option?

The Bangladeshi government has thus far been accommodating the Rohingya refugees, but the large influx of people has strained the country's resources and created significant economic, environmental, and social challenges. As such, third-country resettlement has emerged as a possible solution to address the needs of the Rohingya refugees and the challenges faced by Bangladesh. Third-country resettlement is the process of permanently relocating refugees to a country other than the one in which they first sought refuge. It is an option that can provide refugees with the chance to rebuild their lives in a safe and secure environment while also easing the burden on the host country. However, the rhetoric around third-country resettlement of Rohingya refugees has been contentious and polarizing. Some have argued that third-country resettlement is the only viable solution to the crisis, while others have opposed it, citing security concerns and the potential for increased immigration. Proponents of third-country resettlement argue that it is a necessary step to ensure the safety and security of the Rohingya refugees. The conditions in the refugee camps in Bangladesh are challenging, with limited access to healthcare, education, and employment opportunities. Third-country resettlement provides refugees with the chance to rebuild their lives in a safe and secure environment, with access to basic services and the opportunity to work and contribute to their new communities. Furthermore, proponents argue that third-country resettlement is a practical solution to the challenge of providing long-term assistance to refugees (Bhatia et al., 2018). The Rohingya crisis has been ongoing for several years, and the Bangladeshi government and humanitarian organizations have struggled to provide adequate support to the refugees in the long term. Third-country resettlement can provide a permanent solution to the crisis, ensuring that refugees have access to the resources and support they need to rebuild their lives.

However, opponents of third-country resettlement argue that it is not a viable solution to the crisis. They cite concerns about security, suggesting that resettling refugees in other countries could increase the risk of terrorism and other security threats. Additionally, opponents argue that resettling refugees in third countries could lead to increased immigration, which could create additional challenges for the countries that accept refugees (Siddiqi, 2021). Moreover, opponents of third-country resettlement argue that it is not a sustainable solution to the crisis. They suggest that the focus should be on addressing the root causes of the crisis, including the human rights violations committed against the Rohingya in Myanmar. Opponents insist that resettlement should be a last resort, and that efforts should be made to provide refugees with the support they need to return to their homes in Myanmar.

The rhetoric around third-country resettlement of Rohingya refugees is thus complex and contentious. While proponents argue that it is a necessary step to ensure the safety and security of the refugees and provide them with long-term support, opponents suggest that it is not a viable or sustainable solution to the crisis. The reality is that the Rohingya crisis is a complex issue, and there are no easy solutions. It requires a coordinated and sustained approach, involving the Bangladeshi government, the international community, and the government of Myanmar to address the root causes of the crisis and provide refugees with the support they need to rebuild their lives. Ultimately, the focus should be on ensuring the protection and well-being of the Rohingya refugees, while also addressing the needs of the host communities in Bangladesh. Third-country resettlement may be a part of the solution, but it should be considered carefully and implemented in a way that prioritizes the safety and security of refugees and the host communities.

7 Conclusion

The sustainable management of the Rohingya conflict requires a multifaceted approach that addresses the immediate needs of the refugees, while also addressing the root causes of the conflict. The UNHCR approach provides a useful theoretical lens for managing the conflict, but its implementation has been limited by several challenges. Repatriation of the Rohingya refugees to their home country of Myanmar is a key component of sustainable conflict management. However, it must be done in a safe, voluntary, and dignified manner, with the involvement of the refugees themselves. The Myanmar government must also take concrete steps to address the discrimination and persecution of the Rohingya people and provide avenues for political participation and representation. Third-country resettlement is a potential solution for those Rohingya refugees who are unable to return to Myanmar or remain in Bangladesh. However, it is important to note that resettlement should not be seen as a substitute for repatriation. Resettlement should only be considered after all efforts to find a solution within the region have been exhausted. The sustainable management of the Rohingya conflict also requires a multi-stakeholder approach that involves collaboration among international organizations, governments, civil society organizations, and the private sector. The international community must work together to provide sustained support to the refugees and their host communities and find practical solutions to their displacement.

In addition, efforts to promote human rights, address discrimination and marginalization, and provide access to education, healthcare, and legal protection for the Rohingya refugees are essential to managing the conflict. The unique needs and vulnerabilities of the Rohingya refugees must be taken into account in any approach to managing the conflict. The sustainable management of the Rohingya conflict thus requires a comprehensive approach that addresses the root causes of the conflict, promotes human rights, and takes into account the unique needs and vulnerabilities of the Rohingya refugees. It also requires the involvement and collaboration of the international community and a commitment to finding practical solutions to the displacement of the Rohingya people. Only through sustained efforts and cooperation can a lasting solution to the Rohingya crisis be achieved.

References

Ahmed, F. B. J. (2018). Rethinking UNHCR and OIC response to forced migration. *Al-Shajarah: Journal of the International Institute of Islamic Thought and Civilization (ISTAC)*, 1–26. https://journals.iium.edu.my/shajarah/index.php/shaj/article/view/735

Ashikuzzaman, Gazi, A. K., & Abir, T. M. (2022). The key scenarios of Rohingya refugees in Bangladesh: A narrative study. In *Worldwide inter-disciplinary research* (pp. 252–269). Notion Press India.

BBC News. (2015, June 12). *Papua new Guinea: The camps where Australia sends asylum seekers.* BBC News. Retrieved from https://www.bbc.com/news/av/world-asia-33114230

Bhatia, A., Mahmud, A., Fuller, A., Shin, R., Rahman, A., Shatil, T., et al. (2018). The Rohingya in cox's bazar: When the stateless seek refuge. *Health and human rights, 20*(2), 105. http://www.ncbi.nlm.nih.gov/pmc/articles/pmc6293360/

Greenhill, K. (2004). *People pressure: Strategic engineered migration as an instrument of statecraft and the rise of the human rights regime* [PhD Thesis]. MIT.

Meer, N., Hill, E., Peace, T., & Villegas, L. (2021). Rethinking refuge in the time of COVID-19. *Ethnic and Racial Studies, 44*(5), 864–876. https://doi.org/10.1080/01419870.2020.1855359

Parveen, S., & Sahana, M. (2022). Identity and humanitarian-based approach: Resolution and resolving the Rohingya refugee crisis. *Rohingya Refugee Crisis in Myanmar: Ethnic Conflict and Resolution*, 357–378.

Siddiqi, B. (2021). The 'myth'of repatriation: The prolonged sufferings of the Rohingya. *The Rohingya Crisis: Human Rights, Policy Concerns and Burden Sharing.*

Stedman, S. J., & Tanner, F. (2003). *Refugee manipulation: War, politics, and the abuse of human suffering*. Brookings Institution Press.

Toft, M. D. (2007). The myth of the borderless world: Refugees and repatriaton policy. *Conflict Management and Peace Science, 24*(2), 139–157. https://doi.org/10.1080/07388940701257549

Uddin, N. (Ed.). (2012). *To host or hurt: Counter-narratives on Rohingya refugee issue in Bangladesh*. ICDR.

UNHCR. (2021). *What is resettlement?* The UN Refugee Agency. Retrieved from https://www.unhcr.org/handbooks/ih/getting-started/what-resettlement

UNSW. (2020). *Australia's refugee policy: An overview*. Andrew & Renata Kaldor Centre for International Refugee Law. Retrieved from https://www.kaldorcentre.unsw.edu.au/publication/australias-refugee-policy-overview

The manufacturer's authorised representative in the EU is Springer Nature Customer Service Centre GmbH, Europaplatz 3, 69115 Heidelberg, Germany. If you have any concerns regarding our products, please contact ProductSafety@springernature.com

Printed and bound by CPI Group (UK) Ltd, Croydon, CR0 4YY

30/09/2026

02225314-0009